KATHRYN CASEY

IN PLAIN SIGHT

THE KAUFMAN COUNTY PROSECUTOR MURDERS

wm

WILLIAM MORROW

An Imprint of HarperCollinsPublishers

IN PLAIN SIGHT. Copyright © 2018 by Kathryn Casey. All rights reserved. Printed in the United States of America. No part of this book may be used or reproduced in any manner whatsoever without written permission except in the case of brief quotations embodied in critical articles and reviews. For information, address HarperCollins Publishers, 195 Broadway, New York, NY 10007.

First William Morrow mass market printing: April 2018

Print Edition ISBN: 978-0-06-236350-3
Digital Edition ISBN: 978-0-06-236348-0

Cover design by Guido Caroti
Cover photos: Kaufman County Sheriff's Office (mugshots), © autsawin
uttisin/Shutterstock (striped paper), © STILLFX/Shutterstock (torn
paper), © nfmlk/Shutterstock (paper)

William Morrow and HarperCollins are registered trademarks of HarperCollins Publishers in the United States of America and other countries.

FIRST EDITION

18 19 20 21 22   QGM   10 9 8 7 6 5 4 3 2 1

Praise for *In Plain Sight*

"I love Kathryn Casey—
always smart, always scary, and
always pitch-perfect on Texas true-crime."

—Ron Franscell, bestselling author of
The Darkest Night and *Morgue: A Life in Death*

"Going deeper than anyone has before,
Kathryn Casey transforms solid research on
the Texas prosecutor murders into a deft and
compelling crime narrative. In the style of Ann Rule,
she honors the victims, while also building a
fully-realized villain. Bristling with intrigue,
In Plain Sight takes us into the minds of
justice officials who must identify
and catch the person targeting them
before more of them are killed."

—Katherine Ramsland, bestselling author
of *Confession of a Serial Killer: The Untold
Story of Dennis Rader, the BTK Killer*

"*In Plain Sight*, Kathryn Casey's exploration of a
small-town good citizen turned vengeful killer, is
told with such creeping suspense that it reads like
a crime novel. But the fact that it's real makes
it far more chilling, a vivid and even horrifying
exploration of the making of a murderer."

—Deborah Blum, Pulitzer-Prize winning author of
*The Poisoner's Handbook: Murder and the Birth
of Forensic Medicine in Jazz-Age New York*

By Kathryn Casey

*For all the victims of violence and the good people
who work hard to keep us safe.*

You ended up with men who developed grudges. They became vengeful. Neither one would let it go.

—Sandra Harward

Dear Readers:

When I began researching this book in late 2014, I was told that I would never get interviews with either Eric or Kim Williams. "They aren't talking to anyone," their gatekeeper told me. I wasn't surprised. I'd already heard that Kim and Eric had turned down requests from major newspapers, along with *48 Hours* and *DatelineNBC*.

I was pleased then when, days later, the woman e-mailed me: "Eric and Kim have both agreed."

Over the next eighteen months, I had a series of in-person meetings with Eric and Kim, the couple at the center of three of the most notorious murders of this century. That access proved invaluable. Sections of the book where conversations between Eric and Kim are depicted are based on my interviews with Kim, testimony, and evidence presented at trial.

The result is *In Plain Sight*, a look behind the headlines at how the terror that mesmerized the world unfolded in Kaufman County, Texas, in the spring of 2013.

Kathryn Casey
2017

IN PLAIN SIGHT

Prologue

The parking lot at the Terrell ISD Performing Arts Center gradually emptied after the memorial service. Throughout the event, officers guarded the entrances and exits, patrolled from the roof with binoculars and snipers' rifles. But once the tributes ended and the guests departed, the sentries packed to leave. Only a few lingered, perhaps pondering the unlikely turn of events: The man they'd gathered to honor—a well-known prosecutor—had been mercilessly gunned down in broad daylight in the small city of Kaufman, Texas.

Who would do such a thing? Murdering an assistant DA declared war on law enforcement. In response, local, state, and national agencies flooded the town, including Texas Rangers, ATF, and FBI agents.

While investigators refused to disclose theories, intense nationwide coverage in newspapers and on TV proposed possibilities. Some pundits labeled the assassination the likely work of the powerful prison group dubbed the Aryan Brotherhood of Texas. Others noted similarities to executions of officials south of the border and speculated that the murder could be the work of the Mexican cartel.

While stragglers slowly pulled away from the parking lot, inside the building the nearly deserted auditorium remained set for the memorial service. A somber curtain hung behind the stage. Between two pillars bearing sprays of red-and-white flowers, a table held a framed photograph of the dead man, Mark Hasse, his brown hair combed to the side, wearing glasses and a crewneck sweater.

In the cavernous room, two men remained behind, seated side by side on the stage and dangling their legs over the edge. Mike McLelland, a round, bulky man in a dark suit, was Mark's boss and Kaufman County's district attorney. His thick salt-and-pepper hair combed back, his mustache nearing white, McLelland had a booming presence that commanded attention. An ex–army major, on that day he felt the anguish of losing one of his men. Earlier, he'd delivered an emotional eulogy, telling stories about Hasse, a man he considered a friend.

Now, however, McLelland practically whispered to Mike Burns, a district attorney from a nearby county. If others remained in the theater, McLelland didn't want them to overhear.

"There are people trying to make names on this investigation," Mike McLelland charged, bitterness resonating in his voice. Bringing up the headlines about drug cartels and prison gangs, the rotund DA looked at Burns with a resolute gaze. "This case is local. The killer is somebody bent on revenge." For a moment he paused, perhaps considering what he'd say next. "This is somebody really close to home."

Meanwhile, in a one-story brick house less than two miles from the murder scene, a dough-faced man with dimples, who looked younger than his forty-five years, smiled. On his computer, Eric Williams clicked between competing news reports of the memorial service. Perhaps he felt a swell of pride. More than a week had lapsed, and the massive law enforcement response hadn't connected the dots. Hadn't figured it out.

It appeared he'd pulled off the perfect murder.

Watching the memorial unfold on television, at times he chuckled. How he must have enjoyed that those investigating Hasse's murder had veered off course. How superior he must have felt.

They all had much yet to understand: the most important thing—the killing wasn't over.

Chapter 1

Growing up, Eric was the golden boy.
—Tera Williams Bellemare

Many believe the eyes are windows into the soul, but is there any way to truly look inside a heart? Perhaps the task becomes even more complicated when fantasy takes over. Such an incongruous combination: a happy disposition, an engaging smile, an almost childlike appearance, and festering wrath.

On the surface, little about Eric Williams's upbringing appeared remarkable. For the most part, he could have been any boy raised in rural America, surrounded by loving parents, a younger sister, and a tight group of friends.

One of eleven children, Eric's father, Jim, grew up in a family of sharecroppers in Alvin, Texas. "Jim was like the rest of us, he quit school to work. No one went to college," said one of his sisters. At seventeen, Jim joined the marines and served as a machinist in Korea. Once home, he met Jessie Ruth Lyles at a square dance. After a brief courtship, they married, and in April 1967, their first child arrived three weeks early. For a middle name, Jessie Ruth dropped the final letter from her maiden name, and he became Eric Lyle Williams.

As a young child, Eric had his father's wide smile. Following the style at the time, Jessie emulated the clothing

Jackie Kennedy had favored for her baby boy, and sewed Eric John-John coveralls. Bright and inquisitive, Eric entertained himself, rarely crying for attention. "We're not people given to a lot of emotion," Jim said. "We don't show a lot."

Instead, the Williamses appeared strong and proud. Jessie Ruth had a matter-of-fact manner, and on those occasions when she became emotional, she squared her shoulders and forged on, fighting down her feelings. Describing her own family, she'd say, "Just good people who kept on working without expecting something from somebody."

In their home, Jim and Jessie taught the importance of civic duty. They believed that those who didn't vote relinquished their right to complain. They volunteered during elections and stressed the importance of military service. In stature a small man, just five-foot-seven and wiry, Jim relied on his marine training to gain a job in a lab that built instruments for student projects at Fort Worth's Texas Christian University. On weekends, his beard carefully manicured, he dressed as a Confederate soldier to participate in Civil War reenactments.

Years later, one family story recounted how a young Eric disliked getting dirty. When playing, he refused to sit in the dirt. He didn't like walking barefoot in the grass, and for a time insisted his mother dress him in all white. "Eric didn't like breaking the rules," said an aunt, who added that some of his cousins thought Eric kind of a "goody two-shoes."

When Eric was four, the family home burned down. Jolted from sleep, Jim ran for their son while smoke filled the house. Lifting the sleeping child, he saw the imprint of Eric's small body on the sheets, drawn as the fire's soot settled around him.

Three years later in 1974, the Williams family bought a house on acreage outside Fort Worth, in the small town

Eric with his parents at age six in 1973
Courtesy of Tera Bellemare

of Azle. In the barn and pastures, they kept horses, cows, sheep, chickens, and goats, and Eric adopted a black-and-white dog he named Sweetie. Jim and Jessie Ruth hadn't planned more children, but they expected a girl. In anticipation, seven-year-old Eric carried a miniature plastic baby in his pocket, introducing it as his sister.

After Tera's birth, however, he showed little interest in his sister, their grandmother later telling Tera that Eric seemed reluctant to touch her. "Eric was a lot like my parents. He never showed emotion. He wasn't a loving brother," she said. Still, he was a happy child, always smiling and appearing in a good mood.

Beginning in those early years, Eric escaped into his imagination.

Ordered to clean the chicken coop, a seven-year-old Eric instead lay on his side in the barn reading. On the school bus, too, he habitually opened a book, ignoring the other children.

Yet he did make friends. "We were all nerds," said Brad Pense, who met Eric in the fourth grade. Eric had the first computer in his group, a gift from his father. "He was always one of the smart kids, into technology. His people skills weren't what he was known for," said Pense. "He always seemed really calm. Eric never got angry . . . emotional. I can't remember seeing Eric cry."

In grade school, Eric attended Cub Scout meetings.

Jessie Ruth described her son as diligent about scouting. "Part of it was he could be a leader. He really liked being a leader."

Eric at a Boy Scout camp in 1980
Evidence photo

Before long, an adolescent Eric graduated to Boy Scouts. Jim accompanied the boys on campouts, helping them earn merit badges. One January the director of the Fort Worth Zoo brought animals to hold. At summer camp, Eric took ten-mile hikes wearing a backpack, and cooked over campfires. Under the blue skies, they held outdoor church services. Always conscientious, Eric memorized the scout oath, promising to be courteous and kind, to do his duty to God and country, to keep physically strong, mentally awake, and morally straight.

At fourteen, in 1981, Eric made Eagle Scout, and his parents invited more than two hundred friends and family to the ceremony. "We were proud of him," Jessie said. That day, Eric received a silver ring with a blue eagle and vowed to be trustworthy, loyal, brave, and reverent.

At Azle High, Eric played trumpet in the band and joined the math team. When they traveled to contests, the boys slept on the floor six or more in a hotel room. Eric's parents filled with pride when the local newspaper reported his achievements.

Even then, he seemed slightly peculiar.

Eric with his trumpet
Courtesy of Tera Bellemare

Unusual in most high schools but undoubtedly more so in small towns, Eric routinely carried a briefcase. Among his classmates, he cultivated an image of a smart kid, one who stood a bit apart on the school landscape. On a social level, one friend described Eric as aloof.

Yet despite what could have been considered oddities, Eric experienced a happy childhood. On weekends, over long summer days, he congregated with his circle of friends. Not the popular kids, Eric gravitated toward other bright students, many his counterparts on the math and science teams. The worst insult in the group was being called stupid. Said one parent, "If you wanted to put someone down, that's what you would say."

Surrounded by forests and fields, Eric and his friends shot BB guns at cans in the woods. When they did, smiling and appearing content, Eric rarely talked. Then, at the precise moment called for, he interjected a comment, a punch line, or a pithy observation. "It was perfect," a friend said. "Eric was so funny. We'd all be laughing."

More often they gathered at one of their homes. At times, they brought math problems, approaching them like fascinating puzzles. Other days, they spent hours in make-believe worlds, playing *The Lord of the Rings* or *Star Trek*. Dividing the yard into starships, they portrayed the characters. In their daydreams, they became Romulans, Klingons, captains of the Federation.

Their favorite pastime, however, was Dungeons & Dragons.

In Azle, a Bible-belt town, D&D remained controversial. Many questioned the wisdom of teenagers becoming absorbed in tales of witches and dragons, of heroes and rogues. But Eric and his peers felt drawn to their fictions. In the years before computers took over the role-playing game world, they organized their battles with paper, pencils, and dice. They took turns as the Dungeon Master who laid out the adventures, set up each grand crusade. Inventing voices and mannerisms, they transformed into courageous warriors and villains capable of great evil. As they played, they earned rewards, including knowledge and treasures.

At these pursuits, Eric excelled. "Everyone liked having Eric on their team," one friend remarked. "He was good at strategic thinking. Eric was always good at planning."

A youthful Eric enjoyed wearing uniforms and taking part in organizations with lofty goals; he read books that came alive in his imagination. Playing intricate games where heroes hatched schemes, he righted wrongs and in the process saved the world.

Yet in the real world, when he was not pretending to be a guardian of the universe, his sister saw Eric's actions as troubling. "The truth is that Eric tormented me when I was a child," Tera said. "On the surface, everything with Eric was by the book. But when our parents weren't around, it was very different."

On the farm, Eric seemed fascinated with guns, target shooting, and hunting small animals. Abandoned kittens and cats wandered onto the Williamses' property, many climbing a tree near the house. Eric scrambled onto the roof with his rifle and shot the cats, watching their bleeding bodies fall to the ground. One day, he shot Tera's pet cat through the eye, killing it.

Once in high school, Eric met Tamara "Tammy" Hobbs, who ran in his circle of friends and competed on the math team. Before long, Eric worked at Twin Points, the Hobbs family's lake resort, with picnic tables and horseshoes, a

Eric with his date in high school
Evidence photo

playground, fishing, and swimming. From taking tickets to maintenance, over time he became an ad hoc assistant manager, enforcing park rules, including one that banned cussing. "I always felt safe with Eric," said Tammy. "He wouldn't let bad things happen or would stop the bad things from happening."

While some like Tammy viewed Eric as upstanding, others noted cracks in his veneer. One friend objected as Eric sped down country roads, coasted through stop signs. The friend classified such behavior as lawbreaking. "It's only illegal if you get caught," Eric responded.

It seemed that Eric, the rule enforcer, didn't necessarily view laws as applying to him.

Tera, too, described encounters that strayed from her brother's wholesome Eagle Scout persona. "Eric looked like a normal kid, but he never was," she said. "All Eric ever really wanted to do was play Dungeons & Dragons. It was like he was disconnected, not just from the family, but the world."

If Eric already displayed bizarre behavior, it's unlikely anyone would have guessed at his high school graduation, where he blended into the crowd in his long forest green robe. That auspicious day, the keynote speaker voiced a ubiquitous sentiment at such occasions, that the graduates use what they'd learned to "fly like eagles."

Briefly out of high school, Eric ran a private investigation service with a friend, not a particularly serious pursuit. As expected, in the fall of 1985, he instead enrolled where his father worked, in Fort Worth's Texas Christian University, a stately campus of red-roofed buildings.

At TCU, Eric's talents brought a chemistry scholarship. By then, he appeared a slight young man, standing about five-foot-ten. Despite his choice of a science major, those who knew Eric understood something else appealed more to him. "The paramilitary stuff really got him going," said a friend.

Eric in his 1985 high school
graduation photo
Evidence photo

"From the beginning, that's what Eric was into."

Building on his interests, Eric joined ROTC, the Reserve Officers' Training Corps, and talked of a military career. This, too, wasn't surprising since not only had his father served in Korea, but Eric came from a military family. Nearly all of his mother's male relatives enlisted in the armed services, and every year the Lyles family marked Armistice Day with a get-together honoring his grandfather's service in World War I.

Still, soldiering seemed an odd fit for Eric, who'd grown into a quiet, quirky young man with deep dimples and a sideways smile. Pedantic at times, he appeared particularly proud of not his physical strength, but what he and others saw as his exceptional intellect.

One ROTC friend gave Eric a nickname, "Tennessee Tuxedo." Like Eric, the cartoon character, a penguin in a fedora and a tie, had a superior mind, and the friend saw the moniker as representative of Eric's analytical skills and calm determination. In the cartoon, the penguin often pledged, "Tennessee Tuxedo will not fail!"

By his second year at TCU, Eric wore yet another uniform. At the time as a chemistry major he took theoretical calculus, but then he decided "that the real purpose of college was to finish." Opting for a "less stringent" degree program, he changed his major to criminal justice. Two years after enrolling in the university, Eric added introduction to law enforcement and pistol marksmanship, and legal aspects of criminal justice to his schedule.

In ROTC, Eric also focused on law enforcement, taking classes to become a military policeman. In his evaluation, an instructor described Eric as a model candidate. "His dedication, integrity, loyalty and military bearing are an asset to the . . . program."

Eric in his ROTC uniform (left) swearing in another recruit
Evidence photo

Academically Eric's future, too, looked bright. At TCU, he held a B average, and in spring 1989, his final semester, he made the dean's list. That year his supervisors continued to praise his ROTC performance. The chief of the military police issued a certificate that cited Eric's "special trust and confidence in the valor, patriotism, fidelity."

After graduating from TCU with a bachelor's in criminal justice that May, Eric traveled to army camp in Fort Riley, Kansas. In June, he received a diploma from the army's MP school, his name on the commandant's list. On his evaluation his superiors called Eric a "hard-charging individual who definitely knows what it takes to be an MP."

Eric's desired military career, however, failed to materialize.

That year marked a nationwide reduction in forces, and, unlike many of his friends, Eric wasn't offered a slot in the regular army. One friend thought Eric was passed over because he didn't appear passionate. "He never looked really gung-ho," the man recalled. "Eric was always kind of nonchalant, and that was the way he struck me about the army. Actually, I didn't think he cared. But when he didn't get in, he was really disappointed."

Instead, Eric entered the Individual Ready Reserve as a lieutenant, where he could be called up if needed, and his dream of a career army officer's life came to a screeching stop. It must have seemed an odd turn for someone so many predicted would achieve great success. "I'm sure he was disappointed," his father said. "Eric just wasn't one to show it."

A future in the military abruptly erased with his criminal justice degree Eric applied for a police officer's job in a Fort Worth suburb called White Settlement. There, coworkers struck by his youthful appearance and his shyness nicknamed him "Opie," after the boy played by Ron Howard in the *Andy Griffith* TV series.

In White Settlement, too, however, all didn't go well.

As Eric would later explain it, he enrolled to take a class, but the police chief refused to give him the time off. Once he'd been told no, Eric simply called in sick. Someone reported it to the chief, who called Eric in and asked why he'd ignored orders. Eight months into his stint with the department, Eric flatly said, "Because I want to."

"Well, then you're fired," the chief responded. It struck the man as odd that even while being sacked, Eric never looked upset.

Soon after, he signed on with Springtown PD, a much smaller city half an hour northwest of his last employer. A good friend, Paul Lilly, worked as an officer in the department and recommended Eric to the chief, James Lyons.

In truth, Lyons had mixed feelings about hiring Eric Williams. They had history. Lyons had been on the board that interviewed Eric a decade earlier, when he applied to become an Eagle Scout. For years, Lyons had screened Eagle applicants, and he routinely included a question without a good answer, one to trip the boys up. Lyons wanted to see how they reacted. But when Lyons asked Eric his trick question, Eric had an unusual response. "Eric stared at me until I thought my eyelids would bleed. He had a dead look in his eyes. It gave me a really strange feeling. I thought, that boy's got issues. Something's not right."

When he considered hiring Eric as a police officer, Lyons worried about how Eric would interact with the public. "He struck me as manipulative," Lyons said. "I convinced myself I was probably wrong about Eric."

Then late one night, Lyons received a call from his dispatcher, who said the department's computer system had been hacked, someone accessing the third—the most secure—level. The next morning, the man showed Lyons computer footprints proving Eric had "monkeyed around" in the system. On closer examination, it appeared Eric had changed the log to indicate he had patrolled the streets, when Lyons suspected Eric had actually been at a topless bar.

"The biggest concerns for me are truth and trust," Lyons said when he called Eric into his office. "Did you access the computer system's third level last night?"

"No," Eric said. After seeing the records documenting the breach, he still denied it.

"I looked in that boy's eyes and they were just dead, just like that experience I had with him in Eagle Scouts," said Lyons. "And he had a smirk on his face. I told him, 'Eric, I'm going to have to let you go.'"

At twenty-four years of age, Eric had already failed three times. First, he'd been passed over by the army and then fired by two police departments. Perhaps that motivated Eric, because days later he offered Lyons a gift, a police radio, and asked for his job back. "That hits the bribe button," Lyons said. "Under no circumstances will I rehire you."

At that, Eric turned and left the police station.

Looking back, Lyons thought Eric's actions made no sense. In the older man's opinion, Eric had to have intentionally left the footprints in the computer system. "He was obviously really computer savvy to be able to hack in, and he could have erased the evidence," said Lyons. "I thought he'd left it on purpose. He wanted us to know how smart he was."

In November 1993, at the age of twenty-six, Eric moved with his good friend Paul Lilly to Kaufman County, forty minutes southeast of Dallas, where Lilly had a job with the sheriff's office. In size slightly smaller than Rhode Island, Kaufman was poorer than its neighboring counties, and more rural. With Lilly, Eric rented a small house in Terrell, with sixteen thousand residents, the county's largest city. His law enforcement career stalled, Eric reassessed his future and began studying for the LSAT, the law school entrance exam.

Needing to cover living expenses, however, he applied for jobs. Soon word filtered to Judge Glen Ashworth, who presided over Kaufman County's only district court, the Eighty-sixth, that a bright young man had just relocated to the area. From a mutual friend, Ashworth heard about Eric's degree from TCU, his years in ROTC, that he was an Eagle Scout and a licensed police officer. The timing presented an opportunity, as Ashworth's court coordinator had recently died of cancer. The judge contacted Eric, who drove twenty minutes south to the county seat, the small, quaint city of Kaufman, to meet with the judge in his office behind his courtroom.

Home to fewer than seven thousand, the city of Kaufman had a rustic feel. "It's such a small town, everyone knows everyone," said a local attorney. "I think of it as my Mayberry."

Dominating the town square stood the aging courthouse. Many such Texas institutions were grand, impressive marble and stone structures, some with Victorian flourishes. Instead, the one on Washington Street was a plain, boxy structure built in 1956. If once considered modern architecture, by the time Eric arrived, it merely looked tired. Its only saving grace: large oaks buffered it from trucks rumbling by and offered shade during blistering summers.

The old storefronts that ringed the characterless building, their windows tinted to shut out the strong rays of the

The Kaufman County Courthouse
Kathryn Casey

sun, looked as unremarkable, many redbrick with large windows, housing a smattering of retail stores and law offices. Only a few structures in Kaufman's unimposing downtown displayed any true flavor: a bank building converted to a restaurant, the old Greenslade drug building with its flat canopy, and a small event center.

Although only forty minutes southeast of Dallas, Kaufman felt a world away, a place locked in the past.

When Eric drove into Kaufman, his surroundings may have reminded him of his hometown, Azle. To enter through the courthouse's main door, he passed a Civil War monument topped by a Confederate soldier holding a rifle. On one side it read: "Honor to their memory, glory to their cause, and peace to their ashes."

That day, Eric's interview went well. As they talked, Ashworth asked the young man about his plans for the future, and Eric told the judge that he'd begun studying for the law school entrance exam. Impressed, a few days later the judge contacted Eric and hired him.

Downtown Kaufman storefronts
Kathryn Casey

Chapter 2

Ashworth set Eric up in the county. He made Eric who he was.

—Sandra Harward

For those who work inside, small-town courthouses become second families made up of the staff and lawyers, the regulars who circulate through, crossing paths. Many stop to talk, inquire about each other's lives and health, compare notes on the latest gossip and local events.

A dozen years on the bench, Judge Glen Monroe Ashworth presided over the county's only state-level court and wielded substantial power. His family influential in the area for generations, some called Ashworth "the king of Kaufman County." With penetrating blue eyes and an intimidating scowl, the judge ruled with an iron hand. Ashworth came down hard on those who wasted his time. He knew the law, and he expected the attorneys to know it as well. "He was a good judge, but I'd seen him make attorneys cry," said Sandra Harward, who practiced law in the area.

In March 1994, Eric began working for Judge Ashworth in his offices on the courthouse's second floor, reached by entering the building's main entrance and traveling up a rattling old elevator or a flight of well-worn steps. Near the battered door to the district attorney's office, the judge's chamber connected to his courtroom through a private door. As court coordinator, Eric followed the judge throughout the day, circulating from a desk outside Ashworth's office to one at the head of the courtroom at the judge's right hand.

From his first days as caretaker to one of the county's most important men, Eric, too, exercised considerable power.

His duties varied; Eric managed Ashworth's schedule, worked with lawyers filing motions, and set trial dates. Mornings, he monitored the courtroom, called the docket, and watched over hearings and plea bargains. Evenings, Eric had the judge's calendar organized and desk cleared. Before long, word circulated about the new court coordinator. Eric impressed many of those he met with his intellect, and they often found him amusing with his quirky smile.

Others felt uncomfortable around him. "Eric was strange," said one lawyer. "If it hadn't been for the judge, Eric was wallpaper. He seemed to always be listening, but he was painfully quiet. At the same time, he looked amused, as if he considered himself superior."

Yet only Ashworth's impressions mattered, and Eric appeared efficient, loyal, and discreet, important qualities for someone privy to the interworkings of such an influential office. "No can do," Eric said one day when an attorney stopped in to talk to the judge. Then she listened and heard Ashworth dressing down someone in his chambers. Wearing a grin, Eric shrugged, as if indicating the situation lay beyond his control.

Once home, Eric studied for the LSAT. His dedication paid off. "I scored a 163 out of a maximum of 170," he said.

Life quickly fell into place for Eric in Kaufman. Not long after he hired Eric, Ashworth suggested Eric register as an unpaid reserve officer with the district attorney's office. Once he did, Eric had an official badge that enabled him to wear a holster with a .38 caliber pistol into the courthouse and courtroom. For years, Ashworth lunched with the county surveyor. Soon after Eric arrived, Ashworth suggested he join them, and the three men became regulars at restaurants catering to the downtown crowd.

Later others recalled one particular event, however, and wondered if Ashworth should have realized his clerk wasn't the young man he appeared. The first summer Eric worked at the courthouse, he attended a court coordinators' conference. There he met his counterpart in Coryell County, a woman with a twelve-year-old son, one in the middle of a divorce. Petite and pretty, Janice Gray began dating Eric the following month. They saw each other off and on and talked on the phone often, until she met someone with whom she envisioned a future.

At that point, Gray called Eric to end the relationship. She thought he took it well. Eric called once or twice after that, including the week before that summer's conference in Huntsville. He seemed friendly, and she didn't worry, but when she arrived at the hotel, he waited in the lobby. "Do you want to get something to eat later?" he asked.

"I don't think that would be a good idea," she answered. "I already made plans."

"I have something I want to give your son," Eric said. With that, he reached down and pulled a pistol out of an ankle holster, holding it up to show it to her.

"It's nice," she said, but ignored the offer. Moments later, she turned away to talk to others walking through the door.

That evening, Eric appeared again. In a sports bar where she socialized with friends, he suddenly tapped her on the shoulder, taking Gray by surprise. She hadn't told Eric where she was going. "Could you step back a little? I'd like to talk to you for a minute," he said.

They walked a short distance off from the others and chatted casually for a few minutes, before she said, "I'm going to go back and join my friends."

Ever so calmly, Eric said, "I have a gun. If you walk away, I'll use it. I don't have anything to lose."

Petrified by fear, Gray began softly crying. Perhaps her body language alerted her friends, two of whom walked over. "Come with us," one said, and they escorted her away.

Moments later, Eric had disappeared.

Returning to her hotel, Gray called the conference coordinator, who notified police. They listened to her account and posted a guard outside her hotel room while they looked for Eric. The next morning, they explained that they'd been unable to find him and that they assumed he'd returned to Kaufman. But when an officer walked her to the conference, Gray opened the door and saw Eric seated in the meeting room as if nothing had happened.

"He's in there," she said.

Gray waited in the restroom while the officer pulled Eric out of the conference. After they left for the police station, Gray went into the conference. Later that afternoon, she stopped at the Huntsville Police Department to file a full report.

Recalling that day, Eric scoffed at the notion that anyone worried about his intentions. "They spoke to me, but they did nothing. The police weren't concerned."

In contrast, police told Gray that the local DA talked to Kaufman's DA, and that Judge Ashworth had taken responsibility for Eric. "The judge promised Williams won't bother you," an officer told her. "We'll hold the report, and if he does, let us know and we'll file the charges."

Janice Gray agreed and never heard from Eric Williams again.

Back in Kaufman, Eric returned to work at the courthouse as if nothing had happened. That fall, he officially put down roots and bought his first house, a tan brick one-story about a mile from the courthouse on Anthony Street.

Months later in the fall of 1995 at the age of twenty-eight, Eric Williams began law school at Texas Wesleyan in Fort Worth. From Kaufman, he had a two-hour commute. As long as he finished his work, Eric had Ashworth's permission to leave at three every day. As Eric continued to better his life, many in Kaufman believed Ashworth saw himself as a father figure to Eric. At the courthouse, lawyers and members of the staff predicted Eric would one day follow in Ashworth's footsteps, get his law license and eventually a judgeship.

As the months passed, the closeness between the two men grew. Ashworth gave Eric a key to his house, so that he could care for the judge's pets when he traveled. Then Judge Ashworth told Eric that he had put him in his will. Nearly every day they continued to go out for lunch. After the county surveyor died, his son took his place, and one of the local attorneys joined them, Becky Calabria, who along with her husband had an office across the street from the courthouse.

Two years after arriving, Eric Williams had powerful friends in Kaufman.

Still, at times Eric did say odd things, like one day when he interjected: "If I ever decided to go out, I'd take a bunch of people with me." The group of courthouse friends seated with him fell silent and stared, puzzled by the statement. Later someone mentioned that Charles Whitman, who in 1966 shot forty-nine people, killing sixteen, by shooting from the University of Texas clock tower, was an Eagle Scout like Eric. In response, one of those listening wondered if Eric would one day shoot from the roof of the Kaufman courthouse.

Still, Eric seemed like such a benign young man, no one took it seriously.

Instead, over the years, Eric forged strong ties with many in Kaufman. For the most part, they grew to think of him in fond terms. They liked his slight eccentricities and quiet manner, and thought of him as an odd but amusing friend. When he smiled, he had a boyish look. Gradually, he became accepted as one of them.

By the mid-nineties Eric's career had taken an upward trajectory. Soon he'd be an attorney, with social position and the prospect of increased prosperity. He lacked only the right person to share his success. Then one day in 1996, three years after he arrived in Kaufman, Eric posted on an Internet message board and a woman named Kim Johnson read it. Something about that post appealed to her. The man sounded funny and smart, and she admired both qualities. Kim keyed in a response, and before long, Eric Williams had a partner.

Chapter 3

There were a lot of things about Eric I found out later. I thought I knew him. It turned out that I was wrong.
—Kim Williams

Sometimes couples inspire each other, fostering relationships in which they motivate each other to do things they would never have done alone, the potential outcome great good. Other times they play off each other's insecurities and egos; they build poisoned liaisons, urging the other to the vilest of evils. For yet others events spin out of control for one when a partner takes the reins and leads them to the depths of hell.

For Kim Johnson, Eric Williams became that person.

"I grew up in Dallas," Kim said, her soft Texas drawl punctuated by a slight lilt and a narrowing of pale blue eyes. A petite woman, she had an expressive flair for the dramatic, and a tendency to occasionally flash a sardonic smile.

From the outside Kim appeared to have a respectable, middle-class upbringing. Born in France, her mother, Lucienne, moved to New York. On a trip to Dallas, she met Kim's father, Donald Johnson. They had two children, the first a son, Jamie, followed in September 1966 by Kim. An army reservist, Don made a good living as the owner of an elevator repair company.

Yet, Kim insists, all wasn't entirely as it seemed: "My dad was kind of ornery. It was common knowledge in our neighborhood. He was brutal. I used to hide in the closet or under the pool table."

In school, Kim earned good grades. In ninth grade, she marched with the band. In high school, blond and blue-eyed with big Texas hair, she danced on the drill team, performing during half-time. "I had to run the boys off from her," said her brother, Jamie. "Kim was kind of a prima donna, and the boys liked her. She never gave my parents problems."

Kim did, however, have a shadowy side. For two years, during ninth and tenth grade, Kim hid from friends and family that she battled bulimia. "It was a sort of self-punishment for being the one my dad didn't beat," she said. Her senior year in high school, she stopped purging and never did it again.

In Skyline High School, Kim dated Michael Gregg, and he described her as spunky, someone who knew her mind. "They called us Barbie and Ken, because Kim had a tiny figure and was pretty like a Barbie doll," he said. They solved word scrambles on Kim's front porch, went to AC/DC concerts, and drank root beer floats at the local drive-in. "I wanted more, but Kim didn't. We were friends," he said. "And I was protective of Kim. I cared about her."

When she graduated in 1985, Kim attended junior college before enrolling in Dallas's premier school, Southern Methodist University. Majoring in English, she planned to enroll in law school. In the end, none of that happened.

First, she dropped out of SMU, when she decided law school wasn't in her future. At the time, she worked for an attorney, and what she saw in his office convinced her that she wasn't cut out for a legal career. "I'm not much of a debater. I don't like confrontation. Lawyers are often in confrontational situations. That wasn't for me."

Instead, Kim enrolled in the University of Texas in Arlington, preparing to teach. About that time, she took a summer receptionist's job in a doctor's office. When she liked it, she dropped out of college. "Kim worked hard, and she was fun," said the doctor's wife. "She had big Texas hair and taught line dancing at our son's bar mitzvah. All those soft-spoken Jewish people dancing and laughing."

Kim at the bar mitzvah

At the office, Kim giggled a lot. A Cowboys fan, she pinned a photo of quarterback Troy Aikman on a wall. Each morning, she made copies of the newspaper crossword and competed with the doctor's wife to finish first. Routinely, Kim took small things and turned them into amusing breaks in the day. When a catalogue arrived with photos of male models in scrubs, Kim offered the others chocolates and suggested, "Okay, let's see which guy is the best-looking."

Working at the doctor's office, Kim bought a house not far from her parents' home. At times, the doctor and his wife suggested Kim finish her degree, but she never seemed interested. Then in 1993, when Kim was twenty-seven, they noticed that she snapped at the patients. Kim seemed unhappy. "It had gotten to the point where people irritated Kim," said the doctor's wife. "The job wasn't a good fit for her. She kept getting moodier."

After taking a break to think through what she wanted

to do, Kim quit. Soon after, the doctor heard that she had taken another job, this time as a clerk at a hospital.

Three years after she left her job at the doctor's office, in 1996, Kim signed up for a free thirty-day account with Prodigy, an early Internet service. One evening, she logged onto a message board for individuals in search of friends. A post caught her eye. In a short bio, Eric talked about his courthouse job and described himself as a law student. Something about the tenor of the post appealed to Kim, and she thought that Eric sounded lonely. "I replied, said, 'I'll be your friend.' I didn't expect to meet him. Then I discovered that he lived only forty miles away from me."

For months, they communicated through e-mails. At one point, he asked for her phone number, but Kim refused. He sent his, but she didn't call. Finally, she met him at a restaurant. "I could tell from the e-mails that he had a brain, and that appealed to me." She saw him as "someone I could talk to."

At the restaurant, Kim immediately liked Eric, whom she judged as more intelligent than men she'd dated in the past. While she enjoyed being with him, at first she didn't envision the relationship as romantic. "I didn't feel like we connected that way. He thought so, but I didn't."

"We had the same goals," Eric said. When he described Kim, he referenced intellect, twice: "She was smart, well-read, capable of intelligent discussion, funny and pretty."

On dates, Kim did much of the talking, and slowly she decided Eric had traits that fit her better than those of her previous boyfriends. "Usually they were good-looking but not a lot else," she said. "Eric looked kind of like a preacher or a Bible salesman, but in his own way, he was cute."

That Thanksgiving, Kim invited Eric and his family to her house. Tera brought her six-month-old daughter. As she watched, Tera thought Kim appeared uncomfortable holding the baby, as if she didn't know what to do with her. "I thought Kim seemed like kind of a bimbo," Tera said. "I didn't like that Eric got involved with her."

Eric's mother used the word "different" to describe how Kim struck her. "She didn't seem like Eric's type of person." In fact, she saw Kim with her big blond hair as flighty, and overly proud. Yet she understood why Kim caught her son's attentions. "She was a very attractive girl."

The impressions better on the other side, Kim's dad, Don Johnson, enjoyed talking with Eric about law enforcement. Although working and going to school, Eric maintained his commission with the DA's office and in his spare time continued to pursue higher credentials, earning an advanced police officer certificate.

Once Eric mentioned Kim, his friends at the courthouse noticed a difference in him. Eric seemed more outgoing and engaged, and they thought she had a good effect on him. Some worried that he met Kim on the Internet, but he seemed happy.

All went well, and the relationship deepened. Then, not long after they began dating, Eric lost weight. He seemed tired and inordinately thirsty. Kim consulted a doctor, who suggested Eric have his blood sugar tested. The test showed that Eric had Type 1 diabetes. Unable to regulate his blood sugar, Eric didn't do well with insulin shots, and his doctor installed a small pump he wore on his belt.

Months later when his enrollment came up for renewal in the Individual Ready Reserve, Eric discharged. With his diabetes, he wouldn't ever be called up. "There was no point," he said.

The following year Kim and Eric grew closer, Eric becoming ever more attentive. One night, thinking little of it, Kim told him over the phone that she had plans to meet a friend. Although Kim never mentioned where she was going, Eric walked in the bar moments after she arrived.

Apparently, he'd followed her. "There you are," he said, as if nothing odd had just happened.

"I just thought he was being protective," Kim said. "The following me thing, everything, it just seemed like he loved me."

Once he met Kim, Eric saw less of his own family, and his relationship with his sister continued to be strained. In January 1998, their grandmother died, and he drove Tera to the funeral at what seemed like one hundred miles per hour down narrow country roads. When a police officer pulled him over and asked for his license, Eric flashed his badge from the DA's office. Instead of getting a ticket, Eric asked for an escort. Agreeing, the man drove ahead, his lights flashing and siren blaring. "I figured Eric assumed he was above the law," Tera said.

The following spring, Eric and Kim celebrated their

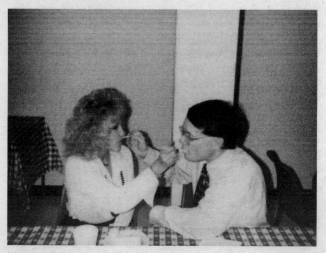

Kim and Eric at their engagement party
Evidence photo

engagement at a party thrown by his courthouse friends. They fed each other cake, and Judge Ashworth, along with the others who attended, toasted the young couple.

Still, they kept their plans quiet from their families. Eric acquired a tux, and Kim a wedding gown. They bought plane tickets, and Kim put her beloved Pomeranian, Penny, in a carrier and took her with them to Las Vegas.

On May 13, 1998, two years after they met, Eric Williams and Kim Johnson wed. Without family or friends, they had a traditional ceremony at the Little Chapel of the Flowers. Kim wore a lace gown, with a bow on the bustle and a keyhole opening in the back covered in a pearl fringe. Eric couldn't have looked prouder as they lit a unity candle, pledging to love and honor each other until death. "We did it up right," said Kim, smiling as she remembered that day.

When they returned to Texas, they formally joined their lives. Kim sold her house and moved into Eric's on Anthony Street, taking a job at Kaufman's Texas Health

Eric and Kim on their wedding day
Courtesy of Tera Bellemare

Presbyterian Hospital as a quality assurance clerk. Less than a mile away at the courthouse, Eric placed Kim's photo on his desk. At times, he held it up and said to the lawyers who stopped in, "Isn't my wife beautiful?" And she was.

"Eric wasn't hot, but Kim was," said a friend. "And he was very much in love. For the first time since I'd known him, he looked truly happy."

Life had treated Eric well. Law school graduation loomed only a year away. In love, he undoubtedly expected decades ahead with an attractive, healthy young wife. They talked of children and a family. Instead, their lives took a fateful turn.

Just nine months after their whirlwind Las Vegas wedding, a bruise on Kim's left upper thigh hardened. A biopsy diagnosed rheumatoid arthritis, a potentially debilitating autoimmune disorder. To ease her pain, her doctor prescribed a narcotic painkiller, Vicodin. "Eric was supportive," she said. "I thought, this isn't good. I was scared. But I thought we'd be all right. Nothing would change. Sure I was sick, but the future looked good."

At that point, Eric appeared to admire Judge Ashworth, and the two men had a strong relationship. Once they were married, Eric and Kim attended the judge's annual Super Bowl party. He invited them for steaks, and one year for Thanksgiving dinner. At home, Eric talked to Kim often of Ashworth in laudatory terms, regaling her with stories about the tight fist the judge held on the courtroom. Impressed by the power Ashworth wielded, Eric seemed proud of their association.

In spring 1999, Eric's family, Kim's parents, Judge Ashworth, and others from the courthouse attended Eric's law school graduation. On that day, the judge looked pleased with his young protégé. At a small party, Eric gave Ashworth a plaque. It thanked the judge for his support, and for inspiring Eric to pursue his degree.

In July Eric took the state bar exam. While he awaited results, he prepared to become a lawyer, leaving his job as court coordinator to sign on with Calabria & Calabria, a well-known husband-and-wife law practice directly across the street from the courthouse. Eric had known Becky Calabria, a regular in Judge Ashworth's daily lunch bunch, for years.

All went as planned, and in November Eric became licensed to practice law in the state of Texas. Despite his diabetes and Kim's illness, which on a bad day made her walk with an unsteady gait, their futures looked bright. That Christmas, Kim's father dressed as Santa, and Eric's parents, Tera, and her family all went to Kim and Eric's home. Kim loved the holidays, and she had a big tree, and decorations spread over the house, covering it like frosting on a cake.

As the new millennium began, Eric and Kim appeared a devoted young couple, poised to live their dreams. Eric

Kim and Eric at Christmas
Courtesy of Tera Bellemare

had worked hard and had become a lawyer. Once licensed, he registered at the courthouse to get appointments. To his benefit, Eric had an advantage any young attorney would covet: a close friendship with the judge handing out the assignments, Ashworth.

Eric worked hard and his calendar gradually filled with clients. Each day he showed up in Judge Ashworth's court meticulously dressed, his hair carefully combed. As the cases came in, the judge called out attorney's names, including Eric's. Diligent, he made his deadlines, and more appointments followed. At times, Eric represented indigent defense clients, those who stood charged with a crime and didn't have money to hire a lawyer. On other days, Ashworth assigned CPS (Child Protective Services) cases, appointing Eric as guardian ad litem to represent children in custody battles and neglect or abuse cases.

His work flourishing and life opening up for them, Eric and Kim went out socially with local lawyers and their spouses. At such gatherings, they laughed and seemed content. Yet the others weren't always sure how to take Kim, because, like Eric, she sometimes said odd things. Although she usually sounded sweet and caring, at times she laced her comments with biting sarcasm. Some found Kim funny, but others walked away troubled.

One night at a party, a clutch of women compared pastimes they enjoyed with their husbands. A few mentioned travel or watching movies. Later one of those at the party said something curious happened. When it was her turn, Kim smiled and said: "Sometimes Eric and I like to sit around at night and plan the perfect murder."

At the courthouse, Eric and Judge Ashworth continued to be close, the judge advising Eric on his career. In the beginning, Eric took a range of court-appointed cases, but as his caseload built, he had ever more clients. After the first year, he went to Judge Ashworth and explained, "I need to make a decision soon, how I specialize."

They talked it over, and Eric came to the conclusion that he'd prefer concentrating on the CPS cases.

Eric liked the CPS work. Overall, he felt that he had more influence representing the children. In the criminal cases he most often negotiated a plea bargain. "With CPS work, I could help plan what would happen. I had a better sense of my work being valued."

The CPS cases also came with substantial power. As a guardian ad litem, Eric offered opinions that carried weight on what happened within families, where children would be placed, even whether a parent or grandparent should be given visitation.

Perhaps a downside, family law often proved emotional. Parents sometimes lost custody and children were often caught in the middle, so it wasn't surprising that while some liked Eric and thought well of his efforts, others saw him as biased and even cruel. "Eric had a lot of influence and he played favorites," said one mother whose daughter had Eric as her ad litem. "He sided with my husband, and it cost my daughter dearly."

At home in the evenings, Kim and Eric's conversations revolved around his work. When he talked of representing the children, Kim viewed Eric as a hero. Working at the hospital, she sometimes heard of abused children admitted for care. In one case a mother claimed a baby fell off a bed, but couldn't explain other broken bones on the X-rays. Representing the child, Eric assessed the suitability of relatives who fought for custody. "I'm going to recommend the grandparents get the baby," he told Kim when she asked what would happen. As Kim listened, he described the details of the case, and she thought her husband genuinely cared.

If the families involved sometimes questioned Eric's

motives, Kim never did. "I always thought Eric saw himself as a champion to the kids. I saw him that way, too."

At first, Eric continued to work under Becky Calabria's umbrella, but his job with the firm ended in a dispute over his earnings. With CPS appointments flowing in, Eric brought in a substantial amount of money. Calabria expected a percentage would go to the firm. Instead, Eric pocketed it. They discussed the issue, Eric later describing it as a misunderstanding. Perhaps he realized that with his career humming along, he didn't need the firm.

The front of Eric's law office on N. Jackson Street
Kathryn Casey

In downtown Kaufman, Eric Williams rented an office on the courthouse square, at 107 N. Jackson Street, from a friend, Taryn Davis. A lawyer, Davis had an office next door, and outside they put a brown plaque edged in white with Eric's name in gold above the one bearing hers. The weathered brown wood-sided building had a leaded glass Texas Lone Star on the door.

In a room just inside the front door, Eric had a receptionist's desk, and he hired a secretary. But as time went on, he sublet the front to a bail bondsman. From that point forward, clients walked a long hallway before reaching his conference room, reception area, and office.

Although the office appeared modest, Eric, into computers since high school, when he was the first in his circle
to own a desktop, brought in all the latest gadgets. "One
thing about Eric was that he always had his office blinged
out with high-tech toys," said a friend. "He was proud of
being ahead of the curve."

Something else in his office attested to his special abilities. While in law school, Eric discovered that his high score
on the entrance exam qualified him to join Mensa, a society for those who scored in the ninety-eighth percentile or
above on standardized intelligence tests. Always proud of
his intellect, Eric paid for a lifetime membership and hung
a Mensa certificate on his wall next to his diplomas. At con-
spicuous places on shelves, he placed Mensa books, leading
one lawyer to assume Eric wanted those who walked into his
office to understand his brilliance.

Most days, Judge Ashworth walked over to collect Eric
from his law office for lunch. His former boss, Becky
Calabria, and Greg Sjerven, the county surveyor, joined
them. "Everybody in the lunch group was smart," said
one attorney. "But Eric was the one with the Mensa certificate."

While Eric's career flourished, the bad news about Kim's
health kept coming. Her mouth parched, eyes chronically
dry, her doctor diagnosed Sjogren's Syndrome, a condition
that inhibits the body from producing moisture. Ninety
percent of Sjogren's sufferers were women, and half of
those had rheumatoid arthritis. When her Sjogren's kicked
in, Kim's arthritis worsened, and her doctor wrote more
prescriptions for narcotics.

Looking back, it seemed that her illness took a toll on
the marriage, and Eric changed.

From the beginning, they'd talked of children. Since
Eric appeared passionate about his young clients, Kim
thought he would be a good father. But one evening he an-

nounced that he "didn't want to bring a child into this shitty world."

Shocked, Kim asked, "What if I get pregnant?"

"You would either have it taken care of, or I would divorce you," he answered.

With that, Eric walked from the room. That night Kim went to bed hurt and angry, and the next morning, Eric acted as if nothing had happened.

Christmas came, and Eric seemed different in another way. In the past, he'd willingly helped Kim decorate. Suddenly, to her surprise, he proclaimed that he'd never liked the holiday and didn't want to spend it with family.

Her situation ever-changing, Kim continued to work at the hospital, until her rheumatoid arthritis left her feeling unsteady on her feet at work. Three years into their marriage, she quit and applied for disability, something Eric had pushed her to do since her diagnosis. After two attempts, the government approved Kim's claim. From that point forward, she received $1,300 monthly payments. "Then I was disabled."

Life slowed. On bad days, Kim took heavy doses of painkillers and remained in bed. On better days, she drove to Eric's office to cover the reception desk and answer phone calls.

Meanwhile, money flowed in from Eric's court appoints, and that year, 2001, Kim and Eric purchased a 2,882-square-foot, three-bedroom house, a mile and a half from the courthouse and Eric's office. At 1600 Overlook, the one-story in the Wellington Park subdivision had a three-car garage. Making Kaufman seem like an even smaller world, Judge Ashworth's cousin had developed the area, in a section the locals nicknamed "Snob Hill," and the Williamses' home had once belonged to the judge's aunt. A field ran behind the house, and Judge Ashworth lived in a house on acreage on the other side.

Eric and Kim's home on Overlook
Kathryn Casey

Along with the new house, Eric indulged his interests. At the courthouse, he showed off firearms, turning them in his hands, letting others hold them to appreciate their weight and balance. When he and Kim married, she had a revolver, and Eric had ten or so handguns and rifles. She didn't know the number grew, but within Kaufman's law community, word spread that in his office on the town square, Eric had a closet arsenal. Yet few thought much of it. "This is Texas," said one Kaufman attorney. "We all have guns."

That year, Eric also bought a black Sport Trac, a small pickup with an extended cab. And for Kim's birthday in September, she bought a Trans Am in the final year Pontiac made them. Nearly daily, delivery services dropped off boxes from Amazon and eBay. At their house as in his office, Eric installed high-tech toys. Laptops covered the white-countered kitchen bar, and in the evenings Eric and Kim played games or surfed the net. When purchases didn't work out, Eric discarded them in closets. Kim complained that he wasted money, but Eric didn't seem to care.

In ways, the tension grew. "Eric didn't ask my opinion on anything," Kim said. "By the time he talked to me, he already knew what he was going to do and how he was going to do it."

In 2002, Ashworth, a Democrat, faced reelection, and Kaufman County had changed, more voters turning conservative. A white-haired, grandfatherly looking attorney named Howard Tygrett, a Republican, registered to run against Ashworth. At that point, Eric's mentor announced his retirement, and Eric's world began to shift.

Chapter 4

Everything Eric did he thought through and considered the possibilities. Everything he said to anyone served a purpose. It was all part of his plan.

—Kim Williams

Ironically, rather than a loss, Judge Ashworth's retirement turned into a financial boon for Eric Williams.

In January 2003, Howard Tygrett took over as the judge in the Eighty-sixth District Court. Whatever the judge's reasoning, he began paying higher fees to the attorneys appointed to handle the county's indigent defense and CPS work. "It started to climb almost as soon as Tygrett took office," said a former county official. "People were suddenly making a lot of money."

Looking back, some would say that by then Eric, who'd been in Kaufman for nine years, had been accepted into the courthouse fold, and that Tygrett began giving Eric the bulk of the CPS work. "Kaufman is really a good-old-boy network, and Eric had become one of the good old boys," said a local lawyer. "Most of us thought of him as one of us. And the judges saw him as the CPS guy, the one who handled those cases."

To some, it seemed, Eric received more than his share. "It was a really unusual situation," said Sandra Harward, a lawyer who worked for the state and specialized in such cases. "I'd never seen it in any other county, where one attorney got so much of the CPS work."

Not long after, something odd happened. Working as a visiting judge, Ashworth circulated to different courthouses. One day in Kaufman, he saw Eric filling out paperwork. When he looked closer, Ashworth realized Eric had a stack of county pay vouchers, the to-be-filled-out sections empty, waiting to be completed with details of hours worked on court-appointed cases. Although largely blank, the vouchers had already been signed by Judge Tygrett. Disappointed, Ashworth reprimanded Eric, suggesting that he shouldn't be filing bills without oversight.

That night, late at night, Eric sent Ashworth an angry e-mail, instructing him to mind his own business and warning that he didn't want to see him anymore. The judge replied that he'd always think of Eric as a friend, and the following morning Eric responded by asking if they could "forget last night's conversation."

The judge agreed, and on days Ashworth worked in Kaufman, their lunch schedule went on unchanged. Yet the criticism wasn't forgotten. From that point forward, Eric fumed about Ashworth, describing his old boss as "a prissy prima donna."

As she listened, Kim realized Eric collected grievances. Over the years she'd heard him rage about clients and lawyers, family members who fell out of his favor. To her, Eric seemed incapable of forgiving any perceived offense. "He let things stew," she said. "It just festered."

Making Eric's position even more enviable, the CPS appointments had another benefit. Over time, his large number of cases earned Eric a reputation as a family law expert. That led to referrals from other attorneys to add to his client list. "Eric made a shitload of money, and he had a lot of control," said Sandra Harward. "The judges respected Eric and often went with his recommendations."

A Facebook photo of Eric in his office

In 2004, Eric hired a secretary to take over Kim's duties at his law office. To his mother, he complained Kim came in late and left early. She spent many days in bed, taking an increasing amount of prescription drugs, including narcotic painkillers. Where she'd once accompanied Eric to social gatherings, he arrived alone, describing Kim as too ill to attend.

Bored at home, Kim set up an Internet company, an eBay concern that sold "tasteful" women's lingerie, named Honey Nuggets after one of their three Pomeranians. Kim treated the dogs, all rescues, like the children she never had. She called them her furry babies and fawned over them. The dogs had racks of clothes, and in the house Kim kept them in diapers. Two clung to Kim, and Eric's favorite, Honey, followed him through the house. Later Kim added pet clothing and toys to her stock. Still, it became little more than a hobby.

Overall, by 2005, Eric spent a diminishing amount of time at the Overlook house.

Late at night, he dawdled in the office, and Sandra Harward received e-mails from him sent at midnight or even later. Some peppered with strong language, he railed against other lawyers and their clients. "Eric, don't you ever go home?" she asked when they got together. He answered with a shrug. Others noticed as well. Eric's landlord at the office told one attorney that Eric practically lived in the office, and that if she installed a shower, he might never go home.

During times they did spend together, Kim noticed Eric drank more, routinely consuming a six-pack of beer in an evening, and he seemed different to her. At a rare party she attended, he introduced her to a pretty young lawyer, someone he advised on family law. Where Kim felt tired and ill much of the time, her hair thinning and dental problems plaguing her from her illnesses, the young woman appeared a stark contrast, healthy and fit. From then on, Eric mentioned the younger woman often to Kim, and she wondered why. "Do you think Eric is having an affair?" Kim asked his secretary one day, when he didn't answer her calls.

"No, I don't," the woman said. She'd seen Eric sleeping on the couch in his office and knew that he stayed long after she left at night, not always working but sometimes playing video games on the office TV.

Once at 3 a.m., Kim called the woman lawyer demanding, "Is Eric there?"

Home alone asleep when the phone rang, she answered,

"No. He's not." But Kim didn't believe her. To Kim it seemed that everyone in Kaufman knew a secret about Eric but covered up for him. One day, she happened upon a receipt for a box of condoms.

In the local legal community, some had suspicions. Once Eric's friends left a house party and saw the windows steamed up on the car of another woman. Someone thought she'd seen Eric inside. "A lot of us thought there was something going on," said someone there that night. "None of us knew Kim well, so none of us felt obligated to tell her."

Eric gone so much, Kim battled loneliness. On the Internet, she reconnected with her high school boyfriend, Michael Gregg. Many of their phone calls revolved around Kim's suspicions about Eric "running around." She also confided in one of Eric's old clients, a man Eric had befriended. She first talked to him when he called the house for Eric, but soon Kim called the man on her own, and then talked animatedly, sounding unhappy, never eager to hang up. "It was strange," the man said. "I didn't really even know her."

The tension rose in the house on Overlook, and Eric came home one evening and announced that he wanted a divorce. While perhaps not surprised, Kim felt devastated. "I asked him to please not leave me," she said. "I still loved him, and I was sick. I was scared."

Characteristically quiet, Eric said little, but days later he came to her and said, "I've decided not to get the divorce. We have more together than we'd have apart." Kim assumed Eric meant their material possessions, the house and cars, the furniture, everything they'd bought during their seven-year marriage.

On New Year's Eve that year, Eric threw a poker party as he often did at the office. The guests, mainly local lawyers and their spouses, brought appetizers, and Kim wore

Kim at a New Year's Eve poker party

a holiday crown. They laughed, celebrated, and she hoped that they'd put the bad times behind them. Yet she wondered about Eric, who seemed changed in so many ways.

But was it all Eric? Sandra Harward saw him often as they worked on CPS cases. She considered Eric a friend, and she didn't like the effect Kim had on him. In the beginning, Harward thought that Eric tried to help Kim, but the longer things went on, the worse the situation seemed to her. "Kim and Eric fed off of each other. They seemed dependent on each other," Harward concluded. "It was a strange relationship."

Only later would others realize that when Kim and Eric

decided not to divorce, a piece of the puzzle clicked into place, forming a picture of the future, one in which their relationship would play a major role. Another chunk filled in when Eric Williams met a man named Michael Elgin McLelland, a bulky, middle-aged attorney. From the first days, the two men clashed.

In the end, that would be the undoing for both of them.

Chapter 5

My father was as bold a man as there ever was.
—JR McLelland

The land around the tiny town of Wortham, south of Dallas, its population hovering at a thousand, is as picturesque as Texas gets: bluebonnets in the spring, deep green summers, rolling hills, cattle and horse ranches, quaint houses, life at a slow pace absent of big-city bustle. No one comes to Wortham for the cultural events or to try the newest restaurant. Cowboy hats and boots aren't a fashion statement but a way of life.

In October 1949, Michael Elgin McLelland was born in Wortham to Elgin and Wyvonne McLelland, the older of their two children. The family lived on the edge of town, in a two-story house with a porch, on a six-hundred-acre horse ranch run by Elgin, a World War II veteran. Wyvonne worked as a secretary. The name McLelland had Scottish roots, and the family went back three generations in the Wortham area. "Our son was a happy child," Wyvonne recalled. Mike played cowboys and Indians. "He was a real boy."

Living an outdoor life, the family cared for their livestock. That rarely worked well for Mike. It wasn't that he didn't like the outdoors, the big Texas skies, galloping down country trails on his horse. Rather, the outdoors didn't

Mike McLelland in 1953
Courtesy of the McLelland Family

like him. From the pine pollen in March to the ragweed in August, Mike sneezed and wheezed and coughed.

That led to the day his father looked at him and suggested, "You get yourself an education, Mike, so you don't have to do this."

The family home lay across the street from a railroad track, and by junior high the whistle on the 10:05 called Mike home each night. Around then, Mike met Pamala Morgan, whose family moved to town to be close to her grandparents. Looking back, Pam described Mike, the first boy who ever kissed her—it happened one night on a hayride—as "always a little arrogant."

Yet there were things that drew them together. "I did love him at the time," she said. "Mike had a dry wit about him."

In 1967 Mike graduated from the redbrick high school, and he and Pam married a year later. From Wortham, they moved to Austin, where Pam took an office job and Mike enrolled in the University of Texas, his goal a bachelor's degree in history. In 1970, their first child, Krista, was born. As he looked at the future, Mike considered pre-law.

His father always told him he'd make a good lawyer. "Because he was good at speeches," his mother said.

Instead Mike considered teaching history, until he joined ROTC and began envisioning a career in the army. It turned out that Mike liked the military lifestyle. "Mike was a real soldier, shoot 'em up, bang, bang. That was Mike," said Pam.

When he graduated from UT in 1971, Mike entered the regular army as a second lieutenant, and the following year he became part of the Eighth Infantry division on a base in Germany. Pam joined him in January 1972, and she worked while Mike continued to build his resumé, enrolling in a correspondence course through Ball State University in Muncie, Indiana, to earn a master of arts in counseling. Looking back, Pam thought Mike seemed happiest in the service. "Mike was born to be in charge," said a family member.

Mike in his army uniform
Courtesy of the McLelland Family

Not long into the marriage, differences arose. One point of contention: Mike didn't like locking doors. He often left their apartment unlatched even while the family slept. It seemed Mike couldn't comprehend anyone would dare come inside. When he and Pam argued, Mike never backed down. Adding to her indignation, Pam thought he diagnosed her based on every new chapter in his psychology textbooks.

In Wiesbaden in 1974, Pam and Mike's second child and first son, JR for junior, was born, and that November Mike received his master's degree. A month later, the family shipped stateside to El Paso, Texas, with Mike stationed at Fort Bliss. There a third child, Josh, arrived.

In 1976, with three young children, Mike transferred to the army reserves and the family moved home to Wortham. With his master's degree, he became a clinical psychologist at the Mexia State School, a residential facility for the developmentally disabled run by Texas's Mental Health and Mental Retardation Department.

At the house, Mike emulated the army lifestyle, insisting the family run on a schedule, difficult with young children. For the most part, his time with his daughter and sons revolved around the types of things he enjoyed in the service, training them to rappel and shoot pistols. "From the time I was eight, I had a gun in my hand," said JR. "My dad was an encyclopedia on guns. He liked old cowboy guns, Smith & Wesson revolvers."

Meanwhile, the marriage deteriorated. In hindsight, Pam said differences doomed the union, and that, although it was a mutual decision, Mike resented her because he'd left the regular army.

After eleven years of marriage, in 1979, with three children ages nine, five, and four, Pam and Mike divorced. She remained in Wortham, but not long after, Mike relocated, continuing his work with MHMR but moving to Dallas, where he administered psychological testing in a clinic.

In Dallas, Mike met his second wife, Patricia Hall. A legal secretary, Trish, as friends called her, married Mike in 1983, when he was thirty-four and she was thirty-one. Living a sedate life, they came home from work in the evenings and read. Mike favored historical accounts and biographies, along with books on the military, tomes on the great wars. Trish, who preferred novels, had no children, so the only distractions were Mike's three. The McLelland brood's visits formed a pattern, a day at a water park, a day at an amusement park, one day shopping, and the children wanted to go home. "At that point, they sat in the house watching Mike and Trish read," remembered Pam. "So I'd drive in early and get them."

In 1990, Mike, at the age of forty, returned to a path he'd considered in college, enrolling in Fort Worth's Texas Wesleyan School of Law, the same institution Eric later attended.

In classes, Mike McLelland met Mike Burns. The two men had a lot in common. Both from small towns, they'd served in the military. A former marine, Burns worked as a police officer in Corpus Christi. Before long, the two joined the same study group.

To Burns, Mike McLelland seemed "a man's man," strong and in control. Burns liked his new friend's sayings, things like "put your big boy pants on" and "when things get tough, get your head down, your butt out of the chair, and move." Off and on, Mike whistled the old Roger Miller hit, "King of the Road."

With his children, Mike McLelland talked excitedly about learning a new discipline. The family agreed that he seemed well-suited for the law. Wyvonne reminded her son how his father, who by then had passed away, always thought Mike should have a legal career. And JR thought his dad would be good in the courtroom. "He could argue with the best of them."

By then, JR was sixteen, and his father pushed him hard to follow in his footsteps, to enroll at the University of Texas and sign up for ROTC. A tall, polite young man, JR wanted nothing to do with college. "It wasn't me. I liked to be outside, on a horse."

While JR's goals didn't include furthering his education, Mike loved the challenge. Despite the long hours, working at the clinic then heading to Texas Wesleyan in the evenings, he flourished. All went well until that same year, in

August, when the first Gulf War began. The army ordered Mike to report to the Mojave Desert to train recruits. Gone for months, when he returned he said little about the experience, and not long after retired from the reserves. After twenty-three years, he departed as a major.

Once back in Texas, Mike reclaimed his life, working during the day and attending law school in the evenings. Since he lived in Corpus Christi, Burns had an apartment, and before long Mike stayed with him, not always returning to the Dallas home he shared with Trish.

Then in 1992, halfway through law school, someone else dropped in at the apartment, bringing home-cooked gourmet dinners and desserts for the two men, to sustain them through long evenings studying for exams. A softly built woman with a bubbly personality and a head of curly blond hair, Cynthia Woodward Foreman had a husband and children. But when she met Mike, none of that mattered.

"I fell in love with Mike McLelland the first time I set eyes on him," Cynthia told a friend. "I knew he was my destiny."

Chapter 6

The thing about my mom, the way I'd describe her,
she was a true believer.

—Nathan Foreman

Opposites do sometimes attract. Love can transcend
divergent beliefs, bridge gaps that might appear insur-
mountable. Such was the relationship of Mike McLelland
and Cynthia Foreman. If in his first marriage Mike criticized
any views other than his own, with Cynthia he ignored such
conflicts. Mike was big and male; the new woman in his life
was a nurturer. Traditionally female, she became the yin to
his yang.

Although they started in similar places, Mike and
Cynthia came of age in dissimilar worlds. Two years older
than Mike, born in Okmulgee, Oklahoma, Cynthia ranked
fourth of five siblings. Her father, Kenneth Woodward,
worked for the Boy Scouts of America's leadership program. Her mother, Shirley, who joked about their many
offspring by saying her husband was a precision bomber,
took temporary jobs and bought rental properties.

Around the time Cynthia turned nine, the family followed their father's job to Texas, where they purchased a
small English Tudor in the affluent central Dallas community of Highland Park. At an early age, Cindy, as the
family called her, became something of a second mom,

cooking and baking. She made pies and cakes she hid so her brothers wouldn't eat them before dinner. "Cindy was a cheerful, jolly soul," said her older sister, Nancy. "Even as a child, she was always smiling."

At seventeen, Cynthia moved to Austin College, a private liberal arts school, where she met Jerry Foreman, the captain of the football team. Homecoming king and queen, they married in 1969, the year Cynthia turned twenty-two and graduated with a degree in psychology.

The newlyweds moved to Denton, and Jerry worked as a building contractor, while Cynthia entered graduate school, earning a master's degree in clinical psychology.

The world in an upheaval with the Vietnam War ebbing, in the early seventies many considered alternative lifestyles. Hippies descended on Haight-Ashbury, and communes sprang up across the nation. In this milieu, Jerry and Cynthia Foreman joined the small community of Stelle, on farmland in northern Illinois.

Cynthia on her wedding day
Courtesy of Nancy W. John

Stelle's founder, Richard Kieninger, billed it as an intentional community, where inhabitants—two hundred families at its peak—worked together to prepare for cataclysmic earth changes he predicted for the year 2000: tornadoes, hurricanes, earthquakes, the realigning of oceans. The inhabitants believed that by living right, sharing responsibilities, they could improve their lives and weather whatever the end of the millennium brought. No doors locked, and families watched over each other's children. There in 1972, the Foremans had a son, Nathan. "My parents were good people trying to improve the world," he said.

Their early years in Stelle were "nearly idyllic," as Nathan remembered it, the children walking from home to home without boundaries, individual families working together for the betterment of the whole. Loving to entertain, Cynthia hosted many of the gatherings. And she focused on her child. Nathan had dyslexia, and she worked hard to teach him to read. "She loved being a mom," he said. "She was passionate about education."

From Stelle, the Foremans settled in other cities in Illinois, where Cynthia worked for a Head Start program and a community action program. In 1984, they returned to the Dallas area, and adopted a baby girl they named Christina.

Four years later, Cynthia took a position as a diagnostic psychologist supervisor for MHMR, the same state mental health system where Mike McLelland held a position. They met, and from the beginning felt a connection. Early on, Mike sent books home for Nathan, who shared his interest in history.

Still in law school, Mike bunked with his friend Mike Burns off and on, and Cynthia visited the apartment often, bringing the two men cheesecakes and cookies. Watching Mike and Cynthia, Burns knew this was an important relationship in their lives. He listened to their discussions on the importance of living each day. A conservative, Mike saw the world in stark black and white, while Cynthia envisioned shades of gray. "Yet you couldn't have a better match than those two," Burns said. "Together they'd be quite a force."

Cynthia and Mike did seem an odd pairing, he the imposing, often gruff, highly regimented military man, Cynthia a new-age free thinker who believed in reincarnation. Yet they spoke the same language, students of the workings of the human mind. They talked shop, about their careers in psychology, and entertained themselves by guessing the IQs of those they met.

In meetings with her family, Cynthia described the exciting person she met at work. Her mother in particular worried about Cynthia's plans. "Mother was very upset. She saw it as a train wreck," said Nancy. "I didn't tell Cindy to stop, because it was what she wanted. I saw it as inevitable. Gradually we came to accept the situation."

In December 1993, Mike completed his classes at Texas Wesleyan. Eyeing the possibilities, he set as his goal a career in criminal law, as a judge or a district attorney. "Mike said he wanted to lock up the bad guys," his mother, Wyvonne, said. "I loved him to death. Whatever he wanted, I hoped he got."

In February, Mike took the bar exam, and the following month Cynthia and Jerry Foreman formally ended their marriage. "My parents had a difficult divorce," Christina said. Nathan was in college; she was only nine at the time.

Complicating the situation, Mike remained married to Trish. A friend would later say that the divorce blindsided Mike's second wife and left her heartbroken. She knew nothing of Cynthia. "Trish truly loved Mike," said a friend. "She had no idea there was another woman."

Despite his situation, that summer Mike and Cynthia moved to Corpus Christi, where Mike shared an office with his law school friend Mike Burns. Although not yet married, Cynthia seemed unconcerned. "He's my soul mate," she said. "You can't worry about what other people think. You have to grab what makes you happy."

Yet that didn't wipe away all consequences. "My dad didn't handle it well," said JR. "He didn't even tell us for a long time." The way the relationship began proved hard on Mike's three children, who'd grown up with Trish as a stepmother.

In Corpus Christi, Mike handled any legal matter a client who walked through the door requested. He filed divorces, negotiated real estate transactions, and wrote wills. At the Nueces County courthouse, he took court appointments. With his background in psychology, most often he handled mental health cases. Once in a while he had a criminal case, never a murder but aggravated assaults, burglaries, DWIs, or felony thefts. For the most part, he disliked his forays into that world.

"We talked about it, and Mike felt most of the criminal defendants were lowlifes," said Burns. "Most of the time we felt like we were on the wrong side in the cases."

His divorce from Trish final that October, Mike and Cynthia purchased a house near a country club, and she decorated it with antiques. When arranging the furniture, true to her new-age leanings, Cynthia enlisted the principles of feng shui, the ancient Asian design philosophy intended to bring harmony to a home. Christina lived with them, and attended a nearby Episcopal school. "Cynthia and Mike made friends, had people for parties. She cooked wonderful meals, including the best squash soup," said Burns. "Life was good."

In November 1995, Cynthia and Mike married in a small service in a quaint stone church. Mike was forty-six, and Cynthia forty-eight. "We felt good, because Mike made her happy," said Nancy. "Cindy liked taking care of him, and Mike liked being cared for. They worked."

In Corpus, while Mike built his law office, Cynthia

worked for the area's state school. Clinical psychologists don't make a lot of money, and she'd considered returning to school for some time. There in 1999, she enrolled in Del Mar College, to work on a nursing degree.

The same year, Mike registered as a candidate for a district judge's seat. Although most of Texas had turned red, Corpus remained overwhelmingly blue, leading him to file as a Democrat. Cynthia, who had once been enough of a true believer to move to Stelle, Illinois, to pioneer a new lifestyle, put as much faith in Mike. That fall they campaigned hard. Yet Mike lost, coming in with less than six percent of the vote.

In another disappointment, that year Mike had a health scare. Tests showed his left anterior descending artery had narrowed, the one euphemistically called the widow maker, because if it closed completely it brought on sudden death. After a triple bypass, Mike had a scar down his chest he religiously covered.

In May 2001, Cynthia graduated and became a registered nurse, and seven years into their marriage, she and Mike moved again, this time back to Dallas, where Cynthia's family remained; Mike's family was nearby in Wortham. Nathan, too, gravitated home after finishing his degree, becoming a Dallas police officer, a career choice Mike encouraged.

While the beginning of her mother's new marriage had been difficult for Christina, she grew fond of Mike. She thought that he and her mom meshed well. As formidable as Mike could be, he softened with Cynthia. He barked and complained, but she said something funny or tickled him, and he laughed, his ample belly shaking.

For a brief time, Mike, Cynthia, and Christina lived in a Dallas apartment. But then in October 2001, Cynthia took a nurse supervisor slot at Terrell State Hospital, a residential psychiatric treatment center, and they bought a one-story home on a quiet street in the small city of Terrell, population hovering near sixteen thousand, in western Kaufman County.

In hindsight, Mike and Cynthia didn't understand as yet the turn this move would make in their lives. On the surface, Kaufman County undoubtedly appeared laid-back, a respite from the big city. Perhaps they felt drawn to it because its conservative bent offered a better fit for Mike politically; he hadn't given up his dream of one day becoming a judge or a district attorney.

Did Cynthia have any premonitions? She believed in many things she couldn't touch or see. When she first met people, it wasn't unusual for her to hold their hands, turn them over, and read their palms. If she'd looked into her own future, saw what awaited her in Kaufman County, could she have convinced Mike to turn and run?

Once back in north central Texas, Cynthia worked at the state hospital in Terrell, supervising the care of twenty-eight women, consulting with their physicians and writing treatment plans. With coworkers, she proved a friendly presence, often arriving with homemade birthday cakes or muffins. As she walked the halls, she hummed old show tunes, frequently pausing to talk to patients, bringing their meds along with a sip of apple juice. From home she brought chewing gum, a small act of kindness, since the hospital didn't stock it and it helped ease dry mouths, a side effect of many psychiatric drugs. The staff grew accustomed to seeing Cynthia huddled with patients, holding hands, talking softly and reassuringly.

From her first days at the hospital, Cynthia talked about her spiritual beliefs, and confided that she sometimes consulted psychic Sylvia Browne, a TV regular, paying hundreds of dollars for a phone session. When one friend pointed out that Browne's predictions hadn't always come true, Cynthia stayed resolute. "Anyone can make a mistake," she said, with a shrug.

Not far from the hospital, Cynthia and Mike purchased an unremarkable single-story, tan brick house with a bay window, surrounded by thick-trunked oaks. A believer in love, she decorated the master bedroom with romantic paintings, trusting that they set the stage for a closer relationship. "I want the last thing Mike and I see before we go to sleep and the first thing we see in the morning to be something beautiful," she told a friend.

In other ways, they made the house their home.

Decades earlier, Cynthia lived with her first husband in Stelle, founded as a place to survive cataclysmic events that threatened civilization. Throughout her life, she carried the sense that the world could change in an instant. In Mike, Cynthia found a kindred soul.

On packed bookshelves, beside her romance novels and his histories, Mike placed volumes on survivalism, manuals on how to prepare for catastrophic events that resulted in political and social upheaval and potentially anarchy. Mike thought about such possibilities, and what would happen if he had to defend his family and his home in a time of lawless chaos.

As a result, Cynthia and Mike prepped, stockpiling survival provisions. One room in their home held stacks of five-gallon buckets of flour and sugar, crates of canned fruit and vegetables, medical supplies, a larder to get them through an earth-shattering event. In nearby Dallas, Cynthia volunteered at Mennonite canning fairs where she helped with food preparation and then returned home with gallon cans of pinto beans and boxes of potato flakes.

With such a mindset, it wasn't surprising that Mike amassed a cache of something else he judged might prove essential in such a crisis: dozens and dozens of firearms.

Throughout the house, Mike scattered handguns, rifles, assault-type weapons, a loaded arsenal. Some sat out in the open, but many were hidden or disguised.

On the back of the couch hung a blanket folded into a sack, one he could reach into to grab a double-barreled shotgun. Next to his easy chair, in the kitchen, the bathrooms and bedrooms, he placed innocent-looking cosmetic bags. Sliced along the zipper with a razor, the bags had pistols inside and openings large enough for Mike's thick hands. If needed, he could grab, aim, and fire without removing the guns from the sacks.

Along with the guns, he accumulated hunting and combat knives, hidden in drawers and on shelves. "My dad's house was like a fortress," said JR.

Some neighbors, had they known, might have been surprised by the substantial storeroom and the hoard of

Mike and Cynthia McLelland
Evidence photo

weapons inside the McLelland home. But from their first days in Terrell, the McLellands blended into the community. Once a month, Mike went to Republican men's club meetings. At the First United Methodist Church, they taught Sunday school, attended Bible study, and sang in the choir. People liked Mike's sense of humor, as on the day he held up the minister's sermon notes and warned the crowd, "Get ready. It's going to be a long one!"

Cynthia had loved to quilt since Nathan's teenage years, calling her pieces "usable art." In a repurposed bedroom, she set up her sewing machine, and shelves overflowed with bolts of fabric "I use the creativity of the quilting to help get rid of tension, just like a lot of people do," she said. "It gives me peace." Once settled into the house in Terrell, she joined the Kaufman Quilt Guild and attended monthly meetings held in a shop across from the county courthouse.

At each of the guild's four annual retreats, Cynthia made a baby quilt, gifts for family or friends or pregnant coworkers. She longed for the day either Nathan or Christina had a child and she became a grandmother. Although Mike had grandchildren, she saw them rarely. And the McLelland brood's rapport with Cynthia, while cordial, had never become close.

On those days when she stitched small blankets meant to warm tiny bodies, Cynthia dreamed of the day she'd hold her own grandchild. "That was the one thing she wanted more than anything else," said a friend. "Cynthia couldn't wait to be a grandmother."

Then, not long after they moved to Terrell, Cynthia's hands began to shake.

The verdict must have been devastating: Parkinson's, a progressive disorder that attacked the central nervous system, causing tremors along with changes in speech and gait. As a nurse, Cynthia must have understood the direness of the prognosis. Although drugs and treatments could lessen the symptoms, science offered no cure.

Perhaps in quiet moments, Mike and Cynthia talked openly about their now uncertain futures. But to family and friends, she refused to acknowledge the disease. Rarely uttering the word "Parkinson's," she instead told those who inquired that the tremors resulted from a shot she'd been given in nursing school. "We respected that," said one friend. "We never pushed."

"I don't want to be looked at as damaged goods," in an unusual moment of candor, she once told a friend. "I don't want people to know."

One quilt guild member Cynthia befriended was Tonya Ratcliff, who after twenty-five years in the navy had moved to the area and become mayor of Combine, another small city in Kaufman County. At one retreat, Tonya and Cynthia sat across from each other. "Where'd you come from?" Cynthia asked. "Where have you been?"

They ended up chatting for hours.

At times when she sewed, as at work, Cynthia burst into song, more often than not a stirring rendition of "High Hopes," the tune Frank Sinatra sang in the old movie *A Hole in the Head*. The song's lyrics, a testament to optimism, praise an ant that achieves the impossible by moving a rubber tree plant. When Cynthia sang, Tonya laughed. One day, Tonya heard someone complain to Cynthia about a trivial disappointment: "You know, let it go," Cynthia advised, patting the woman's shoulder. "In the scheme of things, that's not important."

Cynthia didn't yet realize that true dangers waited in her own future. By then, Mike McLelland worked for the state of Texas. In his new position, he'd soon enter the Kaufman County courthouse, Eric Williams's domain.

Chapter 7

From the beginning, Mike McLelland belittled Eric
Williams. He didn't have any respect for him. And
Eric didn't like Mike, maybe because Mike had done
things Eric wanted to do and never did.
                                        —Sandra Harward

In July 2002, Mike McLelland signed on with the Texas
Department of Protective and Regulatory Services (later
renamed the Texas Department of Family and Protective
Services) as a regional attorney handling CPS cases, the
same job Sandra Harward had filled for years. At times,
he and Harward traveled together to the counties around
Dallas and Fort Worth, working cases. Harward saw Mike
as a good guy and enjoyed the collaboration. Except when
they took a Kaufman County case where a judge appointed
Eric guardian ad litem. It seemed to Harward that from the
day they met, Mike McLelland and Eric Williams barely
tolerated each other.

"I want your gig," Harward told Eric over the years
about what she saw as his near monopoly on CPS cases in
Kaufman County. "You've got a sweet thing going."

They, too, were friends, and Eric took the ribbing well,
flashing a smile, laughing, seeming to acknowledge that
he'd maneuvered into a good deal. The money still poured
in. By then, the commissioner's court had reconsidered

fees paid to private attorneys, but only those representing indigent defendants in criminal cases, spawning plans to cut costs by funding a public defender's office to handle such cases.

None of that affected Eric, since he'd walked away from indigent defense years earlier. As yet, no one seemed concerned with the money paid for CPS ad litems, Eric's bailiwick.

While Mike's path didn't cross Eric's often, when the two men interacted, Harward sensed a palpable tension. With his background as a psychologist, Mike admitted a deep dislike for Kaufman's main CPS attorney, labeling Eric a wannabe with his volunteer deputy badge.

On the other hand, Harward sensed Eric's feelings about Mike ran as negative and every bit as strong. "To Mike, Eric was a fraud, and to Eric, Mike was nothing. Period," said Harward. But then, "Eric didn't have much respect for anyone. He thought he was better than any of them, and he had a lot of power in that county for a long time."

Feeding the situation, Mike became boastful around Eric, bragging about his military experience and his rank as an army major. "Eric didn't like people like that," Harward said.

On top of the tension with Mike, Harward thought Eric had changed. She noticed that he drank more, and she'd grown ever more used to his angry, late-night e-mails. At times, he sounded so enraged Harward wouldn't respond. "Eric liked getting into it with lawyers he didn't like," said Harward. "He was a very cool, calculating guy, but when it was just the two of us he'd say things like, 'I'll blow their brains out or shoot them.'" Sometimes Harward wondered if Eric truly would, but she never believed so. Not really. The thing was, although she knew Eric saw himself as brave, Harward never thought he had the guts.

Something Harward noticed about Mike, on the other hand, was that with his military background he approached the CPS cases differently, seeing them as more cut and dried, not leaving room for interpretation. That, too, put him at odds with Eric, who also considered his opinions the only correct ones. "They quarreled from the beginning, and it only got worse," she said. "It was hopeless." Over the years, although Mike and Eric came face-to-face on a mere handful of cases, Harward always felt uncomfortable when she had to work with the two men.

Then in 2005, Harward discovered something disturbing: that Mike McLelland continued to accept assignments to act as a defense attorney. As Harward understood the rules, this wasn't allowed. "Mike was being paid by the state of Texas. He worked for a state agency. When you sign up as a lawyer employed by the state, you are given time, six months, even a year, to finish your existing cases. But Mike was taking new court appointments."

The next time they drove to a hearing together, Harward brought the situation up to Eric. Afterward, Eric called Nueces County, where Mike had once lived in Corpus, and nearby Hays County. They confirmed that Mike had done what Harward suspected. Eric saw the situation as a direct conflict of interest; Mike worked for the state, but those appointments meant he fought against the state as a defense attorney.

When they talked, Eric told Harward what he'd discovered.

"I called Mike and told him that I was going to have to tell our supervisor," Harward said. "Mike didn't deny that it was true. What he was doing was a violation, and I didn't have a choice. I told Mike, 'You have to quit before you get fired.'"

As summer 2005 came to an end, Mike McLelland left his slot with the Department of Protective and Regulatory Services. When people asked why, he told them he didn't always agree with the way the cases ended. Although she'd confronted him, Mike never appeared to blame Harward, and they remained friends. Perhaps Mike wasn't disappointed about losing the job since he'd made it clear that he'd never liked working for the state. Or Mike may not have held a grudge because he had his eye on a different job, one he'd coveted since law school.

While he and Sandra Harward stayed cordial, Mike McLelland's loathing of Eric Williams intensified. "Mike knew that Eric knew about the situation, what Mike had done," Harward said. From that point forward, "there was bad blood."

Chapter 8

Mike [McLelland] and I talked about the district attorney's job. Mike thought his background would help. He figured a lot of the defendants had drug issues, were self-medicating. As a psychologist, Mike understood the human condition.

—Mike Burns

A dozen years earlier when they graduated from law school, Mike Burns and Mike McLelland dreamed of becoming district attorneys. Burns took that path and became the DA in Palo Pinto, a rural county eighty miles west of Fort Worth. Meanwhile, Mike McLelland practiced general law in Corpus, then headed north and signed on as a staff attorney representing the state of Texas in CPS cases. Yet McLelland's dream of being a DA hadn't died.

In the fall of 2005, not long after he resigned from his state job, Mike registered as a Republican in the Kaufman County DA's race. Some saw it as an unusual move, considering Mike had little background in criminal law. Mike, however, argued that didn't matter. Rather, he claimed DAs functioned as administrators. If he won, he'd have twelve prosecutors who knew what to do in a courtroom. "It's not the DA's job to try the cases," he said. "It's the DA's job to run the office."

That season three candidates vied for the DA's job, all

Republicans: the incumbent, Ed Walton; a former Dallas prosecutor, Rick Harrison; and Mike McLelland. From the beginning, it was a tough race. Though the election was not until November of the following year, 2006, the DA's race would actually end with the upcoming March primary. With the majority of the county Republican, no Democrats filed. That meant the candidate who won the Republican nomination won it all.

Going in, Mike lacked name recognition. Because he'd moved to the area only four years earlier, locals saw Mike as an outsider. Late into the primary campaign, he'd accumulated no war chest, and few backers offered to write checks. That left Mike self-funding, an expensive proposition.

As 2005 came to an end, Mike ordered red-and-white signs that read: "McLelland for District Attorney." For days he drove rural roads, pounding the placards into hard clay at busy intersections, offering smaller versions to shopkeepers for windows. In the evenings, Cynthia and Mike strategized. Their most important task, they decided, was to reach Republicans who'd voted in past primaries. Based on history, it seemed likely that they would vote in the spring.

A list of the voters from prior Republican primaries in hand, Cynthia keyed a database into their home computer. Once it was completed, she laid out the most important areas to canvass. Then, maps in hand, the McLelland clan walked quiet residential streets, rang bells, and knocked on doors. When no one answered, they left a flyer espousing Mike's qualifications and bearing a photo of Mike and Cynthia surrounded by their children and Mike's grandchildren. "Kaufman is a big county," said one area Republican. "There are fish fries, chili cook-offs, church festivals. You have to go to all of them and shake hands. Especially Mike. He didn't have a big war chest. The only way to counter that is on your feet."

To capitalize on what could have worked against him, Mike proposed that as a newcomer he owed no favors. Not involved in politics, he suggested he had a shot at wiping out corruption. Some voters found this appealing. For generations, rumors speculated about what locals called "Kaufman County justice," suspicions that officials looked the other way when those with connections broke laws. Mike played on those concerns and argued that a network of political insiders ran Kaufman County. As in so many campaigns, from small-town mayors to presidential elections, he claimed that as an outsider he had the best opportunity to fix the status quo.

Nightly that winter, Cynthia and Mike ate peanut butter and jelly sandwiches in the car, then walked house to house, bringing campaign literature and his message that he would right things in the old county courthouse. "I think they knocked on every door in Kaufman County," said Tonya Ratcliff. "The odds may have been against Mike, but they believed he could win."

The competition, however, was fierce. Ed Walton had been Kaufman's DA for only one term, but he'd been a criminal lawyer for years. And Rick Harrison, the other candidate, had substantial experience. He'd worked in the organized crime section of the Dallas County District Attorney's Office prosecuting major drug defendants. Both, however, had Achilles' heels. Some in Kaufman's legal community didn't like Walton's management style. And Harrison had a driving while intoxicated conviction on his record from 1994.

On February 2, 2006, the *Kaufman Herald* ran an article entitled "Top Races Produce Big Bucks," detailing the donations that funneled into the DA's race. Harrison had raised $20,208, most from local lawyers, while Mike reported $2,850 in contributions and $12,054 in expenses.

The primary came and went, and suddenly two candidates remained in the race, not the ones most might have predicted. Harrison and Mike had both beaten Walton, and they were headed toward an April runoff.

Walton out of the race, Harrison turned his attention to Mike, focusing on Mike's greatest vulnerability, his lack of criminal experience. Harrison's ads reminded voters that his opponent had never been a criminal attorney or a felony prosecutor. In addition, Harrison touted endorsements from Kaufman County law enforcement organizations.

In response, Mike bought a half-page ad to publicize his resumé, including his ten years as a lawyer, his top security clearance in the army, and his years as a psychologist. Instead of criminal experience, he touted the need for high moral character. As a retired army major, Mike maintained he set an example. In contrast, he pointed at Harrison's DWI.

Then something happened that turned the character question back at Mike. "Dad told us someone wrote a letter that ran in the newspaper and talked a lot of crap about him," said JR.

The letter ran in the *Kaufman Herald*, and the top line read, "Character is essential for our next D.A."

After identifying himself as a local CPS attorney "representing the abused and neglected children of our county," the author wrote that he knew both candidates, and he suggested voters should learn more about the newcomer in the race. The first point read "you must ask for a better explanation from Mr. McLelland as to why he no longer works for Child Protective Services."

Although it didn't spell out that Mike resigned over a possible conflict of interest, the letter implied all hadn't been well in Mike's departure from the agency.

The next point directly contradicted what Mike had told the people of Kaufman County, that he'd been a lifelong Republican. Instead the author revealed that in Corpus Christi, Mike ran for a judgeship as a Democrat. "While I understand that . . . candidates on the local level often switch parties for purely political reasons, it is still no reason to lie."

Advising county residents to be careful with their votes, the letter effectively threw the character issue Mike embraced as his primary selling point back at him, branding Mike a liar and raising questions about his record. That letter was signed, "Eric Williams."

What had he hoped to gain? "I was encouraging people to ask questions," Eric said. "I wanted them to figure it out."

Five days after Eric's letter ran, Rick Harrison won the runoff by a mere sixty-four votes and became Kaufman County's new district attorney.

Days after, a disappointed Mike McLelland drove down rural roads picking up his campaign signs. "I don't know if I have another run like that in me," Mike told Nathan.

When Mike talked about Eric's letter, Nathan came away with the impression that Mike considered it a low blow. If the letter cost Mike only sixty-five votes, it cost him the election. "There's a saying that all politics are personal," said Nathan. "In a small town, it really is true."

In two years, 2005 and 2006, Eric had forced Mike's resignation from his state job and then publicly questioned his integrity, conceivably ending Mike's bid to secure the election. "It was typical Eric, manipulating the situation," said Sandra Harward. "From that point forward, if he didn't before, there was no doubt Mike had his stinger out for Eric Williams."

Chapter 9

Eric was strange quiet. I told people that any time
anyone is that in control of their emotions, it's scary.
—Shawn Mayfield

In hindsight, 2006 appeared a good year for Eric Williams, one in which he nurtured his sphere of influence in Kaufman County.

In January, Eric became an unpaid reserve deputy for the sheriff's office, another of the string of law enforcement positions he'd had since leaving college. Once he did, Eric worked for Sheriff David Byrnes, a tall, white-haired former Texas Ranger. Perhaps the most famous case he handled as a ranger, Byrnes had been in Waco in 1993 for the confrontation with Branch Davidian leader David Koresh. Brought in to accept Koresh's surrender, which didn't happen, Byrnes spent fifty-one days involved in failed negotiations, until the compound exploded in flames, killing Koresh and seventy-nine of his followers.

A captain in charge of the rangers' Company B station in Garland when he retired, Byrnes ran for Kaufman County's sheriff in 2000 and won. Once in office, he helped design a new law enforcement center with a modern jail. "Here

Kaufman County Sheriff David A. Byrnes
Kathryn Casey

we do everything from barking dogs to capital murder," he said about KCSO's duties.

To Byrnes, Eric seemed helpful. Of the ninety-some officers at KCSO, only a handful were volunteers. The most active, Eric happily suited up in his deputy's uniform for parades and events, offered to help with crowd control during bike races and festivals. In crunch times including holidays, Eric took patrol shifts and rode with full-time officers. Every year when a local church held its Lord's Acre Auction, Eric dressed in his uniform, strapped on his gun, and acted as security. "Eric loved the whole law enforcement thing," said a friend. "He reveled in it."

Although they'd agreed to stay married, that summer Eric and Kim struggled. At a birthday party for a local attorney, Kim became incensed when Eric repeatedly disappeared, leaving her to fend for herself. On top of her prescription drugs, she drank, and when she tired of the country-and-western music playing, she drove her car into the driveway and turned her radio on, blasting heavy metal, and dancing alone in the garage. "I can't deal with her," Eric answered, when someone at the party asked him to go out and turn off the radio.

In August, Kim e-mailed Eric photos of her old high school boyfriend, Michael Gregg. "Ah, so now you're exchanging pictures," Eric responded.

Kim called the photos silly and said she felt "PROUD to have YOU!"

She then asked Eric, perhaps hopefully, "You're not jealous of Mike, are you?"

"Well, no, I'm not jealous of Mike," he answered.

Yet at the same time, Kim thought that Eric acted increasingly peculiar. Late that year, their oldest Pomeranian, Savannah, escaped. Frantic, Kim and Eric searched all night. They didn't find the dog until the next morning, at a busy intersection a little more than a mile from the house. Off to the side in a parking lot, they saw a man and woman chasing Savannah.

Behind the wheel, Kim pulled to the side of the road, and Eric jumped out brandishing a pistol. When she could, Kim parked and ran after him. While she thought the couple only intended to corral Savannah for them, Eric waved the gun. The couple rushed to their car and peeled out of the lot, as Kim shouted at Eric to put the gun away.

Five months after he lost the DA's race, in September Mike McLelland got a new job, a slot as an attorney with the Dallas County Public Defender's Office. The agency represented indigent clients in criminal cases, and such experience would have been a way to prepare for another run at DA or a judgeship, but the position the agency offered Mike was in the mental health division. With his psychology credentials, the slot fit him well, representing patients being committed to psychiatric facilities.

If Mike had given up on a bid for the DA's office, Cynthia hadn't. That winter she told a friend, "That last election just wasn't our time. But this is what Mike wants, so we're going to keep trying."

Chapter 10

Law is a conflict-driven system. By its nature, it's adversarial.

—Robert Guest

After Rick Harrison took over in the DA's office in January 2007, Eric Williams popped in off and on. When he did, he walked through the office smiling, then stopped in to see the man he'd supported for the office. It didn't happen often, but the staff noticed that their new boss and the CPS attorney seemed friendly.

Meanwhile, money flowed in from Eric's court appointments, and no one appeared to pay attention to the situation, that one attorney in the county received the majority of assignments. Some noticed that Eric had an enviable position at the courthouse as the only private attorney who had a passkey to get in the back door, bypassing the metal detectors.

Perhaps that made Eric bold, for he seemed increasingly boastful to Sandra Harward. More and more she wondered about him, especially about the vitriolic late-night e-mails railing about other lawyers. "I'm ready to eat barbed wire and spit nails. I'll drink gasoline and piss napalm. Let me loose on these lawyers and tomorrow will be the first day of Armageddon," he wrote in one such missive just before midnight in March. Threatening to try to disbar the attorney who'd caught his anger, to run him out of town, Eric crowed that if he instructed them not to, no landlord in Kaufman would rent the man office space, that the phone company would "fuck up his number," and his computer service would "give him a virus. . . . I have no problem sending him to the hospital with severed vertebrae, removing his children's organs, throwing his wife into a gang bang train, or anything else creative you can come up with. I just really don't like this guy, and he should go somewhere else, if allowed to live."

At the end, he wrote, "How about we don't share this email?—ERIC."

Yet Eric did share it, minutes after e-mailing it to Harward, forwarding it to Kim's e-mail account with the note: "This was a pleasant email also—probably several criminal offices [sic] by me. Love, ERIC."

Apparently there'd been other such e-mails he'd sent to Kim in the past. Despite the issues in their marriage, he wanted her approval. From the tone of his e-mail, it seemed Eric felt confident that Kim would admire his show of male dominance, his pounding of the chest and declaring war, threatening horrific acts upon another man and his family.

On her part, Harward wasn't shocked by the e-mail. She'd heard and read similar things from Eric before, e-mails she'd come to think of as his midnight ramblings. At times he became so embroiled in their cases, so set on getting his way and doing what *he* decided was the right thing for the children involved, that Harward judged it was "to the point of psychosis."

In this particular case the opposing attorney working for the child's parents, Robert Guest, the one Eric threatened to piss napalm about, had been bold enough to question why in Kaufman County Eric Williams seemed to habitually get what he and CPS wanted, "whatever they wanted."

Despite words over the case, Guest had no idea Eric

fumed at him. In person, Eric said little to him, so little that Guest saw Eric as painfully introverted.

Yet Guest and Eric continued to cross paths. In Kaufman, the lawyers took turns serving on the bar association board, at one point Guest as president and Eric managing the law library.

Consisting of a small room on the second floor of the courthouse, tucked to the side, the law library had shelves of books, a conference table surrounded by leather chairs, and a workstation with a computer. In theory, the room gave defense lawyers a place inside the courthouse to research cases and answer judges' questions during trials.

In practice, the room rarely functioned that way. The outdated courthouse offered little space, and judges often commandeered the library to house juries during deliberations. Making matters worse, the library had no wi-fi services, while prosecutors had Internet access in the DA's office. "We kept asking for wi-fi," said one defense attorney. "The people in the county's IT department just kept answering that they couldn't do it. Our question was 'Why not?'"

Increasing their irritation, many couldn't log onto the Internet on their phones and tablets in the building. "Cell service was spotty. For a lot of us, wi-fi was a big issue," said one. "We talked about it, but it seemed like nothing was done."

There were ample funds. The money that supported the law library came from a $10 fee charged every time a civil suit was filed. At one point, the balance in the library's account climbed above $200,000. "I kidded around that we should rent an office and put in a hot tub and bar, kind of a lawyers' club," Guest said with a chuckle. "But Eric explained that we only had certain things we could use the money for, computers and books."

Once in charge of the law library, Eric used the fund to buy the library a new computer, and he talked about other options, most importantly access to wi-fi. "Eric took the lead," one of the attorneys said. "He was trying to help."

Rather than go through channels and contact the county's information technology (IT) department, Eric simply purchased a router and installed it himself. It didn't solve the problem since the library remained unavailable much of the time, but it was a start.

Meanwhile, the days passed, and from the outside, all looked well in Eric's world.

That year, Eric purchased a black-on-black Shelby Mustang, one that he rarely drove but kept in the garage. The car was a special fortieth anniversary edition, and Eric removed the passenger side airbag cover and sent it to Carroll Shelby, the renowned auto designer, who autographed it for him. "Eric never had a sports car, always wanted one. We were trying to decide if we needed a new air conditioner or a sports car," said Kim with a knowing smile. "Sports car won."

Word also spread through the courthouse that Eric had added new firearms to his collection. Sometimes Eric offered those who dropped in at his office a tour of his closet, filled with handguns and rifles. "There was something Freudian and phallic about Eric, with his sports cars and guns," said one attorney. "It seemed out of tune with the person we knew."

On Overlook, too, Kim and Eric appeared to have anything they wanted. "They lived the high life," said a relative. "Kim had nice jewelry. The house was well furnished." Even their dogs appeared spoiled. She changed the Pomeranians' diapers and clothes often during the day. On the living room wall she displayed a life-size portrait of her first dog, Penny. Pomeranian figurines perched on shelves in the hutch beside expired credit cards bearing photos of the dogs, the numbers cut off.

"Eric and Kim acted like they couldn't be happier," said one relative.

Yet that was far from the truth.

Relying on growing doses of painkillers, Kim slept until mid-afternoon most days, then woke groggy. Much of the rest of the day evaporated in front of the television, a large glass of Coca-Cola in her hand. In the evenings, she and Eric sat side by side on bar stools at the kitchen counter, surfing the net and playing games on their laptops. Looking back, Eric characterized that time period as one of deep disappointment. "You start to wonder what's happening in your life," he said. "It came on gradually until one day you realize, wow!"

On the days she left the house, Kim's usual destination was her parents' home an hour north in Lone Oak. To get there, she drove across Two Mile Bridge, spanning Lake Tawakoni. Years earlier, Kim's father had been diagnosed with skin cancer, a dark spot on his cheek that kept spreading, and her mother had suffered a stroke. One night Kim returned home late, and Eric had his computer on. Earlier he'd phoned to tell Kim that he'd gone to get a massage, and Kim glanced through Eric's e-mails. She found one from him that read: "Next time I'll stay long enough to make breakfast for you."

When Kim looked at the e-mail address, she realized Eric had sent it to the masseuse. "What's this?" Kim asked.

"Nothing," he said. "Just junk mail." The next time she looked, he'd added password protection to all his computers.

Chapter II

I wanted out of the marriage, but I didn't know how.
I was so sick. I felt stuck, dependent and distracted.
And I was really afraid of Eric. I have a hard time
admitting that.

—Kim Williams

If her head had been clearer, if she'd taken a step back to
consider, maybe Kim would have read all the signs and realized who Eric had become. One afternoon in the pantry
beside her stash of two-liter plastic bottles of Coca-Cola,
she found a bag holding $6,000 in cash. When Kim asked
for an explanation, he matter-of-factly told her that he kept
it "in case I need to get away quickly." She didn't ask why
he would ever need to disappear.

Then there were the guns.

Over time, Kim came to realize that Eric had built a
formidable collection. Wherever they went, he wore a holster with a loaded gun. At her parents' house, Eric put
whatever pistol he carried on the table, where it sat while
they ate. Don Johnson, Kim's dad, didn't seem bothered
by it, and the two men often talked about guns throughout
dinner.

Kim's father, however, didn't know what Eric said to his
daughter when no one else listened, including several occasions when, in an unemotional tone, as if talking about

grocery shopping, he told Kim, "If I ever decide to take everyone out, I'll kill you and then myself."

At first, Kim just thought it was an odd thing to say, that he couldn't possibly mean it. But slowly she began to suspect Eric might be capable of murdering her. One such day she lay on the den couch watching TV, while Eric cleaned a rifle on top of the white counter at the kitchen bar. Kim stood up and walked toward the kitchen to get a glass of water. As she passed Eric, the rifle discharged in a loud crack, a bullet whizzing past her and slicing into the wall behind her. "He almost hit me," she said, her voice filled with a sense of wonderment even years later.

"I'm so sorry," Eric said, but he didn't appear at all upset.

As a boy, Eric climbed on the roof of his family home to shoot stray cats. Late some nights on Overlook, Kim and Eric's dogs barked. Such nights, he grabbed his .22 and walked out the back door, toward the field behind the house, saying he was going to "kill whatever needed killing." Trying to remain calm, Kim focused on the television, not wanting to acknowledge what unfolded just over her back fence. She turned up the sound, but still heard the gunshots.

A while later, Eric returned, acting as if nothing had happened.

One such night, Kim printed out labels, getting boxes ready to ship for her small eBay company. It hadn't done well, but she kept it going, as much as anything to have something to do. Again that evening, the dogs barked and Eric disappeared out the back door. After she heard shots, the dogs quieted. Then Eric returned to watch the television, as if nothing had happened.

A while later Kim brought her boxes outside. Walking toward the mailbox, she saw a cat in the street. "Kitty, kitty," she said, reaching down to pet it. The animal didn't move. "Oh, man," she whispered, when she realized it was dead.

On the driveway, Kim saw a trail of blood. "It was like drip, drip, drip, from our backyard all the way to the street."

In the house, a shaking Kim told Eric, "If you ever kill anything, I don't want to see it."

He laughed.

Another day, Kim passed Eric in the garage, as she carried a bag of trash. Again, a gun he held suddenly went off, the bullet hissing past her, piercing her car tire. An accident? Kim didn't think so. "He wanted me to know he could get me at any time. He was warning me."

Was he angry at her? Annoyed by her illness, the disappointment in their marriage? Considering the possibilities, Kim thought about how Eric coddled and nurtured his anger, never letting go of any perceived injustice.

After the incident with Judge Ashworth, the one when he questioned Eric's billing, Eric muttered about Ashworth. Although he and the judge still went out to lunch regularly, Eric never forgave the older man for what he saw as disloyalty. One day Eric stopped at the cemetery and e-mailed Kim a photo of the headstone the judge had installed over a plot he'd purchased for his eventual burial.

For years at Christmas, Kim and Eric had their annual argument about putting up a Christmas tree, Eric complaining that he had no use for the holidays and preferred not to participate. For some reason, that year, 2007, Eric covered the house in lights, so many that Kim wondered if it could be seen from outer space. At times, when she looked at it lit up at night, reminding her of the perfect Christmas card, she wondered if Eric had done it to spite her.

Chapter 12

Eric had a sweet deal in Kaufman County. And then they took it away.

—Sandra Harward

Over the years, Dallas spread east and Kaufman County's population mushroomed. In response, four years earlier the state funded a second district court, the 422nd, presided over by Judge Michael Chitty, another white-haired, grandfatherly man who'd been a former defense attorney. Like Judge Howard Tygrett, in the Eighty-sixth District Court, Chitty relied on Eric as one of his go-to ad litems for CPS cases. Combined, the judges' assignments afforded Eric substantial earnings. After so many years, he may have considered the county's ad litem work as his due.

Gradually the judges noticed that Eric made an enviable living off court assignments. In fact, Eric had become one of the county's top-earning attorneys.

Two years earlier, the commissioner's court had founded the public defender's office, cutting the cost of indigent defense. In 2008, Chitty and Tygrett called a meeting to discuss the situation in the CPS cases.

One of those attending, Erleigh Norville Wiley, had presided as judge over Kaufman's County Court at Law court for five years. Raised in the area, Wiley, a frank woman with a kind smile but a stern demeanor, was a former Dallas prosecutor. At the meeting, Tygrett and Chitty asked Wiley to take over assigning the CPS cases. During their talk, the judges voiced concern about the amount of money paid for ad litem work, especially to Eric Williams.

After the meeting, Wiley returned to her office and asked her assistant to pull the billings for the working CPS cases. When she reviewed them, she found Eric listed as ad litem on nearly all of them. At the courthouse, attending bar parties, Wiley had occasionally met Eric. "He was this average-looking guy, but you listened to him and all he talked about were his guns." In the courthouse scuttlebutt, she'd heard about the stash of weapons he kept in his office, across the street from the courthouse.

Looking at Eric's invoices, Wiley thought the hours charged seemed excessive. Wanting to "clear up any misunderstandings," she requested Eric meet with her in her chambers.

That day, Wiley explained that she had taken over the CPS assignments. "As the judge, I believe it is my responsibility to scrutinize the bills," she said.

When Eric agreed, she handed him a CASA report, a page-and-a-half document from the Court Appointed Special Advocates who reviewed such cases. "Please look at this. How long does it take to read it?" she asked.

After glancing at the paperwork, he handed it back. "Thirty seconds to a minute."

"Why did you bill the county two hours?" she asked.

At first, Eric said nothing. Then he became defensive, insisting that he'd built other tasks into the charges, including returning calls. At that, Wiley fanned out the rest of the paperwork. "You already charged for phone calls on this case for this same day. In the future, we need you to bill everything separately, so we can keep track of what the county's paying for."

What Wiley didn't say was what she believed, that there weren't enough hours in the day to do all the work Eric claimed he'd done on the cases. "We're not going to hold this against you," Wiley said, "but we are going to spread the assignments out and bring in other attorneys."

The conversation ended when Eric agreed to do as she'd asked and left. After he walked out her office door, Wiley thought about Eric. She sensed his anger, but she assumed he would shrug it off. The situation had gone on for so long that Wiley decided he had probably just gotten used to being able to bill whatever he wanted.

A short time later, Wiley's assistant told her Eric had called and asked to be taken off the list of attorneys available for CPS appointments. Considering the situation, Wiley decided Eric thought he would teach her a lesson— that he assumed the entire system would collapse without him. "Remove him," Wiley said. "Problem solved. Then I can put more attorneys in, and I don't have to worry about him."

At his office, Eric told his secretary about what had happened. "I'd never seen Eric really mad, but he was upset that day," she said. "He was really disappointed about it."

Later, Eric brought a list of his CPS appointments and his bills to the courthouse, where he showed them to a friend. Eric had made more than $200,000 in county fees in the previous year, a fortune in Kaufman, Texas. Now all that would be gone. "Somebody got mad about the money I was making," Eric said. "Judge Wiley is taking it out on me."

At home, Eric told Kim, too, what had happened, but didn't mention that he'd been caught overbilling. "Eric said that Judge Wiley wasn't paying him like she should and that he wasn't going to take any more CPS cases. He was angry at Erleigh Wiley." Thinking about that, Kim paused, before admitting, "I was mad at Judge Wiley, too. I thought I'd be angry if I was doing the work and wasn't getting paid. I was on Eric's side. I was always on Eric's side."

Perhaps by then Eric Williams had already begun keeping track of those he thought had wronged him, an accounting of the people against whom he someday wanted to seek revenge. If so, two of the names listed were Judge Glen Ashworth and Judge Erleigh Norville Wiley.

Chapter 13

Kim and Eric were almost symbiotic . . . they fed off each other. And the sicker Kim got, she was totally dependent on him.

—Sandra Harward

At the courthouse and other places, Eric mentioned to his fellow lawyers that he worried about losing the CPS appointments. As his existing cases dried up, Eric had less work and less money. Approximately six months after he asked to be removed from the list, in early 2009, he approached Wiley in the courthouse and said, "Judge, I'd like to get back on."

Wiley smiled at him. "Certainly, Eric. You took yourself off. Go talk to my assistant, and make sure she has your information."

"Thank you, Judge," he said, before walking off.

From that point on, CPS cases came his way, but not to the extent they had in the past. His near monopoly on the work and the considerable money the county paid him had abruptly ended. Along with it, Eric lost his power and influence.

Despite his financial situation, Eric didn't rein in his spending. Federal Express and UPS continued to make multiple stops a week at the house on Overlook, many of the boxes containing high-tech gadgets Eric bought online. Even with money tighter, when he purchased something he didn't like or that wouldn't work, he threw it in a closet, irritating Kim and leading to arguments that dragged on and changed nothing.

At times, it appeared Eric had to be trying to be noticed, playing up what so many saw as his quirky image. Ever since moving to Overlook, he'd walked through the neighborhood shirtless, reading from his iPad, even on sweltering summer afternoons.

That year Eric watched Kevin James portray a security guard who rolled around on a Segway in the comedy *Paul Blart: Mall Cop*. Not long after, Eric bought a Segway like the one in the movie, a two-wheeled, battery-powered stand with handlebars steered by balancing and leaning. If he'd looked odd walking and reading, he looked even stranger riding the Segway through the neighborhood, at times again reading a book. If others had Segways in Kaufman, it couldn't have been many. Making it even more unusual, on her good days Kim sometimes joined him, riding an adult-size tricycle.

To his Segway, Eric added all-terrain tires and a side carrier for his briefcase. Soon, Eric left the Sport Trac home much of the time and took the Segway on South Houston Street to his downtown Kaufman office. Amused, an attorney friend played a game with Eric, swinging her car door open as if trying to knock him off.

One neighbor protested when a police officer told his granddaughter that she couldn't drive a golf cart on the street. "Well, she just drives it in the neighborhood," the man said. "What about that lawyer who drives that contraption on the main roads?"

Afterward the officer talked to Eric and explained that he couldn't drive the Segway on public roads. Eric ignored him.

Despite everything that had happened, however, none

of it apparently injured Eric's self-confidence, his sense of being exceptional. That May, he sent himself an e-mail, one that apparently meant something special to him, because he kept it. The e-mail consisted of a single sentence: "Don't underestimate mediocrity."

In Kaufman, Eric continued to establish himself in the community. Along with his position overseeing the law library and attending bar functions, he joined the chamber of commerce and a new group for young Republican men.

That year, Eric also signed up with the Texas State Guard, a branch of the Lone Star State's militia that assists in times of natural disasters. Entering as a first lieutenant, he was assigned to the Nineteenth Regiment's First Battalion. Made up of around twenty-five hundred volunteers—mainly ex-military, police officers, firefighters, and EMTs—the guard also worked with Homeland Security. Unpaid, guard members supplied their own uniforms. The commitment substantial, at least two hundred hours per year, their service included one weekend a month. "Think of it as a militarized Red Cross," said one member.

Stripped of much of his power in the county court system, perhaps Eric saw the guard as a place to build influence. There he could be an officer, commanding a unit. That had once been his dream, before the army passed him over. In an advanced officer course months after joining, he wrote a paper exploring the traits of a leader and expressed lofty goals, including embodying "qualities that others aspire to and respect. A leader must have the character to do the right thing, even when faced with overwhelming odds."

"Eric was the unit's weapon specialist. He was well respected at the guard," said John Sickel, an attorney who worked in the judge advocate general's office. Sickel saw Eric, who seemed gung-ho and dedicated, supportive of the others in his unit, as an up-and-comer, an asset.

Eric in his Texas State Guard uniform

On Overlook, Eric flaunted his renewed connection to the military. He installed a Texas State Guard license plate holder on his Sport Trac and wore his camo uniform with a holster and gun on his Segway tours of the neighborhood. One neighbor thought she remembered Eric on one such ride with an assault-type rifle dangling from his shoulder, resembling a soldier patrolling a hostile zone. "He would do weird stuff," said a neighbor. "I would think, well, okay, he's a little different. Later I would think, well, the signs were all there."

That June 18, 2009, the DA, Rick Harrison, became involved in a minor car accident in Seagoville, west of Kaufman in Dallas County. From the scene, he was charged with his second DWI. Afterward, he issued a public apology: "Someone in law enforcement is and should be held to a higher standard," announcing he'd gone into an eight-week treatment program.

Four months later, candidates registered for the 2010 elections, and Harrison faced the race with the arrest hanging over him. "We asked Rick to pull out," said a high-placed Republican involved in the negotiation. "After the second DWI, we felt it was best."

Harrison refused, perhaps in part because his friend Sheriff Byrnes, the tall, white-haired former Texas Ranger, argued against the idea. "Rick had a little drinking problem," said Byrnes. "He was going to resign, but I talked him out of it."

If Mike McLelland needed any encouragement to enter the DA's race, Harrison's DWI delivered it. "Well, I'm going to run for DA again," Mike told a friend in his booming voice. Ever since his heart surgery, Mike had become sedentary, gaining weight until he topped three hundred pounds, and his loud, gravelly voice fit his round girth, the ample double chin. In November, Mike again filed as a Republican in the DA's race, telling a friend, "This Rick Harrison guy needs to go."

Under the circumstances, after having lost by only sixty-four votes four years earlier, perhaps a second run simply made sense. With his unruly steel gray eyebrows and his proud bearing, he certainly looked the part of someone who could "clean up the corruption in Kaufman County," a prominent promise in his campaign speeches.

To the surprise of many, Eric entered politics that fall as well, not running for the DA's job but for another position, one of Kaufman's four justices of the peace. Many assumed that one day Eric would want the type of power he'd seen his mentor, Judge Ashworth, wield. A justice of the peace slot offered an entry into that world, a first step toward higher goals.

Chapter 14

Eric didn't talk to me about running for office. I didn't think it was a good idea. It worried me because Eric doesn't play well with others, unless the others do what he wants.

—Kim Williams

Actually, Eric had mused about being employed by Kaufman County for some time, considering moving into a position that offered a salary and health insurance. When Kim asked why he wanted a county job, Eric said he'd work for ten years and have a pension. Still, Kim worried enough to attempt to talk him out of it. At that juncture, however, she had little energy to protest.

Eleven years into their marriage, Kim barely resembled the woman Eric married. Numbed by the prescription painkillers she took daily, including liquid morphine, she slept much of the day. Her long, light brown hair fell lifelessly around her shoulders as she shuffled through the house. While rheumatoid arthritis attacked her joints, her Sjogren's Syndrome destroyed her body's ability to make saliva, and her front teeth decayed. "She looked like an old woman," said a neighbor. "If I'd seen her in the grocery store, I wouldn't have recognized her."

When Kim protested Eric's plan, he ignored her. In

truth, however, Eric's likelihood of winning the JP slot appeared slim.

While in the past decade Kaufman County had turned Republican, one Democrat remained in power, the man Eric hoped to unseat: Precinct 1 Justice of the Peace Johnny Perry. Texas law didn't require that JPs be attorneys, and Perry wasn't. A soft-spoken, folksy man, he owned a cattle ranch outside the city. At six-foot-one, with a weathered face, Perry didn't drink or smoke, but he'd chewed tobacco for fifty years.

Johnny Perry in his kitchen
Kathryn Casey

His demeanor that of a good-old country boy, Perry had ruled over his courtroom for eighteen years, settling small claims disputes less than $10,000; handling truancy charges, tickets, evictions, and debt claims; and signing warrants. Most of those coming and going, even some of those appearing before him, called him Johnny, and rather than a black robe, Perry sometimes wore a coat and tie. "I'm not a rocket scientist," he said. "But I'm not a dummy either."

As Kaufman County turned red, based on Perry's popularity his JP slot became *the* Democratic stronghold. Some urged Perry to change parties, but he steadfastly refused, insisting that would violate the trust of voters who'd kept him in office. "If they were giving hundred-dollar bills away, I wouldn't vote for a Republican. I am going to die a Democrat!"

Established in the county, Perry knew most everyone, and he and Judge Ashworth had been friends for years. "Ashworth had cows, too," said Perry. "Sometimes he'd come over to my office just to jaw, visit, and get away for a while."

When Eric filed to run against Perry, those in power didn't believe Eric had a chance. With Perry's reputation, no one had run against him in the prior two elections. Still, Eric believed the changes in the county made Perry vulnerable. As Mike McLelland had in 2006, Eric requested information from the local Republican Party on who voted, and then he narrowed the names down to those within Precinct 1. The list amounted to approximately two thousand residents. That information in hand, Eric knocked on doors.

When he'd filed, Eric told Kim she didn't have to campaign, and she stayed home, often in bed. When she did get up, while watching TV she wrapped candy with his name on it, for him to hand out to children, but otherwise Eric campaigned on his own.

In truth, the marriage had continued to deteriorate. For both of them, Kim's declining health took a toll, and Eric seemed increasingly distant, ever more unpredictable. One night during a family argument with Kim's father, Eric grabbed a high-voltage policeman's flashlight and shone it in the old man's eyes. His cancer advancing, Don Johnson had been ill for years by then, and the way Eric confronted him, the anger, Kim thought that he might hit her father.

Outside the family, others saw indications of Eric's explosiveness.

In November, he held a fund-raiser at Maples Hall, an event venue in a stately old building on a corner across from the courthouse. To announce it, he printed an invitation with a judge's gavel in the center, and that night he rode over on his Segway. Many of the local attorneys attended, along with Eric's courthouse friends. Although Ashworth had given Eric $500 to support his run, the judge didn't appear.

At 10:35 that night, Eric sent his former boss an e-mail:

> Glen,
>
> Tried to catch up with you this evening. Looks like you have a new truck. Since you turned around about three times, I couldn't keep up, so I can only assume you don't want to talk.
>
> Also, since I didn't receive so much as a note, email, or text concerning my election race, I'll count you out of that as well.
>
> Do me one last favor—continue to just stay away. If you do show up, be prepared.
>
> I was your friend.
>
> ERIC

In response the judge, a well-known Democrat, e-mailed back:

> Even if you were my friend, I am still yours. Kaufman politics is an odd thing to me . . . and one reason I have stayed away from your race is because I genuinely believe I would be a detriment in the eyes of many of the more strident Republicans, but surely you must know how much I care about your success; personally, professionally and politically. I'm really sad that you feel this way and if I have

offended you, I apologize. As for consequences, I am always prepared for those, but out of respect for your wishes, I will stay away. Hopefully we can mend this and frankly, I've missed seeing you for the past several weeks . . .

Still my best regards,
Glen

When she heard of Eric's anger toward Ashworth, Harward thought it made sense. She didn't know about the day Ashworth questioned Eric's billing, but she knew Eric blamed the judge for not interceding for him when the CPS work dried up. "When Eric lost it, he thought Ashworth should have supported him . . . Eric was livid."

After the election e-mail, the judge's relationship with his former clerk cooled. The next time Ashworth went on a trip, he had someone else feed his cats. But then, something strange happened. One evening the pet sitter walked into the judge's house expecting it to be empty. Instead, he found Eric in the den, sitting silently in the dark.

"What are you doing here?" the pet sitter asked.

"I just wanted to make sure everything was okay at the judge's house," Eric answered.

Since Eric ran unopposed on the Republican ticket, his win in the March primary was a given. Once he officially became the candidate, the local party gave him $4,000 to help fund his campaign. But few held out much hope for Eric's win. One well-known Republican rang doorbells for Eric, but those who answered mainly wanted to talk about how much they liked the incumbent. "Everyone thought Johnny Perry would win," said the campaigner. "No one would have given Eric a snowball's chance in a Texas summer."

As 2009 drew to a close, Eric brought Kim her medication in bed, where she spent much of the day. In December, he convinced her to sign up for Facebook, and introduced her to Mafia Wars, a popular social networking game where teams worked together as organized crime families. The members collaborated to support one another, to complete missions, to increase their power, and build a criminal empire.

Perhaps the game awakened Dungeons & Dragons memories from Eric's past, for he spent hours in the evenings playing. Before long Kim joined him on Mafia Wars, becoming godmother of her own clan.

Chapter 15

The race got heated. Nearly everyone in the DA's office supported Rick Harrison. So did the sheriff. But we knew it was going to be hard to win with that second DWI.

—A staffer

In Eric's race for the JP seat, the November 2010 election was the prize. Once Eric won the primary, he had nearly eight months to campaign before he'd know his fate. Would he convince the voters of Kaufman County to vote Republican and oust Johnny Perry, or would they stay true to the Democrat who'd been in the office for nearly two decades?

Mike McLelland, however, had a vastly different situation. For him, a victory in the Republican primary held the golden ticket. As he had four years earlier, Mike threw himself into the race. Still employed by the Dallas County public defender's mental health branch, Mike spent days in the state hospitals representing those facing involuntary commitments. At the same time, Cynthia worked at Terrell State Hospital. To campaign they circulated evenings, attending functions, everything from Republican gatherings to church socials.

When no civic events called for their presence, Cynthia and Mike knocked on doors. The family helped, too. Cynthia's son, Nathan, and his wife, Julie, canvassed neighborhoods, as did Mike's mom and sister. His children, Krista, JR, and Josh, pitched in, and from Wortham Mike's mom, Wyvonne, again made phone calls.

Over the years, Mike's relationship with his children from his first marriage had thawed. Although he still didn't see his dad often, JR called and they talked on the phone, and Mike and Cynthia went to hear JR announce a rodeo. With his allergies, Mike couldn't stay for the entire show, but long enough to later tell JR that he enjoyed it. At times, Mike seemed proud of JR, as on the day Mike gave JR a gun for his birthday. JR took it out of the box and cleared it, to make sure no cartridges stayed in the chamber. "That's my boy," Mike said, smiling proudly.

Cynthia's children, too, had grown closer to Mike. The one most like Cynthia, Nathan shared his mother's and stepfather's love of reading, along with Mike's fascination

Mike and Cynthia (center) surrounded by Mike's family, circa 2011
Courtesy of the McLelland Family

with history. "I found him to be an extraordinary man," Nathan said.

To Mike's benefit, the current DA's legal woes worked right into his campaign strategy. Running again on his clean-up-the-county mantra, Mike questioned the appropriateness of a DA overseeing criminal cases, including DWIs, when he faced prosecution in the neighboring county. "Like the first time, Mike played up that he wasn't one of the usual suspects," said one of his advisers. "He ran on a platform of change."

When the *Kaufman Herald* called for comment, Mike said he'd had "a barrage" of phone calls from concerned citizens upset about Harrison's pending DWI case. "The real difference in this race is character and experience," Mike touted in his ads. "Anyone who can command an infantry company certainly wouldn't have any problem with the district attorney's office."

As might have been expected, Harrison also renewed his arguments from the prior race, hitting Mike on his lack of criminal experience. And when it came to Mike's trial skills, Harrison contended that much of Mike's courtroom time consisted of commitment hearings that lasted less than an hour, and that he'd never tried a murder case. Where Mike had no endorsements from law enforcement, Harrison displayed a long list, and his ads quoted Sheriff Byrnes praising the DA's office as "the best I have worked with. We must re-elect Rick Harrison."

When votes were cast in the Republican primary in early March, Mike ranked ahead of Harrison by 369 votes. Since neither received enough votes to win, however, as they had four years earlier Mike and Harrison headed toward an April runoff.

If the March primary had been intense, the runoff proved even more so, Mike and Harrison battling it out in well-placed newspaper ads.

In mid-April votes were again counted, and Mike

McLelland won with what the *Kaufman Herald* called "a commanding lead," fifty-eight percent of the vote. That night Mike and Cynthia threw a victory party, and when Mike gave a statement to the local paper, he said voters had sent a message in the ballot box: "no dual standards for public officials."

Chapter 16

Happy anniversary to the love of my life!!!!:))) . . .
From your wife for the rest of your life:))) Your marriage, first and last.

—Kim Williams on Facebook

While Mike ran for and won the DA's job that spring, 2010, Eric appeared to have a fairly light work schedule. Along with his race for the JP's slot, he went to state guard classes, one in shelter management in April. That month, he sent Kim a photo of his guard unit.

In the guard, Eric earned promotions, up to a full lieutenant's slot. A weapons officer, he took the battalion for shooting practice with everything from an M16 to a Beretta handgun. On his retention recommendation, his superior wrote, "one of the best examples for his unit and the entire regiment . . . a go-to leader," and said Eric had the potential to "rise in the ranks."

Meanwhile, Kim continued to worry about Eric's run for office. "I had a bad feeling."

Often alone, she spent much of her awake time on Facebook playing Mafia Wars. By then, Eric had a second e-mail account under the name Alex Knight to open a second Mafia Wars account. Off and on, he fed Kim rewards and tools, to help her build her crime family.

Then in May, she posted the salute to him for their

twelfth anniversary. That raised questions from her Facebook friends about her marriage. In her responses, she
gushed about Eric, describing him as her perfect match,
saying they had fun together and he made her laugh. "B4
I met him, I had practically given up on finding someone
like him, but we found each other . . . guess it's called
fate . . . It's hard to find someone you like and love at the
same time!"

At times, Kim remained on Facebook well into the
night, signing off at three or later, assuring her Mafia Wars
crew that she'd return soon. Six days after her anniversary
post, she asked for her Facebook family's help in a post that
recalled some of Eric's late-night tirades: "Kick this chicks
BUTT! I didn't do ANYTHING to her and don't even remember her handle . . . She put a bounty on me AND a hit!
Kick her butt until she no longer breathes! . . . here's her
MW profile link, just in case u wanna kill her over and over
again! What she did was NOT right! . . . Thanks again, my
Family!!!:)))"

Along with Mafia Wars, Kim played Farmville, Vam-
pire Wars, and Petville. But she spent most of her time on
the gangster game, earning rewards that included cement
blocks and shipping containers to dispose of bodies, black-
mail letters, assault rifles, and a chop shop sedan.

Over time, Facebook became her support network. With
her Internet friends, she talked about her life and her marriage. If she feared Eric, she never let it show on Facebook.
But then, he logged on as well, so he could see her posts.

In June, another player took a hit out on Kim. Insisting
she'd done nothing to the woman, Kim asked her "familia"
to "pls take her out over and over again until she's DEAD."
Then Kim offered a bounty for anyone who killed the player,
who had a Mafia Wars master thug ranking.

His wife distracted with her online games, Eric ran his
campaign. "The Right Choice!" Eric's ad touted. "Williams. Republican for Justice of the Peace Precinct No. 1."

That summer, Sandra Harward stopped at Eric's office. While they talked, she picked up a small box on his desk. It held a loaded gun. "What are you doing, Eric?" she asked.

Unconcerned, Eric took the gun out and showed it to her, smiling and proud.

Troubled by changes in Eric, Harward pegged it on his drinking on top of his diabetes. The previous year, she'd heard that Eric stocked his hotel room with liquor at a legal conference and entertained lawyers who dropped in, skipping sessions.

Although often numb, even groggy, from her medications, Kim continued to chauffeur her parents from their home to doctor appointments. And off and on, she covered the reception desk at Eric's office. It didn't help their already strained relationship that Eric attempted to kiss a woman at a party. When the woman complained to Kim, she chastised Eric, yet wrote it off as a result of his drinking, contending that the liquor made him "touchy-feely."

One day working at his office, Kim forwarded Eric an e-mail about a client. "Wanted to know if I can get my daughter back. Please call me," it read.

In his return e-mail to Kim, he wrote: "Only because you said be nice am I not stomping her guts out . . . Please call—make her not call any more, Thanks, ERIC." Their pattern continued, Eric talking of violence, and Kim laughing it off and acting proud of him.

In July, Eric's guard unit deployed to the southern Gulf Coast, when Hurricane Alex barreled in with wind and heavy rain. Later that month, Kim wrote on Facebook that she passed out and landed facedown on the ceramic tile. "I didn't tell Eric. He worries too much." She'd been out in the heat pulling weeds and taking care of the dogs. "The swelling seems to be going down . . . I've just been tired, dizzy & hoping that doesn't happen again; the passing out part."

Days later, Kim posted a news story about a woman who put a kitten in a freezer. In her comments, she praised Eric. Despite knowing that he routinely killed cats, she made him sound kind and protective. "He represents the kids . . . I hear about the poor children, but why animals??? I don't understand how anyone could harm an innocent kitten or puppy . . . it just makes me sick."

While Kim lauded Eric's commitment to the children, angry parents attacked him on Internet review sites. "Eric Williams took my children from me! This guy is ruthless . . . because they took my ex-husband's side, I can't see my children," one posted.

"Eric Williams was wrong to think we would forget" wrote another anonymous post.

In March a post attributed to "Anonymous Truth Teller" read: "Kaufman County, do not vote this corrupt lying deceiving man who is now running for JP in Precinct 1 . . . Eric Williams is a sly person. He works undercover but works disaster on families." On another Web site a reviewer wrote "Eric Williams is a family destroying, ruthless and corrupt person—beware! . . . Eric is a full-blown, heartless scoundrel and hypocrite . . . an imposter—an immoral criminal—posing as a child advocate."

At the house, Eric fumed over the posts. As he ran for JP, he found the complaints questioning his character particularly vexing. Kim listened to him rant, and took out a Post-it note and a pen, then wrote down the names of those he bore a grudge against. On the small square of paper along with others went the name of that final Internet poster, who'd called Eric an "immoral criminal." Excited about the list, Eric instructed her to include a state guard chaplain who'd crossed him. Labeling it "Kim's Kick-Ass List," she tacked the note on a kitchen cabinet.

On August 12, 2010, just under three months before the election, the Texas State Guard promoted Eric to a captain's rank and named him executive officer of his unit.

The position usually reserved for a major, some saw the appointment as a testament to the high regard in which Eric's commanding officers held him.

That same afternoon, Eric sent himself another one-line e-mail. It read: "The killer inside me."

Chapter 17

Just wanna apologize to my Facebook friends for being absent. A lot has happened over the last two weeks or more, so I have to tend to other things. Hang in there. It's not like me to just disappear, but I had to.
            —Kim Williams on Facebook, September 2010

The month started out well for Kim. She celebrated her forty-fourth birthday, describing it to her Facebook friends as a "wonderful relaxing day, at home, cuz I can't work. But I didn't realize how many friends I have here where I live & on Facebook who wished me happy birthday."

For her fortieth, Eric had thrown a party, but this year Eric's attentions were elsewhere. Instead she turned to Facebook to feel connected and appreciated.

Despite her seemingly good mood, she complained that her shoulders weren't working properly and said that Eric suggested she might have frozen shoulder, a malady not uncommon for diabetics that he'd had a couple of year earlier. "It's a bummer doing stuff, but I still try cuz I'm a hardhead and refuse 2 let my R.A. turn me into a veggie like a lot of people."

If the month started out with the focus on Kim's health, before long her problems seemed less imposing when pancreatitis landed Eric in a Dallas hospital. Between going to

Kim in a Facebook photo
with a Wombat, the insignia
for her Mafia Wars team

the hospital and taking care of her parents, Kim shuttled
back and forth for nearly a week.

When Kim left the hospital, Eric wasn't alone. His
guard unit tight, members took turns in his room. Eric's
visitors sensed a reverence in the guardsmen who kept Eric
company, treating Eric, their executive officer, with incredible respect. One day a friend dropped in to see Eric, and
a guard member jumped up and stood at attention. With a
salute, the man said: "Captain Williams, with your permission, be back in twenty minutes."

The bout a bad one, for a while Eric's doctors discussed
surgery.

To clear Eric's calendar, Kim cancelled upcoming meetings, explaining that he was hospitalized. One attorney she
called, John Burt, had an office around the town square
from Eric's. On that case, Eric functioned as mediator on a
real estate lawsuit, and he had a session scheduled for the
coming Wednesday afternoon.

Burt quickly agreed to the postponement. "That's fine. I hope Eric recovers well."

After Kim hung up, Burt called his client to inform him. Wednesday afternoon, however, the opposing attorney walked into Burt's office with his clients. "Where is everyone?" he asked.

It was a mistake. Burt thought Kim would inform the other attorney, and she'd assumed that he would. "It's been cancelled. Eric is in the hospital. I guess you weren't called?"

"No," the man said. While the attorney took it well, his clients threatened to file a state bar complaint against Eric.

"I wouldn't do that. Accidents happen," Burt advised.

Days later, when Eric returned to the office, he played his voice mail and heard an angry message from the Dallas attorney.

At nine that morning, Eric stormed into the lobby outside Burt's office shouting, "Where's John Burt? I'm going to kill him, his wife, and his kids. I'm going to burn his house down. I'm going to stab him!"

"Hold on, Eric. Calm down." Burt wasn't in, but the attorney in the next office walked out and warned Eric to "back down."

The next day the attorney who'd heard Eric's tirade told John Burt about the incident. Not understanding why Eric would say such things, Burt worried about Eric's reaction. He'd always thought they had a good relationship.

Chapter 18

Has anyone had a day that you thought you were just completely losing your mind? I mean like a "Twilight Zone." . . . I really need to start drinking again or maybe take a valium. I'm going stir crazy. My puppies are looking at me like I lost my mind.

— Kim Williams on Facebook

So much of Kim's life played out on Facebook in the fall of 2010. Her Internet friends heard her worries about her health, commiserated when she had a bad day. The one area where she never complained, however, continued to be her marriage. On Facebook she flattered Eric. Touting his attributes, she said she enjoyed his company. "He's very sarcastic and with the look and demeanor, when he's being sarcastically funny, I can't stop laughing."

Yet as they sat beside each other at the kitchen bar, clicking away on their laptops, in the same room, a few feet apart, their online lifestyle gradually became alienating. It occurred to Kim that even when physically close, they lived separate lives.

On one occasion when Kim dressed to go out, she attended their neighbor's wedding, held in his home. Eric refused to go. That afternoon as she stood in the yard next door and smoked a cigarette, Kim looked back at her own house. Through the window, she saw Eric where she'd left him, in the kitchen on his computer. Watching him, she felt irritated and sad, alone. She put the cigarette out and went inside.

In October, the general election approaching, the *Kaufman Herald* ran an article on the JP race. When asked why voters should support him, Eric responded: "Three traits—moral, ethical character, good judgment, and trust are essential . . . my life and experience demonstrate the best of those three traits."

In hindsight it would seem that Eric had taken notes on the playbook Mike McLelland used to win the DA's office, extolling his character above all else. But then, Eric was an Eagle Scout, a member of law enforcement, an attorney, and a captain in the Texas State Guard. Why wouldn't he talk of honor and trust?

Meanwhile, Mike made plans to take over the DA's office that coming January. His race over, he went to Palo Pinto County to visit his old law school friend Mike Burns. The DA in that county for three years, Burns had been in office long enough to give Mike a few pointers. Burns enjoyed seeing his old friend excited about taking office.

That week, Mike bunked at his friend's house and went to work with him to watch what went on inside a DA's office. Afternoons, Mike sat in on trials. At night, they talked. "Life was good. We were both living our dreams," said Burns. "This is what we'd wanted when we first started out as lawyers, and now it had happened for both of us."

Later that summer, the men saw each other again, this time with their wives at a district attorneys' conference in Padre Island, near the state's southern tip. One evening, Cynthia confided that she didn't like what she heard in Kaufman. "Some people are saying publicly that Mike doesn't have enough experience to be DA," she said, sounding hurt and angry.

Nonchalant, Mike interjected the same thing he'd told voters, "What the office really needs is a good administrator."

In November, Eric Williams pulled off an upset and won his election. Smiling about it, he later shrugged and said that it wasn't as hard to unseat Perry as everyone thought. Kaufman County had turned Republican, and Eric had watched the voting, saw the shift, and judged that the main reason some considered Perry unbeatable was that no one had run against him.

"Voters add Republican," the *Kaufman Herald* reported. "Perry was not able to overcome the lead." In the vote count, Eric garnered 2,274 votes to Johnny Perry's 1,523. That night, Eric thanked his supporters, "especially my wife and the county Republican Party."

After the win, Eric seemed more content. "He was happy-happy. He joked about running for a district judgeship," said Kim. "We were getting along all right. Doing separate things."

Much of Kim's attention focused on her parents, who continued to have health issues. To make it easier for their daughter to watch over them, that same month the Johnsons moved from their home outside Dallas to one they purchased just a block from Eric and Kim's home, on the opposite end of the U that Overlook formed as it swung through the neighborhood. The Johnsons' rose brick house, elegant with arched windows and a massive oak tree in the front yard, had been the home of Judge Ashworth's cousin when he developed the area.

When Johnny Perry called Eric to concede the election, Perry invited his successor to tour the offices and meet the staff, and soon after the election Eric did. The trip was short to Kaufman County's South Campus, also called the

The sub-courthouse on South Washington Street
Kathryn Casey

sub-courthouse. The JP's office took up one wing of the low-slung, flat-roofed building at 301 South Washington Street. Set back from a busy intersection, it lay diagonally across the field behind Eric and Kim's house.

A modest structure, the sub-courthouse also held a half-dozen other county offices, including the auditor and IT department. The center of the building consisted of Kaufman County's old jail, a somber-looking network of dilapidated cells, empty offices and hallways, abandoned years earlier when the new jail opened.

Visitors accessed the section that would soon become Eric's purview through a manned metal detector. Inside the building, they entered a door marked "Justice of the Peace Precinct 1." A short walk behind the receptionist's workstation, Eric passed his assistant's desk, on his way to the JP's small personal office.

On the day Eric inspected his new quarters, Johnny Perry shook his hand and congratulated him, and Perry's assistant, Regina Fogarty, escorted the newly elected JP to what would be his courtroom, connected to the offices through a private door. Eric's chest must have swelled eyeing the impressive display, Texas and U.S. flags flanking what would soon become his wood-paneled judge's bench.

As the time to take office drew close, Eric gushed to friends about his plans. As withdrawn as Eric had often been, he fomented enthusiasm and ideas for his new office. Preparing, he ordered shirts embroidered with a star encircled by "Justice of the Peace Eric Williams." At a state-run training session for new JPs, Eric quizzed the other attendees about how their courts ran, how they used technology, and he returned home committed to updating Kaufman County's antiquated system. To the lawyers in town, he boasted about what he saw as the centerpiece of his plans, a system that would bring the JP's office into the twenty-first century. High on Eric's list was video magistration, installing an Internet conferencing system. Once it was up and running, Eric and all four of Kaufman's JPs could read inmates their rights and set bonds via a computer hookup, instead of traveling to the jail.

Around the same time, Mike McLelland, too, took a tour of his new offices, the DA's quarters on the second floor of Kaufman's downtown courthouse. On that trip, Mike visited with prosecutors he'd soon supervise. Afterward Mike told a friend how impressive the staff seemed. "I think I'm going to enjoy this," he said.

In the meantime, others noted Eric's win. "A lot of us were really proud of Eric when he won," said Sickel, his friend in the state guard's JAG office. Perhaps Mike McLelland simply went to satisfy his curiosity. Maybe he wanted to look into the possibility of joining. In November, he attended a state guard recruiting session. Afterward, Eric saw Mike's name on the sign-up sheet and e-mailed

Sickel to tell him, mentioning that Mike had been an army major. "He hasn't submitted any paperwork—I just thought it was interesting," Eric noted.

When Mike talked to others about his trip to the recruiting session and his impressions, he laughed, calling the state guard members a bunch of "army wannabes."

In January 2011, excitement filled the room as the election winners took their oaths of office in Kaufman's courthouse. Cynthia held the red-and-gold bound Bible, as Mike raised his right hand. Excited, beaming, she wore a deep red jacket, and she couldn't have looked more pleased. This was her husband's dream, one she'd worked hard to help him attain. Whatever people said about Mike's qualifications, she believed in him. She always believed in him. And she loved him. And the road ahead must have shone as if it held great promise.

The new county judge, Bruce Wood, a former school superintendent, a round man with glasses, swore in Eric, as Kim held the Bible. Eric and Kim both wore gray business suits, and Kim, despite her illnesses, looked beautiful, her hair curled and dyed a soft brown with highlights, smiling at Eric, proud of all he'd accomplished.

They had much to celebrate that day. Eric's new job offered great benefits. His $48,425 salary came with health insurance, a pension, and the opportunity to make vastly more. Many Texas JPs doubled, even tripled their earnings by charging fees to conduct marriages. In addition, the job had enough flexibility to keep his law office open and take on private clients.

Potentially as satisfying, Eric would have the respect afforded a judge. Many saw Eric as well-positioned for a bright future. The hierarchy in the local Republican Party had noticed that he'd unseated the last Democrat in the county. Ambitious, just forty-three, Eric represented a younger generation, an up-and-comer. His trajectory could easily take him on the path he'd seemed to covet since law school, to one day become a district judge, like Glen Ashworth.

Yet even at such a happy event there were shadows over both the McLellands and the Williamses. A few noted the halting way Cynthia walked, her Parkinson's slowly progressing. There also to be sworn in for a new term, Judge Erleigh Wiley noticed that Eric Williams's wife had aged, and that when she talked or smiled, Kim covered her mouth with her hand. By then Sjogren's Syndrome had claimed her front teeth.

"You tell Eric to get you new teeth," Wiley whispered to her. "You're too young and pretty for that."

At that, Kim giggled like a schoolgirl.

On that day, despite any past problems, the lingering concerns about their wives' health issues, both Mike McLelland and Eric Williams undoubtedly felt like the world had opened up for them. In that room as they were sworn in, they showed no signs of any ill feelings between them. Although they didn't seek each other out, and weren't particularly friendly, at one point they shook hands. Perhaps they believed they'd be able to put the animosity behind them.

As DA, Mike moved a large mahogany desk into his office, one that left only a narrow path to squeeze his substantial bulk past. On the walls, Cynthia hung Western art. Further cultivating the look of a Texas DA, along with a sport coat and slacks, Mike wore boots and a black cowboy hat with a wide brim.

On his first day, he called a meeting and told the staff about his history. Some thought the new DA's military background might not bode well, leading him to be inflexible, especially when Mike mentioned that he wanted the office to run like an army unit. Although he said he didn't plan personnel changes, they hadn't forgotten his pledge to clean up the office.

In time many wrote off that concern, as Mike acted more like the office patriarch than a military commander, habitually wandering through carrying his insulated University of Texas Longhorn cup, Diet Coke sloshing inside. Off and on, he paused to inquire about their families.

Before long, some noticed Mike latched on to one person in the office in particular—a slender, brown-haired lawyer—singling him out as a friend. Although in many ways opposites, Mike respected Mark Hasse, describing him as the real thing, a tough prosecutor.

Once a week, Cynthia brought cake and cookies to her husband's office. Perhaps when she first met Mark she took his hand, turned it over and read his palm, as she habitually did with new acquaintances. What did she see? Did she find any indication of the importance the garrulous man with the big glasses would play in her destiny, and that of the man she loved?

Chapter 19

Mark was fearless. Not a big guy, but in a courtroom
he was a giant.

—A friend

Growing up in Dallas, Mark Hasse had what his older
brother called a whip-smart mind. A scrawny kid who gob-
bled junk food and candy bars but never gained weight, he
described himself in junior high as a "science geek," one of
his favorite stories the day he blew up the family's screen
door with a gunpowder experiment. "Mark was an arrogant
little shit," said Larry Cleghorn, who employed a teenage
Mark. "He had girlfriends, but they got fed up. Mark could
be cocky, and the girls got tired of it. He was a good kid,
just really full of life."

A natural, Mark earned a pilot's license in high school.
After graduating from Texas A&M University with a bachelor's degree in history, he found a dream job, working
for King Radio Corporation, an avionics manufacturer,
flying its founder, Edward King Jr., in his private Cessna.
Impressed with his young employee's keen mind, King offered a slot on the corporation's legal team if Mark went to
law school.

Grabbing the opportunity, he enrolled at Southern Methodist University's Dedman School of Law, where he de-
voured textbooks like Snickers bars. Friends later recalled

how he read a book once and recited whole pages. "Mark was a polymath," said Paula Sweeney, who met Mark at SMU in 1979. "He knew everything about everything, and he would tell you so."

Yet people liked Mark. If he overflowed with confidence, he rarely took himself too seriously. Adept at accents and mannerisms, he mimicked professors, at times leading Sweeney to laugh so hard, her sides hurt. A persistent bachelor, Mark dated, but rarely seriously.

Although Mark envisioned law school as a route to a career in aviation, by the time he graduated, King had sold his company. Instead in the fall of 1981, Mark took a junior prosecutor's job working for legendary Dallas district attorney Henry Wade, the man who charged Jack Ruby with the murder of President John F. Kennedy's assassin, Lee Harvey Oswald.

Dressed like all Wade's prosecutors in white shirts and dark suits, Mark wore cowboy boots to lengthen his slight five-foot-seven-inch, 140-pound frame. Starting out in misdemeanors, Mark learned quickly, transferring his swagger and flair to a hardnosed courtroom approach that led to quick promotions. Before long, he tried sex offenders and killers. Never shy, at trials he pointed at defendants, shouting out alleged offenses: "Murderer!"

Sex crimes and ones with children as victims magnified his fury. "When Mark got a burr under his saddle about a particular case, you prayed it wasn't your client," said Dallas attorney Colleen Dunbar. "He went after them with vengeance."

Perhaps even then, Mark Hasse understood his job brought dangers. Dealing with hardened criminals, he must have considered that one day someone might not turn and walk away after a stinging defeat.

Whether or not Mark considered such consequences, his boss did. When he promoted Mark to head the office's organized crime unit, Wade ordered Mark to become li-

Mark in his office at the Dallas DA's office, circa 1985
Courtesy of Marcus Busch

censed as a volunteer deputy with a local constable's office, to enable him to carry a gun into the courtroom. "Mark understood that there were truly evil people," said his friend Marcus Busch. "At one point every prosecutor is threatened. You learn that life goes on and try not to think about it."

Rather than worried, Mark appeared exhilarated. With Busch and his other fellow prosecutors, Mark reveled in describing his courtroom exploits. In long accounts, he impersonated wise guys and gang members as he once had his law professors. "Mark loved telling stories, and he loved putting the bad guys away," said a friend. "He wasn't afraid of anything. Not anything."

In 1988, eager to start his own practice, Mark left the Dallas DA's office. Along with criminal law and personal injury suits, he specialized in a field close to his heart, aviation law. Over the years, he'd bought a plane and continued to fly, earning additional licenses as an airplane mechanic and inspector. Busch also a pilot, the two men frequented

Mark Hasse in the mid-nineties
Courtesy of Morey Darznieks

air shows and fantasized about grand adventures, flights around the oceans.

While those dreams didn't materialize, in 1995, Mark did depart on a grand quest, piloting a World War II aircraft, a single-engine, two-seater AT–6, in Freedom Flight America. A coast-to-coast caravan of vintage airplanes, the event marked the fiftieth anniversary of the end of the war. The day Mark lifted off from Ohio's Wright-Patterson Air Force Base, he had no way of knowing how drastically his life would change. Over Luray, Virginia, in cloudy skies, the engine quit. Mark attempted to land in a field, but instead crashed into an embankment.

Helicoptered to the University of Virginia Medical School in Charlottesville, for days Mark hovered between life and death. When he awoke, doctors couldn't predict the extent of his brain damage. His skull fractured and his left temporal lobe bruised, eventually it became evident that he'd lost much of his short-term memory. His sharp wit gone, Mark returned to Dallas, where Busch closed Mark's office. "He wasn't in any shape to practice law."

For two years, Mark did little but concentrate on his recovery. He lived in his ranch house on acreage in Rockwall, east of Dallas, caring for a menagerie of stray dogs collected from the side of a road, and saw only family and close friends. His speech more deliberate, his reality had changed. With wire holding his broken skull together, never again would he ride the horses he boarded in his barn or scuba dive with friends. His wounds left scars on his chest and legs, a ragged five-inch one on his scalp, and a noticeable hollow on the left side of his forehead.

Slowly he recovered.

In 1997, Mark drove into the parking lot of Air Salvage, on the outskirts of the quiet Lancaster Airport, south of Dallas. Years earlier, he'd used the facility to store blown tires and other evidence for personal injury cases. Inside the modest and cluttered offices, Mark approached Alfred "Lucky" Louque, short and husky, a well-known airplane mechanic. They'd met years earlier, and Mark confided in Louque about his accident. "Brrrrr . . . brrrrr . . ." Mark sputtered, imitating the plane's engine right before the crash.

"I wasn't supposed to survive," he said. Then he hesitated, thinking about what he'd say next. "Since I have, now that I have a second shot, I'm going to do things that make me happy."

To Mark, that meant flying and working on airplanes. Before long, he'd purchased a hangar at the airport and started Intrepid Aircraft Sales, Inc. He bought planes, repaired then attempted to sell them. To Louque, Mark never looked more content than in oil-stained T-shirts and shorts tearing a plane apart, then piecing it back together.

Afternoons, Mark ended most days by walking over to Air Salvage, where he sat with Louque and another airplane mechanic, Curtis Mays, a tall, muscular man with a beard. Close friendships grew, as Mark entertained the men by recounting cases he'd handled, the worst-of-the-worst, during his days in the Dallas DA's office. "Mark said he'd prosecuted somewhere between three and four hundred cases," said Louque. "And he said he'd lost only one, a case where a guy claimed self-defense in an assault."

Over the years, Mays and Louque agreed that Mark had a finely tuned sense of right and wrong. "He didn't back down from anyone," said Mays. "Mark was one of those red-white-and-blue guys who believed in the system."

Years passed. Living frugally, Mark bought airplanes in need of repair, fixed them, and then listed them for sale. At one point, he owned four: a 1948 Luscombe, a high-winged monoplane, an experimental aircraft, and a Cessna. Despite the accident, Mark rarely looked happier than in the cockpit, especially flying low with the windows open, the wind on his face.

To Louque and Mays it appeared Mark made few sales. Yet Mark didn't complain, any more than he did about the aches and pains he still suffered from the crash. More often he made fun of his situation, laughing about how the brain damage had resulted in the loss of his sense of smell. One afternoon at the airport, he stirred a pot of gumbo, not realizing it had turned rancid. When someone told him, he shrugged and said, "It's a good thing I didn't eat any."

Despite not practicing law, Mark never formally relinquished his license. As the years passed, when he again felt capable, he did small jobs for friends, writing wills, advising on real estate transactions, reviewing contracts, but his focus remained on the airplanes.

The years Mark worked on his planes at the Lancaster Airport would be among the most content of his life. His brain healed, restoring his memory and his sense of humor. In time, the old Mark returned, the quick-witted lawyer who loved a good story.

In late 2009, Mark reflected in conversations with his friends about the possibility of restarting his legal career. While he loved repairing airplanes, he admitted it had proven a financial failure. With his medical history, he couldn't find health insurance. And at fifty-four, Mark wanted a job with a pension. Considering possibilities, Mark settled on a slot with a DA's office. Rather than Dallas with its big-city crime, he preferred a rural county. Along with money and insurance concerns, he told Louque that he'd missed "putting bad guys behind bars."

Months later, Mark announced that he'd found just such a position in Kaufman County, where an old Dallas friend, Rick Harrison, was district attorney. "I think I'm going to play that gig for a while," Mark told Louque. "I'll be a prosecutor again. That's what I'm good at."

Certainly Kaufman was lucky to get Mark Hasse. He had all the right credentials, especially his years of prosecuting in a busy courtroom. His mind, if not as sharp as it had been before the accident, had recovered to the extent that no one doubted his abilities. "Mark was still one of the smartest people I knew," said Marcus Busch.

In July 2010, Mark began work in Kaufman County, half an hour's drive from his home in Rockwall. It must have seemed like the perfect match. His $74,000 salary came with health insurance and a pension. A predominantly rural county, Kaufman had little big crime, a murder or two a year, a couple of dozen assaults, some domestic violence. Instead, the cases involved meth labs; DWIs; public intoxication; stolen cars, cows, and horses; and dog bites.

In the old, rundown courthouse, Harrison assigned Mark the chief prosecutor's position in the 422nd District Court, the one presided over by Judge Michael Chitty, and Mark settled into an office next to Brandi Fernandez, the office's first assistant and the chief prosecutor in the county's only other district court, Judge Tygrett's Eighty-sixth.

Quickly, Mark's life fell into a pattern.

In the mornings, he drove in from his ranch in Rockwall and parked on a side street behind Lott's, a dry cleaner that had been on a corner across from the courthouse since

Mark Hasse in his Kaufman County ID photo

1959. Still so thin one friend said he resembled a grey-hound, Mark stocked a desk drawer with junk food and his office refrigerator with Country Time lemonade. Word spread of his sweet tooth, and when items turned up missing from lunches, more often than not the owner sought out Mark.

Around the office, like a character in a beach movie, Mark stuck his head in offices and called the men "dude." With the women, the lifelong bachelor bantered and indulged in practical jokes. When he told his assistant that he'd lost his sense of smell in the plane crash, she hid cheese in his office. Soon others complained of the stench, but not Mark. "Okay. What did you put in my office?" he asked after one attorney made a face and held her nose.

"Mark didn't have a filter," said Fernandez. "The women

teased him about being skinny, and he teased them about being chunky. Somehow Mark always got the last word."

On non-court days, he wore what many agreed ranked among the ugliest sweaters imaginable. "We thought his mother must have given them to him decades ago and he just kept wearing them," said one of the secretaries. Perhaps because he had so little body fat, Mark felt perpetually chilled, so much so that he sported sweaters in the summer and in the winter long johns under his business suits.

In the afternoons, Mark, as he had for years at the airport, made the rounds, looking for an open door, landing in someone's office, and then regaling them with stories of the bad old Dallas days when he'd taken down major criminals. "Once Mark walked in your office, you had to figure that you'd lost at least thirty-five minutes," said one attorney with a laugh. "It wasn't going to happen that he was going to let you get back to work."

No one complained, however, because they appreciated the other Mark, the slight man who became a giant in the courtroom. There his stories became the facts of the cases, the evidence that, pieced together, formed pictures of horrible wrongs, ones he pleaded with juries to make right. "Mark could connect with jurors like few prosecutors I'd ever seen," said one lawyer. His fellow lawyers saw Mark as fair, unless someone tried to manipulate him or had truly injured another. Then Mark became relentless.

In hindsight, Mark Hasse must have understood when he walked in the door at the Kaufman County DA's office that first time that the office faced a potentially tumultuous transition. Three months before Mark started, Rick Harrison had been defeated in his bid for reelection by Mike McLelland. If Mark did any research, read any of Harrison's ads or listened to office scuttlebutt, he knew how little criminal experience the incoming district attorney had. At times, Mark mused with the others about what it would all mean. Would the new DA understand the cases they prosecuted?

"You can't learn criminal law by sitting in on a few trials," Mark told one friend. "How's this guy going to know what we're up against? How's he going to understand who should be prosecuted, and who shouldn't?"

Chapter 20

Mike loved being DA. He came home every night with stories to tell Mom. It had been a long time since he felt such joy from his job. And Mom loved being the mother hen.

—Christina Foreman

If Mark initially worried about his new boss, he either hid his concerns well or getting to know Mike McLelland put him at ease. Early on, it became obvious to many in the office that the two men had forged what was perhaps not such an unlikely friendship.

Most mornings, Mike found his way to Mark's office. Despite their disparate pasts, they had much in common, including a love of telling stories, Mark of his years as a Dallas prosecutor and Mike from his army days. Within weeks of taking office, others noticed that Mike relied on Mark, going to him when he sought advice. Yet Mike reveled in the fact that he ran the office and made the decisions, that he didn't have a boss. At noon, Mike walked over to a smokehouse for barbecue, sometimes with Mark beside him, Mike, bulky and round, more than six feet tall, and Mark whisper-thin and half a foot shorter. "If Mike was a bulldog, Mark was a pit bull in the courtroom," said the county judge, Bruce Wood.

Over plates of brisket, potato salad, and coleslaw, Mike and Mark bonded. To others, Mike talked often about the frail-looking prosecutor who wore worn-out sweaters and spent much of the day munching on junk food. Mike bragged about Mark's courtroom prowess and repeated Mark's Dallas stories, when he'd taken on organized crime figures and drug lords.

On days Cynthia brought in homemade baked goods for the staff, some were taken aback when she insisted on hugging them. Still they munched happily on her peanut cookies rolled in sugar or her cheesecake, the top perfectly cracked and a golden brown. She, too, seemed to take a particular interest in Mark, the perennial bachelor, bringing extra cookies for his desk.

In the office, Cynthia cooed over Mike, straightening his shirt collar, snuggling up to his side, as he smiled proudly. "Some of us started joking that they were grossly in love," said one secretary. "It was like she couldn't keep her hands off of him."

Not long after he took office, Mike hired his first lawyer, Michelle Sutton, an amply built woman with shoulder-length dark hair and an engaging smile. Mike and Cynthia had been friends of Michelle and her husband, Rob, for years. A former judge in a Dallas CPS court, Michelle had presided over cases when Mike represented clients. The Kaufman job appealed to her since Dallas's political changes were the opposite of Kaufman's, and as a Republican she faced re-election in a county quickly turning blue.

In addition, Mike brought on Bruce Bryant, Nathan's former sergeant at Dallas PD, as an investigator. Mike assigned Bryant to the 422nd, Judge Chitty's court, where Mark was chief prosecutor. A husky man with thinning salt-and-pepper hair, Bryant lived in Terrell and was commander of the local American Legion post. When Mike hired him, he confided in Bryant that he felt certain there was corruption in the county. "He didn't want to continue the old practices, looking the other way," said Bryant.

From all appearances, Mike settled quickly into the DA's office, but he must have realized that he had much to learn. "Well, you got your arms around it yet?" a friend asked.

"It's like a greased pig," Mike responded. "It keeps spurting out of my hands."

Their prospects improved, a few months after Mike took office, the McLellands sold the house in Terrell and purchased a sprawling four-bedroom in Forney, Kaufman County's most affluent city. On Blarney Stone Way, twenty minutes' drive from the courthouse, the house was in the Shamrock Ridge subdivision, streets of large, one-story brick homes on acre lots cut from former cotton fields. "The house seemed a better fit for Mike's new job," said a friend. "Cynthia said it was a great entertaining house."

The McLellands' new house featured an open floor plan; the front door led to a hallway with a study on the right, which Cynthia and Mike filled with books, and

The house on Blarney Stone Way
Kathryn Casey

a dining room for parties on the left. Straight ahead, the living room bordered a kitchen where Cynthia had wide open counter space for baking and cooking. The living room was furnished with an entertainment center against one wall, a fireplace, two lounge chairs, and a couch behind which Cynthia placed her sewing machine so she could quilt while Mike watched TV.

Cynthia turned the house's master bedroom into a fabric room, because feng shui deemed its location, to the right of the front door, as less advantageous. Instead, Mike and Cynthia took a bedroom at the front of the house on the left. As in the old house, they turned one spare bedroom into their larder, filling it with a substantial stock of flour and sugar, canned beans and vegetables, all the survival supplies they'd amassed in case the world fell into upheaval.

In the kitchen, Mike put kennels for their two Scotties, ones neighbors grew used to seeing Cynthia walk down the pencil-straight street as the sun rose and set.

Along with Mike's position in the community, the election brought new friends into the McLellands' lives. A Vietnam War vet, Skeet Phillips wore a mustache and gray hair. After he lost a bid for a county commissioner's seat, he and his wife, Leah, thin and girlish with long blond hair, had pitched in to help Mike with his campaign. They had three sons, two together, and lived nearby on a horse ranch.

When Cynthia met C.J., Leah's son from an earlier marriage, Cynthia asked with a conspiratorial smile: "Do you believe in arranged marriages?" Like Nathan, C.J. worked as a Dallas police officer.

"You know I have a beautiful daughter. She and C.J. would be perfect together," Cynthia told Leah, not dissuaded by the fact that both dated others. As if she had a premonition, she added, "It'll work out."

Before long the couples met for dinners, including at a little Italian restaurant. Although Cynthia didn't mention her illness, it didn't take long to realize that she wasn't well, and Leah grew used to seeing Cynthia standing helpless, her legs locked in place, unable to move. It happened most often in the evenings, when her medications wore off. When it did, Leah put her arm around Cynthia and nudged her to get her moving again.

At times, Cynthia did things that made Leah shake her head and laugh, like one night in a restaurant when Cynthia emerged from the ladies' room carrying a stranger's baby. "Oh, I offered to hold it while the mother used the restroom," she said.

Soon, the two couples grew so close, they thought of each other as family. Cynthia made each a quilt and cooked birthday and holiday dinners, Leah jumping in to help with the McLellands' annual Christmas party. They had keys to each other's homes and usually walked in without knocking. Seventeen years younger, Leah thought of Cynthia as a big sister. And Skeet was impressed with Mike, whom he saw as someone who wouldn't back down from a fight. "The thing about Mike was that he wasn't going to let anyone tell him what was right," said Leah. "Mike wasn't afraid of the old devil himself."

Chapter 21

Eric was back in the arms of the income stream that was Kaufman County government. On his own, he hadn't been a great success, so this was important to him.

—A local attorney

While Mike McLelland settled into the DA's role, Eric Williams took possession of the Precinct 1 JP's domain. Mornings, he rode his Segway the few blocks from the house to the sub-courthouse. In his private office, Eric placed two barrel-shaped aqua leather chairs around a table topped by a collage depicting the Alamo, longhorns, and an oil well. In town he wore his shirts with the embroidered JP insignia, but on the bench, in his black robes, Eric looked like the judge he'd become.

Underneath he strapped a holstered handgun to his hip.

From his first days, Eric moved to modernize the office, and when his lawyer friends stopped in, he crowed about the improvements he'd slated, video magistration high on the list. Those who worked with Eric understood why he needed the latest high-tech tools. In the legal community, much of Eric's image relied on his intelligence and computer acumen. His new assistant, Fogarty, noticed something else; unlike her old boss, Perry, who enjoyed traveling to the jail, she thought Eric appeared more at ease behind his desk, working on his computer.

Quickly after taking over, Eric began updating, walking a copy of an ad for a Dell laptop to the other side of the sub-courthouse, to the county's IT department. On it he'd written, "JP 1, please. Thanks, ERIC." In the cluttered IT room filled with computers and parts, Lori Friemel, who did the ordering, explained the process. Supplied by a $4 fee on each ticket paid in his court, Eric had at his disposal tens of thousands of dollars in his technology fund. "You have plenty of money," Friemel told him. "Just let me know if you need anything else and I'll order it."

"Nothing else right now," Eric answered.

Graying hair and friendly eyes, Friemel put through the order for his computer.

These were heady days for Eric, who made noticeable changes from the way Johnny Perry functioned as JP. Overall, Judge Eric Williams adopted a more formal presence. When a deputy who'd known Eric since he first came to Kaufman called him by name, he corrected her, saying, "It's Judge Williams." When deputies and constables dropped in to get warrants signed, a brusque Eric complained that they weren't filling out forms correctly.

The new JP's attitude rankled some who thought Eric enjoyed reminding others of his nascent power. One afternoon, Precinct 1 Constable Shawn Mayfield brought in an eviction notice. In the past, Perry would have signed it and had him out the door in minutes. "With Eric it took an hour and a half," said Mayfield, who was left to stew as Eric took a recess.

"Eric was king for a day in that courtroom," said one lawyer. "Some of us started talking about Eric having 'black robe syndrome,' feeling powerful because he was a judge."

That winter at the sub-courthouse, emboldened by his

new stature, Eric did as he pleased, ruling over his domin-
ion. Ignoring channels, he bypassed the purchasing department and personally bought a separate mailbox for the JP's
office. Rather than file a request for a county worker to
mount it, Eric did it himself. Again without notifying the
county, Eric procured and installed a safe to hold ticket
payments kept overnight.

Along with making changes at the sub-courthouse, Eric
turned his attention to an old project. At the main courthouse, lawyers continued to complain about a lack of wi-fi.
By then many carried laptops into the courtrooms, ones on
which they wanted to be able to do research during trials.
The router Eric installed in the law library two years earlier barely extended beyond the door. "We'd complained to
Eric that we'd talked to IT and they did nothing," said one
lawyer.

Again, Eric circumvented the system.

Rather than approach Lori Friemel or her boss, George
York, Eric personally made inquiries, calling AT&T directly to review pricing to bring wireless to the entire
Kaufman County courthouse. In charge of the law library
with its hundreds of thousands of dollars, Eric had ample
funds and saw no reason to ask permission.

Yet that wasn't the way the county worked, and this
time someone noticed that the new JP overstepped his
boundaries.

When the AT&T installer dropped into the IT offices to
ask questions about services already in the building, a surprised George York sought Eric out. Not mincing words,
York informed Eric that the IT department oversaw all the
computers, phones, and other equipment used on county
property. "Anything that gets plugged in, we order, install,
and fix."

Although Eric backed down, York walked away thinking
the conversation hadn't gone well. "Eric was very offended
that we told him that was not the way to do it."

For the most part cloistered at home, Kim grew increasingly frail. That winter, with the trees bare outside his JP office window, Eric could look out across the field and see the back fence of the Overlook house. Inside, Kim spent much of the day either sleeping or on the computer. "We hardly ever saw her outside," said a neighbor. "When we did, she kind of shuffled."

One day Eric told his assistant, Regina Fogarty, all the medications Kim took, including liquid morphine and hydrocodone, some twenty pills. "How does she function?" Fogarty asked.

"I give her the pills to make sure she takes the right amount," he said with a shrug.

When she asked if they had children, Eric said no, citing his diabetes and Kim's health. Then Eric said something Fogarty thought odd. "If anything ever happens to me, if I ever get in trouble, call Taryn Davis."

It seemed so strange, and Fogarty wondered, "Why would a justice of the peace worry about getting in trouble and needing a lawyer?"

Along with his new job, other things fell in place for Eric. In February, he took over as the head of the local Republican men's club. Politics makes strange bedfellows, and at a meeting, he and Mike McLelland stood next to each other for a group photo.

Then in March, the state guard published the latest edition of its magazine, *Guidon*. An essay by Eric ran on page 17 under the headline, "Why I Serve in the TXSG. Duty, Honor, Country: There's Nothing Better That I Do." In the piece, Eric wrote: "Honor, while unfortunately lacking in many aspects of our society, is essential. . . . I don't spend my time in the guard because I have nothing better to do; I spend my time in the guard because there's nothing better I do."

At the same time, Eric continued to move ahead with

his plans to update the county's computer systems, adding the video conferencing. One afternoon, he invited the three other JPs and Judge Chitty to his office. Eric hooked up a Skype link between his desk computer and his laptop, one in his office and the other in the adjacent conference room, to demonstrate how video magistration could work. "They all seemed impressed," he said.

Along with wi-fi in the courthouse, video magistration wasn't a new idea in Kaufman County. There'd been talk of it for years, yet nothing had been done. "They wanted committees for everything," said Eric. "Everything had to be studied. I thought it wouldn't be that hard."

Yet with tens of thousands of dollars sitting in his court's technology fund, Eric didn't discuss his plan with George York and York's assistant, Lori Friemel. Information technology was their department, their territory, but Eric had never been one to bow to rules.

Overall, Regina Fogarty, Eric's assistant, liked her new boss. More hands-on than Johnny Perry, Eric used a computer and typed up his own reports. Still, Fogarty wondered about some minor events she saw as odd. The first was the day she mentioned to Eric that Xerox dropped off the wrong toner for the copy machine. When she said she would call to have the Xerox rep pick it up, Eric told her to instead return it to Terrell Office Supply for a credit. Since Xerox, not the office supply, had billed for the toner, Fogarty left perplexed about Eric's advice.

Not long after, Fogarty ran out of ink in her laser printer cartridge and asked Eric to order a replacement from IT. "Don't worry, I'll get some," he said. "I know where they keep it."

Later, Eric showed up with the cartridge, and as Fogarty installed it in her printer, she wondered how and where he'd gotten it.

Then on a Monday morning, May 16, 2011, four and a

half months after Eric took over as JP, Lori Friemel walked into the IT workroom and eyed the boxes of brand-new computer monitors next to her desk. The Friday before, she'd had her laptop perched on top of the stack. Now the boxes looked less than half the height. When Friemel pulled the records, she realized three monitors were missing. Somehow they had vanished over the weekend. Considering possibilities, Friemel called her boss, York, and asked if he'd picked up the monitors. When York said that he hadn't, Friemel sat back in her office chair, surrounded by remnants of computers, phones, cable and printers, equipment waiting for repair.

"Well, where did those monitors go?" she wondered.

Chapter 22

I was in bed when the phone rang. Eric said, "Be quiet. Listen to me. The big computer monitor on the bar, put it in the box next to it and take it to your parents' house. Do it now." I did what he told me to do. I always did what he told me to do.

—Kim Williams

When he called Kim on the morning of May 24, 2011, Eric was at the Kaufman County Sheriff's Office. Three deputies had shown up that morning and asked Regina Fogarty to let Eric know they needed to see him. As JP, Eric routinely signed search and arrest warrants for the deputies, so Fogarty asked, "Do you have warrants for the judge?"

"We have one for the judge's arrest," one deputy said. Fogarty thought they were kidding, but moments after they met with Eric in his office, they marched him out in handcuffs. Remembering what Eric told her, Fogarty called Eric's friend Taryn Davis at her law office.

At the sheriff's office, Eric waited in an interview room, and Chief Deputy Rodney Evans walked in along with another investigator. By then, Evans had been filled in on evidence Lori Friemel had pulled together. On the sub-courthouse surveillance video from Sunday, May 15, Eric wove through the building from his JP office, down a long hallway and through unlocked doors into the IT department. Moments later, he emerged carrying a Dell monitor box. On another trip, he left carrying two more such boxes. In a clip from an outside surveillance tape, Friemel had Eric in the parking lot putting two of the monitor boxes in his Sport Trac.

The security cameras kept video for only thirty days, then taped over, but when she pulled previous weeks, Friemel found that two weeks earlier, again on a Sunday, Eric had similarly circulated to the IT room, this time leaving with something they couldn't identify. Based on the videos, Friemel's boss, York, installed cameras inside the IT room. The following Sunday, days before Eric's arrest, he'd returned. This time the video cameras caught Eric calmly perusing the IT room, and then walking out with what appeared to be a laser printer cartridge.

Was it a mistake? Perhaps his office monitors had broken.

At first, Friemel assumed Eric would call or send her a note explaining. But he didn't. When Friemel saw him afterward, Eric didn't mention the monitors. More troubling, his body language seemed suspicious on the video. He peered out windows and doors, hesitating as if to make sure no one would disturb him. In two videos, he carried what appeared to be a police scanner, as if monitoring dispatch. Something else odd: On the Sunday he walked out with the monitors, he came in through a back door, where there'd be no record he entered the building. Also suspicious, the DVR that monitored the video surveillance system for the side of the building that included the JP offices was missing from the closet where it was kept.

Even stranger, days after the monitors disappeared, Friemel went to Eric's office to help him with an Internet issue and spotted a new nineteen-inch Dell monitor on his desk. "When I saw Eric carrying out the monitor boxes on the video, I couldn't believe it," Friemel said. "I mean, he could have ordered anything he wanted for his office. Why would he steal them?"

Once Friemel and York turned over the evidence, at the sheriff's office there'd been talk about what to do. Everyone knew Eric. Captain Ernie Zepeda, who'd been given the case, considered Eric a friend. Yet he saw little wiggle room: although the value of all three of the monitors added up to less than $600, it clearly appeared that Eric was stealing. After Zepeda showed the sheriff the video, both men agreed they had to pursue it.

In the DA's office that same week, Zepeda reviewed the evidence with Mark Hasse and Mike McLelland, and they talked about options. At first, Mark and Mike seemed ready to get a warrant for Eric's arrest, but the following week Zepeda returned, and this time Mark wasn't available. As Zepeda recapped the case, another assistant DA scoffed. "I don't see why you're doing this. If you don't find those monitors, you don't have anything."

Unsure about what to do, Zepeda left and returned when Mark and Mike were there. Mark said little, but this time Mike, too, sounded worried. Perhaps he'd consulted with the other assistant district attorney, and she'd told him her view. If the monitor on Eric's desk wasn't one of the missing ones, Mike worried that none of the three would be found. "I just don't see that we have a case without the monitors."

"He has them somewhere," Zepeda responded. "And we have the video."

After Zepeda told the sheriff that the new DA seemed averse to pursuing the charges, Sheriff Byrnes said he would talk to Mike. Later Zepeda recalled a conversation in which the sheriff told him, "McLelland said he doesn't know what you're talking about . . . He's ready to go."

Judge Chitty signed a warrant, and Zepeda went to the JP's office.

While others transported a handcuffed Eric to the sheriff's office, Zepeda handed Fogarty a search warrant. Quickly, they focused on Eric's desk, inspecting the monitor. Comparing the serial number, Zepeda confirmed it matched one of the missing monitors.

As they continued to search, in Eric's closet, they found the monitor assigned to his desk. When Zepeda plugged it in, it worked, verifying that Eric hadn't taken the new monitor to replace a broken one. In the closet, Zepeda also found a black canvas bag with a wallet inside that held $1,800 in $100 bills, much like the stash Eric kept in the pantry at home, the one he'd told Kim he kept in case he had to leave in a hurry. On Eric's desk, Zepeda also found a police scanner like the one Eric held in the videos.

Then in the parking lot, Zepeda popped the door on Eric's Sport Trac. Combing through the cab, Zepeda uncovered a Dell monitor in the backseat concealed beneath a small blanket. Again the serial number matched the list. That meant two of the three missing monitors had been recovered. Yet both were on county property, albeit one in Eric's truck.

Inside the Sport Trac, Zepeda also noticed something else of interest, an AR–15 assault-type weapon strapped to the headliner. Beside it hung a semi-automatic rifle, and scattered throughout the truck were two Glocks and three other handguns.

At the same time in a sheriff's office interview room, Chief Deputy Rodney Evans—a broad-shouldered man with thick dark hair speckled with strands of gray, and startling blue eyes—had Eric's handcuffs removed. In the 1960s, Evans's great-uncle, H. L. "Caggie" Evans, had been Kaufman's sheriff. Since Eric was a reserve deputy for the Kaufman County Sheriff's Office, Rodney Evans knew him. Before they walked in, Evans thought about his impressions of Eric's personality and his pride in his intellectual superiority. "We're going to play country dumb," Evans instructed the investigator who accompanied him into the room.

After Evans read the Miranda warning, Eric, wearing khaki pants, a blue shirt and a tie, confirmed that he understood. "We're going to talk about the computer monitors," Evans said.

"Well, okay," Eric replied, shaking his head and raising his hands as if perplexed. With that, Eric said, "Everything I've done to improve my office, I've done myself, including putting up a mailbox. . . . I had to scrounge for Post-its and pens."

At that point, Evans didn't know about the one found in Eric's truck. "There are three monitors missing. One was on your desk. Where are the others?"

During the interview, Eric often appeared nervous. At times, he rubbed his chin and acted amused. During other moments he raised his hands, as if exasperated. The computer monitors, he said, were for the video magistration system he planned for the JP courts. The one in his office he intended to hook into the system. The one in the Sport Trac, he planned to install at the jail.

What Eric didn't have an explanation for was the third monitor.

Although he'd asked Kim to take a monitor to her parents' house, when questioned about that third monitor Eric claimed he didn't remember it. "Unless I took one back," he said, suggesting he may have tried a third monitor, decided it didn't fit, and returned it.

While admitting he hadn't filed a request for the equipment, Eric maintained he'd taken the monitors for county use. And while he hadn't gone through channels, he pointed out that there'd been an ongoing conversation about video magistration that included the other justices of the peace and Judge Chitty. More often than not, Eric acted puzzled at even being questioned.

Throughout the interview, the exchange lobbed back and forth. When Evans suggested Eric should know he couldn't take equipment without filing paperwork, Eric said some businesses ran that way. After Evans said county equipment was inventoried, Eric compared the monitors to toilet paper, asking why employees were free to take some supplies and not others.

The questioning continued past three that afternoon. After being booked, Eric signed two consents to search, one for his law office and another for the Overlook house. Kim hadn't been home long after dropping off the monitor in its box at her parents' house, as Eric had instructed, when the doorbell rang. Deputies waited outside. After they showed her Eric's signed permission, she let them in. They walked through, found nothing, and left.

At Eric's downtown law office, the deputies also departed without the third monitor. But they found something else, Eric's closet filled with weapons: rifles and handguns.

By then, Taryn Davis had bailed Eric out.

That night, Kim asked what had happened, and Eric said that he'd bought the Dell monitor he'd had her move, but that he didn't have the receipt, and he thought the deputies might mistake it for the third, missing monitor. "I don't know why they thought I stole the monitors," Eric told her. "I thought at first that they were playing with me."

In the *Kaufman Herald* Eric's arrest made front-page news, and the local law community chattered about it. "There were a lot of us who thought it was just plain silly. It seemed really political," said one lawyer. "We all knew Eric was working on that video system for his court."

Many brought up Eric's support of Rick Harrison, Mike's opponent in the DA's race, and the letter Eric published questioning Mike's qualifications. "It was three computer monitors worth around $600 and two of them were found on county property. The third one was less than two-hundred dollars. What were they going to start going after folks for? Stealing paperclips?"

At the DA's office, some second-guessed as well, questioning why Mike went after the JP over something so small. Others didn't see a conflict. "Eric wasn't on our radar," said Brandi Fernandez, the first assistant at the DA's office. "The only reason he was on our radar was because the sheriff's office brought over the case. Nobody went looking for it."

The day after his arrest, Eric called his JP staff into his office, along with the constables from Precinct 1 who had offices in the building. At the meeting, Eric said, "I didn't steal anything. I just stepped on the wrong toes. This is ludicrous. It's all going to go away."

Constable Shawn Mayfield hadn't liked Eric from the beginning. Something about the new JP troubled him. He knew about Eric's fascination with guns, but that wasn't it. "I am, too. Red-necked old boys love guns." On that day, listening to Eric, Mayfield walked out.

For her part, Eric's assistant, Regina Fogarty, believed her boss, assuming it was political and that the people in charge had "done him wrong." What she particularly didn't like was the way Eric was arrested. Instead of allowing him to turn himself in, the deputies descended on the office and dragged him out in handcuffs. Many of the lawyers in Kaufman also talked about the lack of professional courtesy shown Eric. "You'd have thought he'd stolen hundreds of thousands of dollars from the county, or that he was an armed robber."

That day, Eric e-mailed John Sickel, his friend at the state guard's JAG office, self-reporting that he'd been arrested. When Sickel read the e-mail, he thought Eric jested. "No joke," Eric responded. With that, Sickel looked up Eric's name on the Internet and saw it was true. "What the [expletive]?" he responded.

When Eric asked what the arrest meant for his guard service, Sickel explained that he'd probably be suspended pending the outcome of the case. "Eric thought this would be straightened out. I did, too. Surely this was a mistake," said Sickel.

"Don't worry. I'll be fine. I didn't do anything wrong," Eric assured an attorney friend when she called. Yet Eric acknowledged that there was a lot on the line. If convicted, Eric stood to lose everything he'd worked hard for: his judgeship, his law license, even, perhaps, his freedom. "This is all trumped up," he said.

Eric used that same argument days later when he met with the county judge, Bruce Wood. The former school superintendent had just taken office when Eric did five months earlier. Both Republicans, they didn't know each other well. Scheduled weeks earlier, the purpose of the meeting was to discuss the budget for Eric's JP court. Instead Eric said he wanted to clear the air about the "800-pound elephant in the room."

When Wood asked what he meant, Eric said, "This charge against me is a misunderstanding. My attorney said not to give this to you, but I want you to read it." He then handed Wood a note.

A teacherlike man used to giving patient explanations, Wood read what Eric offered, an account of what had happened in which he took responsibility for taking the monitors, but argued that he'd broken no laws. "I did not steal or intend to steal any equipment." In the letter, Eric argued that the DA's and sheriff's offices were unwilling to back down. "I am hoping that you can stop this chain of events from getting any more out of control. . . . I am asking that you determine if things can be de-escalated. . . . I have learned my lesson."

After he finished reading, Wood, a large man with a pensive look, stared down at Eric. "I need you to stop the investigation," Eric said.

"Eric, I don't have the authority to do that," Wood replied. "I would be in trouble if I tried to do that."

That finished the conversation, and they went on to the

JP's budget. As they did, Wood had the impression Eric, despite what he'd written in the letter, had no idea of the gravity of the charges he faced. As his first order of business, Eric brought up his salary. "I need a ten-thousand-dollar raise," Eric said, matter-of-factly.

Although shocked, Wood calmly explained that the county didn't have the extra money at that time. "Well, I wanted to ask for it, because I think I deserve it," Eric countered.

To Wood, considering Eric's situation, the exchange seemed out of touch with reality.

When Eric's old boss from his short time as a deputy in Springtown PD, James Lyons, heard about Eric's arrest, he felt no surprise that Eric's actions were caught on video. Recalling how Eric left evidence when he hacked into the department computers, Lyons saw it as another example of Eric bragging about what he'd done, and of Eric assuming he'd be able to talk his way out of any consequences.

At the DA's office, Mark Hasse pursued Eric's case. "I don't remember him saying anything other than that Mike wanted Eric tried," said one of the assistant DAs.

While he seemed determined at work, however, with others Mark voiced concerns.

At the airport over the weekends, where he worked on his planes, early on Mark told something very different to his friends. "I want my boss to assign a special prosecutor on this thing," Mark said, looking troubled. "The courthouse is close quarters, and everyone knows everyone else. This is too personal. Plus there's something about this guy. He worries me."

Chapter 23

In the beginning, Mike tried to handle it profession-
ally, treat it like any other case. But Mike didn't like
Eric. He didn't trust Eric. Things got out of hand.
                                        —Michelle Sutton

As the summer wore on, the seriousness of Eric's situation crystallized. In late June, after Mark notified it of
the charges, the state's judicial board suspended Eric
without pay from his job as justice of the peace. As John
Sickel predicted, the state guard also removed Eric from
active duty. That happened after Mike McLelland personally mailed the video to the guard's Austin headquarters.
From that point on, Eric went to his law office off and
on, handling his private cases, but slowly became increasingly isolated.

It didn't help that word spread of his substantial arsenal.
One afternoon, Eric walked into the courthouse. Someone called the deputies, and they detained and questioned
him, asking if he had any weapons, searching through his
briefcase. Where he'd once been a trusted member of the
courthouse elite, it became clear that many had grown to
view Eric as a possible threat.

It surprised some how hard the prosecutors focused
on the case. "There'd been people who'd worked for the
county and done bad stuff equal to Eric in the past. They

got caught. They slapped their hands," said Johnny Perry, who was called on to temporarily replace Eric as JP until the case was decided. "They made them give the money back and gave them deferred adjudication . . . let them move on."

To Eric, it made his situation worse that the commissioner's court appointed Perry, the man he'd defeated in the election, as his replacement. Voicing his dissatisfaction, Eric wrote to a higher-up in the Republican Party, but the complaint went nowhere. To explain their actions, the commissioners said Perry was the only one in the county who fulfilled the statutes, which required four-and-a-half years' experience.

For his part, returning even briefly delighted Perry, since the extra months in office increased his pension. He moved back in, easily settling into his old office, still with Eric's Texas table and matching aqua leather chairs across from his desk.

Meanwhile, the Kaufman legal scene mulled over Eric's situation that summer and fall, many calling the prosecution purely political. "If anyone else had been DA, they would have said, 'Eric, put the monitors back,'" said one attorney. "It would have been swept under the rug."

"It seemed like a political witch hunt," said another. Although with what she pegged as "Eric's arrogance," she believed that he hadn't gone through channels to get what he wanted, she still didn't see it as stealing. "Most of us didn't think Eric should be prosecuted."

From the beginning, Eric believed that as well. He argued that the people at the courthouse understood he was attempting to set up the video conferencing. Like the wi-fi for the library, he only intended to update county services. The monitors, he said, were never intended for his personal use. That Mike McLelland didn't recognize that, he contended, smacked of revenge. "I always recognized the actions that led up to the charges, the motivation behind it. It would be hard not to believe that it was a personal grudge," he said.

One day in June while the situation unfolded, Sheriff Byrnes crossed paths with Eric's lawyer, Taryn Davis, and in their conversation Eric's case came up, the sheriff offering that they had substantial evidence, saying, "It's right there on the surveillance tape."

To the sheriff's surprise, Davis didn't appear to know about the video, so he sent a copy to her office. Meanwhile, at the DA's office, Sheriff Byrnes talked to Mike and Mark about offering a deal, suggesting they work something out instead of taking the case to trial. Days later, Mark extended an offer, one that would have allowed Eric to plead guilty to a class A misdemeanor, abuse of office. While Eric would lose his judgeship, Mark argued that Eric would keep his law license. In contrast, a felony conviction would have resulted in automatic disbarment.

"Mark wasn't excited about the case," said Brandi Fernandez, the first assistant at the DA's office. "He saw it as a glorified misdemeanor. He had better things to do."

Around Kaufman, the prosecutors talked the deal up to the local lawyers. Mike even called on Judge Ashworth to convince Eric to agree. But by then Eric had assessed the situation and come to an opposite conclusion. In his opinion the abuse of power charge, since it involved a theft, would be considered a crime of moral turpitude, a designation that would result in the state bar revoking his license. When Ashworth talked to Eric, he refused, instead making a counteroffer, to pay $600 restitution and walk away from his JP job, but not plead guilty to anything.

When that offer arrived at the DA's office, Mike planted his feet and declined. "Eric Williams is a crook," he said. "He doesn't get to pick what he pleads guilty to."

The animosity between the men always seemed to fester

just under the surface. When Mike looked at the situation, he contended he had Eric figured out. In his view, Eric couldn't plead guilty to anything. Always having to play the hero, Eric simply didn't have it in him. Mike viewed Eric as incapable of admitting any wrongdoing, accepting any responsibility.

Once Eric refused the plea, the mood at the DA's office hardened even further against him. "In my opinion, that's when it became personal for Mike and Mark," said Judge Wood. "They both saw it as a slap in the face, and they were angry."

"Williams didn't take the deal," Mark told Captain Zepeda, the lead investigator on the case. "I'm walking it up to the grand jury." The indictment came down days later, officially charging Justice of the Peace Eric Williams with burglary of a building, and a theft of more than $500 and less than $1,500 by a public servant. Despite the small amount, charging Eric as a public servant raised the theft charge from a misdemeanor to a felony.

"I'd been against escalating it," said Sheriff Byrnes. "It was penny ante. Eric wasn't a repeat offender. He wasn't going to do it again."

In the courthouse hallways, attorneys continued to discuss the case as it unfolded. Some still thought Eric wasn't being treated fairly. Like the sheriff, they saw the amount of the alleged theft as small stakes, especially when compared to the ongoing case of a woman who worked in the county tax office. She'd been arrested just a week before Eric, charged with stealing more than $100,000 from the county coffers. The woman's alleged theft vastly dwarfed the value of Eric's three monitors, and many saw her punishment, by comparison, as more lenient and more in tune with what the county had done in the past. In exchange for pleading guilty, the woman served no jail time. Instead she agreed to reimburse the county $123,724, serve ten years' probation, and complete three hundred hours of community service.

With so much controversy surrounding the case, perhaps it wasn't surprising that Taryn Davis withdrew as Eric's attorney.

After Davis pulled out, Eric talked to John Sickel, his friend from the guard, and asked Sickel to represent him. "I don't think I should, Eric, because we're friends and you have a lot riding on this," Sickel responded. "Hire someone else, and I'll second chair." For his main attorney, Eric contacted a friend of Sickel's, David Sergi, a colonel in the guard who had a practice in San Marcos. To pay his attorney fees, Eric borrowed $50,000 from Kim's parents.

When Sickel looked over the case, it seemed to him that the charges smacked of overreaction, lacking any common sense, and one day in a motion hearing, he talked to Mark at the back of the courtroom. "Is there any wiggle room here?" Sickel asked.

Although Mark had referred to the case as "a piece of junk," he shrugged and answered, "No way." Sickel interpreted Mark's body language as suggesting he had no say in the decision, and that the die had already been cast. To Sickel, none of it made any sense. Although within their rights to pursue the charges, if the prosecutors won they would ruin Eric, taking everything he'd worked for, including his ability to practice law. This seemed extreme for something that Eric had done—while admittedly not following protocol—for the betterment of the county.

When Sickel listened to the attorneys in Kaufman, they shared his opinion, and he heard overwhelming support for Eric and criticism of the prosecutors. More than one of Eric's lawyer friends made that clear to the prosecutors. "You shouldn't be doing this. It's not right," Jenny Parks told Mike one day at the courthouse.

"You don't know everything, Jenny," Mike answered.

Looking back, some wondered if Mark would have gone ahead with the case if it had been left up to him. Michelle Sutton, the assistant DA assigned to assist Mark on the case, didn't think so. She had the impression that Mark pursued Eric only as a favor to Mike.

Aware that the law community had lined up against them, Mike and Mark began a campaign, waylaying attorneys who circulated in and out of the DA's offices into a room where they played the surveillance video of Eric taking the monitors, pointing out the odd way Eric acted, looking through windows and carrying a police scanner. Even then many of the lawyers didn't agree with the charges, and dislike of the prosecutors' actions smoldered.

At home, Mike described Eric as a narcissist, someone with a large ego who saw only his own needs, a person who felt entitled to whatever he wanted. On Wednesday evenings when he and Cynthia met Leah and Skeet Phillips for dinner and ice cream, Mike ate his chicken strips and Cynthia her jalapeño burger while they talked about Eric, Mike voicing the opinion that his prosecution would send a message that the county wouldn't tolerate thieves.

Meanwhile, word spread through the Texas State Guard about Captain Williams. "I heard it was a trumped-up bunch of political crap," said one member. "That it was all a raw deal."

Chapter 24

I stopped over to see Mark working on a plane. He had on ratty old shorts, his skinny legs hanging out, a stained T-shirt, and a holster with a gun. When I asked, "What's up?" he said there was a crazy guy he was worried about.

—Curtis Mays

At the sub-courthouse, after Eric's arrest, George York added locks to the IT department doors and a security system to the building. Meanwhile, in the DA's office, Mark Hasse hadn't routinely carried a gun since his days as a Dallas prosecutor. But in mid-July, just short of two months after Eric's arrest, he signed up under the auspices of the Kaufman DA's office and registered with the state as a member of law enforcement, allowing him to carry a gun into the courthouse. From that point forward, he routinely wore a gun in a holster under his suit coat.

Meanwhile, Eric studied his case. On his computer the same week Mark took steps to be armed, Eric wrote a note under the heading, "What to do?" In it he mused about repercussions from a conviction, that it would take away his livelihood. "What does a disbarred attorney, ousted judge, revoked police officer, discharged military officer and convicted felon do?" The options included working as a landscaper or selling cars, "but the convictions would be a problem . . . medical billing or some other goofy deal?"

While willing to relinquish the JP seat, he grieved over the potential loss of his law license, writing:

IF THIS RESULT OCCURS WITHIN OUR PRESENT LEGAL SYSTEM, THE ONE ABSOLUTE IS THAT I WILL NOT WORK AGAIN IN ANY LEGAL FIELD POSITION. I MAY BE THROUGH WITH THE LEGAL FIELD NO MATTER WHAT!

The loss of health insurance also loomed large. Without it, Eric wouldn't be able to continue paying for his insulin pump for his diabetes. And who would cover the costs of Kim's frequent doctor appointments and mounds of medications? Worsening the situation, the county tried to drop his coverage right after his indictment, but Eric's attorneys pointed out that he was merely suspended. If convicted, it would only be a matter of time before his insurance ended.

All summer Eric worked on his case, writing long letters of instruction to his attorneys, some pointing at areas where he believed the prosecutors' case could be attacked. One was that the surveillance video had time lapses, starts and stops. Since it was triggered by a motion detector, that seemed understandable, but Eric thought it could be argued that it was defective. "It is my opinion that the video should be suppressed because it is not a complete record. It is extremely possible that civil rights violations are occurring here," he wrote.

The day Lori Friemel saw the Dell monitor on Eric's desk, she also noticed its box in the sub-courthouse Dumpster. That, too, Eric characterized as suspicious: "The way she located the Dell box in the trash is highly suspect."

In an e-mail Eric wrote:

NEVER STOP FIGHTING—THE BATTLE HAS JUST
BEGUN!

At home, Eric complained that the county refused to
pay nearly $10,000 in fees he had pending for cases he'd
worked. Kim, too, felt it unfair, judging all the misfortune
that had befallen them stemmed from small-town politics
and clashing personalities. "Eric could be arrogant. I knew
that. That ticked some people off. I figured the whole thing
was just a foul-up, and that it was just that Mike McLelland
didn't like Eric."

Despite continuing to reassure her that it would all be
cleared up, Eric evidently worried, most apparent when he
talked about Mark, describing him as "a really good attorney, a bulldog."

With little money coming in, just the few fees he collected for his private legal work and Kim's $1,300 monthly
disability check, Eric appealed to the judicial board to
change his status to suspended with pay. The request was
denied.

At the commissioner's court meeting in mid-July, Judge
Chitty brought up a new matter pertaining to Eric: his oversight of the law library fund, which had a balance in excess
of $300,000.

Weeks earlier, more allegations had surfaced. The
manager of Terrell Office Supply called the DA's office to
explain that for years Eric had supplies ordered for the library delivered to his law office. It never seemed strange,
because no one manned the law library to sign for the deliveries. The amounts weren't large, but many of the items
ordered seemed odd for the library, including gaming earphones, special computer controls, keyboards, a calculator,
flash drives, micro cards, Post-it notes, and gel pens. Captain Zepeda scouted through the library and found none of

the purchased equipment. In response, he turned the matter over to the DA's office, which forwarded it on to the Texas Rangers' public integrity division.

In his appearance before the commissioner's court, Chitty asked that the court take over responsibility for the library and appoint one of the judges to oversee it. Becky Calabria, a friend of Eric's who'd lunched with him for years, seconded the motion. All four of the commissioners voted in favor of the resolution.

While Mark Hasse initially appeared ambivalent about the case, like Mike McLelland, once the indictment came down Mark appeared ready to pursue it. Or perhaps his opinion changed when he learned more about Eric Williams.

One day a Kaufman PD officer dropped in and told Mike and Mark how Eric rode his Segway at three in the morning through his neighborhood, wearing camouflage clothing, an assault rifle strapped to his back. "It seemed like strange behavior to say the least," said Bruce Bryant, Mark's investigator.

They also heard about Eric's run-in with John Burt the fall before, when Eric burst into Burt's office shouting threats. Then someone told Mark about the Huntsville incident, the evening Eric told Janice Gray that he had a gun, and "I'll use it. I don't have anything to lose."

Another day, a woman stopped in to talk to Mike, one who'd been Eric's friend. In a closed-door meeting, she said that around 2008 Eric sent her threatening e-mails. Knowing Eric, she warned that everyone involved in his case needed to be watchful, because the man she knew would view anyone who didn't back him as against him.

"If Eric knew I talked to you, he'd kill me," she said.

The tension mounting, one day Mark drove to the subcourthouse to talk to Johnny Perry. In the office that used to be Eric's, Mark told Perry that he had concerns about what Eric might do. "We're going to hang him," Mark said. "We've got him."

"You be careful," Perry warned, seated at his desk in front of the window.

"You need to watch out, too," Mark said. Standing at the window, looking out over the parking lot and the street, Mark pointed in the direction of Eric's house, as the crow flew little more than a block away. "If he crossed that field toward the office, if Eric has a scope on a gun, he could aim at the back of your head."

After Mark left, Perry pushed his desk away from the window.

"**E**ric Williams was supposed to be one of the good guys. A judge," Mark told a friend one day. "By God, I'm going to put him *under* the jail!"

The animosity festered. During Monday morning office meetings, Mike and Mark talked often of the case. In many ways, it ranked among the smaller matters the office handled, a minor theft. But it was a public official, and it was Eric Williams, whom Mike and Mark increasingly saw as unstable. At the same time, their fervor built, and they became more committed to convincing others that Eric wasn't the mild-mannered attorney they knew, but a dangerous man.

To many it sounded like prosecutor hyperbole when Mike labeled Eric a sociopath in front of local attorneys. "I thought they were going overboard," said one. "Especially when Mike said they wanted jail time. They were prosecuting the shit out of this guy for those monitors."

News trailed back to Eric's attorneys about what others saw at the DA's office. At one point, they heard Mike hung a wanted poster with Eric's mug shot on a wall with "CAPTURED" scrawled across it. John Sickel asked the attorneys who described it to get a picture, but they balked, concerned they'd be seen and the prosecutors would hold it against them.

In docket calls, the attorneys gathered in the jury room, and in the 422nd, where Mark was chief prosecutor, he often turned the conversation to Eric, sometimes referring to him as "that fucking crazy ass Eric Williams." When Mark mentioned Janice Gray, telling the others about Eric's threats, he became particularly agitated. It seemed he no longer cared what the others thought. In the hallway, Mark stopped one attorney and asked, "How's Williams, your thief friend?"

When she asked him not to say that, Mark laughed.

When anyone remarked that Eric's prosecution appeared personal, Mark mentioned the rejected plea bargain and insisted, "I'm just doing my job."

Watching the actions of those around her, the prosecutor assisting on the case, Michelle Sutton, didn't like what she saw. She knew something others didn't, that not only did Mike have political reasons to be angry with Eric, but that Mark had a conflict as well.

Off and on after Eric's election, Mark had mentioned that some in Kaufman had told him he should have made a run for the JP seat. And once Eric was charged and out of office, Mark talked about the idea, even driving around the county looking for a house to buy, one that would make him a resident and eligible to run for Eric's judgeship.

Meanwhile, all wasn't well at the house on Overlook, where Eric spent much of the day on his computer playing Mafia Wars. "Kim nagged at Eric about losing his job," said Jim Williams, Eric's father. "She was angry about it, and the money."

At times, Eric's phone rang, one attorney friend or another telling him what they saw at the DA's office, how Mike and Mark talked about Eric as if they were taking out a major crime figure. In response, Eric reassured his friends not to worry, that he would eventually be cleared.

Conference calls and e-mails went back and forth that

summer and into the fall as Eric and his attorneys prepared for the trial. Hands on with the decisions, Eric vetoed filing a motion to have his trial moved out of Kaufman, arguing that he had friends in the county, and that the voters there liked him enough to elect him justice of the peace.

Although they had enough against him in the pending charges to potentially take everything from him, in November, Mike secured a second indictment against Eric, this one for theft between $1,500 and $20,000, for supplies billed to the law library but delivered to Eric's law office.

Rather than knocking on his door and handcuffing him, this time the prosecutors let Eric turn himself in at the jail for booking. When he did, Lieutenant Jolie Stewart, a tall woman with long dark hair, came down to check him in. Stewart had known Eric for years, since his tenure as Judge Ashworth's assistant, and she'd seen him change. One day at the JP's court, she'd referred to him as Eric, as she always had, and he'd stopped her: "It's Judge Williams."

From that haughty point, he'd fallen until she now patted him down for booking. "You have any weapons of mass destruction on your person?" she joked, to try to ease the tension.

"No," he answered, followed by an uncomfortable silence.

As Eric's attorneys prepared for trial, David Sergi brought in a private investigator to help the defense: Sharon Holbrook, a former treasury agent. Her task was to talk to the principal witnesses, including George York and Lori Friemel; type up her recorded interviews; and turn them over to Eric and his attorneys.

From the beginning, Holbrook liked Eric, thinking that he resembled a high school chemistry teacher. They talked the same language, law enforcement, and she thought he was perhaps a bit odd, but interesting. In college, Eric had been nicknamed "Tennessee Tuxedo." At one of his first jobs they'd dubbed him "Opie," after the youngster in Mayberry. Holbrook and Sergi began calling him "Dudley Do-Right," after the *Rocky and Bullwinkle* character, because "he bungled but he was a good guy trying to do the right thing." Something about Eric seemed to attract such comparisons. With his crooked grin, he reminded others of a young boy and two cartoon figures out to save the world.

One night at Eric's office, Holbrook went to refill the paper in the copy machine, but when she opened the door to the bin she found an AK–47 inside. "You expecting Armageddon or something?" she asked.

"I work family law, Sharon," Eric said. "People get upset when you take kids away. You don't know who is going to come walking into the office."

Working closely, Holbrook listened to Eric's account of the case and decided it was "a cluster fuck" from the beginning, and that "he'd just gotten in crossways with the wrong people."

In December, Holbrook waited on a hallway bench in the Kaufman County Courthouse for documents to be turned over. Before long, Mark sat on the window ledge near her, apologizing for the material not being ready, and began opening up about the case. "It was like he forgot I work for the defense," Holbrook said. "He liked hearing himself talk."

As he did, Holbrook reached into her purse and turned on her digital recorder.

That day, they spoke for three hours, Mark answering Holbrook's questions about discovery, what documents he had, how he understood the case. Sounding sure of himself, he seemed full of confidence. The longer they talked, the more open Mark became. Unaware of the running tape recorder, he called Eric a thief, and said "everybody knows it." Citing what others said about Eric's arsenal, he labeled him a "massive gun nut." Talking of Eric's threats against John Burt, the attorney he threatened the previous fall, Mark labeled Eric a "total whack job."

"You know, I was thinking, I feel sorry for Sargi," Mark said, mispronouncing the name of Eric's attorney, David Sergi. When Holbrook asked why, Mark said, Sergi's "got a narcissistic, goofball client with two indefensible cases . . . And [Sergi's] really trying to kill himself to do something for this guy. But, you know, some clients you don't get to pick. And he's got a guy that's got a ton of [extraneous offenses] on him that are gonna piss the jury off."

After Holbrook transcribed the tape, she sent copies to the lawyers and to Eric. Perhaps, if Mark had known he was being recorded, he would have realized that everything he said would land on Eric's computer, and that it would only feed Eric's hate.

At the DA's office in December 2011, Mark wore one of his infamous sweaters, a thick, fuzzy one, and easily won the ugly Christmas sweater contest.

On Blarney Stone Way, Cynthia and Mike showed off their new house one Saturday and had a Christmas party. Excited about how well the house accommodated a crowd, Cynthia baked for weeks preparing. As always, she loved to entertain, and now that Mike was the DA, most of the elected officials in the county came, along with neighbors and friends. She had sandwiches and a table of appetizers and desserts, and Mike wore a bright red shirt and laughed often and loudly.

Still, with her Parkinson's progressing, entertaining had become increasingly hard. Cynthia took longer to do things, and when she baked, her hands shaking, it appeared as if it had snowed in the kitchen, flour and sugar blanketing the countertops. To a friend, Mike mentioned that at night when Cynthia sat quilting, as she grew tired, her hands trembled so hard, he'd walk over and tell her to turn off the sewing machine. It was time for bed. Then he helped her walk to the bedroom.

To pull the party together, Leah Phillips pitched in

A Christmas party at the McLelland house, Mike with an unidentified woman

along with a mutual friend, Samantha Keats, whom everyone called Sam, a tall, outdoorsy woman in her fifties with long, dark blond hair. A major landowner, Keats ran an eight-hundred-acre tree farm in Forney. Although a Democrat, she'd worked to get Mike into office by convincing independents to vote for him. Like Mike, Keats had a bad feeling about Eric Williams, who'd been her daughter's ad litem in her divorce. To Keats, Williams seemed all ego. At a party, she'd once heard him refer to himself as a genius.

By then, Cynthia got stuck more often, her feet tying up underneath her, so much so that Sam, like Leah, routinely walked over to give her a nudge. Toward the end of the party, Cynthia looked tired and drawn, but as guests left, she smiled and told them to come back soon.

Chapter 25

I moved my chair in the courthouse, so I wasn't in line with the window. Out of the 422nd, you could see Eric's office across the street. We all knew he had a mess of guns. We were all nervous.

—Mark Ragsdale

In Kaufman, unease stirred about Eric's upcoming trial. Some talked of his arsenal of weapons, and his odd behavior, strange statements he'd made over the years, and how he'd become withdrawn in the community. Others considered the unusual nature of a case in which many of the parties involved had prior relationships. In hearings, the defense attorneys argued those shared histories impacted who should and shouldn't be allowed to participate.

Instead of his usual perch, weeks before the trial Judge Michael Chitty took the witness stand. Eric's defense attorneys, John Sickel and David Sergi, had filed a motion to remove the judge from the case. Instead of behind the bench, they wanted the judge in the witness box.

Judge Chitty, the defense argued, was essential to their case. The reason: he'd attended Eric's video-conferencing demonstration the previous year. That made the judge aware of Eric's motives, able to back up his contention that he'd taken the monitors for county use.

Judge Chitty on the witness stand
Courtesy of Ken Leonard

A visiting judge presiding, Mark asked Chitty questions, first verifying that since Eric was a family law specialist, many of Eric's cases were tried in Judge Chitty's courtroom. "Is there anything about any case of his . . . which would make you biased against him or rule differently?"

"No, sir," Chitty answered.

The judge did acknowledge being aware of Eric's interest in setting up the video magistration system. "There have been general discussions of that here in the county for months," the judge said. Still, the judge denied knowing of any conversation in which Eric was assigned to obtain the equipment to design such a system.

"Is there anything Eric Williams has ever done to you or in your court that would make you in any way biased against him . . . ?" Mark asked.

The man with the snow white hair answered with a confident "No, sir."

When David Sergi, a bulky, scholarly man who'd been born in Germany, took over, he returned to the conversations Judge Chitty had with Eric regarding teleconferencing, asking what the judge remembered from the demonstration in Eric's office.

In response, Judge Chitty described his memories as hazy and said that he couldn't recall exactly what had been discussed.

After Judge Chitty left the courtroom, the two sides laid out their arguments. To Sergi, Judge Chitty's testimony could bolster his client's defense.

"I'm curious as to what he's going to be able to testify to besides I don't remember," said the visiting judge hearing the motion.

"My client may not have followed all the administrative rules of Kaufman County, but that is certainly not theft what he did. . . . Short and simple. Short and sweet," said Sergi. "And his conversation with Judge Chitty is material."

In contrast, Mark described the video of Eric taking the monitors, the way he furtively glanced out windows. Rather than a misunderstanding about being in charge of setting up the video-conferencing system, Mark said Eric was "sneaking around on a Sunday theft case."

In the end, the defense attorneys lost, and Judge Chitty remained on the case, blocking him from being called as a witness.

A week later, this time with Judge Chitty on the bench, Sergi argued to have someone else taken off the case: Mike McLelland.

A month earlier Mark's assistant on the case, Michelle Sutton, had fallen ill, suffering from what she'd later discover was stage four breast cancer. Once Sutton left, Mike decided to replace her as second chair. "I will put myself out there, and if anyone has a problem with it, they can talk to me," he told his family.

Before the judge, Sergi pointed out that bad blood existed between Mike and the man on trial, and contended that alone should disqualify the DA. To prove his point, Sergi asked Mike if he and Eric were political foes, based on the letter Eric penned supporting Rick Harrison.

"I never attributed that to Eric Williams," Mike said. "I attributed it to Rick Harrison, who simply found somebody dumb enough to sign it."

Seated next to his attorney, Eric, proud of his intellect and his Mensa membership, must have blanched. Having Mike besmirch his intelligence in a courtroom, one where he'd been a prominent lawyer, had to rankle. The situation didn't improve when Mike admitted he'd personally reported Eric's arrest to the state guard. "I thought they'd want to know."

The portrayals of the DA's and the former JP's relationship in the courtroom that day would be diametrically opposed. Sergi suggested Mike had it out for his client, that Mike held a grudge. In contrast, Mike insisted he had no problems with Eric, and that they'd barely said twenty words to each other.

From calling Eric "dumb" to playing a hand in appointing Johnny Perry to replace Eric, Mike, Sergi argued, shouldn't be involved in the trial. "This whole case is personal. You need someone who can prosecute objectively and that is what this motion is about."

In the end, that motion, too, failed. As a result, as Eric's trial loomed, those involved all occupied the same incubator, the rundown Kaufman County courthouse. When the gavel fell on the first day of Eric's trial, Judge Chitty would preside, with Mike McLelland seated beside Mark Hasse at the prosecutors' table.

As David Sergi said, it would all be exceedingly personal.

That was something Mark was well aware of, and he took precautions. Since starting at the courthouse, he'd habitually parked his pickup each morning on a side street behind Lott's dry cleaner's, stopping to drop off his clothes in the mornings and pick them up in the evenings. As Eric's trial date neared, Mark changed his routine, instead parking his maroon Ford Dually in the county lot, a block from the courthouse, behind the tax office, where more cars came and went during the busy morning and late-afternoon hours.

One day in the lot, Mark told a woman who worked at the courthouse that he'd heard from others that Eric had made threats.

"He's crazy," she said.

"I know," Mark answered.

Looking at his slender frame in his suit jacket, she said, "You need a bulletproof vest."

With a shrug, Mark said, "If Eric wants to kill me, he'll just shoot me in the head."

The woman thought about that for a minute, then asked, "Do you think Eric's the kind of guy who would blow up the courthouse?"

"No," Mark said, shaking his head. It seemed he'd considered that scenario and dismissed it, coming to another conclusion. "Eric wants to be the glorious one. He'd come out both guns blazing."

Chapter 26

The week before the trial Mark told me that the sheriff's department was watching Eric closely. They had a plan to stop him, if he avoided the metal detectors and brought a gun in through a back door. They thought Eric might hurt someone.

—Ron Herrington

On the afternoon of Monday, March 19, 2012, Eric Williams's theft trial began. Because of concerns about what he might do, precautions had been established to text those involved when Eric entered the courthouse, and when he left.

In the 422nd, Judge Chitty sat in his usual chair behind the bench, while at the prosecutor's table Mark reviewed his opening statement. If worried about the volatility of the man on trial, Mark appeared confident and eager. "Mark had his game face on," said Ragsdale, the bailiff.

At Mark's side towered Mike, as big and bulky as Mark was slender. Eric must have looked like a gift to a DA who'd run on a "regain integrity in Kaufman County" platform. That the suspended justice of the peace backed Mike's opponent undoubtedly made the trial loom even sweeter. Perhaps buoyed by her husband's enthusiasm, in the back row Cynthia nodded and smiled at well-wishers, as usual her hands busy, this time twisting and turning yarn as she knit. She appeared eager to watch Mike's first trial as DA as he took an errant public official to task.

At the defense table, David Sergi and John Sickel sat beside Eric, his face as placid as on the day deputies arrested him. In his mind, Eric estimated he had a fifty-fifty chance of an acquittal.

Noticeably absent was Kim, who despite her husband's crisis spent her day at home in bed, after downing a heavy dose of prescription meds. Over the months, Kim had seen Eric's resentment grow. Around the house, he ridiculed Mark's rail-thin build, calling him "Fuck Stick." At other times he mocked Mike, whom he'd dubbed "Sluggo."

Although she felt weak and tired, Kim, who remained convinced Eric would prevail, had wanted to go to the trial. Eric didn't want her there. Instead, to gain sympathy, he preferred the jury and judge believe she was bedridden.

Throughout the trial, the courtroom crowd ebbed and flowed, local lawyers filing in and out, listening to snatches of evidence between their own obligations, leaving to meet with clients or file motions. Curious, they wanted to see the evidence.

On the stand, Lori Friemel recounted the day she discovered the monitors gone, and how she saw Eric on the surveillance tape walking them out the IT department's door. On a schematic of the building, she explained his route, one that didn't require using his passkey, ensuring there wouldn't be a record he'd been in the building. When she'd looked at video from previous weeks, she tracked Eric walking out with other items, acting as if shopping in her office.

When it came time to show the video to the jurors, David Sergi renewed a previous objection, charging that it wasn't a complete record. Judge Chitty ruled against him, and in the courtroom, the lights dimmed. On the screen Eric, just as Friemel described, circulated through the building into

Eric Williams carrying out two monitor boxes in a still taken from
the surveillance camera
Evidence photo

the IT room, and then walked out with three boxes marked
Dell.

To prove Eric hadn't simply made a mistake, that he
knew how the county handled equipment purchases, Mark
asked Friemel questions about the laptop she bought for
Eric soon after he took over the JP court, putting into evidence the written request with Eric's signature.

The testimony damaging, Eric paid little notice. Behind
the defense table, he acted like one of the attorneys, writing notes. "Whatever was going on around him, he never
changed expression," said Bruce Bryant, an investigator
on the case. "I thought he must have been wired different
than most people. He looked as unconcerned as if he was at
home watching TV."

For those in the courtroom throughout the trial, the evidence disproved many of the rumors that had circulated in Kaufman's law community. One was that Eric had taken the monitors out of frustration, after having requested them for months without IT following through. Instead, Friemel testified that Eric had never asked for the monitors, and that if he had, she would have ordered them, since he had more than ample funds in his technology account.

In response, Sergi hammered on where the two monitors were found, one on Eric's JP desk in the sub-courthouse, the other in his Sport Trac in the parking lot, the vehicle he used to go back and forth to the jail.

"Did you at any point . . . give Eric Williams your consent to enter the IT offices, to take the monitors?" Mark asked George York when he took the stand.

"No," he said.

Back and forth the questioning went, as the tension in the courtroom mounted. No exchange was more heated than the one over the authenticity of the video, which Sergi insisted was incomplete and unreliable, and Mark countered simply missed segments of time because the motion-activated camera turned off and on.

On the stand, Ernie Zepeda, wearing his captain's uniform from the sheriff's department, explained how they set the trap, installing cameras inside Friemel's office to watch Eric. Again a video played, this time of Eric walking out of the IT room with a laser cartridge. After Eric's arrest, Zepeda searched his truck. "There was a lot of weaponry, a lot of firearms in there."

"Did you ever find the third monitor?" Mark asked.

"No," Zepeda answered.

On cross-exam, Sergi repeated his accusations that there were flaws in the state's case, most importantly how the video had been made, simply copying it onto a thumb drive. And he insisted that his client had returned the third monitor, the missing one. "Eric is maybe not the most politically astute person . . . He steps on people's toes?" Sergi prodded.

"I wouldn't know," Zepeda answered.

"You are aware that Judge Williams had a county car allowance and he was allowed to transport county property in his vehicle?" Sergi asked.

"Yes, I am," Zepeda answered.

One question brought consequences the defense hadn't intended, when Sergi asked: "You've known Eric Williams a long time. You've never known him to steal anything, correct?"

Zepeda agreed, but Mark latched on to that question, arguing before Judge Chitty that Sergi had put a "skunk" in the jury box by insinuating "there's no other thefts."

The defense attorneys vigorously objected, but in the end Judge Chitty agreed with the prosecutor. "Are you aware that Eric Williams has been charged with a theft over several periods, several different episodes, stealing money from the county by accessing improperly the county law library fund?" he asked.

"That's correct," Zepeda answered.

Perhaps Eric's attorney could have argued away the one charge involving the monitors, but knowing of other theft allegations had to have affected the jurors.

Later, many would say Mike, a big, bustling presence in the courtroom, looked proud throughout the trial, sometimes glaring at Eric, at other times almost grinning. It was his first trial as DA, and he relished the experience.

Eric's situation only worsened when Mark listed the items ordered for the law library. A goose-necked light for a laptop, for instance, that couldn't have been warranted since the law library didn't have a laptop. The gaming headphones perhaps could have been useful for dictation, but another item was a global positioning system for a laptop. "Is there anything like that in the law library?" Mark asked.

"No, sir," Lori Friemel answered.

From scissors to Post-it notes, from pens and envelopes to memory sticks, door stops, and DVDs, none of it had been found in the law library. Eric had purchased four computer mice, but the library had only one.

The defense did what they could. Regina Fogarty described Eric as a hands-on JP who'd worked hard to improve the office. Lanith Derryberry, a former designer for Texas Instruments, voiced the defense's view of the surveillance tape by labeling it unreliable. Yet Mark defused the argument, and Derryberry admitted he looked through the video and hadn't seen Eric return the third monitor to the IT room.

These actions have thrown a cloud over every elected official in the county!" Mike railed in closing arguments. "Eric Williams is a judge. He's supposed to protect the good people from bad people. He was supposed to protect them from people like him.

"This is a classic case of the fox watching the hen house . . . We expect more from our leaders . . . you have to be able to show everybody else out there that the people of Kaufman County will not tolerate this from their regular citizens or their leadership, elected or not elected. . . . We pay the price for it being held to a higher standard. He took an oath to do just that. He spat on that oath."

"You know the defendant is, as has been pointed out, an army officer, member of the Texas military forces, an elected official, a licensed lawyer. He is really an American hero," David Sergi countered. "Now, did he do something silly? I kind of compare Eric to a Dudley Do-Right. He tries to do the right thing. He's trying, but he makes mistakes . . . a rookie JP in a courthouse that I think you can see is a snake pit."

Rather than stealing, Sergi said Eric simply tried "to bring the JP office into, frankly, into the 20th century, not even the 21st century."

When it came to the supplies ordered for the law library, Sergi offered multiple explanations, including that the earphones were for the lawyers to plug into the computer to listen to continuing education classes. "The district attorney's office has done its best to make mountains out of mole hills. . . . It doesn't rise to the level of criminality."

Before he asked the jurors to find Eric not guilty, Sergi said, "Violation of some administrative policy? Maybe. A crime? No, sir."

The last to speak, Mark attacked: "You just heard about me trying to paint an evil picture of Eric Williams. Well, I don't think I need to do that. I think the pictures that are in evidence, the video, the still photographs clearly paint an evil picture of Eric Williams, an elected politician who's a thief. There's no worse thief than that. You put him in office, you give him a key to a building . . . and he steals from you. That's evil."

Over and again, Mark suggested jurors review the video, paying attention to Eric's body language as he "cased the joint." If Eric had been there to "do good for the county," as he claimed, why did he make sure no one saw him before he walked out with the boxes?

"This guy's sitting over at the end of counsel table," Mark said, pointing at Eric. "He's an elected public servant who is just a flat-out thief and burglar and needs to be removed from office and convicted of being a thief and a burglar."

Less than four hours after they retired for deliberation, the jurors did as Mark and Mike requested. In the courtroom, one spectator watched as the guilty verdict was read. "Eric was really still. Hardly moved," she said. "But I thought I saw a tear in his eye."

Chapter 27

This is the sort of thing that people elected me for
in the first place. They were tired of the wrongdoing
being done in county government and nothing being
done about it.

> —Mike McLelland, as quoted in the *Terrell Tribune*
> regarding the Eric Williams theft trial

After the guilty verdict, Eric's attorneys asked the judge
to rule on punishment, rather than the jury. Earlier they'd
discussed that Judge Chitty would better understand all
Eric had already lost with the guilty verdict. At that point,
the jury was released, and soon after the case was put on
hold to give time for a pre-sentencing study.

When Eric returned home that night and told Kim what
had happened, she felt stunned. She'd never considered
that the decision could go against him. Throughout, he'd
seemed positive, in the evenings telling her about the day's
events, sometimes laughing about how reporters followed
him through the courthouse, calling them his paparazzi.
With the guilty verdict, his mood became somber.

That same night, Eric sat at his computer and franti-
cally wrote recommendations for his attorneys for the next
part of the trial. He sent them a list of character witnesses.
On it were the names of officers in the Texas State Guard,

Kaufman attorneys, and Kim. "I think she should be the last witness for us, to have the most impact," he wrote.

Undoubtedly fuming over the day's events, Eric also logged onto Kaufman County's LexisNexis account, an online service used to look up publications, cases, and information on individuals. Although he was suspended, no one had cancelled his password. What thoughts needled at him as he searched for personal information on Mark Hasse, including his home address?

In the days that followed, Eric closed his law office. Convicted, he would be disbarred, prohibited from practicing law. He'd worked hard to get his degree and build a business. At one time, he'd had a near monopoly on the guardian ad litem work in Kaufman County, wielding power over families and children, making hundreds of thousands of dollars a year. Now, unless an appeals court overturned the verdict, he had no future as a lawyer, no livelihood.

In Kaufman, many continued to worry. One day the sheriff walked down the street in civvies, and a woman called out, "Where's your gun?"

"In the car," he answered.

"You know, Eric is kind of a goofy guy, and he has all those guns," she said.

Making light of it, the sheriff replied, "Well, he's not a very good pistol shot. I'm not in big danger there. If he's going to shoot me with a long gun, I can't do anything about it."

In the DA's office, Mark pulled together witnesses for the punishment phase. Many were people Eric had threatened over the years. One of the first Mark called was Janice Gray. On the phone, Gray sounded frantic. Still afraid of Eric, she didn't want to testify, but Mark had a subpoena issued for her to appear.

Meanwhile, in an interview with the probation officer

assessing his case, Eric lamented the loss of his judgeship, his license to be a law enforcement officer, his law license, and his place in the state guard. "I will have to seek another career with a felony, and I will not be able to earn what I am used to. My life has taken a drastic turn."

With the jury's decision against him, the best Eric could hope for was probation, to avoid prison.

Afternoons at the house, Eric worked with Kim, preparing her to testify. Her feet swollen from a rheumatoid arthritis outbreak, he suggested she wear a casual outfit, and they settled on a loose top, knit pants, and tennis shoes. He wanted her hair in a ponytail, and asked her to wear little makeup. "I want you to act sick. Limp a little," he told her. "I want the judge to feel sorry for you. You know, if I'm sent to jail, it won't do you any good. You need me here."

Thinking about her situation, her deteriorating health, her mother's stroke, her father's ongoing battle with cancer, Kim thought that was true. "I couldn't take care of myself. I rarely left the house. I barely ate."

Each day Eric reviewed the questions she'd be asked, and Kim practiced her answers.

On June 9, 2012, the 422nd again filled with Eric's attorneys, the prosecutors, and curious spectators for the punishment phase. Kim dressed as Eric instructed, and she felt nervous. He'd also told her about some potentially disturbing testimony from a woman at the trial, one he'd dated. He laid out what Janice Gray would say about a night he threatened her. "None of it is true," he said. "Her friends talked her into calling the police. I didn't do it."

"I believed him," Kim said. "But I always thought there had to be some truth to it. I wasn't sure, but it sounded like things he'd done to me. It sounded like the Eric I knew."

The prosecutors went first, and they put on John Burt, the attorney Eric had threatened a year earlier. On that day,

Eric screamed, "I am going to kill him, his wife, his kids. I'm gonna burn his house down." Yet when the defense asked if Burt feared Eric, he said that he didn't. "I've been concerned about him. Eric and I have always had a good relationship."

When the attorney who heard the threats testified, he reiterated what he'd heard Eric say but agreed with Burt. "Society would not benefit with Eric going to the penitentiary."

"He told me he had a gun . . . if I turned around and walked away—he would use it 'cause he didn't have anything to lose," Gray said. Near tears, her hands shaking, she remained frightened of Eric. When David Sergi asked if she knew what Eric intended to do with the gun, she replied, "I was afraid he was going to shoot me, if that's what you're asking."

The first to testify for Eric, his commanding officer in the Texas State Guard appeared genuinely confused at having to come to court on behalf of a man that he thought well of, one he trusted. Eric had keys to the guard's armory, which held hundreds of thousands of dollars of equipment, none of which had ever come up missing.

Into the record, the defense attorneys entered Eric's personnel folder from the guard, with his many commendations. His college and law school transcripts became evidence as well, along with his long record as a registered law enforcement officer.

As the last defense witness, Kim hesitantly walked toward the stand, barely resembling the woman Judge Chitty had seen eighteen months earlier at Eric's swearing in for the JP slot. Instead, her complexion sallow, her eyes weary, lacking her front teeth, she appeared ill, her senses dulled. While Eric had insisted she stare at Mike and Mark, Kim didn't do that. Instead, she felt uncomfortable just being on the stand.

In their fourteen years of marriage, Kim explained she'd

suffered from a cluster of illnesses, including her rheumatoid arthritis, which she described as similar to having the flu but ten times worse. Just driving, she had to fight to stay awake, and at times had to pull over to rest.

"Who takes care of you at home?" David Sergi asked.

"My husband," she answered, later adding that he watched over her parents as well.

"Has Eric ever threatened to kill you? . . . Is there any domestic violence in your home?"

"No," Kim answered. "I came from a home where domestic violence was a daily occurrence, and I decided a long time ago I was not going to take that. I was not going to allow a man to hit on me or treat me bad."

In spite of all the problems they'd had, that she'd later say she feared him, Kim stood by her husband. "The Eric I know is a loving man. A helpful man. He wouldn't do anything to hurt anybody. He's a good man : . . I can't imagine my life without him."

The testimony ended.

In an emotional closing argument, Mike charged, "I think what's at stake here . . . is the credibility of the courthouse to the people in Kaufman County. Every night they see corrupt public officials and corrupt businessmen and things like that arrested on the TV. They watch their proceedings, and in the end they get something like some slap on the wrist, like probation."

Instead, Mike asked Chitty to give Eric jail time, saying Eric "took all kinds of different oaths. He didn't honor any of them. He's a man bereft of honor."

Defending his client, John Sickel disagreed, pointing out how minor taking three monitors ranked in the scope of the crimes Judge Chitty saw on a regular basis. Rather than a man bereft of honor, Sergi contended that Eric helped his country and the county and lived an honorable life. "The prosecutors want you to throw Eric under the jail!"

In truth, Sickel proposed, Eric had suffered enough, and he didn't deserve to also serve time in prison. "I cannot stand here before this court and imagine what Mr. Williams is going through right now. . . . To see everything that you have worked hard for come crumbling down. . . . He's lost his law license. He has lost a bench. He will lose his military commission. All of those things that mean something to him he will lose."

The final argument Mark's, he cited pre-sentencing interviews, ones in which Eric expressed no responsibility or remorse. And he recapped all the people Eric had threatened. "To scare people . . . To steal from people. Even if you're not a public official, this is unacceptable conduct demanding pen time. Then you add to that that he's a public servant, using his public access to a public building to steal public money, this guy's got to go to prison, Judge. Two years in prison is nothing compared to his history of committing crimes and what he deserves. Two years is not nearly enough. It's just the best you can do."

Despite the prosecutors' arguments, Eric escaped time in a Texas prison. Instead, Chitty placed him on probation for two years, ordered him to do eighty hours of community service, and fined him $2,500. "This conviction carries with it removal from office, and I hereby remove the defendant from office as Justice of the Peace, Precinct 1 of Kaufman County, Texas," Judge Chitty said. "And I understand an additional consequence will be the loss of his law license."

As the session ended, Eric's defense attorneys informed the judge that they intended to file an appeal.

While lawyers often shake hands at the end of a trial, on this day in the 422nd, that didn't happen. Instead, a funereal atmosphere filled the courtroom. Eric's attorneys knew that although the sentence could seem light, their client had paid dearly.

If Eric's chest filled with a sense of injustice, of being persecuted, Mike seethed just below the surface as well. He'd wanted to see Eric behind bars. As the gavel came down, it might have seemed like an ending. Only later would those gathered realize that day marked a beginning.

Chapter 28

I was driving back to San Marcos after the trial with another investigator who'd worked Eric's case. At one point he said, "Yeah man, Eric is going to go in and pepper all those bastards," kind of jokingly. I didn't take it seriously.

—Sharon Holbrook

Bearing the scarlet letter of his felony, Eric even more resolutely withdrew from public, rarely seen except for the odd sighting. One day a local restaurateur noticed Eric pacing in the intense summer heat in a grocery store parking lot, screaming into his cell phone. When the man walked out forty-five minutes later, Eric was still shouting into the phone.

Days spent at home on his computer playing Mafia Wars, Eric no longer had his JP office to go to, or his law office. No court appointments or clients streamed in. Everything had stopped. When lawyer friends called to inquire, he insisted, "We're fine. We'll be fine."

Few believed him. Some saw what had happened as a death sentence of sorts, killing all Eric had worked hard to become, leaving him with nothing to build on. At one point, Kim noticed that her husband had begun taking antidepressants.

That he'd lost so much hadn't quelled the prosecutors.

"We heard that Mark Hasse and Mike McLelland were crowing about the victory," said John Sickel. "In the local newspapers, Mike in particular celebrated about what they'd done."

One newspaper quoted Mike saying, "While we're not happy that he got probation, it was important to get Eric Williams convicted and removed from the bench."

In courthouse hallways, Mark and Mike bragged about their victory, Mike branding Eric as "too stupid to take the deal." One day someone asked him to name the best thing he'd done in office, and Mike replied, "I took Eric Williams's law license."

"Eric Williams isn't the smartest guy in the room anymore," Mark told one local lawyer, with a hearty laugh.

Many of those they boasted to liked Eric and didn't join in. Some thought Mike and Mark made a mistake chuckling about Eric's fate where they could be overheard by those who might repeat the conversations to Eric. "You never rub someone's face in it after you beat them," said one attorney. "You shake his hand and say, 'Nothing personal,' and go on. What we heard is that they shamed him."

An odd event took place inside the DA's office not long after Eric's sentencing. Sam Keats, the tree-farm owner who helped Mike win his job, sat in his office one day. She'd dropped in to visit, and they talked about things they wanted changed in the county, when someone knocked on the door and delivered a sheet of paper. "What's this?" Mike asked.

"It's a list that came over about Eric Williams. The woman who sent it said to give it to you."

"I don't know what this is," Mike said, as he looked it over. "Is this a hit list?"

Perplexed, Mike showed the list to Keats. Looking at the five names on the sheet of paper, Mike speculated, "Some kind of enemies list?"

Still appearing unsure what to do, Mike folded the piece of paper and put it in his wallet. A little while later, he took it out, looked at it again, then put it in his desk drawer.

"Are you going to tell those people?" Keats asked.

"I suppose I should call them," he said.

Recalling the names on the list, Keats said: "Sheriff Byrnes, Judge Chitty, Mark Hasse, Mike McLelland, and Denise Bell."

"**A**fter the trial, Eric was really mad at Mike McLelland and Mark Hasse. He never used their names, just Sluggo and Fuck Stick. And he was mad at the sheriff, because he said the sheriff should have just called him and asked him to come over and talk to him about the monitors, not had him arrested. Judge Chitty. Erleigh Wiley. He was mad at both of them," said Kim. Then she brought up another name that wasn't on that faxed list. "Maybe, more than anyone else, Eric was furious at Judge Ashworth. Eric thought the judge told them about that woman, Janice Gray. He said no one else knew about her."

Perhaps an odd addition to the written list, Denise Bell managed the *Forney Post*, an online newspaper that covered Kaufman County's most affluent city, the community where the McLellands lived. Short, with shoulder-length dark hair, a plump woman who talked fast and enthusiastically, Bell had reported on Eric's trial, snagging a photo of him during a break. One day she rode down the elevator with Eric and his lawyers, standing near him because she sensed that it bothered him. "Don't talk to her," she heard one of his attorneys whisper.

Later there would be questions about whether that written list ever existed. No one would be able to find it. No one questioned at the DA's office would recall receiving it. Yet Sam Keats insisted it did. Perhaps confirming her memory, Mike did take steps to warn at least one of those mentioned on it. At an event, he pulled Bell to the side. "Denise, Eric

Williams is upset, and he has a list of people he's unhappy with. You're on it. Do you know how to shoot a gun?"

"Yes, I do," she said.

Mike looked at her long and hard as he said, "If it goes bad, run."

Chapter 29

Whenever I ran into Mark in the courthouse, he wanted to talk about Eric. Mark said, "Ron, I think Eric Williams is going to kill me. I've become target number one."

—Ron Herrington

A former cop who'd gone to law school, Ron Herrington knew Mark from his first tenure as an assistant DA. War horses, they enjoyed trading stories about the bad old Dallas days, when Herrington worked assaults and Mark ran the organized crime unit. Herrington also knew Eric and liked him, but he took Mark's concerns to heart. It had been Herrington's experience that when someone worried about another person's intentions, the concern often turned out to have merit. At times, Mark focused on Eric's guns, his night vision equipment, ballistic vests, and high-powered ammo. "He's that kind of guy, Ron," said Mark. "He might hurt someone."

Thinking about Mark, Herrington doubted his friend would do well if Eric did come after him. Not trained for combat, Mark also had trouble with his right elbow. He needed surgery.

Despite his concerns, Herrington wondered if Mark wasn't too fixated on Eric, so much so that he'd inflated the danger. There'd been a time, back in the Dallas years, when

Mark might not have worried about an Eric Williams. At fifty-seven, however, Mark had already faced death once in the plane crash. Others hadn't noticed a change, but it seemed likely that Mark no longer had a young man's hubris and sense of invulnerability.

At the Lancaster Airport, where Mark kept his planes, his friends heard similarly disquieting statements. Mark seemed on edge, nervous, jumping at loud noises, like the day a car backfired. "He threatened me," Mark told one friend. "After the trial, he threatened to kill me."

Still, in Kaufman all appeared quiet, even if during Monday morning meetings Mike reminded his staff that they needed to be on guard. He, too, said that he'd heard that Eric made threats. "Better watch your backs." As a man who'd based his life on the importance of being pre-pared, he asked his staff how many had a gun and knew how to use it. Some did, but for those who didn't, Mike sug-gested they take concealed handgun courses and buy one.

Even after his conviction, Eric's name remained front and center.

One day in a meeting in Mike's office, he, Mark, and one of the DA's investigators talked to Captain Ernie Zepeda, from the sheriff's office, about the importance of Eric rid-ding himself of his weapons. As a convicted felon, once the appeal process ran out, Eric wouldn't be allowed to own a gun in Texas. From Mike's office window he could look out and see Eric's old law office with his name still on the sign. "Are you worried about Eric doing anything to your wife?" someone asked Zepeda, whose wife worked for an attorney in town.

"No, I don't think so," he answered.

The room grew quiet. Someone then said, "It's just a matter of time, you know, before Eric Williams comes across the square to the courthouse and shoots everyone up."

Zepeda thought about that, but shrugged it off with a "Nah."

Yet Mike worried. Around the office, he wore a holster with a snub-nose .38 that resembled an old detective's gun. At home, he continued to have guns scattered throughout the house, on tables or shelves, in drawers. He cautioned Cynthia to be careful as well, and she and her friend Leah Phillips took a concealed weapons class to become licensed. Typical Cynthia, she brought snacks to the classes, graham crackers to dip in white chocolate.

For his part, Sheriff Byrnes doubted trouble lay ahead. "I figured Eric would sit back and figure out where to take his life." Yet when Eric's firearms were brought up, Byrnes agreed they needed to be proactive. Someone from the sheriff's office called Eric's attorneys and asked to have him compile a list and to remind Eric that he needed to start getting rid of them, so he wouldn't be a felon in possession of a firearm. As instructed, Eric typed up the requested document. On it were twenty-three handguns, a tranquilizer gun, five shotguns, and fifteen rifles.

If others worried about his client—preparing for what they feared could be a day of reckoning—John Sickel thought that Eric appeared calm about the situation, anticipating success with his appeal. "He seemed certain that it would be overturned."

What no one other than Mike and Mark yet knew, however, was what would happen with the other indictment against Eric, the theft charge for the $1,700 of supplies they accused him of misappropriating from the law library. That still hung over Eric, threatening to hurl him back into a courtroom, this time possibly to a jail sentence.

On Overlook, Eric and Kim visited his parents not long after the trial, and afterward his mother called his sister, Tera, and told her about the encounter. That day, Eric said little, but Kim became incensed, shouting that they would sue the city and the county, screaming, "We're going to own Kaufman County!"

To Jim Williams, it was what he'd expected from her. Like his wife, he'd never had good feelings about their daughter-in-law. "Kim liked living high on the hog. She was mad about the whole thing. She didn't like it that Eric wasn't bringing home big money anymore."

At the house, Eric watched movies on TV or played on his computer. Kim urged him to look for work, but he refused. "I'm going to get my job back," he told her.

"How are you going to do that?"

"Win the appeal."

The only money coming in her $1,300 a month in disability, they began cashing in her IRAs. She started out with nearly $50,000, but each month the amount dropped. "At times, Eric became excited, talking about how he'd win his appeal and it would all go away. He came up with some idea, what to argue," Kim said. "But then Eric talked to his attorneys, and he'd hang up and said it wouldn't work. The only ones he talked to were his attorneys and his buddies from the state guard."

At the guard, many of those Eric had commanded saw his conviction as a miscarriage. One guard member set up a meeting with a state representative, Dan Flynn. At lunch, Eric explained his situation, contending that he'd been unfairly prosecuted. "There's nothing I can do," Flynn told him. "If you feel it's unfair, talk to the Texas Rangers."

Living in the house on Overlook, Kim and Eric had reminders of their new situation all around them. After he fired the landscaper, the yard overgrew between his attempts to cut the grass and shape the bushes. He trimmed the trees so high off the ground that a neighbor complained. The pressure built, and one day, Eric said, "If I were going to go off, I'd go to the high school and start shooting and just keep on going from there."

Not knowing what to say, Kim responded, "Oh, really?"

"You know those prosecutors set me up," he said, and Kim believed him.

Little to occupy their minds, they spent days side by side at the kitchen bar playing on their computers. On Facebook, Kim opened an account under the name "Holly Hatchet" to feed supplies to her Mafia Wars crew. To her, Eric seemed more upset about not being in the guard than the other repercussions. "He liked dressing up and playing soldier."

Afternoons, Eric grocery shopped and picked up Kim's medications, then doled them out to her throughout the day. In the evenings, he cooked dinner. Although he no longer carried a gun, he still dressed in camo and rode his Segway around the neighborhood. Police officers saw him, but there was nothing they could do. He wasn't breaking any laws.

Those long days with nothing to occupy him, Eric's anger built. One afternoon that summer, he nonchalantly told Kim he'd been thinking, and he had people he'd like to take revenge against. The names didn't exactly match those on the list Mike received at the DA's office. Instead, Judge Ashworth held the top slot, followed by Mark, Mike, and Judge Erleigh Wiley, who'd taken away his CPS assignments. "These people ruined our lives. I was angry, too," Kim said. "His emotions were my emotions. But I didn't believe he'd kill anyone. For a long time, I tried not to listen."

Sometime that summer, Eric picked up temp work through the Internet, writing documents for other attorneys. On the net, he also rented out the house IP address, the designation used to track online activity, to companies who specialized in hiding the origins of Web site browsing and e-mails. For the company to use, he cleaned off Kim's old laptop and left it plugged in. At times it suddenly clicked online, there'd be activity, and then it shut down. Checks occasionally came, but rarely more than a hundred dollars.

Money tight, Eric compiled a resumé, listing his most recent employment as justice of the peace. In a cover letter he described his situation as complicated. "I was elected to be a judge in Kaufman County, but have now lost all those opportunities because of criminal charges, including burglary and theft by a public servant. My attorneys are working hard to appeal, but I must begin to move on with my life and find my next positive step," he wrote. ". . . Second chances are very hard to ask for, and in my circumstance very hard to get. My resume is attached, and with this letter I am asking for the chance to interview and for you to judge my potential for your company."

Looking into another alternative, Eric downloaded the form required to send to the Texas governor to request a full pardon.

One friend called and offered grocery money to tide them over, assuming Eric and Kim were growing short of funds, but Eric refused. "We're okay," he said. "We'll manage."

Once the IRA money disappeared, Eric and Kim began drawing on $30,000 she had in a savings account, composed of gifts from her parents.

Eric's talk of killing increased in the fall of 2012, six months after the trial. "The first one Eric was going to kill was Judge Ashworth," said Kim. "He was really mad at him about the trial, that he'd helped the prosecutors."

When Eric drank, his moods strayed even darker, and at the house, he laid out his plans. Ashworth's house, across the back field from Eric and Kim's house, made him accessible. "I'm going to cut through the fence with bolt cutters," Eric told her. "Then I'll shoot him with a crossbow. I'm going to gut him and fill his stomach with napalm."

Shocked, Kim said later that she just stared at her husband. Yet she understood. She blamed Judge Ashworth, too.

A while later, Eric returned from a shopping trip with

her father and showed her a crossbow he'd bought. On another day he walked in with a sticky, bright yellow substance he made in pickle jars in the garage, a concoction he described as napalm. For weeks, killing Ashworth dominated Eric's conversations. Explaining how the plan would unfold, Eric said the judge would die on Super Bowl night, after the guests left his annual party.

Another day Eric told Kim that he'd modified his plan. At that point, he planned to kidnap the judge and bring him to their house, kill him, and bury him in the backyard. Not long after, she woke up one afternoon and saw Eric in the backyard with a shovel, digging up a bed of roses. "What are you doing?" she asked.

"I want to see how far I can get, if it will hold a body," he said, continuing to dig.

Rather than argue, Kim ignored him and watched TV.

Then there was the day Kim heard a thunk, thunk, thunk outside the patio doors. When she looked out, she saw Eric in the backyard loading arrows into the crossbow, shooting them into a paper bull's-eye tacked on their wooden fence. Rather than address what he intended to do with the weapon, she complained, "You're making holes in the fence."

For weeks, Eric talked about Ashworth's murder. Then, suddenly, without explaining why, Eric told Kim that he'd changed his mind. Instead of the judge, Mark's name had moved to the top of Eric's list. The lawyer who prosecuted the case that crippled Eric would die first. When she later went in the backyard, Kim noticed that Eric had refilled the flower bed, patting the dirt down as if he'd never dug it up.

Meanwhile, life went on in the DA's office. In August, Brandi Fernandez, the chief prosecutor in the Eighty-sixth, Mark's counterpart in the other district court, tried a case against a member of the white supremacist prison gang Aryan Brotherhood of Texas. The accused punished another member who skipped a meeting by kidnapping him, which led to a shootout. Fernandez got the man two life sentences. "I'm just ecstatic about the sentence," Mike told the local newspapers. "It shows that those people can't come down here and run roughshod over folks in Kaufman County."

In the DA's office, more attention centered on such cases. "Our emphasis was to clean up Kaufman County from gang activity," said Fernandez. At the same time, Mark looked into cartel activity, groups that used I–175 to transport drugs. "In our little rural county there were pockets where people had meth labs," Fernandez said. "They were running drugs."

On weekends at his hangar, Mark restored an old Mustang, and one of the women from the courthouse brought her Corvette for him to work on. At night after long days at the office, Mark returned to his house in Rockwall, his dogs waiting. He didn't know that by then Eric Williams had brought Kim out to the house, to show her where Mark lived.

Perhaps Kim found it exciting. Or, numb from the drugs, she couldn't focus, didn't understand or want to admit the seriousness of her husband's plans. Later she'd maintain that when Eric mentioned scouting Mark's house, at first she refused to go.

"I don't feel good," she told him.

"You're going, and you're driving," he responded.

By then Kim's hair had turned a dirty blond gray, and she rarely ventured out except to her parents' home. In the passenger seat, Eric watched cars drive by, and played on Kim's phone. "Maybe I'll just shoot him as he comes down the driveway to go to work," he said a few days later. As he described it, he could shoot through Mark's truck window. Once he did, Mark dead behind the wheel, Eric thought the truck would lurch forward and crash into the fence across the street. "They'll think it's an accident," that he'd been hit by a stray bullet.

But then he paused. "That's too risky," he said. "There's a better way."

Chapter 30

I believed everything he told me. Eric's anger was my anger. It was Mark Hasse's and Mike McLelland's fault. They'd done this to us.

—Kim Williams

"Mike and I think that Eric Williams has the personality type that means he can't stand being publicly humiliated," Cynthia told her friend Tonya Ratcliff while quilting. By then Ratcliff had resigned as Combine's mayor and been elected Kaufman County's tax assessor. During the day, she worked in the annex building, across the street from the courthouse, backing up to the county parking lot.

From behind her sewing machine, Tonya looked at Cynthia and frowned. She knew her friend worried about Eric. Mike seemed apprehensive about him, too. Making matters worse, Ratcliff had noticed that Cynthia's Parkinson's appeared worse. When Cynthia walked, a leg slightly dragged. When quilting, she needed help. At the retreats, Tonya and others cut her fabric, something Cynthia couldn't do with her trembling hands.

Others saw similar signs.

The phone rang at Leah and Skeet Phillips's house one evening, Mike looking for aid. Dinner and later continued to be his wife's bad time. "We're out at a restaurant, and I need someone to drive Cynthia's car home. She can't," he said. As she hurried to help, Leah thought about how even as the disease progressed, Cynthia still refused to discuss it.

While Cynthia rarely rested well, she now slept little, staying up quilting until late into the night. Despite her illness, in many ways Cynthia hadn't changed. She still laughed and cried with little provocation, broke into show tunes at odd times, and remained preoccupied with the unseen. At some point, she'd decided that in a previous incarnation her older sister, Nancy, had been her mother. Cynthia also believed that Leah had been her sister. Based on that imagined relationship, Cynthia made Leah a quilt and sewed on a patch that read: "Presented to: Leah Rhea Phillips with much love. Your sister, Cynthia Woodward McLelland."

In September 2012, Cynthia and Mike attended a DAs' meeting in Padre Island and spent time over dinner talking to Burns, Mike's law school friend. They laughed and told stories, and Mike turned the conversation to their time in Corpus, when he'd had the bypass. "You know, Cynthia was almost a widow," he said, reminding Burns that doctors called his clogged artery "the widow maker."

"I'm too young and beautiful for that," Cynthia said with a chuckle. Then, uncharacteristically, she admitted her disease, teasing, "I live with Parkinson's, and I live with this man, too."

Patting her hand, Mike laughed.

In Kaufman that fall, Eric received a suspension letter from the state bar, formally prohibiting him from practicing law as he awaited a decision on his appeal: "It is ordered that Eric L. Williams immediately surrender his Texas law license." His only hope, the briefs for his appeal had been filed in Dallas, at the Fifth District Court of Appeals. In them, Eric's lawyers argued multiple issues, including that the surveillance video was altered.

Perhaps the state bar's letter solidified Eric's commitment to do what he already planned. "You're going to help me kill Mark Hasse," he told Kim one day in the house.

"No, I'm not," she said.

"You're my wife," he said, staring at her. "You don't have to do anything, but you're going to come with me and sit there while I kill Fuck Stick. Because you're my wife."

In the days that followed, that conversation replayed, Eric insisting and Kim refusing or walking away, or turning over in bed and trying to block out his words.

At Kaufman's Scarecrow Festival on a weekend in late October in the town square, the quilting guild had a booth, and Cynthia staffed it one afternoon with her sister Nancy. While the two women talked to those who walked up, Mike sat at the rear of the booth, calling out to people and waving. When they finished their tour of duty, they went inside the courthouse, and Mike brought the women to his second-floor offices. Once there, he played voice messages on the office recorder. From another room, Nancy heard a menacing voice say, "You'll get yours."

"Here it comes again," Mike said to no one in particular, never explaining, never identifying the caller.

As they left the office, Nancy thought that maybe it came with the DA's job, that people became angry and some voiced that, whether they actually intended to fulfill the threats or not.

At a Halloween party, Cynthia wore a dark blue peasant dress and displayed a Merry Christmas banner she'd quilted. Around that same time, Mike visited Michelle Sutton, whose breast cancer had landed her in the hospital. Among his first hires at the DA's office, before her illness, she'd assisted Mark on Eric's case. That day, Mike remarked about the close relationship he and Cynthia had with Leah and her husband, Skeet Phillips, and all they did together, the new house, and his job as DA.

Cynthia (right) showing off her banner

"I've never been happier," he said.

On Saturday mornings, Sam Keats often ran into Mike and Cynthia at Costco, where they bought in bulk to restock the substantial storeroom they kept in the house. Cynthia walked Keats around the store, arm in arm, and they picked up samples to taste from the vendors. "You're too skinny," Cynthia chastised. When Cynthia tried to reach for an item on a shelf, her hands shook and she couldn't grab it. Sam snatched it for her, and Cynthia giggled.

At the Kaufman DA's office, business went on as usual as winter approached.

Across the state, a push had begun against gangs, and in Houston that November, the FBI issued a press release announcing the indictments of four senior Aryan Brotherhood of Texas (ABT) leaders on charges of conspiring to participate in a racketeering enterprise. In all, the grand jury indicted fifteen members on seventeen counts. "Today's takedown represents a devastating blow to the leadership of ABT," Assistant Attorney General Lanny A. Breuer said. An FBI special agent added, "It sends a clear message that we will relentlessly pursue and prosecute the leaders and members of those criminal enterprises regardless of where they lay their heads."

Describing the effort as a multi-agency task force, the FBI thanked those who'd helped, including the U.S. Marshals Service, the Texas Rangers, Houston PD, and many others. Based on Brandi Fernandez's case, the one in which she'd prosecuted an ABT gang member for kidnapping, the final mention was the Kaufman County, Texas, District Attorney's Office.

"You're going to get caught," Kim told Eric at the house when he again talked about killing Mark Hasse.

"I'm not going to get caught," he said with a shrug. Sitting at home, Eric had gained weight, and when he smiled, his dimples cut into fleshy cheeks. "Who's going to know?"

In addition to murdering Mark, Eric insisted Mike McLelland had to die. Only then would a new DA be named. Once that happened, Eric told Kim that a fresh set of eyes on his case would come to the conclusion that he'd been railroaded. As Eric framed it, any other DA would have to clear him. For weeks, Eric had been telling Kim that his attorneys weren't hopeful about his appeal. "I'm going to kill Fuck Stick and Sluggo," he said. "Then I'll get my job back."

"We don't kill people," she said, her head hurting just thinking about it. "What are you talking about?"

"This is the only way I'm going to get my law license back," he repeated. "I need to get rid of Fuck Stick and Sluggo, so someone else takes over. They aren't going to back down."

"Well, we don't kill people," she said, still not believing he'd go through with it, although she had the sense he'd mulled over the idea for a long time.

At that, Eric dropped the conversation, but he returned to it days later. "I can buy a car, use it to kill Fuck Stick and Sluggo, and then dump it," he said.

Chapter 31

We watched movies a lot. Eric liked Westerns, and one of his favorites was *Tombstone*, with the shootout in the O.K. Corral. One day he told me how he was going to kill Mark Hasse. He said, "It's going to be Fuck Stick's Tombstone."

—Kim Williams

Considered the most famous shootout in the history of the Wild West, the thirty-second gunfight in the O.K. Corral in 1881 pitted legendary lawman Wyatt Earp, his brothers, and his friend Doc Holliday against a group of desperados called The Cowboys. In 1993, George P. Cosmatos directed a film in which Kurt Russell portrayed Earp, and Val Kilmer an ailing Holliday. In truth, the deadly battle actually took place not in the O.K. Corral but an empty lot down the street from it in Tombstone, Arizona, in broad daylight.

Eric hatched a similar plot to ambush Mark. As he described his brazen plan, he'd confront Mark a block from Kaufman's town square, in the county lot where Mark parked his maroon Dually, in the morning as Mark arrived for work. Kim's job would be to drive Eric to the scene and wait. When Mark pulled in, Eric would jump out, shoot him, and then hop back in the car. By the time police responded, Kim would have spirited them away.

For weeks, Kim refused, while Eric insisted she had to. "You're my wife. You're going to help me."

At times, Eric explained marital privilege, a law that prevented spouses from being forced to testify against each other. Sharing Eric's anger at the way he was treated, she found herself thinking about Mike and Mark, what they'd done to Eric and to her. Still, she said no.

"You're going to help me!" he ordered.

Inside, her stomach churned. Her head hurt. "I was really afraid of him," she said.

Around Thanksgiving, he told her, "If you don't help me, I'm going to kill your mother, your father, and then I'll come back and shoot you."

"That was when I knew he was serious," she said. From that point on, any time she left the house, even to walk to her parents' home, Eric shadowed her. "He kept a real close eye on me after that. He knew threatening my parents would get to me."

On December 6, money dwindling and in search of a new income stream, Eric filled out the paperwork to apply for disability, claiming that he suffered from diabetic neuropathy. In his application he wrote that it limited his movement and made him unable to work. In addition, Eric contended that he suffered from bouts of frozen shoulder, a malady he'd had in the past that sometimes incapacitated his arm. When he answered a question assessing his ability to get along with authority figures, Eric wrote: "Fine, don't come in contact with them."

Although he had cut off contact with his friends at the Kaufman courthouse, Eric talked occasionally with members of his guard unit. Looking back, one member described their former captain's conviction as a "significant event" for the battalion. "We couldn't understand how this could have happened. We were all in disbelief."

Many in his unit supported Eric, adhering to military

fidelity as if they went into battle together and counted on one another to cover their backs. "We are trained to be loyal. Our values are loyalty. We never betray a member of our unit," said one guardsman.

On the day he'd joined the guard, almost three years earlier, Eric met a man in a hallway outside the commander's office who wasn't related to him but shared his last name: Barton Williams. The unit's command sergeant major, Barton Williams went by his middle name, Roger. He bridged the chasm between enlisted men and officers, moving freely among both. With a bushy salt-and-pepper mustache, Roger worked for AT&T as a senior training manager.

Before long, Eric and Roger became friends, and others saw the two men eating lunches during training sessions. "The one Eric was closest to at the guard was Roger Williams. No doubt," said another member.

In November, Eric began an e-mail dialogue with Roger Williams, writing: "I have a favor to ask. Can we meet to discuss some details? I'm open most anytime. My treat for lunch or dinner. No rush just let me know. Thank you, ERIC."

As their communication developed, Roger learned that the help his former executive officer requested involved renting a storage unit. Although not true, Eric said Kim's brother, Jamie, planned to move in with his parents, to care for them, and needed a place to store his things. Although he didn't understand what role Eric had in mind for him, Roger agreed.

"I found what I was looking for," Eric e-mailed Roger in mid-December. "Let me know when you've got some extra time & I'll meet you for lunch."

On December 10, Eric received a bill from David Sergi for $5,557 to pay for work on the appeal. Eric responded that he would get the money to him soon.

At the house on Overlook on the fourteenth of that month, Eric and Kim, like much of the nation, watched the horrific mass shooting at Sandy Hook Elementary unfold on television. The news from Newtown, Connecticut, where Adam Lanza murdered twenty six- and seven-year-olds along with six adults, devastated the nation. On that terrible morning, Lanza rushed into the school with a Bushmaster XM15–E2S rifle, fired, and didn't stop until police arrived and he shot himself through the head.

For days, the news reports centered on the tragedy at the school, the initial reporting on the killings and the aftermath including the funerals. One day as Eric watched, he turned to Kim and said, "If I was going to do something like this, that's what I'd do."

"You'd go in and shoot a bunch of little kids?" Kim gasped.

"Yeah, get the generation while you can, before they grow up. After I finished at the school, I'd go to a Wal-Mart and take as many people out as I could. Then I'd shoot myself."

With that, Eric laughed.

The McLellands had more than a hundred guests at their home on Blarney Stone that December for their annual Christmas party. Pitching in, Leah Phillips and Sam Keats spent the evening in the laundry room making sandwiches. As always, many laughed and patted one another on the back. Cynthia hugged everyone as they arrived and again as they left.

The holidays approached, and that Christmas Mark Hasse dropped in at the hospital in Kaufman to spend time with a young girl, the victim in a sexual assault case he'd worked. No one else visited her, just Mark, who brought a teddy bear and lingered, telling her stories.

Late that month Eric met Roger Williams at a restaurant for lunch. After small talk, Eric said that he'd found the right storage facility. Still unsure of his role, Roger had brought cash with him, in case Eric needed help with the rent.

Instead, Eric explained that he wanted Roger to put his name on the unit, to sign the paperwork and then turn it over to him to use. The reason Eric gave involved his conviction. As a felon, with his name on the contract, he said, the unit could be subject to search. As he explained it, Eric didn't want his in-laws to have to endure such an intrusion.

On December 28, Eric and Roger drove to Gibson Self Storage in Seagoville, a half hour west of Eric's home, closer to Dallas. The modest facility Eric had found bordered a business park on a side street off U.S. 175, behind a Chicken Express. Once there, they met with Larry Mathis, the manager. In his sixties, his glasses in the shadow of his ball cap's brim, Mathis was the brother-in-law of the owner. After retiring from selling insurance, he took over supervising the facility, repairing the keypads at the entrances, handling the rentals. While Gibson's had gates, it didn't have surveillance cameras.

On the wall behind his desk, Mathis displayed a poster that read: "Expect the Unexpected." On a placard, he had the rates.

To begin, Mathis escorted his potential renters outside to look at Unit 18, measuring ten feet by twenty feet, the size of a one-car garage. An end unit, on the right Unit 18 bordered a driveway. Once there, Mathis raised the door, and Eric and Roger looked inside. After Eric approved it, they returned to Mathis's cluttered office.

As Roger filled out the rental agreement, Mathis noticed that Eric stood with his back to them, staring out the window, watching the traffic on the street. Although it seemed a bit odd, Mathis thought little of it.

"Who'll be accessing the unit?" he asked.

"Eric will," Roger answered. At that, Mathis asked Eric to fill in his name and other information on the paperwork, and show his driver's license. In addition, Roger listed Eric as the emergency contact for the unit. Based on their shared last name, Mathis assumed the two men in his office were related. Finally, Roger handed Mathis $1,020 in cash, money Eric had supplied to cover the unit's rent for one year. In Mathis's experience paying cash wasn't particularly odd, since renters sometimes didn't want the bother of monthly bills.

Before they walked out, Mathis handed over a gate code specific to their unit.

Outside the office, Roger gave Eric the contract, the code, and the key to the lock. "I really appreciate this," Eric said.

"No problem." Roger then offered to help move in Eric's brother-in-law's possessions.

"No, I'll just take my time doing it. None of it is too big," he answered. "I can handle it."

The next day, Eric began settling into Unit 18. But rather than Jamie's things, he lugged in his arsenal of weapons: duffel bags of handguns, rifles, shotguns, along with boxes and trunks filled with ammunition, night vision gear, police clothing, badges, and ballistic vests. Mathis didn't notice Eric come and go, since Eric made a point of entering through the far gate, on the driveway closest to the Chicken Express pick-up window.

As 2012 came to an end, Ron Herrington noticed that Mark Hasse rarely brought up Eric Williams any longer. It seemed that the nearly seven months since the trial had calmed him. Herrington didn't mention Eric, either, wanting to let Mark relax, hoping it had just been nerves.

In the DA's office, too, the focus moved on.

That month the Texas Department of Public Safety, which included the Texas Rangers and the state troopers, issued a report on the Aryan Brotherhood of Texas, warning that it could "be planning retaliation against law enforcement officials" who worked on the case that resulted in the

Houston indictments, the one in which the FBI thanked the Kaufman County DA's office for its contribution.

New Year 2013 would later be a fog for Kim. Heavily medicated, she slept.

On January 4, Eric met another guardsman, Scott Hunt, at the Angry Dog, a restaurant on Commerce Street in the Deep Ellum section of Dallas. When Hunt arrived, Eric was sipping a beer. The two men shook hands, and then ordered lunch.

A high school photography teacher, Hunt was in charge of marksmanship for Eric's old guard unit. While he didn't know Eric well, Hunt thought of the former executive officer as quiet but confident, a good officer. Before he'd agreed to meet with Eric, Hunt had called his command sergeant major, Roger Williams, and asked if he thought it was all right.

After he got a go-ahead, Hunt set up the lunch, and at the table, he and Eric initially discussed Hunt's experiences in officers' candidate school and then the outcome of the most recent shooting competition. To Hunt the conversation felt awkward, and Eric appeared nervous.

After a while, Eric turned the conversation to guns and ammo, asking about the capabilities of 5.7 rounds. "What about glass penetration?" Eric asked. Perhaps he still considered shooting Mark Hasse through the Dually's window.

"I don't know," Hunt answered. "Do you have a 5.7?"

"No," Eric answered, again making Hunt think that something about the conversation seemed strange. Yet there'd been so much interest in Sandy Hook that Hunt wondered if that explained Eric's question. In light of worries about renewed gun control efforts and predictions that some types of weapons could be banned, sales of assault-type weapons had soared. Hunt thought Eric, like many others, might be considering buying out of a fear of government actions.

Without explaining further, Eric turned the conversation to AR rifles. They talked, and then the food came. "So, what is this favor you want of me?" Hunt asked.

"Can you help me get rid of an AR upper?" Eric asked, referring to the section that connects onto the lower and anchors the barrel. The traceable part of such a weapon, the upper had a serial number, and it could be matched to a shell by comparing tool marks.

At first, Hunt thought little of it, assuming that Eric had disposed of a lower and had an upper he wanted to sell. Prices on uppers—the more valuable part of the rifle—had gone up in the wake of Sandy Hook, again because of gun control fears. Earlier in the conversation, Eric had vented about the unfairness of his prosecution and admitted that not working took a heavy financial toll, so selling an upper seemed like a reasonable request. In fact, when they talked of money, twice during the conversation Eric had said, "I'm at the end of my rope."

"Why don't you take the upper to a gun show and sell it?" Hunt said, mentioning one scheduled that same weekend. Then Hunt had another thought. "What type is it? Maybe I'd be interested."

When Eric didn't respond with a manufacturer or model number for the upper, Hunt said, "I'm not really understanding. What do you want?"

"If I had an upper, could you—if I gave it to you—would you make sure it never sees the light of day?" Eric asked.

Increasingly uncomfortable with the conversation, Hunt didn't respond.

In the parking lot as they left, Hunt wondered if Eric could be so desperate he'd hurt himself. "Now don't do anything stupid, okay?" he said as they parted.

At 10:25 that night, Hunt e-mailed Eric and said he'd enjoyed seeing him. "Sorry I can't help with your request. . . . I'm sure everything will work out in short order . . . like you, I'm just keeping my head down and slugging away toward the finish."

Minutes later, Eric responded. "I appreciate our open discussion on various topics," he wrote. "I do look forward to bringing the truth to light through the proper legal process . . . Frustration is sometimes best expressed in a safe way . . . I get past it every day, and my best tactic has been to stay UTR (under the radar)."

The day after his lunch with Scott Hunt, Eric logged onto Kaufman County's LexisNexis account. Once on the site, he again searched for information on Mark and checked driver's license information that included where Mike McLelland lived.

Throughout January, the door opened and shut every few days at Unit 18 at Gibson Self Storage, presumably Eric moving in more of his combat gear and weapons and organizing the space. In the middle of the month, he clicked onto eBay and ordered size XL Value-Tek blue anti-skid clean-room shoe covers, the type worn by medical personnel in operating rooms. He paid $32.68 on his PayPal account for 280 covers.

On the net, Eric also looked for a car, reliable but cheap, one that would blend, not stand out. At the house, he called Kim over to look at possibilities on Craigslist. She noticed his excitement building as his plan took shape. More often than not, she refused to look, but sometimes he ordered, "Come look at this!"

And she did.

Chapter 32

Mike was so entrenched in bringing Eric down, it was just ridiculous. I told him, "You really need to leave this guy alone."

—Sandra Harward

Sometime around the beginning of the year, Sandra Harward drove into Kaufman for a consultation on a case and dropped in on Mark and Mike in the DA's office for a friendly chitchat. She also wanted to talk to them about the charge still hanging over Eric: the law library theft.

"Do you really need to keep pursing Eric? You need to leave him alone," she told Mark.

Saying that Mike planned to go forward with the charges, Mark admitted that it wasn't something he initially wanted to handle. Instead, he told Harward what he'd told others, that he wanted Mike to appoint a special prosecutor. Then he said, "Mike and I are both carrying guns all the time."

"So now everybody's got a gun. It sounds like the Wild West," she answered.

After her conversation with Mark, Harward talked to Mike in his office. "You aren't going to keep this going, are you? You've done enough, right?"

"We're going to bring Eric Williams to his knees," Mike answered.

"Why are you pursuing this?" she asked. "You've already nailed him to the cross."

"Until we get him for everything we can, we're not stopping," Mike answered.

"You won. You got his license, Mike, it's time to stop. No good can come of this."

Then Mike said, "We're going to destroy Eric Williams."

Not long after, Mark called an old friend, Colleen Dunbar, about a case she was handling in Kaufman, and she mentioned that she'd decided to refer it to a local attorney, maybe Eric Williams. "You haven't heard?" Mark said. He then recounted all that had happened, and that Eric had been disbarred.

In that same conversation, he said that he'd been threatened, although he didn't identify by whom. "Now I'm carrying a gun. I leave the courthouse by a different door every day."

At the house on Blarney Stone Way, Mike McLelland had been trying for months to connect with the installer for his new ADT security system, but kept missing the appointments. Finally, he met the installer at the house, and Mike and the man discussed what he wanted: a state-of-the-art system, one with sensors on all the doors and windows, with cameras. The Pulse system hooked up to the Internet to allow remote surveillance. In the living room, a camera was placed to catch the inside of the front door.

That month at the Kaufman DA's office, Bill Wirskye worked as a special prosecutor on a murder case. He'd been appointed before Mike took over as DA, tried the case, and got a conviction. When it was overturned on appeal, Mike asked him to prosecute it again.

A former college basketball player, Wirskye stood nearly six-foot-eight. Out of law school, he'd hired on at the Dallas DA's office and stayed for a dozen years, although long after Mark left. Working his way up to chief prosecutor in charge of a court, he tried the infamous "Red Bird Rapist" and alleged serial killer David Wayne McCall, getting two life sentences for sexual assaults.

A partner in a firm with an office in downtown Dallas, despite his expanding forehead, the forty-seven-year-old retained a boyishness about him, with his ready smile, except in the courtroom, where he turned markedly serious.

Although he'd never met Mike McLelland before, Wirskye immediately liked the big man with the deep voice, and one day he met Cynthia when she brought cookies up to the office.

As Wirskye's trial unfolded, Mike sat in often. And off and on, Mark popped into the courtroom to watch. During downtimes, Wirskye waited in the DA's office, and Mark kept him company, as always eager to tell stories. Some days, Mark talked about his mother, whose care he oversaw, his brother, and his niece. He seemed proud of all of them. And Mark talked about his dreams, retirement plans that included flying his airplanes around the country.

Bill Wirskye in his office
Courtesy of Nicole McGuire Photography

For years before they met in Kaufman, Wirskye had known Mark Hasse's name from hearing about him in the Dallas DA's office. Other lawyers still talked about Mark and the cases he'd tried. The wiry prosecutor with the outsize courtroom presence hadn't been forgotten.

During the trial, Wirskye heard rumors that the killer's family fumed at him, leaving him on edge. Mornings when he parked in the county lot, he fought off a nagging anxiety. Although nearly in the center of town, the site seemed secluded. As he walked to the courthouse, he glanced around, considering the lonely place. The county tax office and stores backed up on it, but none looked out over the lot, no windows with people to see what transpired. Across the street, curtains blocked the view from a row of small frame houses.

"The sheriff is worried about this family making threats," Wirskye told his law partner, Toby Shook, one evening. Then Wirskye went on to describe the disquieting feeling he'd had parking his car in the lot. "It would be a great place for an ambush."

"Do you think it's serious?" Shook asked.

"I don't know," Wirskye answered. "But it is isolated. You could get picked off easy."

During closing arguments, Mike and Mark sat in the courtroom listening to Wirskye lay out the case and ask for justice. While the jury deliberated, Mark waited with Wirskye for the decision. Often a nervous time, it can drag. As they talked, Wirskye thought Mark wanted to help him take his mind off what was unfolding in the jury room. "Do you find enough to keep busy in Kaufman? To keep you interested?" Wirskye asked.

"I do," Mark answered, looking satisfied. "I like it here."

While he noticed the gun Mark wore in a holster, Wirskye thought little of it. Some prosecutors wore guns. Being worried about one's safety came with the job.

Word came that the jury had a verdict, and the men went to hear the defendant pronounced guilty.

That same month, someone else had an odd feeling about the county parking lot. Brandi Fernandez, too, had received a threat, and when Mark heard about it, he insisted on walking her to her car each evening. "I don't want you going out there alone," he told her.

"Mark, they're not *that* mad at me," Fernandez protested, but not too much, rather touched by Mark's protective urge. As they walked, they talked shop, and one afternoon Mark remarked about how impressed he was with Bill Wirskye's courtroom skills. "You know," Mark said. "If something happened to me, that's who I'd want to prosecute my case."

On Saturday, January 26, Eric had Kim drive him to downtown Kaufman to the county parking lot. Looking around at the deserted scene, even lonelier on a weekend, he said, "This is where I'm going to kill Fuck Stick."

The killing would take place early in the day, he said, when people arrived at work, because that would benefit from the "shock factor." The brazenness of the murder would stun witnesses enough so that they wouldn't recall details. "They won't believe their own eyes."

As they sat in the lot talking, Eric pointed to where Mark habitually parked his Dually. Apparently Eric had been watching and knew the spot. Not objecting, Kim nodded. She'd long since given up arguing. By then, Eric hovered constantly over her. He drove with her to the store to buy her cigarettes, and trailed her outside the house when she smoked, followed her on her daily visits to her parents' house. "I felt trapped," she said. "I felt as if his eyes were always on me."

In the days that followed, Eric prepared.

At Gibson Self Storage, he continued to come and go, and at home he watched Craigslist for a car. The day after they assessed the parking lot, Eric responded to an ad for a Mercury Sable, silver with a gray leather interior, listed for $1,500. It had 235,000 miles on it, but the transmission had been overhauled a couple of years earlier.

That day, January 27, Eric and Kim drove in his black Sport Trac to the owner's office on I–35 in Dallas to take a look.

"It's for my daughter," Eric told the man. Kim stayed in the car, and Eric had dressed in khaki pants and a bland shirt, clothes he thought a dad would wear.

Multiple things struck the man selling the car as odd that day, including that Eric didn't take a test drive. The man thought that if he wanted a car for his daughter, he'd be concerned about its condition. But Eric said he had a good mechanic, so he wasn't worried.

To pay, Eric pulled out $1,500 in cash. The man hand-wrote a bill of sale and gave Eric paperwork from the auction where he'd purchased the car. With that, the man left, assuming Eric and the woman with the ponytail, who still hadn't left the car, would soon drive off.

Instead, twenty minutes later, the man returned to find a tow truck taking away Eric's Sport Trac, which had stopped running. After the tow truck left, Eric and Kim departed in the Sable. On Overlook, Eric pulled around the house to the back, hiding his purchase behind the three-car garage, where it wouldn't be seen from the street.

The next day, Kim followed Eric in her car as he drove the Sable to Seagoville, to a parking lot close to Gibson Self Storage, behind an auto parts store in a nearly deserted strip center. He parked the Sable, locked it, and they left. As they drove, Eric explained that he'd watched carpoolers leave cars in the lot, which convinced him no one would notice one more parked car.

At the house on Overlook, he showed her two handguns he had hidden in the bedroom.

"I'm going to use these," he said.

When he played his games as a boy, Eric pretended to be great heroes and evil villains. Later that day he modeled his murder costume for Kim, all black like the gunmen in the *Tombstone* movie. As she watched, he turned so she could appreciate the nylon jacket with a bulletproof vest underneath, dark pants, and a strange hood with mesh over the face. He offered her a similar hood, a dark purple. Considering it, Kim refused, worried it could prevent her from seeing well enough to drive. When Eric mentioned that after the shooting the police might come to their door, he ordered, "If anyone shows up, just don't talk to them."

As to when it would happen, Eric gave Kim a date: the coming Thursday morning, on January 31. That night, Kim took more than her usual meds, "to knock myself out, because now it was real."

Chapter 33

Eric left, and I suddenly realized I was alone. I got in the car, and I drove to JJs, the convenience store where I bought my cigarettes. I thought there'd be a pay phone there. But the phone was broken, smashed. I just drove back home.

—Kim Williams

Later Kim wouldn't remember who she planned to call the day she drove to the convenience store, or why she couldn't use her own phone. She also couldn't explain why she didn't drive to another pay phone. "The drugs made everything hazy," she said. "I couldn't think."

That week at the DA's office, one of the secretaries tired of Mark's practical jokes and threatened to throw him out the window. She complained to Brandi Fernandez, who walked into Mark's office planning to give him a jab about it. But when she looked at him, he wore one of his old threadbare sweaters. "You know, you make it too easy," she said with a laugh.

Perhaps Mark understood, for at lunch he drove over to the Tanger Outlet Center in Terrell and bought a new suit, one he wore back to work that afternoon.

That Wednesday, January 30, at 5:30 p.m., Eric deactivated his Facebook account. An hour and a half later, he opened the door on Unit 18, at Gibson. By then the manager,

Larry Mathis, had left for the day. That night, Eric pulled out at 9:02.

Thursday, January 31, 2013, Eric woke Kim early. Dragging out of bed, she fed their three Pomeranians, and then Eric let the dogs outside, while Kim pulled on a dark navy blue sweat suit. When she returned to the kitchen, Eric wore the clothing he'd modeled for her, all black with combat boots.

"Leave your phone at home," he told her. "They can track them."

Outside the sun rose, and the day had a bright blue sky, the winter weather a few degrees above freezing. In the Sport Trac, Kim drove to the parking lot behind the auto parts store. There, Eric popped the trunk and transferred something into the Sable—the guns, Kim assumed.

In the truck, Kim followed Eric driving the Sable toward Kaufman. Once in the city, Eric turned toward the hospital where she'd once worked, then drove down a quiet street with few houses, much of the land undeveloped. Kim parked, and then got out. Eric moved over. In the driver's seat, she grasped the Mercury's wheel. With that, they headed toward the downtown business district, and the courthouse parking lot.

As Kim drove through the town square past the old Scott Pharmacy building that backed up to the lot, Eric pulled the hood over his head, securing it. "Park there," he said, indicating an area behind the stores and offices backing up to the lot. Kim did and they waited, but a man walked out and stood a short distance away and didn't leave. It made Eric nervous.

"Park in the lot," he ordered, pointing. "Over there."

In the lot, Eric told her to position the car facing an exit. "Keep the engine running," he muttered, as he unfolded a shiny silver sunshield across the front window. To Kim the tension inside the Sable was palpable as Eric ordered, "Watch for Fuck Stick's truck."

The lot wasn't particularly crowded at just after 8:30, although Thursdays could be one of the busier mornings at the courthouse. Instead, the spaces around the Sable remained empty. Without speaking, they waited, how long Kim couldn't estimate. Across the street, in the front yard of a small house, a parent displayed a sign cheering on the local high school football team, the Kaufman Lions, and no one had yet opened the garage-type doors at the Gomez Paint and Body Shop.

Nervous, to Kim every moment felt like hours. Then Eric pointed at Mark's maroon truck as he pulled into the lot, drove past them, and parked in his usual spot, halfway down the next row. Saying nothing, Eric jumped from the car.

As usual, Mark was running late. That morning he had a meeting with Andrew Jordan, the head of the county's public defender's office. Afterward, they had a hearing on an upcoming trial. Grabbing his canvas bag with his sack lunch inside, Mark exited the truck and walked toward the town square and the courthouse. As he had for more than a year, he wore a holster and gun, but on this cold winter morning, Mark buttoned his gray-and-white tweed coat over it.

In the Sable, Kim closed her eyes. "I hurt inside. I couldn't watch."

Country music blared in Lenda Bush's car as she drove into Kaufman. A salt-and-pepper-haired lawyer with an office in Terrell, she had a scheduled routine hearing. As she approached the courthouse, driving down Grove Street a block from the county lot, she saw a man in an overcoat walk toward the sidewalk that led to the courthouse. Just then another man, a heavier one dressed all in black, rushed toward him. When they met, the heavier man pushed the smaller man. She thought the men talked, before the heavier man bumped into the smaller man again. The altercation reminded Bush of boys in a school-yard.

Then the heavier man jammed his hand into the smaller man's neck, and she heard the crack of a gunshot. More gunfire followed, and the smaller man stumbled. The gunman shoved the other man again, hard, and the smaller man fell backward onto the pavement.

By then, Bush had approached the lot. She drove past as the gunman pulled a second gun, shot the man on the pavement, then shot into the air twice as he hurried toward a car in the lot.

Shocked, adrenaline surging, Bush turned into the lot and drove in front of the gunman's car, looking for a license plate, but didn't see one. As the sedan pulled away, Bush followed. The car drove fast but not too fast down Kaufman's quiet streets lined with wood-sided bungalows with small fenced yards, children's toys strewn about on the winter brown grass, flowerbeds covered by the previous fall's withered leaves.

On her phone, Bush tried to punch 911. Brand-new, her first smart phone after finally disposing of a flip phone she'd had for years, her hands shaking, she hit 991 instead. She tried again with the same result. After more tries and a couple of blocks, frustrated, Bush turned the car around. If she couldn't reach police, she needed to help the injured man in the lot.

When Eric jumped in, he'd slammed the Sable's door shut. Pulling the sunshade off the window, he ordered, "Drive!"

Kim didn't notice Lenda Bush's small blue car following. As she drove, Eric cautioned Kim not to speed, ordered her to turn right out of the lot, then take a quick left. Trying not to think about what had just happened, Kim did as in-structed, slowing to a crawl at the stop signs but rolling through. Behind the wheel, Kim's chest tightened with fear, but Eric looked excited.

At the street behind the hospital, Kim got into the Sport Trac to follow Eric in the Sable.

"It's a lawyer. Someone I know," Lenda Bush thought as she ran toward the man on the pavement. The slender man in the coat lay on his back, his eyes open, blood beginning to pool near his head and shoulder. Bush couldn't see his chest rise as he took in air. Falling to her knees, she began methodically pumping his chest, starting CPR. "Call 911!" she shouted at the people who had started to gather. "Get an ambulance!"

At first, she didn't recognize the man on the ground, as she worked hard to try to save his life. He'd fallen next to the street, at an entrance to the lot, under a bright yellow metal arch intended to keep out large trucks. The man's glasses, twisted in the altercation, lay nearby, along with his canvas bag. Every once in a while, the man struggled as if trying to take a breath. At first, Bush thought the man had freckles, but then realized he had blood spatter on his face.

Someone in the lot, a woman, cried out: "It's Mark."

Mark? Bush looked down at the man's face. "Of course it is," Bush thought. She knew Mark Hasse. She liked him, enjoyed talking to him and hearing his stories. In fact, if she'd arrived in the lot minutes earlier, she would have rushed to walk to the courthouse with him. Instead, he lay on the ground, bleeding.

"You okay?" she said as she pushed on his chest. In the distance she heard sirens. "Of course you're not, but you will be. Help is coming. Hang in there."

Half a mile away, Kaufman PD officer Jason Stastny, a husky man in a dark blue uniform, heard the shots. In his patrol car, he followed the sound, and as he rounded the corner near Grove Street, found Bush hunched over a figure on the pavement. He ran to her, shouting, "I'll do that."

Tired from the effort, Bush moved away. By then, officers, passersby congregated. "He got shot in his face," Stastny said, his dash camera picking up his words. "He's not breathing."

As Stastny pressed on Mark's chest, the injured man's lower body jerked up, then collapsed like a lifeless mannequin. "Come on Mark, buddy. Come on," the officer urged. Sporadically Mark gasped, a hoarse, unnatural attempt at pulling in air. "There you go. There you go!" Stastny urged. "Come on Mark, take a breath!"

Five minutes after Stastny arrived, another siren blared. His voice raspy from the effort, Stastny said, "EMS is almost here. The ambulance is coming."

A minute later, the rig pulled up and EMTs rushed toward the men carrying a yellow backboard, while Stastny shouted a rundown of Mark's condition.

"Anyone know anything about him?" one of the EMTs asked.

Police and EMTs clustered around Mark Hasse in the parking lot
Evidence photo

"He's one of the DA prosecutors," Stastny answered. He estimated Mark had been down perhaps five minutes, but by then at least ten minutes had lapsed since the gunshots, and it had been three minutes or more since Mark had taken a breath. As in the background officers strung yellow crime scene tape around the parking lot and street, the EMTs loaded Mark into the ambulance.

While the others struggled to help Mark, Lenda Bush returned to her car and pulled out a pad of paper and a pen. Still fresh in her mind, she drew the shape of the taillights on the car she'd followed, the one with the gunman inside, hoping to help police identify the type of car. She'd been in a panic, and she couldn't remember the color of the car. She didn't know what make, but she thought some kind of light-colored sedan. Maybe a Ford Taurus.

As soon as she could, she gave the drawing to one of the officers, but then later saw it lying on the ground. This time she handed it to a state trooper and asked, "Do you know what kind of car this is?"

On the highway, Kim drove the Sport Trac, following Eric in the Sable. Nervous, she missed the exit to Gibson, circled back, and when she arrived, Eric waited in the lot across the street. He then drove to the gate, pressed the code associated with Unit 18, and she followed him through at 9:12 that morning, approximately thirty-four minutes after the shooting.

In front of Unit 18, Kim waited while Eric pulled the Sable inside. She lowered the door, but not all the way, leaving a gap at the bottom. Standing outside, she heard Eric spray something on the car, and she assumed he wiped it for fingerprints. Tense, the time dragged for Kim, until eighteen minutes later when Eric popped the door open and walked out wearing blue jeans and a shirt. He turned the key in the lock, and minutes later, back on the highway, they headed toward their house. "That car is FBI," Eric said, sounding almost gleeful as a black car passed them on the way to Kaufman.

"Did he say anything?" she asked.

"Yeah," Eric said, looking proud. "Fuck Stick said, 'No, no, please, please, no!'"

At the house, they parked the Sport Trac around the back. Once inside, Kim took more pills, this time Valium, and went to bed, while Eric turned on the television.

"There's a shooting!" a man yelled as he ran across the street in front of the courthouse. "Someone's been shot."

At the scene, police asked questions of the witnesses. Lenda Bush described what she saw. She thought the gunman and Mark talked, but she hadn't heard the conversation. The gunman was the larger of the two men. At one point an officer asked, "Could the gunman have been Eric Williams?"

Lenda knew Eric. They'd worked on cases together. But she hadn't been in Kaufman during the trial, and didn't realize how contentious it became. She also hadn't seen him in years and didn't realize that he'd put on weight, or that he might have worn a flak jacket that made him look heavier, or considered that the gunman stood on the high side of the entrance ramp, making him look taller. "Why would I think it was Eric?" she said. "No, it wasn't Eric. This guy was too big to be Eric."

"I heard the man say, 'I'm sorry. I'm sorry,'" another witness said in Spanish. That morning the man opened the doors to the Gomez body shop, across the street from the lot, just as he heard gunfire. There to prep a car for painting, he hid and watched, and he saw the gunman fire into Mark's body, then up in the air as he walked away. The man emptied one gun, pulled another, eight shots in all. "I think the two men knew each other. The man who got shot tried to push the gun away."

At first police doubted Patricia Luna saw the shooting

from inside the small gym the county had for employees in what used to be a bank drive-through on the edge of the parking lot. Working out when she heard the shots, Luna peeked through the blinds and saw a man dressed in black shooting up in the air as he walked away. She did recall that he wore a bulletproof vest and army-type boots. Like the other two witnesses, Luna described the car as a light-colored sedan. "Someone else was driving," she said. "The man got in the passenger side."

At the tax assessor's office that backed up to the lot, one of Tonya Ratcliff's employees told her she heard shots. "Lock the doors," Ratcliff ordered. "Everyone needs to stay put."

At the courthouse the county judge, Bruce Wood, watched through his office window as the street filled with police cars. Seconds later a secretary came in and said, "Judge, Mark Hasse's been shot."

In the DA's office, many gathered and stared out the windows. No one yet knew what had happened, just that someone heard what he thought might be gunfire. At her desk, Mark's assistant, Amanda Morris, expected him in. She called his cell. When he didn't answer, she called again. "Maybe it was a car backfiring?" she wondered. Sometimes Mark forgot to turn on the ringtone, so maybe he just didn't hear his phone.

"Someone's been shot," she heard one of the lawyers say.

"Oh my God. What if it's Mark?" Her hands shaking, Morris called again.

Another member of the staff, Michelle Bork, had just arrived when she heard there'd been shots fired. Word spread quickly through the office that it was an assistant district attorney, and that the man was gravely injured, but they had no other information. Around Bork, people paced, whispering about who it could be. By then offices and stores throughout downtown Kaufman barred their doors, and the schools in the city had gone on lockdown.

"Everyone stays put," Brandi Fernandez announced. With Mike not in yet, Fernandez, as the first assistant, took charge at the DA's office. For information, she dispatched two of the office's investigators to find out what happened. One, Bruce Bryant, worked for Mark. At the parking lot, Bryant ran up moments before the EMTs loaded Mark into the ambulance.

"Bruce says it's Mark," one of the staff told Bork, after Bryant reported in. "It doesn't look good."

In the office, Bork thought the others looked the way she felt: stunned, "ghost faced." Her heart racing, she felt frantic. Picking up her phone, she called Mike McLelland, who had stopped at a meeting on his way in to the office. Around Bork, people cried.

"Mark's been shot," she said. "It's bad."

At 9:48 that morning, the *Dallas Morning News* reported a shooting outside the Kaufman County courthouse. On the paper's Web site, the victim was identified as a county employee, who'd been shot several times. A minute later, they identified the man as an assistant district attorney. In their first official statement, police announced that two suspects dressed in black fled in a light-colored sedan, maybe a silver one, perhaps a Taurus.

Not long after, Mark's mother called the Kaufman DA's office. She'd heard the reports, tried Mark's cell phone, and he hadn't answered. "Is he okay?" she asked.

"We're trying to contact everyone and account for them," the person answered, not wanting to tell her the bad news over the phone. Instead, a state trooper had been dispatched to talk to her in person.

Chaos spread through the Kaufman courthouse. A trial was interrupted in Judge Wiley's courtroom, the jurors locked down inside. In the DA's office, Brandi Fernandez stationed officers holding AR–15s at the doors. "We didn't know if we were under attack," one said.

The sub-courthouse went on lockdown as well, and in the IT department Lori Friemel immediately thought of Eric Williams. She bolted the door, and took out her pistol.

As soon as he heard, Mike drove directly to the hospital. When he arrived, an ER doctor broke the news: Mark was dead. Moments later, County Judge Wood walked in and the two men gathered with Sheriff Byrnes, who'd been driving in to work when he heard the news.

Looking at the sheriff, Mike said, "Eric Williams did this. He killed Mark."

The sheriff looked uncertain, but he didn't dismiss the possibility. Instead he turned to one of his deputies and said, "Go find Eric Williams."

A short time later, Mike stood over Mark's body as Johnny Perry, in his official duty as justice of the peace, conducted a death investigation, counting gunshot wounds and writing up an autopsy order. From the failed attempt to save him, Mark still had a ventilator in his throat. Perry noted a large, bloody hole on the left side of Mark's neck, and other injuries scattered across his body. When the ER nurse cut off Mark's clothes, a bullet fragment had fallen out, one she placed in a sterile cup to preserve as evidence. Under his coat, she found his holster still holding his Glock. The leads from the heart monitor hung from his thin, bare chest.

"Eric Williams killed Mark. I know he did!" Mike said to Perry, seething.

Perry didn't disagree. He remembered the day Mark warned him that Eric could turn to violence. As the DA and the JP talked, Perry signed the autopsy order, writing "Please Rush" across it. Although Perry didn't respond to Mike's suspicions, he said, "I shared his thoughts."

"The MF killed Mark," Mike told Michelle Bork when he called the office. Although he didn't use Eric's name, Bork understood. "Get the staff together and come here."

Not everyone showed up at the hospital that day. One frightened woman, an assistant DA, got into her car, and never returned. But the others congregated at the hospital, many emotional, some crying, as Mike brought in a chaplain to console them.

"It looks like Mark was targeted," Mike told his staff. "We're going to work together and figure out who did this."

As they talked, some in the office voiced the opinion that it appeared to be a professional hit. "But the heavy prevalence was that it was Eric," said Brandi Fernandez.

The chaplain said a prayer, as the DA's staff joined in, fighting back fear and disbelief. "We all knew it could happen. We got threat letters from inmates all the time," Fernandez said. "But this was reality. This was your worst nightmare coming true."

Once alone, Mike talked to Bruce Bryant. The two men knew each other well, and Mike quickly told him his theory focused on Eric's involvement in the killing. While Mike doubted that Eric "had the guts" to kill Mark, he thought Eric manipulated someone else into doing it.

One way or the other, "I know Eric Williams is responsible for this," Mike said.

About 10:30 that morning, two hours after the shooting, Constable Shawn Mayfield, at his office across from Eric's old one at the sub-courthouse, received a phone call from a sheriff's deputy who wanted to know if Mayfield knew where Eric lived. When Mayfield said he did, the deputy asked Mayfield to show him the house. A short time later, five sheriff's deputies and Mayfield pulled up outside the Overlook house. While the others went to the door, Mayfield hung back, wondering if Eric watched from inside, feeling exposed on the street. Like Mike, Mayfield thought of Eric as soon as he heard of the shooting.

The deputy at Eric's door rang the bell, and they waited. No one answered.

As the deputies turned to leave, however, a contractor working on the house across the street called to them. "There's somebody in that house." The man had heard sirens downtown, and a while later saw someone driving fast turn onto Overlook and swing into Eric's driveway. The brakes squealed when the black pickup disappeared behind the garage.

As the deputies listened to the man talk, Eric suddenly opened his front door. "Why are you here?" he asked. He had his arm in a sling.

"Mark Hasse's been shot," one said. "We need to know where you were this morning."

Looking shocked, Eric huffed, as if taken off guard. Then Eric said he'd just returned a short time before from picking up a prescription for Kim. When the deputy asked Eric about the sling, Eric said he'd recently had rotator cuff surgery.

"We'd like to swab your hands for GSR," the deputy said. Eric agreed, and the deputy opened a kit with a glue stick inside, ran it over Eric's hands, and then sealed it to send to the lab.

"We'd like to come in and look around," he asked. "Do we have your permission?"

"Not you," Eric said, but then he pointed at Mayfield. "But Constable Mayfield can come in. I know him."

Walking into a house with a man who might have just committed a murder was not a pleasant idea, so Mayfield brought another deputy with him. As they entered, Mayfield kept Eric where he could watch him. As he scanned the rooms, Mayfield had specific things on his mind: the dark clothing matching the description of what the gunman wore, anything with blood on it, weapons.

Since the gunman got in the passenger seat, Mayfield

also looked for another person, the getaway driver. The first room Eric walked them into was the master bedroom. "Please be quiet. My wife's very sick, and she's sleeping," he said.

In the dim room, Mayfield saw a woman in bed. He wouldn't have taken her for Eric's wife. She looked older. Much older. Hearing the men walk in, Kim propped up on her elbows and looked at them. "What's going on?" she asked.

"They're just looking around," Eric said.

With that, Kim lay back down, and Mayfield thought no more about her, never suspecting she could have been the accomplice. Later she'd say she didn't know what she would have said had Mayfield or the other deputy questioned her, although with Eric peering at her through the door, perhaps she would have said nothing.

Walking through the house, Mayfield was shocked by the chaos surrounding him. Clothing, books, boxes, computer gear stacked haphazardly on countertops and the floor, piled high. Empty two-liter plastic Coke bottles filled a bathtub. The disorder didn't fit Mayfield's observations of Eric Williams. At the JP office, he'd always been meticulously dressed.

In the living room, Mayfield noticed two or three TVs, and on the kitchen bar, computers.

In stark contrast to the disheveled appearance of the house, the garage looked nearly immaculate. Mayfield saw no silver or light-colored sedan, no Taurus or similar car as described by those who'd witnessed Mark Hasse's execution.

Back in the house at the front door, Mayfield thanked Eric. Outside, the constable relayed what he'd seen to the others, and they scattered and drove away.

Later that afternoon, Kim climbed slowly out of bed, her senses dulled by the drugs. In the kitchen, she found Eric watching television and chuckling, on a high from the murder. "I put that old sling on my arm, so they'd think I couldn't fire a gun," he said, appearing proud. "They won't question me anymore."

When she went to throw clothes in the wash, she couldn't find the navy blue warm-ups she'd worn. "You don't have to worry about that," Eric said, proudly. "I took care of that, too."

At the same time, the investigators on the scene bumped Mayfield on the radio in his squad car, and asked him to report downtown. There he described his walkthrough at Eric's house, and said that he saw nothing to tie Eric to the crime. Still, Mayfield's instincts needled him.

"We need to watch for his truck," he said. "I feel like I just talked to the killer."

Things moved quickly that morning. By 11:15 a.m., the dead assistant DA's body was on a table at the Southwestern Institute of Forensic Sciences in Dallas, and the chief medical examiner, Jeffrey Barnard, M.D., inspected the corpse. Two representatives of the Kaufman sheriff's office stood by, one of them Lieutenant Jolie Stewart, and two Kaufman PD officers. As might be expected, the victim's identity complicated the task. Everyone gathered knew Mark Hasse. Stewart had talked to him often over the years and liked him. "I had to put that in a box and separate it out," she said. "If I was going to do my job."

As Barnard assessed the body, he wrote in his notes that Mark looked older than his fifty-seven years. The physician then went on to document the dead man's scars, many dating back to the plane crash. When Barnard cut back the skin on the scalp, he uncovered metallic sutures and brads, where seventeen years earlier surgeons had pieced Mark's skull back together.

Quickly Barnard turned to the new injuries. Documenting five gunshot wounds, the physician focused first on the one would-be rescuers noted at the scene, labeled "GSW #1." That bullet entered in front of the left ear and fractured the skull. Once inside the skull, it shattered and spread, hemorrhaging and bruising a large section of Mark's brain. As he worked, Barnard recovered fragments he placed in envelopes for the lab.

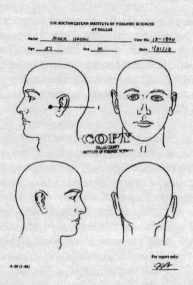

The autopsy diagram depicting the bullet to Mark Hasse's head

The next two GSWs entered from the back. Number two traveled toward the right, cutting through the trunk. On the way, it pierced the upper lobe of the left lung, perforating the trachea and the esophagus, before entering the right chest cavity, where it cut into the upper lobe of the right lung. Number three pierced Mark's left mid-back, damaging a lung before escaping through the chest. In the autopsy report Barnard explained that GSWs two and three combined to result in a blood pool inside the dead man's right chest cavity.

Under conclusions, Barnard wrote: "It is our opinion that Mark Edmund Hasse died as a result of injuries from multiple gunshot wounds." Under manner of death, he wrote: "Homicide."

Chapter 34

I asked the Kaufman PD captain where his chief was. Chief Aulbaugh was in Dallas at a conference. I said, "If you don't want to work it, we'll work it." A while later, I was told the chief said Kaufman PD would work Mark's murder. At that point, Chief Aulbaugh took the lead on the case.

—Sheriff David Byrnes

After he left Mike McLelland at the hospital, Sheriff Byrnes drove back to the scene. By then, the roped-off area had grown to two square blocks. The sheriff's department moved in their mobile command center, and the forensic team searched for evidence. One of the first things they noticed was a lack of any. Everything they did find tied back to Mark. They had the blood pool on the cement, his twisted glasses, his briefcase with his lunch, but nothing attributed to the killer. Most notably, they discovered no spent casings littering the pavement. That suggested the gunman fired a revolver, which doesn't expel but retains shells inside the cylinder.

While the forensic team worked, the area flooded with law enforcement, official cars from throughout the area. The media followed. Word spread, and soon the press swarmed just outside the yellow tape line. TV satellite vans with their mobile towers ringed Kaufman's downtown, parked on narrow side streets, waiting to beam reports to Dallas TV stations, ones that would then proliferate the news across the state and eventually the nation and the world.

None yet revealed the identity of the victim.

After the autopsy, Lieutenant Jolie Stewart, too, returned to the scene. Something struck her as she listened to Lenda Bush's account of the killing. The way it took place, that Bush thought the gunman talked to Hasse, the bumping into him before he shot, not only seemed incredibly aggressive, but very personal. Considering the situation, Stewart thought about how angry someone would have to be to carry out such a scheme, how much they were willing to lose to kill in the light of day and in front of witnesses. The word "brazen" occurred to Stewart.

Going with the accounts of the witnesses who thought the gunman had an accomplice, the alert issued via radio to law enforcement was to be on the lookout for a light-colored sedan, possibly a silver Taurus, and, based on Eric's costume at the scene, two men dressed in black.

A who's who of the county's law enforcement responded. Chief Deputy Rodney Evans from the sheriff's department and Texas Ranger Eric Kasper, assigned to work the Kaufman area, drove the area roads, watching for the sedan. By then Kasper, a tall man with a long face, wearing the rangers' official silver belly cowboy hat, badge proudly displayed on a crisp white shirt, had called in for help, and DPS helicopters circled overhead, taking photos. Yet none happened upon the getaway car.

Although he'd followed the theft trial in the newspapers, Kasper hadn't been involved in Eric's prosecution. Yet he wasn't surprised when he heard the sheriff's office had sent investigators to find the former JP. "I knew Eric probably wasn't happy."

At the courthouse, Eric's attorney friend Jenny Parks walked around a corner and heard Mike McLelland say, "Eric Williams did this."

Texas Ranger Eric Kasper
Kathryn Casey

"No, he didn't, Mike," Parks interrupted him.

"Yes, he did," Mike insisted.

A short time later she e-mailed Eric her phone number and the message: "Call me."

When he did, Parks told him, "Some folks are saying that it's you."

"Don't worry, Jenny," Eric assured her. "I'm at home watching TV. They were already here and did a GSR test on me. They left. They know it wasn't me."

"Okay. Just wanted to make sure you're okay and you know what's going on."

"It's terrible," Eric said.

In Dallas, Bill Wirskye was in his law office working on a defense for a client indicted on a murder charge when his phone rang. One of the assistant prosecutors in Kaufman, an old friend, told him that Mark Hasse had just been murdered outside the courthouse.

"Let me know if you need any help," Wirskye said, saddened at the realization that Mark, a man he'd spent hours talking to just weeks earlier, was dead.

"We'll probably need a special prosecutor," she said. "We'll keep in touch."

Wirskye's law partner, Toby Shook, was at the Dallas courthouse that morning when word spread that one of their former prosecutors, Mark Hasse, had been gunned down. When Shook had been a young up-and-coming assistant DA, he used to sit in on Mark's trials, watching his passion in the courtroom.

Shook, a short, fit, intense man with dark eyes and hair, felt the tension in the air, heard people talking all around him about what sounded like an execution near the town square. During his decades as a Dallas prosecutor, many times Shook had been asked if he was afraid. He'd always told himself that no one would come after a prosecutor. But now it had happened, and Mark was dead.

The irony didn't escape Shook when Wirskye called and described where Mark died, in the exact location Wirskye had worried about weeks earlier, the secluded county parking lot. "It all felt eerie," Wirskye said. "I had this chill run through me when I heard. I could picture the spot, how it took place."

Ernie Zepeda's wife called him that morning to tell him that Mark had been murdered. "It's probably that darn Eric Williams," he responded. Months earlier, Zepeda had quit his job at the Kaufman County Sheriff's Office (KCSO). The rest of the day after Mark's murder, Zepeda assumed someone from the sheriff's office would call him, wanting to talk to him about Eric, but no one did. So Zepeda drove to KCSO headquarters in the law enforcement center just outside town. When he got there, everyone appeared too busy to talk, and he told one person, "Listen, if anyone needs me, tell them to call."

No one called.

Other friends of Mark's called KCSO that morning and got similar responses, including one who specifically told the investigator that they needed to look into Eric. "We already did," the investigator answered.

At home, Ron Herrington, the former cop turned lawyer, clicked on the television and saw the news reports. When he found out the victim was Mark Hasse, he, too, called KCSO headquarters and got patched through to an investigator. "You know that Eric Williams probably did this," Herrington said.

"No, we talked to him," the man said. "Eric had his arm in a sling. It couldn't be him."

"Bullshit," Herrington hissed. "If he didn't shoot Mark, he hired someone to do it."

As they talked, Herrington considered all the times Mark predicted that Eric might kill him, and now Mark was dead. Who else was in danger? Herrington wondered how much Eric might be capable of. Would he blow up the courthouse? "When you've got somebody saying 'I think this guy might kill me,' that's a good suspect," Herrington said to the investigator.

The man responded, again saying, "We already checked Eric out."

Wary, Herrington said, "Well, maybe you're right, but I don't think so."

Concerned, Herrington then called Kaufman PD headquarters, the inconspicuous, flat-roofed building tucked behind the city hall on Chestnut Street, where nineteen officers worked, mainly responding to nuisance calls, minor felonies, and the occasional domestic violence call. Most years there wasn't a murder in the city of Kaufman, and now they were overseeing a major homicide. "Tell the chief that I think it might be Eric Williams," Herrington said. The man said he would, but no one ever called Herrington back to ask why he believed that might be true.

At 10:50 that morning, Kaufman PD's chief, Chris Aulbaugh, gave his first press conference announcing that the victim, an assistant DA, had died. As yet, Aulbaugh, the head of the lead agency on the case, wasn't releasing the dead man's name, although word of mouth spread quickly within the city. By then downtown Kaufman appeared awash with federal agents in dark windbreakers, the names of their agencies stenciled on their backs. They'd driven in to offer help, a not unusual occurrence when a killer targeted a member of law enforcement. The FBI, ATF, even Homeland Security responded, and as the head of the investigation, Chief Aulbaugh became the point person, the one issuing orders.

With a narrow reddish mustache and eyebrows, his short hair graying, formidable bags under his eyes, Aulbaugh had worked at and retired from Dallas PD. On the day Mark died, he had been chief in Kaufman for a year. Few working the investigation that day knew that like Eric Williams, Aulbaugh was a member of the state guard, in the same regiment, the Nineteenth.

Sometime that morning a message came through to the chief's phone from Command Sergeant Major Roger Williams, the same man who a month earlier had rented a storage unit for Eric. The text was on the order of: You don't think the captain could have done this, do you?

The man Roger referred to was former Texas State Guard Captain Eric Williams.

"Oh my God, Eric," Sharon Holbrook, the PI who worked on his theft case, texted to Eric that morning. "I just heard about Hasse. . . . The guy was a shit, but no one deserves to die for doing his job."

"Yeah, I know," Eric responded. "What a shock. It appears it was a professional hit."

Not long after, John Sickel called Eric, worried. "Where are you?"

"At home, in my kitchen eating a bowl of cereal," Eric said, and his attorney immediately felt calmer. "Why?"

"Mark Hasse was murdered."

"Really?" Eric said, and Sickel thought that his client sounded surprised.

In her oncologist's office waiting for an appointment, Michelle Sutton heard the news. "It's Eric Williams," she said. "He killed Mark. No doubt."

"Are we in danger?" her husband, Rob, asked.

"Well, if it is him, I was second chair on his case at first. Maybe we are." Instead of driving home, after her appointment they detoured to their local police department and asked to talk to an investigator. "I think Eric Williams killed Mark Hasse," she told an officer, and then she explained why.

Around that time in downtown Kaufman, the blood spatter expert from the department of public safety (DPS) inspected the crime scene and thought he could picture how the murder took place. He diagrammed a trail of blood where EMTs moved the body to the ambulance. But in three other places it appeared someone had dripped blood. Considering the pattern, the blood expert surmised that as each bullet hit Mark, he'd taken a step or two, staggered and bled, until he finally fell, the pool of blood collecting near his head.

On the scene, another investigator found grooves in the concrete, places that resembled bullet strikes. Treated with chemicals, the areas tested positive for lead and copper, confirming the suspicion. As they searched, the forensic team recovered two bullet fragments that they bagged and checked in as evidence.

While the investigation ramped up in Kaufman, in Houston that morning, federal prosecutors announced that two members of the Aryan Brotherhood of Texas pleaded guilty on federal racketeering charges from the indictments that came down three months earlier, the same cases in which the Kaufman County DA's office played a small part.

Before long, a Dallas reporter published an article speculating that there might be a connection between Mark's murder and the plea bargains, based on the theory of an anonymous source. At noon, her story hit the Internet: "Authorities with knowledge of the [murdered] assistant DA's caseload said he had been heavily involved in the investigation of members of the Aryan Brotherhood."

Mark hadn't been involved in the ABT cases, but from that point on, it seemed the news stories routinely cited a possible connection between his murder and the prison gang. As far away as the United Kingdom, London's *Daily Mail* reported: "Manhunt for gunman as county prosecutor involved in Aryan Brotherhood investigation is shot dead."

Although word leaked and some sources had already reported it, Mark's identity wasn't officially confirmed until 1:25 that afternoon by Sheriff Byrnes during another press conference. "We have no concrete information . . . we are pursuing every avenue right now." Regarding the killing of a prosecutor, he said, "I've been [in law enforcement] for forty-three years, and I have never experienced anything like this before."

At the same press conference, Chief Aulbaugh told reporters he didn't see Mark as a random victim. Instead, he believed he'd been specifically targeted: "The fact it was not an ongoing rampage, it was one individual being shot and then [the gunman] leaving the scene. It was very small, very confrontational."

As events swirled around them, Mike brought his staff back to the DA's office, inside the locked-down courthouse. He had lunch brought in, so they could share their grief. Family and friends called, checking on them. Brandi

Fernandez's daughters, in lockdown at their school, spent hours wondering if the dead prosecutor was their mother.

So much would later seem a blur in the bedlam that descended upon Kaufman. News dripped out slowly, sometimes wrong, as that afternoon when the Dallas DA, Craig Watkins, wrote to his staff that an arrest had been made in Mark's murder. In the e-mail, Watkins urged his employees to be "aware of your surroundings. This is probably an isolated incident but until further notice if you plan to work past dark today, please be careful and ask security for assistance escorting you to your vehicles."

Soon after in Kaufman, Chief Aulbaugh held a news conference and labeled the Dallas DA's remark a mistake; no suspects had been apprehended. As part of the announcement, Aulbaugh informed reporters of added security measures around the courthouse, and that for the foreseeable future security would escort employees walking to and from the parking lot.

At Aulbaugh's side stood the sheriff and Mike McLelland. After the chief and sheriff talked, Mike took over the bank of microphones, splayed out in front of him like the ears of the world. Wearing his black cowboy hat, Mike embodied the bold man his family had always known, his deep voice edged in anger. With reporters he confirmed that his office—although not specifically Mark—had worked ABT cases, and that many possibilities existed, since each DA handled hundreds of cases. "We lost a really, really good man. He was an excellent friend and a spectacular prosecutor," Mike said. Then in a speech carried around the world, he challenged, "I hope that the people who did this are watching, because we're confident we're going to find you, pull you out of whatever hole you're in, bring you back, and let the people of Kaufman County prosecute you to the full extent of the law."

Judge Wood stood beside Mike and thought the DA's

Mike McLelland at the news conference, with Texas Rangers Major
Dewayne Dockery (left, behind him)

speech had one target: Eric Williams. To Wood, it seemed
Mike intended to taunt the man he suspected of the murder.
"Perhaps Mike didn't realize how dangerous it was to poke
a stick at a sociopath," said Wood.

"Anything you can do to help us get our hands on this
scum would be appreciated," Mike told the public. After
the press conference, Mike walked back into the office, and
some in the staff noticed tears in his eyes.

At the house on Overlook, Kim stood next to Eric in the
kitchen as he watched the press conference, a cocky grin
on his face. "Look at Sluggo," he said, followed by a hearty
laugh. Kim paused a moment, listened to Mike mocking
the man she knew to be her husband. After the newscast
clicked off, she took another pill and walked back to the
bedroom to sleep.

At the sheriff's mobile command post, Ranger Eric Kasper and others worked late into the night. When he thought about how Mark died, it didn't seem real. A masked man all in black sounded more like a fictional character, someone out of a movie or a video game.

Late that night, the sheriff relocated the command post from the trailer into the old National Guard Armory Building on South Houston Street. Being used as a training center, the white brick building had a sign out front with a picture of a badge. As the head of the investigation, Chief Aulbaugh claimed a room and put a hand-lettered sign on the door that read: "COMMANDER'S OFFICE." Before long others settled into desks, investigators from Kaufman PD, the sheriff's office, an ATF agent, and Texas Rangers. When he arrived, Ranger Kasper looked around and saw resources pouring in, to an extent he'd rarely experienced in any case.

The public responded as well. At the local Crime Stoppers branch, reward money funneled in, the amount rising in less than a day to more than $20,000 for information leading to the arrest of the killer or killers.

While many struggled with the new reality—that in Kaufman an assistant district attorney had been gunned down in bright sunlight on a downtown street—Judge Glen Ashworth packed a bag and left. His destination Dallas, he planned to spend his nights there for the duration. As soon as Ashworth heard of Mark Hasse's murder, his thoughts turned to his former protégé, Eric Williams.

Chapter 35

The normal role of an investigator we didn't have, where we would go out beating the bushes. Instead we followed up on tips coming in. . . . It was Kaufman PD's case, and that's what we were told to do.

—Texas Ranger Eric Kasper

The following day, Friday, February 1, the Kaufman County Courthouse reopened, but nothing felt normal; armed police escorted employees from the parking lot. A formidable law enforcement presence covered the quaint downtown, officers on corners and patrolling the streets, state troopers, Texas Rangers. The TV vans, too, remained, and reporters circulated to stores and offices, stopped passersby asking for comments.

Across the state, Mark Hasse's murder had spread fear, and district attorneys openly expressed anxieties. The Dallas County DA told *USA Today* that prosecutors "are people on the front lines. . . . we have a lot of individuals who have ill will toward our profession. Maybe this unfortunate circumstance will provide a wakeup call."

Much of the press coverage repeated the misinformation from the day before, labeling Mark Hasse as heavily involved in an investigation of the Aryan Brotherhood. Some noted the timing, Mark's murder occurring just hours before the two gang members pleaded guilty in Houston.

Something else popped up later that day in news reports: that Mark had told friends he was frightened, and that in the past year, he'd started carrying a gun.

Despite the rest of Kaufman's downtown reopening, the DA's office stayed shuttered. Yet the entire staff gathered behind locked doors, many distraught, some crying, banding together talking, comparing stories about Mark, wondering who murdered him. Eric Williams's name came up often, especially from Mike, who warned the staff to watch for the disgraced JP. In the office, many wondered about Mark's caseload, if Mark's files held clues.

The news reporters, too, delved into those possibilities, some wondering if the murder could be tied to Mark's past as head of the Dallas DA's organized crime unit. In all, as a prosecutor, there were hundreds of possibilities in Mark's past and present caseloads. Only a few news articles mentioned two high-profile Kaufman cases: a recent murder Mark prosecuted, and the case of a public official convicted of theft—former justice of the peace Eric Williams.

At the command post that day, Dallas-based FBI special agents Michael Hillman and Laurie Gibbs joined the investigation. With decades in law enforcement behind them, they'd worked many cases together. Their boss offered their services as soon as he heard of Mark's murder, but at first they'd been turned away. Gibbs and Hillman drove to Kaufman anyway, and when they suggested they could organize the command post, Chris Aulbaugh accepted. Before long, Gibbs and Hillman brought in desks, new computer lines, and supplies.

When Lieutenant Jolie Stewart saw federal and state agencies pouring into Kaufman, she wondered what part they'd play and if they'd all get along. She'd heard of local departments pushed to the side when the feds arrived. "I thought

FBI Special Agents Laurie Gibbs
and Michael Hillman
Kathryn Casey

maybe the Kaufman County Sheriff's Office wouldn't have much of a say."

Instead, all eyes looked to the smallest agency, Kaufman PD, headed by Chief Chris Aulbaugh. His organization in charge, Aulbaugh made the decisions.

"Regarding this tragic Hasse incident," Eric wrote in an e-mail to his attorneys the day after the murder. "I can meet the police chief anytime, any day."

At least from all appearances, Eric Williams wanted to cooperate.

That Friday, the day after the murder, Ranger Kasper reached out to Eric through Chief Aulbaugh. Yet the situation quickly became cumbersome. As soon as they contacted him, Eric asserted his Sixth Amendment right to counsel, and referred the investigators to his theft trial attorneys, John Sickel and David Sergi. From that point forward, any requests for interviews or information, any contact from any member of law enforcement involved in the case, had to go through Eric's lawyers.

After considering the situation, Sickel and Sergi agreed that Eric would talk to Ranger Kasper, and negotiations began to make that happen. They discussed options, and scheduled an interview two days out, for the coming Sunday.

Meantime, Eric watched TV news coverage and read

online articles about Mark's murder. To Kim, her husband appeared on a post-killing high, smiling broadly, laughing, happier than he'd been in more than a year. At times, he looked amused. Curious, Eric e-mailed Jenny Parks and asked, "Any news? Or am I still public enemy number one?"

He must have been pleased when she responded: "I think it was the Mexican Drug Cartel that they have been getting a case together on . . . some think it was the Aryan Brotherhood . . . THEY HAVE NO CLUE as far as I can tell . . ."

"Well, frankly the 'NO CLUE' part doesn't surprise me," Eric wrote back.

In the DA's office, Mark's assistant and others reported for work over the weekend, to help FBI agents search Mark's files. The active case folders, hundreds of them, covered a wall on shelves outside his office. Perhaps Mark had made a notation in one indicating he'd been threatened. While not knowing what precisely they looked for, the agents thought something about a particular case might catch their attention and offer a possibility.

At the command post, Hillman and Gibbs directed much of their attention toward gathering video, hopeful that some camera, somewhere, recorded either the murder or an image of the getaway car. Urgent because surveillance cameras often loop and tape over, investigators rushed to collect video from private companies, homes, and commercial buildings in the area. They secured dash-cam footage from police cars responding to the scene, thinking one might have unknowingly passed the getaway car. Some responders drove in from Dallas, offering a web expanding out from the murder scene. Yet as they considered maps, they saw a myriad of routes, making it impossible to predict where the gunman headed after Lenda Bush stopped following.

A major disappointment involved the camera on the back of the county tax assessor's office, which backed up to the crime scene. Pointed in the right direction, it could have recorded the murder. Instead, it turned out that the building had been painted the prior year, and no one had noticed that workers sprayed red paint over the camera lens. Instead of a video of the murder, they came away with nothing.

As big a disappointment, Lenda Bush spent the day at the command post reviewing video as it came in, hoping to pick out the killer's car. Weary, her eyes strained by the effort, it proved a worthless exercise. Tense and tired, she felt only more so after an FBI agent pulled her to the side before she left and suggested she have her car's license plates changed. Someone had noticed that newspaper photographs of the crime scene included images of Bush's car. "They said the killer could come after me," she said. "To get rid of a witness."

As a multi-agency task force worked on the nitty-gritty of searching for evidence, behind closed doors at the command center, top-ranking officers from the various agencies met to strategize. Early on, some expressed doubt about the gang angle. The Aryan Brotherhood, while powerful within prison walls, had little influence in the outside world. Yet with a dearth of information funneling out to the media, speculation of the possible link flourished. In hindsight, it would have a profound effect on the investigation.

"The AB loved the attention," said an investigator. "It played right into their hands."

Within twenty-four hours of the first reports of possible AB involvement in Mark's murder, gang members across Texas called their attorneys or asked to talk to authorities in the prison system, claiming they had valuable information. Most had a motive. Some AB members wanted tickets out of prison in exchange for what they claimed they knew. Others wanted to "piss on a case where a prosecutor was murdered," said one investigator, to lay their scent on it and stake claim. That brought prestige inside prison walls, making enemies and rival gangs view them as dangerous. Any inmate able to engineer a hit on a public official from behind prison walls "had a lot of cred in the system."

Before long, so many AB leads poured in that Ranger Kasper thought pursuing them felt like trying to drink from a fire hose.

Attempting to stem the flow, Chief Aulbaugh called a news conference and told reporters, "We have no indication that Mr. Hasse had directly worked on cases recently that were directly related to the Aryan Brotherhood."

It came too late. Rather than stop the AB media coverage, it mushroomed.

While investigators across the country fanned out following AB leads, many into prisons for sit-downs with convicted criminals, two days after Mark's murder, communications lobbed back and forth between Eric's attorneys and Ranger Kasper.

That day, a Saturday, Kasper checked in with Sickel and Sergi, in anticipation of his scheduled interview with their client the next day. At first, the two attorneys assured Kasper that Eric did want to meet with him. But then Sickel called Kasper and said that he and Sergi had advised Eric not to talk, worried it could hurt the appeal he had pending on his theft conviction.

Disappointed, Kasper asked instead that Eric sign a release for his medical records. Kasper had heard about the sling Eric wore the morning of the murder and his claim that he'd had surgery. "What I heard people saying was that Eric couldn't have done it," said Kasper. "I kept hearing about his messed-up shoulder." Sickel told Kasper he'd get back with him.

"There are no significant advances in the case," read that day's release, which included an announcement that Chief Aulbaugh had cancelled his press conference.

On the following day, Super Bowl Sunday, Eric had

once planned to murder Judge Ashworth by shooting him with a crossbow, gutting him, and filling his abdomen with napalm. Instead Eric had ambushed and murdered Mark Hasse, and, unaware of how close he'd come to a horrific death, the judge watched the Baltimore Ravens beat the San Francisco 49ers.

That afternoon John Sickel notified Ranger Kasper that Eric would sign a release allowing authorities access to his medical records. Once he coordinated the details, Kasper requested more, this time Eric's cell phone records. Later that day, Eric again agreed.

"Maybe it's not Eric Williams," Mike told Skeet and Leah Phillips, along with Sam Keats, that evening, relating how Eric voluntarily took a gunshot residue test and allowed officers to walk through his house. From the instant he'd heard of Mark's murder, Mike sounded resolute that the killer had to be Eric, yet with so much talk of the Aryan Brotherhood floating around the investigation and Eric agreeing to supply evidence, Mike voiced second thoughts. "Maybe Eric didn't do it. Maybe it is someone else."

"No. It's Eric. He's the kind who would do this," Cynthia said, reminding her husband of the discussions they'd had about Eric. "He's got the right personality."

Listening to his wife, Mike nodded, and Keats thought "a light went on," convincing Mike that he hadn't been mistaken. Eric had to be the killer.

Leah and Keats knew the investigation wore on Mike. He talked of little else. One thing in particular seemed to bother him, quotes in the media indicating Mark had been frightened. A handful of Mark's friends had given interviews recounting how he'd told them that he'd been threatened and that in response carried a gun. Mike called that "fairy-taleing," telling stories. "Total BS," Mike said. "Mark was not afraid of anybody or anything." Mike may have believed that. Or maybe Mike, who took such pride in his manhood, thought Mark admitting fear made him look weak. In his denials, Mike defended his dead friend's honor.

When it came to his own safety, Mike insisted he had no qualms. "There are no holes for me to hide in, and that's not my style anyway," he told a *Dallas Morning News* reporter who found Mike and Cynthia at the quilt shop in downtown Kaufman that weekend.

Those who knew Mike understood that he told the truth. The Mike McLelland they knew never worried about his ability to protect himself. Big, strong, and trained, he'd amassed a household stocked with firearms. Mike didn't tell reporters but confided in friends just how certain he felt that he'd have the upper hand in any confrontation: "I hope the SOB comes after me. I'm always armed."

In contrast, Cynthia admitted to a reporter, "I feel like my husband could be in danger."

Chapter 36

People were tense. We didn't know what was going
to happen next. People locked their doors who never
locked their doors. These things happen in big cities,
not here.

—A Kaufman resident

The DA's office reopened on Monday morning, and later
that day a ceremony took place in memory of Mark outside
the courthouse's front doors. About four hundred people
attended, bagpipers played, and an honor guard raised a
special flag that traveled to ceremonies honoring fallen
law enforcement officers. A trumpeter played "Amazing
Grace" and taps.

"Mark would have gotten a kick out of this," Mike told
a reporter.

Meanwhile, upstairs at the DA's office, Mark's assistant
and others continued to comb through files with the FBI
agents, looking for clues. One after the other, the folders
came off the shelves. They reviewed and assessed each
one, searching for possible connections to his murder. Few
potential leads turned up, little that looked promising, and
they discovered no notations on any case tying it to the
killing. Nothing suggested any defendant had threatened
to retaliate.

In the office, one possibility did stand out, however: a

shooting range opened by an Iraq War vet on one of the county's many rural roads. The previous May, Mike had filed a restraining order to close it, calling the range a clear and present danger to neighbors who feared ricocheting bullets. On the day Mark died, Mike had been scheduled to file a motion in the case.

It took little time for investigators to realize the man who started the range wasn't a suspect. Still, they wondered if a gun rights proponent angry about the case could have struck. Like so many other leads, at the beginning the prospect appeared encouraging, but then dried up.

In Kaufman, Ranger Kasper continued to push Eric's attorneys for an interview with their client, but with no links appearing to tie Mark's murder to any of his other recent cases, the rest of the investigators moved on. At a command post meeting, Chief Aulbaugh, Sheriff Byrnes, the FBI and ATF agents, and others gathered, this time to discuss widening the net by focusing on Mark's earlier cases, those he prosecuted in Dallas and as a defense attorney in private practice.

While the others looked for leads in decades-old cases, in a room at Kaufman DA's office, FBI agents individually questioned Mark's coworkers, asking his fellow prosecutors, the legal assistants, clerks, and secretaries if they noticed any changes in Mark in the months, weeks, and days before his murder. Could he have been worried about anything? Do you know of anything in his personal life that could have led to his murder? "Who do you think did this?" an investigator asked one employee.

"I think it's connected to Eric Williams," the woman replied.

In fact, the name the FBI agents heard most often was Eric's. "We kept telling them about Eric," said Mark's paralegal, Amanda Morris, a matter-of-fact woman with long, dark hair. After Mark's murder, Morris's nine-year-old daughter, who'd liked her mom's boss, drew a picture of Mark with his big glasses and wrote a poem in which she said he'd never be forgotten. Morris brought it to work and posted it outside Mark's office door. When Morris and others talked to the investigators, they were adamant about whom they believed was responsible. "We told him that Eric had a real dark side, and that we thought he could have murdered Mark."

Yet what the FBI agents and others heard from local law enforcement was that they doubted Eric was behind it. While some speculated that Eric could have hired someone to murder Mark, others insisted he wasn't involved. With his ever-present smile, his quirky mannerisms, his intelligence, he just didn't strike them as capable of the killings. "From local law enforcement we heard Eric Williams was this bungling ex-JP," said one investigator. "We were looking at him. He wasn't off the list. But no one seemed to think he was the guy."

Working through Mark's old cases, investigators reached out to Mark's friend from his days at the Dallas DA's office, Marcus Busch, by then a federal prosecutor in Washington, D.C. In interviews, Busch ran down the possibilities involving cases he'd prosecuted with Mark. There had been those they'd worried about at the time. Some of the convicted killers and organized crime figures had recently paroled out of prisons. "These were very bad people," said Busch. "And they were out on the streets."

When he considered the possibilities, Busch grew anxious about his own safety. If Mark's killer held a grudge from a case they'd prosecuted together, perhaps Mark's death hadn't ended the matter. It didn't seem unreasonable to Busch to think that he, too, could be in danger. Reacting, Busch and his family took precautions. "We wanted to know where this came from," said Busch. "And we wanted to know when it would end."

Busch wasn't alone in his fears. As the headlines shouted that the Aryan Brotherhood of Texas could be responsible for the killing, an assistant U.S. attorney in Houston who handled ABT cases resigned, citing fears of threats from the prison gang. Meanwhile, in Kaufman the Crime Stoppers tip line continued to overflow with calls connected to the ABT.

From the command post, Gibbs and Hillman doled out the leads, sending FBI agents across the country for prison meetings with AB members and their attorneys, people who said they had valuable information. Some claimed that they overheard inmate conversations about the murder. "It mushroomed and took over," said Hillman. "Pretty soon it was out of control. People got their fifteen minutes of fame by saying they knew something."

It all seemed out of scale to what they knew about Mark. When the investigators asked about AB cases Mark handled, his assistant, Amanda Morris, and others continued to say that there weren't any. "Then we repeated, 'Talk to Eric Williams,'" Morris said. "We told them, he's the one Mark worried about."

At Crime Stoppers, the reward for information on the Hasse case climbed to $71,150. And in Kaufman, "We had cops coming out of our ears," said Bruce Bryant, the DA's investigator assigned to Mark's court.

On Overlook that first week after the murder, Eric drove past the old armory. When he returned, he told Kim that it looked like the sheriff's office had turned the building into a command post. He laughed about it, that they'd set up on South Houston Street, so close to his front door. He and Kim could walk down their street, past the house next door, look to the left, and see the building and the squad cars outside. Dozens of men and women, many in uniform, came and went throughout the day.

"They're right there," Eric said, snickering. "I'm a block away. They don't have a clue."

When Kim needed cigarettes, she drove and Eric rode

with her. As they passed the armory, he put down the window, took out a camera, and pretended to take a video.

"Stop that. They'll see you!" Kim ordered, but he didn't listen.

"You know how easy it would be to get an AR and blast them?" he said. "So easy."

"Quit poking sticks at them, Eric," she chastised. When he only laughed, she said, "Eric, you need to stop it before they start shooting at us! Don't do that!"

During one such trip past the armory, someone noticed and walked inside to tell the others that Eric Williams took photos of the building as he drove by. Few realized that their command post had been set up in a building Eric could eyeball from the end of his street.

Once the crime scene tape came off Mark's office door, Amanda Morris and others cleaned out his personal effects. So much reminded them of the dead man, including the stash of candy bars and cookies they found in one drawer, and the small refrigerator he kept in his office stocked with cans of Country Time lemonade. Someone took the drinks and put them in the main office refrigerator. When Brandi Fernandez saw the cheerful, bright yellow cans, she couldn't tolerate the idea of someone else drinking it. "Get rid of those," she ordered.

"What's the part about this that hurts the most?" a reporter asked Mike.

"That I can't reach out and grab somebody and do something about this right now, because I want to really bad," he said.

The more Mike thought about it, the more he seemed sure Eric was behind Mark's death. He wouldn't tell that to reporters, but he sometimes lowered his voice when he gave interviews and advised them to be careful of the Aryan Brotherhood angle, that he had his doubts.

At times, Mike contemplated how Eric could have

pulled it off, and who helped him. The DA's theories centered on Eric's friends at the Texas State Guard. "I want to corral that whole battalion, all those toy soldiers," Mike told Bruce Bryant. "I want to lock them in a room until they answer questions."

At the command post, Chief Aulbaugh held morning and late-afternoon meetings, when the senior investigators reported on what their sections were doing. Mike showed up off and on, one day cornering the FBI's Michael Hillman, insisting that the investigation needed to focus on Eric and his guard battalion. Hillman didn't disagree, but with Eric lawyered up, options appeared limited. Like Ranger Kasper, Hillman tried to set up a meeting with Eric, only to be rebuffed by his attorneys.

Midway through that week, Mike took Bruce Bryant with him to the command post for the express purpose of confronting Chief Aulbaugh about the guard unit. That day in the old armory building, Bryant watched as Mike pulled two chairs together and he and Aulbaugh talked. Even from a distance, Bryant sensed Mike's agitation. By then, Mike had told Bryant that he believed Eric's battalion was the "key to cracking the case." As he watched, Bryant noticed Aulbaugh lean back, away from Mike, distancing himself, and Mike lean forward, invading the other man's space. From across the room, Bryant saw Mike's temper building.

After an hour or so, Mike stood up to leave, walked over to Bryant, and they headed toward the door. As they talked, Mike bitterly complained to Bryant that he had the impression Chief Aulbaugh had already marked Eric Williams off as a serious suspect. "Aulbaugh just won't do it. He won't look at Eric Williams and those armchair commandos," Mike complained.

Bryant knew something he hadn't mentioned to Mike before.

Not long after Chief Aulbaugh hired on in Kaufman, he and Bryant went to lunch. That day, the chief mentioned something that now seemed perhaps important. "I told Mike, 'You know, Aulbaugh is in the Texas State Guard,'" Bryant said. "It was like scales dropped from Mike's eyes. He said that was probably why Aulbaugh wasn't cooperating."

Sheriff Byrnes was at the command post that day, and after Mike left, Chief Aulbaugh walked over to talk to the sheriff. "What did Mike want?" Sheriff Byrnes asked.

"He's upset. He thinks Eric Williams is the one who did this," the chief answered. He then went on to explain that Mike wanted the commander of the battalion to call a muster and keep everyone locked up until they got to the truth, whether anyone in the unit knew anything about Mark's murder. "I explained we couldn't do that, and he got angry."

Meanwhile, the situation continued to complicate. When no one could find the holster and handgun Mark wore under his coat the day of his murder, the hospital was contacted. Instead of retaining it as possible evidence, they said that they'd turned it over to the DA's office. "Who has Mark's gun?" the sheriff asked Mike when he called.

"I do," Mike said. "It's out in my truck. I unloaded it."

For days, the sheriff and Ranger Kasper had pondered what to do about a prosecutor for the case. Sheriff Byrnes worried that Mike's friendship with Mark could complicate matters if they needed to negotiate a deal. Now he felt certain Mike needed to step down. "You're going to have to recuse yourself as the prosecutor," the sheriff explained. "Since you took the weapon, you're now potentially a material witness. You need to appoint someone."

Not happy, Mike ultimately agreed. That same day, he filed a motion to remove himself and the Kaufman DA's office from the case. Then the question became whom to appoint. Brandi Fernandez reminded Mike what Mark had once said, that if anything happened to him, he'd want Bill Wirskye to take the case.

"Let's call him," Mike said.

That afternoon, a friend in the Kaufman DA's office called Wirskye and said Mike wanted him and his law partner, Toby Shook, to take over the Hasse murder as special prosecutors. Wirskye had been half expecting the call.

Chapter 37

Eric got really excited about that Christopher Dorner
[the ex-Los Angeles cop] running around killing
people. He watched the news constantly. Eric said,
"This guy really knows how to do this."

—Kim Williams

At the command post, Ranger Kasper reviewed Eric's
cell phone records, finding nothing that appeared tied to
the case, and sent subpoenas out to Eric's doctors for medical records. Meanwhile, the other investigators continued
to look into the leads that multiplied daily, including ever
more phone calls and letters from prison inmates across the
country about gang involvement. Each one had to be followed through, first to see if they were legitimate. "These
were bad people, some killers," said Ranger Kasper. "We
couldn't just write the leads off."

Secondly, if they'd ignored leads, once Mark's killer
was on trial in a courtroom, his defense attorney could
use uninvestigated leads to contend law enforcement had
tunnel vision.

Meanwhile, on Overlook, Eric had the big TV in the
living room, the smaller one in the kitchen, and his laptop
all on news reports coming in about the search for Christopher Dorner, who'd assassinated the daughter of a former
LAPD captain and her fiancé. Like Eric, Dorner was dis-

gruntled, and he had a hit list. His included the names of forty LAPD personnel he blamed for his firing. Off the Internet, Eric printed Dorner's manifesto, a long, convoluted explanation for his actions. Addressed to America, the subject line read, "Last Resort."

"I've lost everything because the LAPD took my name and new [sic] I was INNOCENT!!!" Dorner had written. "I lost complete faith in the system." The killing would stop, he said, when LAPD "states the truth about my innocence PUBLICLY."

The news on Dorner came on the same reports as updates on the killing of Mark Hasse, making it especially interesting, it seemed. Perhaps Eric identified with Dorner. Both men had been part of the system and then became outcasts. Kim watched as Eric read and reread the manifesto, until she believed he'd become "mesmerized by it."

As the days passed, Kim thought Eric worried about the investigation, wondering if they focused on him. He'd turned over months of cell phone records and signed the medical release. It was part of his plan to appear to cooperate. But his attorneys still said no to an interview.

When she walked outside, Kim saw unfamiliar cars on the block, including a dark one parked across the field behind the house on a dirt road. She worried that police had the house under surveillance. When she went inside, she told Eric, "I know they're watching us."

"They may have planted listening devices," he said. "They could hack into the computers and listen to you through the computer."

Kim didn't know what to think. Before long, Eric speculated that the sheriff had put the command post close so that police could monitor their house. "From that point on, whenever he wanted to talk to me about his plans, he motioned for me to go in the pantry, and we talked there." By then, her husband's thoughts had moved past Mark

Hasse. Huddled together, Eric reviewed his list with her, ruminating about who deserved to be killed next.

The two names mentioned most often were Mike McLelland and Judge Erleigh Wiley.

As his paranoia grew, Eric became more concerned about eavesdroppers and reluctant to say names. "He started doing this thing with a deck of cards. If he wanted to talk about Mike McLelland, Sluggo, he held up a king. If it was Erleigh Wiley, he held up a queen," Kim said.

Her husband's obsession with the news out of California continued for all nine days of Christopher Dorner's rampage. In the end Dorner killed four people, wounded three others, and died in a burning mountain cabin. By then, Eric had reopened a Facebook account. On his computer, after Dorner's death, he found the killer's page and clicked the add button, as if to let the dead man know that he considered him a friend.

In Kaufman, nerves continued to be on edge. One local police officer drove by the Denny's at the Washington Street underpass and glanced over at a filling station. Someone had spilled what looked like a pail of red paint on the pavement, and for a moment he thought it looked like blood. Briefly he wondered if it could be a bad omen.

The day after Bill Wirskye received the call from Kaufman, he and his law partner, Toby Shook, drove from their Dallas office to the command post. In the car they talked about Mark, and openly wondered what they might encounter working with a DA's office where someone had murdered a prosecutor. Their workloads heavy, as they drove Wirskye told Shook not to worry, that as the lead prosecutor on the case, he'd "do the heavy lifting."

The two men knew each other well, going back to the ten years they'd overlapped at the Dallas DA's office, where Wirskye worked for Shook. They'd met during a drunk-driving trial. In some ways, they were opposites. As tall as Wirskye was, Shook was short. But they got along. When they worked cases, both tended to overprepare. "We share an intense fear of failure," said Shook, with a chuckle. In fact, the two men laughed often, seeming to relish their roles.

As early as the seventh grade, Toby Shook followed sensational trials in the newspapers and dreamed of becoming a prosecutor. "I thought it would be a fun job. I liked to argue a lot, so my mom thought I'd be a good lawyer."

Two years after Shook left the DA's office, Wirskye followed and joined Shook's firm. Off and on, they agreed to take cases as special prosecutors. Yet no case had quite

Toby Shook in a courtroom
Evidence photo

been like this, where they both knew the victim. After they arrived in Kaufman that day and were sworn in by Judge Chitty, Shook and Wirskye drove to the command post. The place teemed with members of law enforcement, including Texas Rangers in their pale silver belly cowboy hats, ATF agents, FBI special agents, some barking orders, others rushing in or out.

After being introduced to everyone, they were given a briefing, much of it centered on interviews of the ever-growing list of Aryan Brotherhood members who claimed to have insights into the murder. One strange aspect: everyone in the Kaufman DA's office was considered a potential witness, because it could turn out that any one of them worked on a case with Mark that resulted in his murder. So they had to be kept out of the investigation.

While there, the two prosecutors reviewed the first lab reports. The Texas Department of Public Safety (DPS) experts pegged the one bullet recovered in the hospital, the one that fell out of Mark's coat, as fired from a .38 special or .357 magnum revolver. Possible manufacturers of the handgun they surmised "included but not limited to" Ruger and Smith & Wesson.

After the briefing, despite all the activity and so many agencies working the case, Shook left the command post thinking that the investigators had no real suspects.

From the command post, Wirskye and Shook drove back to the courthouse, this time dropping in at the DA's office to check in with Mike. Just walking in the door, Wirskye sensed the tension. "You could cut it with a knife. They were all scared."

Much of their time together Mike spent reviewing the Williams case, saying Eric "was the kind of guy who would do this," talking about threats he'd made against others and his love of guns. When they left, both Shook and Wirskye thought Eric Williams sounded like a strong suspect, yet when Wirskye brought his name up with local investigators, he heard the same things the FBI agents and others had, that they didn't consider Eric a likely suspect.

That week Lenda Bush returned to the command post, this time to be hypnotized. The horror of that day still haunted her. Whenever she drove to Kaufman, her heart beat fast remembering the gunman and Mark dying on the pavement. As she met with the DPS hypnotist, Bush fought a cold. Every time he told her to take a deep breath, Bush coughed. In the end, she wasn't sure she'd been hypnotized, but Ranger Kasper told her that she had gone back in her mind to that day, and that she hadn't seen a license plate on the getaway car. She did, however, describe an unusual pattern on the car, something like fleur-de-lis, which struck her as odd.

At the DA's office during Monday morning meetings, Mike continued to warn his staff. "I know this is Eric Williams. Be aware of your surroundings. Watch your backs."

Once he'd recused himself from the investigation, Mike complained that he was kept in the dark. At times, Wirskye dropped in to reassure him that the investigation continued. Mike often found ways to return the subject to Eric, and Wirskye listened. At one such meeting, Mike repeated to Wirskye what he'd wanted Chris Aulbaugh to do, call a muster and lock up the guard members, keep them locked up until they talked. Wirskye explained that they couldn't do that; it wasn't constitutional. On the other hand, he understood the DA's frustration. "His technique wouldn't work, but he had valid concerns."

What Wirskye didn't discuss with Mike was that he and Shook both had doubts about the entire Aryan Brotherhood angle. The scenario just didn't fit what they knew about the gang, and they didn't see killing a prosecutor as something the AB would do, mainly because it would bring too much heat down on the gang.

In truth, for what Wirskye and Shook knew about the

case, Eric Williams seemed a better fit. When they reviewed the evidence, they both came away believing that Mark's murder had been highly personal. Mark knew the killer. Otherwise, why would he have said, "I'm sorry. I'm sorry," as the car repair worker heard?

Back in Dallas, their law office staff fended off calls from reporters. At times, it appeared they'd walked into a West Texas twister. Yet neither worried about the case being high-profile, as headlines spread across the world. They'd worked together on the infamous Texas Seven trials, the inmates who escaped a Texas prison and went on a killing spree. And Shook had prosecuted Darlie Routier, the mother whose two sons were murdered one night in their suburban Dallas home. The case made international headlines for months, and Shook had helped put Routier on death row.

Not long after the two special prosecutors came onboard, however, Mike complained bitterly one afternoon in Brandi Fernandez's office, that people were griping about Wirskye's and Shook's appointments, throwing out names of others who could have been hired. As he talked, Mike reviewed for Fernandez all the good work Wirskye had done on the murder case he'd tried in Kaufman earlier that same year. He talked about Shook's strong reputation. "I don't think I made a mistake," Mike said, shaking his head. Echoing what Mark said weeks before his death, Mike then added, "If I was the victim, that's who I'd want, Bill and Toby."

"**D**on't worry. Mike has security all over this place," Cynthia whispered to her friend Leah at Mark's memorial service at the Terrell Performing Arts Center on a Saturday afternoon nine days after his murder. The semicircular rows of seats filled with family, friends, and prosecutors from Dallas and Kaufman, along with members of law enforcement. As she talked, Cynthia pointed to armed officers in the balcony. Outside, more officers manned road-blocks, checking credentials, and snipers watched from the rooftop.

The weather cold and damp, the staff at the DA's office had met in Kaufman, then arrived together in a bus with a police escort. Inside the cavernous theater, Mark's mother sat beside her surviving son, Paul, whose daughter sang a moving rendition of "Amazing Grace." From the podium, he thanked those who attended, "especially those of you who are looking for whoever did this."

At one point, for some unknown reason, the lights blinked off in the auditorium. In the darkness, those gathered heard shuffling. When the lights flashed back on, the officers had moved forward in attack position. But it had just been a mechanical error.

Mark's mother asked Marcus Busch to talk, and he did, at times his emotions overwhelming him, as when he said that he would have preferred "being in a courtroom trying a case with Mark than in this room" memorializing his friend. "This world is a better place because of Mark, and so are we," Busch concluded.

Ending the ceremony, Mike walked over with a folded flag and gave it to Mark's mother.

As the crowd filed out, Mike talked to Lucky Louque, Mark's friend from the airport. The Texas Rangers had been out to talk to Louque, Curtis Mays, and others at the airport, and they'd said the same thing the people close to Mark at the DA's office had said, that the only one Mark worried about was Eric Williams. "Be careful," Mike told Louque. "That guy's still on the loose. Watch your backside."

Then, after the crowd dispersed, the bulky DA sat on the edge of the stage with his old friend Mike Burns, their legs dangling, and said, what he'd been thinking since days after Mark's murder: "This is local, and everyone is trying to make it a national news event. . . . It's somebody bent on revenge, and it's somebody close to home."

"Are you all right?" Burns asked. Mike seemed shaken, his face red and angry. Burns could tell that his friend felt as if on a mission to find the killer.

"My greatest fear is that it was one person working alone, who doesn't drink," Mike said, suggesting that then perhaps no one would ever talk and reveal who'd murdered Mark. "If he's coming after me, he better come prepared. There'll be a fight."

Chapter 38

After the GSR test came back negative and Eric answered the door with that sling on his arm, I had the impression that convinced some folks that he couldn't have done it.

—Bill Wirskye

As one of his responsibilities as lead prosecutor, Wirskye dropped in at the DA's office at times. The staff continued to be tense, although they'd picked up their workloads and forged on. For his part, as soon as Wirskye walked in, Mike consistently asked, "Is everything being done on Eric Williams that can be done?"

"I'll talk to the investigators about it again," Wirskye said. And he did, repeating Mike's concerns at the meetings. Some of those investigating appeared to agree, growing frustrated that they hadn't made more progress looking into Eric. Others shrugged it off.

At the sheriff's department, while not writing Eric off the list of suspects, some doubted he was capable of the murder. "In my mind, I didn't see Eric pulling the trigger," said Sheriff Byrnes. Many like the sheriff did still wonder, however, if Eric could have hired or manipulated someone else into committing the murder, but few saw the pudgy former JP as a brazen killer.

"Everything I heard was that Eric Williams was a

coward," Wirskye said. "No one talked about him like he could be a first-person shooter." Except for in the DA's office, where so many remained certain Eric had to be involved.

The weeks passed, and Aryan Brotherhood tips continued to filter in, fewer but new ones most days. At one point, Wirskye heard a theory that the gang had coordinated to continue the onslaught of leads simply to toy with the investigation. One tip suggested that the ABT had a list of officials in Kaufman County it intended to kill, including the chief of police and the judges.

Meanwhile, more reports arrived from the DPS lab on the only physical evidence, the fired bullets and fragments recovered on the scene and from Mark's body. When compared, they all tied back to the same type of weapon, a Ruger or Smith & Wesson type revolver.

Across Kaufman, nerves remained on a sharp edge, especially among those who like Mike believed Mark's murderer was local and that Eric could be behind it. Others had worked Eric's theft case, and they worried he might come for them as well.

Ever since the murder Bruce Bryant, the DA's investigator, carried a loaded gun. At times, he couldn't sleep. At night, he left the house and stood in the darkness on his front porch, watching and wary. One morning around four, he heard his newspaper slap down outside. He walked out, and a car eased past, slow. Watching, wondering if it could be Eric, Bryant put his hand on his gun, and he kept it there until the car left his sight.

In his nearly two decades as a JP, Johnny Perry had never seen an investigation as tight-lipped as the Mark Hasse case. "No one talked about it," he said. In the back of his mind, he often thought of the day Mark warned him to be careful because Eric could be gunning for him.

After Mark's death, in particular, Perry made sure he was armed. Then it happened. One day he drove to a small Asian restaurant in a convenience store with three friends, looking forward to a $6 lunch special. Behind his truck, Perry noticed a black Sport Trac. "We've got company," he said. When one of the men asked what Perry meant, he told them not to turn around to look, but that Eric Williams was trailing them.

"I'm going to see how far he follows me," Perry said. Driving the eight miles to the restaurant, Perry watched the rearview mirror, and Eric shadowed. Finally Perry pulled into the restaurant lot, Eric turning in behind him. Perry parked. The Sport Trac parked. With that, Perry and the three other men opened all four doors simultaneously and jumped out, all brandishing guns. In one hand, Perry held an AR–15, a pistol in the other.

They waited and watched.

At first, the Sport Trac didn't move, but then the driver swung the truck around, back out onto the road, and drove toward Kaufman. "I figured Eric was mad at me because I took his job," said Perry with a frown. "I figured Eric wanted to let me know how unhappy he was."

In mid-February, the *Dallas Morning News* ran an article reporting on assistant U.S. Marshals across the nation spreading out to prisons to talk to Aryan Brotherhood members about the Mark Hasse murder. "Authorities are no closer to finding out who gunned down the highly respected assistant district attorney." In the article, an official with the San Antonio U.S. Marshals office described the focus of the murder investigation as on the ABT.

While some had wondered if someone out of Mark's personal life could have committed the murder, that theory fell away as well. Three of his old girlfriends showed up at his memorial, all of whom he'd stayed friends with over the years. At one point, evidence that Mark had once Googled information on how to marry a Russian mail-order bride brought up the possibility of the Russian mob, but that didn't pan out, either.

Time passed, but Mark's killing never seemed far from the McLellands' thoughts. He continued to talk to friends about Eric's list, one with five names on it, people the former JP was angry with. Tonya Ratcliff asked Mike if he thought his name was on it, and he admitted that could be true. Another day, he talked to a local political leader and repeated the information about the list. "Mark was on the list," Mike said. "I think I'm next."

Of the two, the one who appeared more fearful was Mike's wife.

Walking their two dogs, Cynthia stopped and talked to a neighbor. When the woman asked about the investigation, Cynthia teared up. "I'm worried that Mike made someone mad. I'm afraid he might hurt us."

At the quilt guild meeting in downtown Kaufman one evening, Cynthia talked to a small group of friends about Mark's death. After she announced it was Eric Williams who'd killed Mark, someone asked, "Well, if you know it's him, why don't you do something about it?"

"Mike's working on it," she said.

Although she still sang and smiled often, those who knew her understood how nervous Cynthia had become. At the hospital, she talked of Mark's killing often, calling Eric the killer. To her coworkers, she confessed that she feared that Eric would come after her and Mike. For the first time, she didn't feel safe at home alone. When she finished work each afternoon, she went to the Phillipses' house, or met Leah to go shopping. "She was so frightened," Leah said.

Worried about his friends, Skeet, Leah's husband, tried to talk Mike into installing driveway sensors to beep if anyone drove up. Mike refused. They did have the new security system, but old habits die hard. Most of the time when friends arrived on Blarney Stone, they found the McLellands' doors unlocked and the system turned off.

When Cynthia's sister Nancy heard Cynthia talk about

Eric, Nancy felt her anxiety build. "It came up enough times that it registered that Cindy was terrorized."

Yet at other times, Cynthia seemed determined to fend off her apprehensions, like the day she told a friend that she talked to a psychic who told her that she and Mike were safe.

The biggest stumbling block remained so little physical evidence.

At the command post, assignments piled up, like perusing dumps of information from cell towers around the courthouse, to see if any interesting telephone numbers showed up the morning of the murder. Tedious work, each report had to be analyzed. In the end, nothing came of it.

At the same time, others studied the masses of video that continued to arrive from surveillance cameras and dash-cam footage from the responding police cars. Hundreds of hours evaporated reviewing the tapes, looking for something, anything tied to the murder, to no end.

As one of its contributions, the FBI brought in behavioral analysts from Quantico, Virginia. The profilers evaluated cases based on statistics generated by analyzing similar crimes to compile psychological profiles of criminals. There'd been so few murders like Mark's that when Sheriff Byrnes asked for a personality assessment of the type of killer to look for, the experts offered little. Their only hint: it appeared to have been someone with a personal grudge.

At the same time, inside the Overlook house, Eric waited and watched.

One day he drove Kim to the storage unit, talking about the next killing. Mike McLelland remained high on his list, but so did Erleigh Wiley and Judge Ashworth. Once there, Eric turned the key in the Sable and the engine kicked in, but then the car rumbled, smoke poured out, and they heard a bang. The transmission had blown.

"Shit," Eric said.

With Kim's help, he rolled the car out of the storage unit. Then he steered as she pushed with the Sport Trac. Throughout, he yelled, shouting orders, angry. At the back of the lot, he abandoned the Sable near an embankment, where it wouldn't be visible from the highway. Before they left, he wiped the car down.

Not knowing who owned it, the facility's manager had it towed away.

On Valentine's Day, Mike and Cynthia attended a banquet at the First Assembly of God Church in Kaufman, to show people they didn't cower in fear. "We want folks to understand life's gone back to normal," Mike said.

That same day on Overlook, Eric searched for a replacement car to use to kill his next victim. By then, his plan had taken shape, and he wanted a car that fit his scheme. "I want something that looks like a cop car," he told Kim. "A Crown Vic."

Heavily medicated, Kim slept, while Eric sat at his computer perusing Craigslist.com, comparing cars. One caught his attention, a white Ford Crown Victoria police interceptor. "Hi—I am interested in looking at your car for sale . . ." Eric e-mailed, using an account he'd opened in a fake name.

Once Eric's doctor supplied his medical records, Ranger Kasper leafed through and found nothing about rotator cuff surgery. After he finished, he sent the file to Lieutenant Jolie Stewart at the sheriff's department. They talked, compared thoughts, one of which was that Eric might have gone to a specialist. If so, since the records had come from his regular doctor, it seemed plausible that the surgery wouldn't be mentioned. "Maybe we need to find out if he has an orthopedic surgeon?" Kasper asked, and Stewart agreed, disappointed with yet another delay.

The two FBI agents on the case felt frustrated, too. They'd heard Eric's name repeatedly mentioned. A few townsfolk stopped in to talk to them, giving them information on Eric, but when they followed up, none of it checked out. And Eric's lawyers still rebuffed interview requests. "What we needed was actual proof," said Michael Hillman. At the same time, he'd grown to see the AB cases as a dead end. "We burnt a lot of manpower and got nowhere."

Mark's murder unsolved, the press never quite left Kaufman, stopping back off and on to check on the investigation. "I'm ahead of everyone else because I'm basically a soldier," Mike told a reporter that month who asked if he worried about his own safety. After he mentioned that he even wore his gun while walking his dog, he said, "People in my line of work are going to have to get better at dealing with danger."

On February 21, Eric received a letter from Kaufman County's human resources director, notifying him that his COBRA health insurance benefits would end on March 31, a little more than a month away. "We disagree that your status is simply 'suspended without pay.' . . . You should take all appropriate steps to obtain other insurance benefits."

The following day, the command post at the armory closed. As the investigation stalled, leads dwindled to a halt, and Sheriff Byrnes suggested that the investigators still trying to solve the mystery of Mark Hasse's murder could set up an office in a conference room at the law enforcement center. By then, Chief Aulbaugh, for the most part, only came in for meetings once or twice a week. Two of his officers were assigned to the task force, along with the sheriff department's Lieutenant Jolie Stewart, Texas Rangers Lieutenant Eric Kasper, a representative from ATF, and the two FBI special agents, Laurie Gibbs and Michael Hillman.

The investigation winding down, some worried whoever

murdered Mark might get away with it. "I started hearing from folks that maybe we wouldn't have an arrest," said Wirskye.

Perhaps Eric had waited for that, to see the command post close, knowing that meant that the bulk of the investigators had left.

The following day, he and Kim drove to Greenville, near Dallas, and using the name Richard Greene, giving a false address, he paid a seventy-year-old man $3,200 in cash to purchase a retired police car, a 2004 white Crown Victoria with tinted windows. It had 104,220 miles on it, and the license plate holder held a paper advertisement that read "FRONTIER FORD."

The money handed over, the seller wrote out a bill of sale in longhand. Getting rid of the car because his wife didn't like it, Ed Cole thought it odd when the only test drive Eric took was to back it up in the driveway.

Days later, Cole realized he'd left his garage door opener in the car. He e-mailed the man he knew as Richard Greene, and before long it showed up in Cole's mailbox.

On February 26, Special Agent Michael Hillman called John Sickel and tried again to set up an interview with Eric. By then, the investigators had few other leads, nothing that looked particularly good, and they talked more about Eric Williams, the one suspect that had never been fully investigated, the one possibility who had never been eliminated.

In response, Sickel e-mailed his fellow attorney Sergi and Eric, saying he had conflicted feelings about the best course of action. He worried that cooperating, rather than helping Eric, could result in even more attention focused on him. While the easiest thing might have been to agree to the interview, Sickel wasn't sure that was the best decision for their client.

"Clearly it appears that there is no prime suspect," Eric

responded. ". . . So I ask myself if there is anything I could tell them in an interview which would make them conclude, 'Okay, take this guy off our lists'—and that answer is no." Instead he suggested Sickel remind the FBI that after Mark's murder he'd voluntarily had a GSR test and allowed a search of his home.

Sickel responded that the FBI knew about the GSR test and the search. As Eric's attorney, Sickel worried that nothing short of an arrest in the case—the indictment of another suspect—could remove Eric from suspicion.

In the end, Eric and his attorneys rejected Hillman's request for an interview.

The following morning Bill Wirskye drove in for a meeting at the new command post in the sheriff's conference room. Chief Aulbaugh, as usual, held the meeting, and all the investigators attended: the two Kaufman PD officers assigned to the case; Lieutenant Stewart; the two FBI agents, Gibbs and Hillman; an ATF agent; and Ranger Kasper. As they talked, Hillman recounted how he reached out to John Sickel yet again to attempt to set up an interview with Eric, only to be told no. Talking options, they had few leads to work. By then the dozens of Texas Rangers who'd been brought in, FBI agents across the country, and local law enforcement had run down thousands of tips, all to no avail.

Like some of the others in the room, Wirskye felt frustrated that they hadn't been able to fully explore the man Mike McLelland continually pointed to as his prime suspect. It seemed to Wirskye that with leads pouring in, the investigation had become more reactive than proactive. To him, Chief Aulbaugh seemed enough out of his element so that he'd allowed the flood of ABT tips to divert the investigation instead of focusing on what needed to be done. Wirskye thought they needed to take a step back and rethink where they were heading.

Toward that end, Wirskye suggested that they explore Eric's involvement to a conclusion. Then Wirskye repeated what Mike had said, that perhaps someone at the state guard might have information. While Mike's idea wouldn't work—they couldn't call a muster and lock the guard members up—Wirskye thought Mike's concerns valid. "What do we know about these people?" Wirskye asked. "We have to do something with Eric Williams. We either need to include him or exclude him."

Over the weeks, someone on the task force had pulled together a list of the guard members in Eric's unit, and he marked off those with whom Eric appeared to have a relationship. Throughout the meeting, Wirskye pushed the guard as the way to find out more about Eric, and the others agreed. Yet the one who knew some of the potential sources on the list, who understood the organization's culture, Chief Aulbaugh, never mentioned during the meeting that he was a guard member.

The plan they agreed on revolved around interviewing Eric's neighbors, family, friends, and people he'd worked with; obtaining the rest of his medical records, and pulling together a grand jury to bring in the guard members to be questioned.

As they talked, they decided to form teams. One would focus on Eric Williams, another on general tips coming in over the Internet, two others on the Aryan Brotherhood and Mexican cartel theories. Instead of working the others first, however, the emphasis had turned to Eric.

Still, when he left that day, Wirskye felt unsure that they'd refocused the investigation. Back at his Dallas law office, he told Toby Shook that he had begun questioning his contribution to the case. "They all look at me like the pro from Dover," he said, resurrecting an old term for an outside expert.

A while later Wirskye learned that Chief Aulbaugh was in Eric's Texas State Guard regiment. Frustrated and disappointed, Wirskye wondered why the chief hadn't spoken up and offered advice on how to proceed.

"I have to go to the storage unit, and I want you to go with me," Eric said near the end of the month.

Kim agreed. Once they arrived, Eric picked up two long guns, assault-type weapons. Back in the car he showed them to Kim, and then said, "I want to see how they shoot. . . . I found an underpass with big concrete pillars and there's no traffic."

They arrived at a lonely underpass, with cars speeding by on the highway overhead. There he instructed her to stay in the car and be the lookout, to let him know if cars approached. He got out, loaded the rifles, and began shooting at the pillars, the guns making a loud crack and the bullets whizzing then pinging as they hit the concrete. Kim watched for cars, ready to tap the horn if anyone approached. When Eric returned to the Sport Trac, he appeared exhilarated, as if looking forward to the next murder.

A few nights later, perhaps trying to direct the investigators away from him or simply amusing himself, just before midnight, Eric e-mailed an anonymous tip on the Hasse case to Crime Stoppers. "Overheard this guy talking about the 'hit' on that DA guy. Said his buddy and another guy did it and got a cool vacation down south Mexico Way—free girls, drugs & booze. They're supposed to be back next week in Athens [Texas]. Didn't hear nothing else. Some guy named Bull. 6 foot, 240 pounds, 30 y o. Drove a blue Chevy pickup."

"Look what I did," Eric said, showing Kim the e-mail. "I'm going to screw with them."

"Don't do that," she fumed. "Do you want to get caught?"

The possibility police could ring the doorbell and arrest them at any moment never left Kim's thoughts. Only the drugs kept her anxiety at bay.

Kim's brother, Jamie, visited their parents that month,

and Kim and Eric walked down the street to the Johnsons' for a barbecue. Their mother, Lucienne, had already told Jamie that she worried about Kim. Her illness had gotten worse, and she seemed heavily medicated. "I think Eric controls her," Lucienne said. "He never leaves her alone. When she's here, he follows her room to room."

When Kim arrived, Jamie understood his mother's concern. Kim didn't look right, her eyes cloudy with dark circles, her hair brittle, and she had a large gap from her missing front teeth. Kim had physically aged. Even stranger, some things she said struck him as odd. At one point, she looked at him and asked, "Jamie, what's prison like?"

Chapter 39

When something is on the streets, people talk. What was so odd about Mark's murder was that there was no street chatter. By the time March hit, the silence was deafening.

—Lieutenant Jolie Stewart

The bills from David Sergi kept arriving, and Eric e-mailed saying that he'd have a $500 payment within a week. One morning he nonchalantly mentioned to Kim that by the end of that month, March, they would lose their health insurance.

At the new command post, after Ranger Kasper and Lieutenant Stewart reviewed Eric's medical records, Laurie Gibbs looked through them, interested in any mention of shoulder surgery. She saw none. Despite the way Eric appeared to cooperate, Gibbs and her partner, Michael Hillman, shared Wirskye's sentiment that more had to be done. To that end, Hillman made another attempt to find out specific information about Eric's shoulder surgery, including the name of the surgeon.

"I'll get back to you," John Sickel responded.

Meanwhile, in early March, Chief Aulbaugh mentioned to the two FBI agents on the case his position with the guard, and that he'd had a text message on the morning of Mark Hasse's murder, one that said something like: You don't think the captain could have done this, do you?

The text had come from Barton Roger Williams, Eric's guard friend.

Frustrated that the chief hadn't mentioned it sooner, Special Agents Hillman and Gibbs put a call in to Roger Williams, asking him to meet with them. That happened on the sixth, and Gibbs and Hillman asked the command sergeant major about Eric Williams, their relationship, and why Roger sent the text message the morning of Mark Hasse's murder. It seemed interesting, at least, that he'd considered the possibility that Eric could be Mark's killer.

That day, Roger Williams denied he had any reason to believe Eric might be involved in Mark's murder. Throughout the conversation, Hillman and Gibbs marveled at the way Roger continued to afford Eric the respect of calling him "Captain Williams." As he talked to the agents, Roger Williams never mentioned that a month before Mark's murder, he signed the paperwork and rented Eric a storage unit.

About that time the DA's investigator, Bruce Bryant, stopped at the sheriff's office on business and saw a member of the Hasse task force in the parking lot. Bryant started to walk over to him. The Kaufman PD officer quickly turned and rushed toward his car. It would have been funny, Bryant said later, if it hadn't been so maddening. "I thought he was going to break into a run. I figured he'd been ordered not to talk to me."

On March 15 at 3:45 p.m., Eric sat at his computer surfing porn sites. That day, Cynthia baked a peanut butter pie for a friend, who posted on Facebook, "I am in sugar heaven." When she had requests for the recipe, Cynthia listed it in the comment section.

Six weeks after Mark's murder, life in Kaufman appeared normal. "People stopped talking about it every day," said one staffer in the DA's office. "We were trying to go on."

Yet reminders made that difficult, like the day Mark's mom dropped in at the office to talk and hear stories of her dead son. "I just wanted to spend time with people Mark loved," she told one of them.

One evening that week, Leah and Skeet Phillips drove the McLellands home. As they came down Blarney Stone Way, Skeet continued past the house.

"What are you doing?" Mike asked.

"You didn't see those people over there?" Skeet asked, pointing at a couple walking on the road. "You need to watch your surroundings. The people who killed Mark are still out there."

About that time at the house on Overlook, Eric pulled Kim into the pantry to talk about his plans, holding up the king card so she'd know that he referred to Mike, whom he still called Sluggo. Mark's murder having gone so smoothly, Eric discussed ambushing Mike the same way, on his way to work. The symmetry may have appealed to him. Maybe he thought it particularly brash to repeat the same act.

Days later, Eric had changed his mind. "I'm going to do it at their house," he told Kim. "We'll drive up, and you can wait in the car. I'll pretend I'm a cop, to get her to open the door."

"Who?"

"Mike's wife. If she's there, I'll kill her, too."

For some reason, Kim had never thought about Cynthia dying, and that bothered her. "She doesn't deserve that."

"If she's there, she's collateral damage," Eric said. "This is the way I'm going to do it."

Excited about his plan, Eric crowed about how distracting the false leads had become for the investigation, and how his plan would bolster those theories. "They think it's the Aryan Brotherhood. They think it's the Mexican Mafia. That'll make it seem even more likely. Because gangs and the cartels go in people's homes and kill them. It'll fit."

Later it would seem as if events across the nation created a perfect storm of sorts, preventing the investigation from focusing, as Mike McLelland wanted it, "close to home."

Giving more credence to the AB leads, on March 19 in Colorado, someone executed Tom Clements, a prison official, in his home. The investigation focused on Evan Spencer Ebel, a member of the 211 Crew, a white supremacist prison gang similar to the Aryan Brotherhood. Some speculated that the gangs wanted to broaden their reach by killing public officials. Further suggesting the Colorado murder could be linked to Mark's, two days after Clements's killing, Ebel died in a shootout in Wise County, Texas, a hundred miles northeast of Kaufman County.

The gangs in the news, another brazen killing, apparently even Mike wondered if he'd been wrong, and if the ABT could be behind it all. When reporters asked him about Ebel's death, Mike didn't pin Mark's murder on the ABT, but he suggested that perhaps there might be a link: "Well, we've put some real dents in the Aryan Brotherhood around here in the past."

If Mike had second thoughts about Mark's killer, Cynthia didn't. That month she went to a quilt retreat with friends. She made yet another baby quilt, and in one of the booths set up by local vendors, she bought a chunky blue stone necklace and a matching ring. Rather than pack it to bring home, she wore it, telling one friend that she wanted to enjoy things and not save them for tomorrow. "I love it," she said. "And I might as well wear it."

Perhaps tomorrow felt too uncertain. One morning, another quilter awoke early and found Cynthia drinking coffee. "You know, this isn't over," she said.

"Don't you think whoever murdered Mark Hasse got out of Dodge?" the woman said. "If it were me, I'd still be running."

"No, it's Eric Williams. And he hasn't gone anywhere,"

Cynthia in her necklace and ring

Cynthia said, appearing worried. "I feel like Mike and I could be in danger."

Days later, Cynthia's thoughts again focused on her situation. "If something happens to me, will you promise me that you'll take care of my kids?" she asked Leah.

"Well, of course I would," Leah said. "But nothing is going to happen to you. And you have to promise the same, that if something happens to me, you'll take care of my boys."

"Of course, I will," Cynthia said, and the two women hugged.

Cynthia's older sister, Nancy, felt on edge in March. She worried about Cynthia and Mike. "I could feel it," she said. "Something built. I couldn't explain it, but it made me feel sick. I told Cindy I was concerned, and I asked her to be careful."

At the Terrell State Hospital where she worked, Cynthia helped decorate for spring with flowers and bunnies. One of her coworkers thought that Cynthia's hands shook more, the Parkinson's becoming ever more noticeable. The third week of March, Cynthia brought in a quilt she made for a coworker expecting a baby and seemed intent on presenting it that day, telling someone that it had to be soon, not explaining why.

"If something happens to me, Eric Williams did it," Cynthia told one coworker. The comment came out of context, thrown out as if never far from her mind.

"Did you receive a threat?" the woman asked.

"No. But if something happens to me and Mike, be sure to tell them Eric Williams did it."

In Kaufman, Mike got a call at his office from his old law school friend Mike Burns, who asked about the Hasse investigation. "Well, this thing has taken on a life of its own," Mike complained, with a sigh. "And we're getting nowhere."

At the house on Overlook, Eric continued to Google "Mark Hasse Murder" to keep up on the news articles. It must have been gratifying to read speculation that it could have been tied to the Colorado prison official's murder and the dead 211 Crew member. Days after the shootout Evan Ebel died in, the FBI announced that their investigation included considering any possible links between Ebel and Mark's murder.

Off and on, Eric traveled to Gibson Self Storage and opened the door on Unit 18, perhaps organizing his supplies and planning.

On Palm Sunday, March 24, the McLellands attended services at United Methodist in Terrell. Easter a week away, Cynthia bubbled with plans. She'd invited Nathan and his wife, Julie; Sam Keats; Leah and Skeet Phillips and their sons. She'd already begun shopping for candy and presents to stuff Easter baskets, and she planned to hide eggs around the house and yard. Christina had to work, but she dropped in early that week to visit her mother and stepdad.

Meanwhile, from Wortham, Mike's older son, JR, texted in hopes of setting up a weekend visit. JR and his girlfriend had plans to go dancing with Mike and Cynthia the week before, but had to cancel because JR had to work. The father and son had begun talking more, sometimes multiple times a week, texting back and forth, and JR felt as if they were finally getting close. Not long before, Mike's oldest, Krista, visited their dad with her family. If there'd been hard feelings at one point, they seemed to be melting away.

On March 25, Denise Bell, the *Forney Post* editor, held a meet-and-greet at her house for candidates running for city council, and Mike and Cynthia attended. The previous fall, Mike informed Bell that her name was on Eric Williams's list, the one sent to his office.

This night Cynthia approached Bell and told her not to be too worried. "My Mike is going to prove that Eric did it. But you be careful."

Mike stood beside his wife, holding her purse. "Denise, you do need to be careful," he said. "And remember what I told you. If it goes bad, just run."

"Are you serious?" Bell asked.

"Yes, I'm very serious," he said.

"**I** want you to drive me by their house," Eric said. That evening, after dark, Eric directed Kim to Blarney Stone Way. As they approached the McLellands' sprawling one-story, he ordered Kim to slow down. She did, and he snapped photos.

By then, Eric had informed Kim that he had chosen a date for the murder, the coming Saturday, the day before Easter, March 30.

On Wednesday, March 27, the Mensa association e-mailed its Dallas-area members, including Eric, informing them of the annual gathering, "Culture in Cowtown," to be held in July in Fort Worth.

That afternoon at the courthouse, Mike dropped in to talk to the county judge, Bruce Wood. They chitchatted, and Wood asked if Mike still believed Eric murdered Mark. "Yup, more convinced than ever," Mike said.

"Anything new happening?" the judge asked.

"No, but if you look at Eric Williams, he's a narcissistic psychopath," Mike said, explaining his opinion, drawing on his training as a psychologist. When Wood got home that evening, he Googled the term and read the definitions, descriptions of people without consciences who cared for no one but themselves and displayed aberrant or violent behaviors.

The next day, Thursday, as she had so many other days, Kim played Mafia Wars. "Need help fast on a war declared on me," she posted. Another player had singled her out, attacking, and four in Kim's crew jumped to her aid. "Thanks, y'all. ☺"

That morning, Bruce Bryant had a meeting about a different case with the sheriff. After they finished, Bryant asked, "Anything going on with the Hasse case?"

"No," the sheriff said, then adding, "We probably have to look at Eric closer."

Bryant had heard something similar from Wirskye when they talked the day before, that he planned to convene a grand jury and call in the guard members to be questioned. When they'd talked, Bryant thought Wirskye looked "beat down," from the investigation dragging. "We'll tell them this is your chance to talk," Wirskye said, reciting how he envisioned the questioning. "You don't tell us what you know and it turns out to be important later, you're in trouble."

When Bryant repeated those words at the DA's office later that afternoon, Mike smiled and looked happier than he had in the two months since Mark's murder.

The courthouse closed the next day, the DA's office prepared for a long weekend. Before heading home, Mike stopped in Judge Chitty's office, behind the 422nd. "Judge, just wanted to remind you to watch your back," Mike said.

"You, too," Judge Chitty countered.

"I'm prepared," Mike answered.

On Good Friday, March 29, John Sickel called Eric to tell him that his appeal on his theft conviction had been set for oral arguments in May, little more than a month away. That same afternoon, Mike stopped at a gun shop near his house in Forney to get a price on a new handgun. While there, he stood in front of a glass case filled with pistols and inquired about guns for his staff. "I want them to be armed," he told the owner.

When the gun shop owner asked about Mark's murder, Mike replied, "I think we're getting close."

That evening on Overlook, Kim was scrolling through Facebook when Eric walked out dressed all in dark clothing with a helmet, looking like a SWAT officer. He wore a bulletproof vest and goggles. A black mask obscured much of his face. "I think this is what I'm going to wear," he said. As part of the costume, he had a sling to hold the rifle. That way he could push it to the side and leave his hands free to gesture when Mike or Cynthia came to the door. If he showed his hands, he explained, he wouldn't appear threatening, and they seemed more likely to unlock the door.

"Okay," Kim said. There appeared to be no end to the chaos in her life. Weeks earlier, her mother had suffered a stroke, and her father's condition had deteriorated enough that hospice workers had been called in. Her gait hesitant, heavily medicated, Kim walked to their house daily, but Eric trailed her on the Segway, shadowing her wherever she went. She could still hear his threats, that he'd kill her parents and then turn the gun on her.

In the pit of her stomach, it all made her sick, but she said nothing. "I was afraid to act at all negative. I knew he was in that mindset. He'd already threatened me. It seemed best to act like I wasn't afraid."

On the occasions when she had admitted that she felt uncertain about his plans, Eric smiled at her and said, "Oh, honey, I'm going to protect you the best I can."

Before bed, Kim took her medicine, and Eric set the alarm clock for 5 a.m.

The phone rang off and on at the McLelland house that evening. Mike's mom called. She worried and asked if he felt safe. "I've got a gun in every pocket," he answered. They talked about Easter plans, but then Mike had to go. The last thing he said to her, "Momma, I love you."

Nathan called that night, and he and Cynthia discussed the holiday, too. "Can you and Julie come early? Then you can help hide the eggs and baskets." The hunt Cynthia's favorite Easter tradition, she wrote clues to lead guests to their baskets. Nathan said that they would, and Julie agreed.

Every year, Cynthia labored over what she put in each guest's basket. One year Julie, a Star Wars fan, had a Yoda doll, and another a fuzzy yellow stuffed duck. "Cynthia was like a five-year-old in her heart," said Julie, affectionately.

Cynthia and Leah texted back and forth that night. The table already set for Easter dinner, Cynthia planned to serve a pork loin, green beans, asparagus, a salad, and a strawberry cake. Excited about the holiday, she looked forward to the next event, asking Leah what she wanted for her coming birthday dinner. "Who are we inviting?" Cynthia texted.

Christina had to work Easter Sunday, but late that evening she called her mother and they talked for fifty-eight minutes, with Mike in the background. Going over what she put in the baskets, Cynthia mentioned she had a difficult time spearing the Peeps, the small spongy yellow and pink marshmallow ducks and bunnies, on sticks. Her Parkinson's made the effort harder, her hands trembling. At one point Mike suggested Cynthia rest, but she seemed determined.

"I'm fine," she said, excited about the next day.

After she hung up, Cynthia dressed for bed, putting on a brown plaid nightshirt. Following her belief in holistic medicine, she slipped on gloves that held crystals. To prevent trembling, she put on hand braces. At 11:14 that night, the motion detectors on the alarm system inside the house stopped noting movement in the living room. By then, Mike and Cynthia must have been in the bedroom, not the master where shelves filled with quilting fabric covered the walls, but the one to the left of the door, the one Cynthia had chosen because it fit feng shui principles and brought harmony and good fortune to the house.

Mike slipped off his class ring and watch and placed them next to his iPhone on the counter. They turned out the light and fell asleep, with no way of suspecting what the morning would bring.

Chapter 40

Eric was a planner. The reason he picked that Saturday was that he figured a lot of the deputies would be off for Easter. He based that on what he'd seen as a reserve deputy.

—Kim Williams

Heavy storms rocked Kaufman County that night and early the next morning. At 3 a.m. the skies crepitated over Forney, white-hot, jagged bands of lightning, pounding thunder that echoed through the darkness.

On Overlook, Kim wearily climbed out of bed at five to let the dogs out and feed them. Already up, Eric dressed in the outfit he'd modeled the night before. When Kim had their three Pomeranians diapered and back in their kennels, they walked out the door.

The drive to Gibson Self Storage felt excruciating to Kim. The storm brought with it wind, and although the rain finally stopped, gusts pummeled the Sport Trac. The gates at Gibson were accessible at six, and they arrived six minutes later. Eric pulled over and keyed in his code, 2072, and they entered as he always did from the far gate, the one near the Chicken Express drive-through.

The door on Unit 18 up, he drove out the white Crown Victoria. Kim got in the car's passenger seat while he parked the Sport Trac inside the unit and lowered the door,

locking it. In the car, Eric put blue surgical-type booties on
his feet and wore latex gloves. They pulled out of Gibson's
at 6:18, turned right as they exited the gate, and headed
east on U.S. 175 for the twenty-minute ride to Forney. As
Eric drove, Kim slumped in the seat, drifting off on her
medication.

At times, her eyes fluttered and she thought about where
they were going and what Eric intended to do. "It's Easter
weekend. What if they have family there?" she asked.

"I'm going to do it anyway," he answered. "If anyone
else is there, I'll kill them, too."

When they got to the McLellands' house, Eric parked
in the driveway and got out, leaving the driver's side door
open behind him. The car's dome light didn't go on, and
he'd turned the headlights off. She watched as he hurried
toward the front door, an assault rifle hanging from the
sling over his shoulder. A light went on in the left side of
the house, in the bedroom where the McLellands slept. The
porch light went on, and then Eric disappeared inside.

A second later, Kim heard the rat-a-tat-tat of gunfire.
"Oh my God," she thought. "Oh my God." She waited,
nervous, her stomach churning, her head throbbing. More
gunfire. It seemed longer, but less than two minutes after he
entered the house, Eric hurried toward the car. He opened
the car's back door and tossed the gun on the backseat, shut
the door, got behind the wheel, and then backed out of the
driveway. As he drove, he pulled off the helmet, throwing
that, too, onto the backseat. Resolutely quiet, Eric looked
nervous, until they pulled out of the neighborhood.

Once on their way, he smiled and laughed.

The route Eric took back to Gibson differed from the
one he'd taken there, veering toward the north. On 1641 he
turned left just before the Forney Community Park, with a
playground and tennis courts. Kim didn't ask about what
had happened in the house, not wanting to know, but it
seemed Eric wanted to talk.

"His wife didn't die right away," Eric said suddenly. "She was still moaning, so I put a bullet through her head."

When he said it, Kim's stomach roiled, but she thought Eric sounded proud.

In the Crown Vic, Eric took a right on I–20, then a left on Beltline Road. He used his code to open Gibson's gate again at 7:07 a.m., forty-nine minutes after they'd driven out. At Unit 18, Eric backed the Sport Trac out. While she waited, he drove the Crown Vic back into the unit. Once he did, she pulled the door down but left a foot-high gap at the bottom. Then, just as after Mark Hasse's murder, Kim heard Eric spray the car down, cleaning it, and he walked out in other clothes, blue jeans and a green shirt with Velcro slits on the side. "I didn't think anything. I was just mostly scared," she said. "Being around him. Getting caught. I was scared."

Seventeen minutes after they returned to Gibson, they drove out the gate. On Overlook, they stopped at Kim's parents' house, dropping in to check on them. Later, at their own house, Eric logged onto his computer and turned on all the TVs, watching news reports.

"I'm going to lie down," Kim said.

"Okay," Eric said, appearing to barely notice her.

When she woke up, they returned to her parents' house, and Eric, smiling and laughing, grilled steaks for all of them for dinner. By then, she'd put the morning's horror behind her, relieved to have it over. So much so that she felt happy watching him celebrate.

At 8:30 that morning, Sam Keats picked up rose plants to bring to the McLellands' house. She'd been invited for Easter the next day, and Cynthia wanted help planting the roses in the garden before everyone arrived. As she drove, Keats called Cynthia's cell, but didn't get an answer. She called again at 9 and 9:30. No answer. She left a message.

Wondering if Cynthia's plans had changed, Sam called Leah.

The rain and thunder had roused Leah off and on during the night. She woke up early and went to the vegetable co-op to pick up her produce and Cynthia's. When Keats called, Leah thought about Cynthia not answering her phone and assumed that she'd been called into work. That happened sometimes, and sometimes Cynthia simply forgot appointments. Neither Keats nor Leah worried.

About eleven, Keats, with her dogs in the back of her pickup, drove to the McLelland house, thinking that she would deliver the roses. When she got there, the house looked strange. She rang the doorbell, and no one answered.

Sam Keats on the McLellands' front walk
Kathryn Casey

At first, she couldn't isolate what bothered her, but then she noticed the light on and the ceiling fan churning in the window on the left, Mike and Cynthia's bedroom. That seemed odd. The newspaper lay in the wrapper on the driveway. Keats thought about walking in. The door was nearly always unlocked, but something told her not to try it.

Keats left, deciding to bring her dogs home. She drove a little, and then called Leah again. "Mike's truck is there, and so is Cynthia's car," she said. "Something is wrong."

"Well, I'm supposed to bring their vegetables to

them," Leah said. "Maybe Mike went somewhere with someone."

"Can you call them?" Keats asked. "They'll answer the phone if you call them."

Leah agreed, then put in calls to both Mike's and Cynthia's cell phones. They didn't answer. At her house, she walked outside the front door and looked out at the sky and the grass. "That's weird," she thought. Considering the possibilities, she decided that maybe Mike and Cynthia had gone to a movie, and they'd turned their cell phones off.

Still, something bothered her. She called again. No answers. "Have you heard from your mom today?" she asked Nathan when she reached him later that afternoon.

"No," he said. "I'll call and see if someone else has heard from them." He talked to Cynthia's mother, her sister Nancy, and Christina. No one had talked to his mother or Mike. Nathan didn't know that Mike's mother, Wyvonne, had been calling off and on all morning and afternoon, too, without an answer. Again he tried his mother's number, but she didn't answer.

Leah sat in the rocking chair in the house when Nathan called back. "No one has talked to them. Can you go over there?"

"Okay," Leah said. "I have their vegetables. I'll run them over."

After she loaded a crate of strawberries and a box of vegetables and fruit in her car, Leah drove toward Blarney Stone Way. At the house, she pulled into the driveway. Holding the crate of strawberries, she rang the doorbell. No one answered.

Walking around the house, she saw Mike's truck, and then she noticed Cynthia's car turned around and pointed down the driveway toward the street. Leah thought about how Mike habitually parked his wife's car that way each night to make it easier for Cynthia to pull out onto the road.

That meant Cynthia hadn't taken her car out that day. That seemed odd. And the newspaper in the driveway bothered Leah. Cynthia loved reading the newspaper. Each morning she picked it up when she walked the dogs. That it remained outside didn't seem right.

Leah had her key to the McLelland house. She knew that often the front door was unlocked. But she stood on the threshold still holding the crate of strawberries and stopped before grabbing the storm door handle. Behind it the heavy wooden front door blocked the view. Usually she would have walked right in shouting, "Cynthia! Mike!"

Instead she took the strawberries back to her car. Then she walked farther around the house. She checked the back door. Closed. She looked inside the cars. Nothing unusual. She heard Mike and Cynthia's dogs barking in their crates. Feeling queasy, she returned to her car. She pulled out of the driveway thinking she'd get an iced tea. A short time later, her phone rang.

"Did you go to Mom's?" Nathan asked.

"They aren't there."

"Did you go in?"

"No. I could hear the dogs in the crates. They must have gone somewhere."

"Can you go back?" Nathan asked. "You have a key."

She didn't want to. "Only for you, Nathan," she said. With that, she turned around and headed back to Blarney Stone, fighting an overwhelming sense of dread.

On the way, Leah called C.J., her oldest son. He and Skeet were working on a project they'd planned for weeks. "Something is wrong," Skeet said, when C.J. repeated what Leah told him. "Call your mom and tell her not to go in the house. We'll be there in a few minutes."

When Skeet and C.J. arrived, they walked with Leah to the McLellands' front door. Leah felt sick to her stomach as C.J. opened the screen door, then pounded on the wooden inner door and yelled, "Mike." Again, without an answer.

As Leah watched, her oldest son grabbed the handle and pressed down on the lock. The door swung open. It was unlocked. C.J. stepped inside shouting, "Mike! Cynthia!"

Falling to her knees, Leah screamed.

When C.J. looked back, his mother pointed at the floor. Her voice suddenly hoarse, she said, "Your feet! There are shells between your feet!"

C.J. glanced down and saw spent casings on a beige throw rug between his feet. At that, C.J. took a few more steps forward and saw Cynthia on the floor, on top of an oriental rug in front of the fireplace, a pool of drying blood near her head. Immediately, he backed out of the house. Once he and Skeet had Leah upright, C.J. said, "I'm going to the car. I'm going to get my gun."

By the time C.J. walked his mother back to the driveway and returned with his gun, Skeet had entered the house, going far enough inside to find Mike's body sprawled on the floor in a small hallway.

Leah waited near the car, as her husband and son walked toward her. "Mom," C.J. said. "I'm so sorry . . . They've been dead for a long time."

Leah screamed slightly, just as Sam Keats drove back up to the house and got out of her truck. She saw the look on C.J.'s face, pale as if all the blood had been pulled from his body. She looked at Leah. "I knew it was bad."

"They're gone," Leah said.

Chapter 41

It was the most ironic thing that's ever happened in this world. My dad got shot, and he'd been preparing for a gunfight forever.

—JR McLelland

Leah waited in the car with Sam Keats, while Skeet called the sheriff. Sheriff Byrnes's son answered the phone. Just out of the shower after spending the afternoon working in his garden, tending his beds of corn, pole beans, and black-eyed peas, the longtime lawman took the phone. "We're at the McLellands," Skeet said. "Mike and Cynthia are dead, shot, inside the house."

"Call 911," the sheriff said.

"If I do, this house will be flooded with people, and the media," Skeet said. "We can't help Mike and Cynthia. They've been dead a long time. Let's get the right people out here."

The sheriff agreed. He hung up, put in a call to Chief Deputy Rodney Evans and to Ranger Kasper, instructing them not to put it on the radio.

After he hung up with the sheriff, Skeet called Nathan. "It's bad," he said.

About five that evening, half an hour after the call went out, the sheriff arrived at the house. Moments later, Ranger

Kasper pulled in, followed by Chief Deputy Evans. "Everyone stays off cell phones," Kasper ordered. "We don't want the media to hear about this."

Once they gathered, the sheriff and his chief deputy decided they needed to go inside, to verify that the McLellands were truly beyond medical help. Inside their crates the McLellands' two small dogs barked and yelped, as the sheriff and his deputy entered the living room and saw what C.J. had, Cynthia's dead body in front of the fireplace. A few more steps and they noticed drops of blood in front of the entertainment center. Steps farther lay Mike McLelland, the Kaufman County DA, bare-chested, wearing sweatpants, barefoot, eyeglasses still on, dead on a hallway floor.

"It looked like a war in there," Sheriff Byrnes said referring to all the blood and spent casings scattered on the floors.

When they walked out, other officers had arrived, stringing crime scene tape. Sam Keats walked up to Byrnes and realized how shaken he appeared. "I've been to a lot of crime scenes," he said. "But this is different. I know these people."

Each time Evans called an investigator and told him what happened, he sounded stunned.

Hours away outside Houston at a family picnic when the call came in, Lieutenant Jolie Stewart felt as if she'd been "sucked into a vacuum." Since the McLelland house was in the county but not within city limits, the murders came under the sheriff's authority. In the car on the way to the scene she worried about what it all meant. That the killer had murdered Cynthia had ratcheted it up to a higher level. Who was next? Were all their families in danger?

"It was an oh-shit moment," FBI Special Agent Laurie Gibbs said. She and her partner, Michael Hillman, were both at their homes when called. "There had never been two prosecutors killed like this in the history of the United States."

At about seven, Bill Wirskye's phone rang. Chief Aulbaugh said, "Bill, the sheriff asked me to call. The McLellands have been found dead in their home, and the sheriff wants you and Toby out there."

"Please tell me that it's a murder-suicide," Wirskye said. His mind racing, he thought about how much pressure Mike had been under. While horrible, that seemed preferable. If they were both murdered, the situation had become vastly more serious. Another murdered DA meant a war against law enforcement.

"No, it's a murder-murder."

Shaken, Wirskye said, "Okay. I'll get with Toby and get out there as soon as possible. I'll see you there."

Although heading the Hasse murder investigation, Chief Aulbaugh, however, said he wasn't going to the McLelland murder scene. The reason? He worried about being on "the list." What Wirskye assumed Aulbaugh referred to was the tip that the Aryan Brotherhood had a list of targets, and Kaufman's chief was on it.

Toby Shook had just finished a family Easter egg hunt when Wirskye called. "This ain't gonna be good," Shook thought. What he said was, "Well, we know it's Eric Williams now, don't we?"

"Yeah. He's the common denominator. The only thing Mike and Mark did together. The sheriff wants us out there."

"Whoa, they're killing prosecutors. You going?" Shook asked. When Wirskye said he was, Shook told him, "Well, come get me and we'll go together."

"Don't answer the door for anyone," Wirskye told his wife, before he left to pick up Shook. It all seemed surreal.

At his house, Toby Shook reminded his wife where they kept a gun. "You think I might need one?" she asked.

"We don't know what this guy will do," he answered. "I'll call before I come back. Unless you know it's me, get ready to shoot." When he got in Wirskye's car, Shook had a .38 revolver in his pocket.

The two men habitually broke the tension by sharing a joke, and Wirskye teased, "Don't shoot me before we get there."

As his law partner had hoped he would, Shook laughed.

On the drive to Forney, Shook and Wirskye analyzed the situation, that they'd been appointed special prosecutors on a case where someone murdered prosecutors. They wondered about their families. Like the others, they realized that the person behind the killings had increased the danger when he killed Cynthia.

By then, the sun had set. On a dark night in the countryside, the two prosecutors had a hard time finding the McLelland house. When they arrived, crime scene tape had been strung, and the scene felt deathly quiet. As soon as they walked up, Wirskye and Shook noticed the worry on Sheriff Byrnes's well-lined face. With all his decades of experience, it took the two prosecutors aback. By then Ranger Kasper's boss, Major Dewayne Dockery, a tall, bald man with tired blue eyes and a crooked frown, wearing a cowboy hat, had arrived on the scene, along with the two FBI agents, Hillman and Gibbs. The rangers had called for their mobile crime scene lab, built into a converted horse trailer, but it hadn't yet arrived.

"Boys, I've never seen anything like this in all my years," the sheriff said.

"What about Eric Williams?" Shook asked.

"We have someone looking for him."

Unaware of the scene unfolding, Christina worried. Ever since she heard from her brother, Nathan, hours earlier that no one could contact their mother, she'd been on edge. Driving with a friend, she said, "I need to go out there."

Joking, trying to ease the situation, Christina said, "God only knows what my mom and Mike are doing."

The friend offered to go with her.

All the way to the house, Christina called Nathan, but he didn't answer. On the road, she pulled into a store parking lot. "I need some cigarettes."

"You haven't smoked since college," her friend pointed out.

"I'm going to need one." Back in the car, Christina lit a cigarette and said, "I'm really sorry. I don't have time to take you home. My parents are dead."

"They're not," the woman replied. "How do you know?"

"I just know."

When she pulled onto Blarney Stone, Christina saw Nathan's car and the street lined with police cars. "That fucker killed my parents," she said.

JR McLelland was driving in his car with his girlfriend and his kids on their way to go country-western dancing at the Elks lodge, when he got the call that his father and Cynthia had been shot. He couldn't figure out how to tell the others, what to say. Instead, he drove to his aunt's house. Once there, he called his sister, Krista, still not knowing if their father had survived. Once Krista arrived, they called Kaufman PD and the sheriff's office, but no one who knew anything answered. Finally, they called Nathan, who told them that Mike and Cynthia were both dead.

The first thing JR wondered was how long his dad and stepmother suffered. And then he wondered if the killer could come after him or his family.

At the house, Christina and the others hung together, supporting one another. Waiting. Some worried about Mike and Cynthia's two dogs, locked in their cages. They asked to have someone bring them out. Michael Hillman, the FBI agent, agreed to go in and carry them out.

Afterward a group of the investigators, along with the two prosecutors, congregated near the front door. The first name that came up was Eric Williams. As he had earlier, the sheriff told the others that he had someone looking for Williams. "By then, we'd all decided he had to be the focus," said Hillman. "It just made the most sense."

As they talked, they remarked that it seemed odd that they saw no signs that the front door had been broken into. That suggested that either Cynthia or Mike opened it for the killer, or that it was unlocked and he walked in. Perhaps something else made that second scenario sound possible. The expensive alarm system Mike purchased wasn't turned on.

While the investigators conferred, Christina called her family spreading the news. She asked her father, Cynthia's ex-husband, to drive to the scene, to stay with Nathan and Julie, while she went to the assisted living center to tell their grandmother. "I couldn't tell someone who is ninety-eight that her child died before her on the phone," Christina said.

Chapter 42

There was a profound sense of fear that this thing was much worse than it had been with Mark. To murder Cynthia, who was completely innocent, took it to an unimaginable level.

—Marcus Busch

That evening, Brandi Fernandez parked in her driveway, and another Kaufman County prosecutor waited for her. "Hey, did you hear about Mike?" the man said.

"What are you talking about?"

One of the assistants in the DA's office sent out texts and phone calls, asking the staff to meet at her church. Many departed from family dinners, their homes, one left a bonfire in a pasture cooking hot dogs when the text came in.

With everyone from the office accounted for at the church, one woman explained that the sheriff had called and Mike and Cynthia were dead. They had no more information. They waited, the room tensely quiet, until an hour later when a police officer walked in and announced that the McLellands had both been murdered. "Don't go home tonight," he said. "Go somewhere else and stay there, until we figure out what happened."

One person not particularly shocked was Mark's assistant, Amanda Morris. Looking back, she'd been waiting for something else to happen, because "they hadn't caught him."

"Please, just come home," Morris's mother pleaded on a voice mail that night. "We want you home. You need to find another job."

Some of the DA's staffers gathered their spouses and children and stayed with family, while others checked into hotels. Those who returned home took turns sleeping and watching, peering out into the darkness, a rifle or a shotgun nearby, until the morning.

Constable Shawn Mayfield's wife saw on Facebook that the McLellands were dead, murdered. Through the grapevine, Mayfield had heard that Eric had a hit list. Wondering if he might be on it, Mayfield helped his wife hang blankets over all the windows in the house, to prevent anyone from watching them, making it harder to shoot from outside.

Meanwhile, Judge Erleigh Wiley's court coordinator tracked her down after a stressful night of calling without answer. At a friend's house, Wiley had her ringtone turned off. The court coordinator finally called Wiley's husband, who handed her the phone. As the judge listened, the other woman cried so hard that at first Wiley couldn't understand her.

Once Judge Wiley arrived home, someone rang her doorbell. A police officer stood outside. "Ma'am, we'll be posted around the house for the night," he said. The judge thanked him, and closed the door, thinking about Mike and Cynthia and wondering, "Who was next?"

After the steak dinner with her parents, Kim and Eric returned to their house, and Kim decided she wanted to go for a ride. She felt anxious and thought that might ease her restlessness. Eric agreed. When he got in the car, he carried something that looked like a black bag. From the way it hung, Kim knew it held something heavy. Without asking, she assumed it had to be guns.

They headed out, and Kim drove not knowing where to go. Before long, Eric suggested she head north on Highway 34 toward Lone Oak, where Kim's parents used to live. "Let's go up to the lake," he said, referring to Lake Tawakoni.

A reservoir with a long, ragged shoreline, Lake Tawakoni was a dammed-up, flooded section of the Sabine River, fifty minutes northeast of Kaufman. Cars crossed it via Two Mile Bridge, descriptively named for the length of its concrete span.

On Highway 34, Kim drove past horse and cattle ranches and through the rolling countryside. While affluent homes bordered other Dallas-area lakes, as they approached Tawakoni the surrounding area looked depressed: small restaurants, businesses that catered to boaters and fishermen, mobile home and RV parks, and clusters of cottage-like houses. On the bridge, the car thump, thump, thumped over the rough concrete, and Eric told Kim to slow down. Then he ordered her to stop not quite halfway across at an incline, a high point from which he could see cars approach. He got out, walked a short distance, and then threw something into the lake. In the darkness, Kim couldn't see, but assumed he'd disposed of the heavy black bag.

"Let's go," he said once back in the car. "Turn around and let's go home."

As Kim drove on, she thought about the lake's muddy water and assumed what Eric had thrown away would never be found.

Minutes later, Eric's phone rang. A sergeant from the sheriff's office, Robert Ramsey, asked for his location. "I'm up around the Quinlan area with my wife," Eric said, citing a town west of the lake. "Why?"

"The McLellands have been murdered," Sergeant Ramsey replied. "I need to talk to you."

They agreed to meet at the Denny's on South Washington in Kaufman, not far from the law enforcement center and the sheriff's office, less than a mile from the house on Overlook. Sometime after ten, Eric arrived, and Ramsey waited with three other officers.

Kim stayed in the car, while in the parking lot Ramsey ran a glue stick over Eric's hands, testing for gunshot residue. When they asked Eric to account for his whereabouts, he said he'd been with Kim all day, and that they'd helped her parents. About 8:30 that evening, they decided to drive up to the lake.

"When's the last time you fired a gun?" Ramsey asked.

"Not since my arrest," Eric responded indicating his theft arrest nearly two years earlier.

Then Ramsey asked if they had phones on them. Eric did, and he turned it over to the sergeant. Ramsey followed them home and they surrendered Kim's as well.

At the house, Eric turned on the television. By then, local and national news bulletins announced that in Kaufman, where nearly two months earlier a prosecutor had been murdered, the DA and his wife had been killed. Video feeds from helicopters and the street showed lines of police cars and officers in dark windbreakers with "SHERIFF," "FBI," "DPS," and "ATF" across the backs. Kim saw a small smile on her husband's face as he watched. Before long, she left him with the TVs and computer news blaring, and she went to bed wondering why Eric had taken his phone with him to the lake and if what he'd told her earlier was true, that police could track cell phone signals.

"Can you give me a quantitative threat assessment? What do you think our threat level is?" Sheriff Byrnes asked the FBI profiler he talked to on the phone from the scene.

"We don't know," the man said, explaining there'd never before been a case in U.S. history in which two prosecutors and one of their wives had been murdered. "We have nothing to compare this to."

Facing the unknown, the sheriff ordered all his deputies back from their holiday plans.

One of those who'd responded to the murder scene was Ranger Kasper's boss, Major Dewayne Dockery, a tall, bald man with cold, pale eyes. In charge of Company B, the entire Dallas regiment, Dockery issued an order that brought in rangers and DPS troopers from throughout the region. He also notified the U.S. Marshals office. Until they had the killers in custody, all public officials in Kaufman County needed round-the-clock security details.

When Sheriff Byrnes called his wife, he found her at the grocery store shopping for Easter dinner. "You need to go home," he said. "The McLellands have been murdered." When she arrived home, their daughter and her husband, a police officer, waited to watch over her.

"It is a shock," Chief Aulbaugh told a *Dallas Morning News* reporter who asked if the McLelland murders were tied to Mark Hasse's. "Until we know what happened, I really can't confirm if it's related, but you always have to assume until it's proven otherwise."

"They need to shut the DA's office down for a while," a local attorney said. "Everybody is a target. They're not safe on the streets of downtown Kaufman. They're not safe in their homes."

A local councilwoman went to Denise Bell's house to tell her that Cynthia and Mike were dead. Bell drove out to the house and saw Cynthia's children, Leah and Skeet Phillips, and Sam Keats. "People were scared to death," said Bell. "It was like the killer sent a message that he'd go to their homes and take their wife and kids, too."

From the scene, Denise drove home. Crying, she filed a story on her Web site, and then packed. In her head she heard Mike's voice, "Denise, if it goes bad, just run." That night she went into hiding. Days later, an FBI agent came to her hotel room. She had a .45 caliber pistol.

"That's not going to protect you against the Aryan Brotherhood," he said.

"No, it won't. But this isn't the Aryan nation. It's Eric Williams."

When the crime scene unit responded, Ranger Kasper took them inside the house for an initial walkthrough. Careful where they stepped, they assessed the scene. Inside the door, they saw the first spent casings. They appeared to be .223 caliber, the type shot by a high-velocity, assault-type rifle. That made sense, since those types of weapons expelled the casings to the right, where these were found. Kasper and the others followed the casings in and walked over to Cynthia. There more spent casings lay near her body, one in the blood pool above her head, where it appeared the killer had walked up and pumped a bullet into her.

Looking at drops of blood in front of the entertainment center, Ranger Kasper thought that was probably where Mike stood when the first bullets hit him. Then he ran back, attempting to flee, as the killer continued to shoot. More casings scattered about the floor near Mike's corpse, so Kasper reasoned that the killer must have kept firing as he walked toward him, then shot from directly above Mike into his body as he lay on the floor.

So much blood. So much hate.

The ranger wondered if the door had been unlocked, or if Cynthia opened it and let the gunman in. On the dining room table, set for Easter dinner, Kasper saw a sack of guns. If the door had been locked and Mike had been the one to answer, the ranger had no doubt Mike would have had a loaded gun in his hand.

At the house on Overlook at 11:30 that night, Eric downloaded an article on the killings, undoubtedly relishing the excitement of sitting in the shadows watching as the world reacted.

At one or so that morning the DPS forensic team placed yellow tentlike, numbered evidence markers inside the McLelland house beside spent casings, holes in the walls, and blood. The decision had been made not to remove the bodies until the morning. The evidence markers in place, a cameraman videotaped the scene. He started outside the front door where a small cement angel sat beside one of Cynthia's souvenir rocks on the front stoop. The audio picked up a loud squeak when the storm door opened, then a rustle as it slammed. In the entryway, he focused the camera on the spent casings on the floor.

Inside, the house felt eerily quiet, as the camera scanned the floors and walls, pausing over fired casings, documenting damage to furniture, bullet holes in the walls, blood, and Cynthia's and Mike's bodies, still, cold, and pale, on the floor.

At 2:30 that morning, Bill Wirskye and Toby Shook arrived back in Dallas. At his house, Toby relit a bonfire he'd built earlier to toast s'mores. The two seasoned prosecutors, shaken by what had happened, held loaded guns on their laps. "We sat there around the fire like two little kids," said Wirskye. "Every time a breeze came through, we jumped."

Still wired from the night, they discussed what they needed to do. As they talked, they decided they had to push the others even harder to investigate Eric Williams. He was the only connection between Mike and Mark and their best suspect. They also talked about the fact that the situation had changed, that since the second murders had happened in the county, the sheriff, not Chief Aulbaugh, would be in charge. In another positive development, Major Dockery, the head Texas Ranger in the area, would become more involved.

"Whether or not it's that JP, we need to know for sure," Shook said.

Chapter 43

Eric said that he rang the doorbell and Cynthia answered. She let him in, then turned and walked back to yell for Mike. Eric walked in and started shooting.
—Kim Williams

That night Sheriff Byrnes drove Skeet and Leah Phillips home, because their car remained parked in the McLellands' driveway inside the crime scene tape. When she got out of his car, Leah gave the sheriff a hug. "David, if he can walk in and kill Mike and Cynthia, he can come to your house. You need to get protection."

"I've already got somebody there," he said.

When Lieutenant Stewart returned to Blarney Stone early the next morning, the coroner's van had arrived to remove the bodies. She went inside and did a walkthrough. Like the others, Stewart reflected on the limited scene, confined to the front entry and living room, Mike's body in the small adjacent hallway. "It looked like target practice," she said. "How quick it must have happened."

Helping to bag the bodies, she felt overwhelmed by sadness.

At 5 a.m., Judge Tygrett and others began showing up at Leah and Skeet Phillips's house asking questions. Tygrett and the other public officials all came accompanied by guards, security details provided by the sheriff, Homeland

Security, DPS, the U.S. Marshals, and others. Some wore bulletproof vests.

At 7 a.m., Mike McLelland's children arrived in Forney. After talking to investigators on the scene, they drove to Forney PD headquarters, where they met with FBI and ATF agents. JR wanted to know what they could tell him, but instead the agents questioned them, asking where they were the day before, when Mike and Cynthia died. The investigators probed their relationships with their father and stepmother, looked at their phones and read the text messages. On JR's he had a message from Mike, one about their cancelled night out dancing and plans to get together in the coming weeks.

None of them minded answering the questions. They understood. "But they wanted to know who did it, and they wanted an arrest right then," said one investigator. "And that was something we couldn't give them."

That morning, Easter Sunday, at a meeting in the re-opened command post in the old armory building, the FBI agreed to take a greater role. That meant additional agents brought in to track leads, and the profilers would return to Kaufman to reassess and advise. By then, those gathered had initial reports from the crime scene unit, confirming that the murder weapon fired .223 caliber cartridges, the type often used in high-velocity, assault-type rifles.

Many marveled at how fast it must have been, leaving Mike McLelland unable to grab a weapon. The forensic team found rifles and handguns scattered throughout the house, including three in the entertainment center where Mike stood when first hit by a bullet. As they pieced together how the assault took place, some thought Mike might have been in the bedroom, and came out when Cynthia opened the door. Others thought that Mike was sitting in his chair near the fireplace, next to the entertainment center, when the gunman burst in. The killer shot Cynthia. She fell, and then he turned his gun on Mike, who tried to flee to a guest bedroom. He never made it, instead collapsing in the hallway, as the gunman stood over him and fired.

With the sheriff's office the coordinating agency, Lieutenant Jolie Stewart acted as lead on the case. Decisions included that the evidence would be picked up from Kaufman PD and moved to the sheriff's headquarters.

Once the McLellands' neighborhood woke up, Ranger Kasper and others spread out, canvassing the families who lived on or near Blarney Stone. Their first hope centered on finding a home surveillance camera that might have caught the killer or the car. As they knocked on doors, they also recorded descriptions and license plate numbers of the cars owned by the McLellands' neighbors, to identify their vehicles on surveillance videos they'd collect from intersections, businesses, and homes in the area.

"Did you hear or see anything suspicious?" they asked.

For the most part, no one did. Some heard loud bangs, but they assumed it had to be thunder since the storm had passed through. One man who lived behind the McLellands did hear gunshots early that morning. "I didn't call 911 because it's not all that unusual around here," he said. "This is a rural area and people hunt."

While investigators worked the scene, the first news accounts of the murders appeared. Unaware that much of the investigators' interest had turned toward Eric Williams, the reporters continued to focus on the Aryan Brotherhood. Some predicted the Kaufman killings presented a disturbing precedent. In media reports, experts described the "troubling boldness" of the killings, ambushing Mark Hasse on the street; storming, guns blazing, into the McLellands' home. One speculated that such audacious assaults worked to the gang's advantage. "Part of the goal of a domestic terrorist organization is to instill fear."

As prosecutors and public officials read their Easter Sunday newspapers, the murders instilled fear not only in Kaufman County, but across Texas. Throughout the state, law enforcement brought in officers to stand guard at homes. In Houston that day, Harris County District Attorney Mike Anderson announced he had twenty-four-hour protection for himself and his wife and children. "District attorneys across Texas are in a state of shock," he told a reporter.

Meanwhile, the scene on Blarney Stone Way remained somber. Late that afternoon the crime scene tape came down, and once it did, someone drove a cross into the McLellands' front lawn. Before long neighbors, friends, and townsfolk dropped by bringing flowers and candles, short handwritten notes and sympathy cards, piling them around the cross.

On Overlook that Easter Sunday, Eric's word of the day from Urban Dictionary arrived on his e-mail account. "Jesus: man who was nailed to a plank for saying how nice it would be if everyone was nice to each other."

For the most part, the day unfolded without incident. Late that morning, Sergeant Ramsey stopped over and returned Eric's and Kim's cell phones, after downloading the information. In the afternoon, Kim woke up and walked into the kitchen to find Eric laughing at a statement released by Governor Rick Perry, one that said his thoughts and prayers were with the McLelland family and the residents of Kaufman County.

After the sun set, Kim went back to bed, leaving Eric at the kitchen bar at his computer keyboard.

A block away at the command post at 9:57 p.m., an e-mail arrived, and the investigator managing the Crime Stoppers tips carried it over to show the others. The system designated it as tip number W695–196. It read: "Offense type, homicide. Victim information: Mark Hasse. Do we have your full attention now? Only a response from Judge Bruce Wood would be answered. You have 48 hours."

Monday morning the FBI profilers waited at the command post when Bill Wirskye arrived early. Many of the investigators already working, the place buzzed with activity; much of the discussion centered on Eric Williams.

The result of Eric's gunshot residue test further fueled speculation that he could be the killer. Eric claimed that he hadn't fired a weapon in more than a year. But the swab of his hands tested positive.

The test had been taken more than a dozen hours after the murders, so it seemed unlikely that gunshot residue would have remained from the actual killings. But there was another possibility. The GSR could have come from handling a recently fired weapon. That seemed logical in the context of another piece of evidence: Eric's cell phone records. The evening after the murders, his phone pinged off towers near Lake Tawakoni. It took little imagination to picture Eric handling the murder weapons when he threw them in the water.

The investigation kicked into gear that morning, and one of the first pieces of business involved assessing the anonymous tip from the night before. At the meeting, they decided to reply in hopes of starting a conversation. Toward that end, at 10:15 a.m. they responded: "You have our attention. How can the judge contact you?"

As Judge Wood arrived downtown that morning, Kaufman resembled an armed encampment with local, state, and federal law enforcement stationed for blocks around the courthouse, many carrying rifles on slings over their shoulders. At the county lot, guards waited to escort employees, and reporters milled around shouting out questions. With the McLellands' murders, the news coverage exploded, and photos of the small city of Kaufman showed up on the front page of the *New York Times* and other newspapers across the nation.

Although officially closed, at the DA's office the entire

staff reported for work. Despite the fear that surrounded them, they wanted to send the message that they hadn't been defeated. Some clustered together offering sympathy to those who cried. Many found comfort in camaraderie with others who understood their anxiety. For the most part, they felt more relaxed in the office surrounded by guards than in their homes. "We felt safe in the office, but when we walked out that door, that was when it hit," said one woman.

Grief counselors talked to those who asked, while others kept to themselves, facing the horror in their own ways. They'd consoled each other after Mark's murder. The McLellands' deaths drew them even closer, leaning on each other more like family than coworkers.

As Mike's first assistant, Brandi Fernandez took over as interim DA. One of her first duties, she appointed Bill Wirskye and Toby Shook as special prosecutors on the McLelland murders. Again she considered the odd circumstances. Mark had told her if anything happened to him, he'd want Bill Wirskye handling the case. And months earlier Mike sat in her office and told her that if anything happened to him, he'd want Shook and Wirskye.

All that day, a large display grew outside the courthouse, people dropping off flowers, notes, and religious items, as they had at the house on Blarney Stone. All the judges and county officials arrived under heavy guard. Judge Chitty had a SWAT team at his house day and night, and Homeland Security installed surveillance equipment in his yard. One assistant DA carried an AR–15 into the office, along with his bag lunch.

Once everyone reported to the DA's office, deputies ushered the staff into Judge Chitty's courtroom, where a representative from the sheriff's office asked if anyone had theories about who murdered the McLellands. As they had after Mark's murder, many would later say they called out, "Eric Williams."

The man in the front of the room may not have wanted to tip the investigators' hand. Or he didn't know that by then many considered Eric the prime suspect. It was also possible that he knew about the theories but had his own doubts that the nerdish ex-JP would commit three such cold-blooded murders. But what Mark's assistant Amanda Morris and others said he replied that day was on the order of "I need something more reliable than that."

As was done with Mark's office two months earlier, upstairs on the second floor behind the door marked "District Attorney," authorities cordoned off Mike's office with crime scene tape. When the others returned after the meeting, they found FBI agents rifling through his files, looking on the dead DA's computer. Where they had hundreds of cases to look at after Mark's murder, this time that part of the investigation moved quickly. The only case Mike personally prosecuted in Kaufman was assisting Mark on the Eric Williams theft case.

Meanwhile, at the command post the number of investigators swelled. With two more deaths, Texas DPS responded with dozens of Texas Rangers and state troopers. The FBI brought in fifty agents, earmarking the Kaufman killings their number one priority in the nation. "We were told we got whatever we needed," Michael Hillman said. "Anything was at our disposal."

At the briefing sessions, between one hundred and one hundred and fifty people gathered. Again the tips poured in, and again coverage about the Aryan Brotherhood brought leads from inmates across the nation. In addition, theories mushroomed about possible Mexican cartel involvement.

Law enforcement under fire, the agencies collaborated. Although they had a main suspect, they couldn't afford to block out other possibilities. At the command post, those gathered broke off into teams: one to explore ABT tips, one for the cartels, one to follow miscellaneous tips. Each had representatives from multiple agencies, the Eric Williams squad manned by Ranger Kasper, Lieutenant Stewart, and the two FBI agents, Gibbs and Hillman.

Another group focused on dissecting the victims' lives. They'd question family and friends, looking for the possibility of someone close to the victims, perhaps motivated by insurance money or inheritance. As after Mark's murder, one team would do nothing but secure video from surveillance cameras in the area. Another examined dumps from cell towers, looking for phone numbers that tied to possible suspects.

While the others pursued their tasks, Bill Wirskye e-mailed David Sergi and John Sickel, Eric's attorneys, informing them that he and Toby Shook had been appointed as special prosecutors on the McLelland murders and requesting an interview with their client.

For years, Eric had a history of e-mailing late at night, after he'd had a few beers. Kim had warned him not to e-mail Crime Stoppers. She'd said, "You'll get caught."

Ignoring her warnings, that Monday night at 10:13, almost exactly twelve hours after he received a response on his anonymous Crime Stoppers e-mail that said simply "You have our attention," Eric responded: ". . . Your act of good faith will result in no other attacks this week. As proof, Mark Hasse was killed with .38 caliber +P ammunition, 147 grain Hydra-Shok ammunition, fired from a 3-inch .357 5-shot revolver." Then Eric demanded: "Judge Wood must offer a resignation of one of the four main judges in Kaufman County, district or county court, list stress or family concerns or whatever else sounds deniable. The media will understand. My superiors will see this as the first step to ending our actions. Do not report any details of this arrangement. You have until Friday at 4:00 p.m. We are not unreasonable, but we will not be stopped."

When that second e-mail from the same unnamed sender arrived, those who knew the contents of the DPS lab reports on the bullet fragments recovered from Mark Hasse's body understood that the tipster had firsthand knowledge of the case. "No one else would have known what kind of firearm and ammo was used," said Wirskye. "He was taunting us."

Chapter 44

I'm a human being. I have family members I dearly love. To say we're not concerned would not be truthful. But to walk around in fear? My life goes on, as does the other elected officials.

—Judge Bruce Wood to CNN

A picture of the McLelland murders developed as investigators collected evidence. While Mike and Cynthia didn't have the alarm set on the house on the morning they died, front door sensors established when the gunman entered and left. After investigators received the records from ADT, they knew that the killer spent less than two minutes in the house, from 6:40 to 6:42 a.m.

In that brief time, the McLellands' killer pulled the trigger twenty times. "It was an assassination," Lieutenant Stewart said. "Plain and simple."

Those involved understood the importance of finding evidence as quickly as possible, so the McLelland autopsies were rushed, completed at Dallas's Southwestern Institute of Forensic Sciences that same Monday, the day after Easter.

Cynthia's plaid nightshirt was cut off, her arms and legs remaining bent, as when she'd been found. On her hands

she still wore her gloves with the crystals she'd put on for
bed and the braces to immobilize her wrists. Around her
neck hung a cross pendant with another crystal. And on
her ears, heart-shaped earrings adorned with even more
crystals.

Dr. William McLain noted that Cynthia, pudgy, her
hair graying, appeared as expected for a sixty-five-year-
old woman. When her toxicology screen came in, it would
show she had nothing surprising in her system: no alco-
hol, only a mild sleep aid, her high blood pressure and
Parkinson's medications. Throughout the autopsy, McLain
focused on documenting eight gunshot wounds, GSWs,
scattered around her body.

The first, GSW #1, was a gunshot wound to the head.
First McLain shaved Cynthia's hair, to get an unobstructed
view. As he magnified the injury, he observed no soot or
stippling, indicating the weapon had not been within four
feet when the killer fired. In his report, McLain described
the entrance wound as keyhole-shaped, a straight line
where the bullet gouged out a circle of skin before entering
at the top of the skull.

Assessing the angle, McLain knew Cynthia couldn't
have been standing. The angle of the bullet wouldn't have
allowed that, not unless the killer somehow suspended
himself above her. Instead, McLain judged, this particular
shot had been fired while Cynthia lay on the floor.

When the physician pulled back the skin, he found the
bullet had fractured the skull. "The brain is massively lac-
erated," he'd later write. "The bones of the mid-face are
fractured." As he traced the path, he found no bullet. Instead, he documented an exit wound, just below the chin.

GSW #2 entered on the right chest area, above the
breast and toward the shoulder. As it traveled through the
body, this bullet collapsed Cynthia's right lung and hit her
spinal cord. Before moving on, McLain collected bullet

fragments, photographed them as he found them, and then placed them in marked evidence bags to be transferred to the crime lab.

Number three lay a short distance away, in the center of the chest, just above the breasts. Following the bullet's trajectory, downward front to back and slightly right to left, Dr. McLain recovered a larger bullet fragment.

As he worked, evidence bags collected on a tray near the autopsy table. The next fragment, from GSW #4, in the center of the chest, larger but badly damaged, hit bone as it traveled through the body.

No bullets or fragments were recovered from the next gunshot wound, number five, which entered from the front near the left shoulder and exited out the back. McLain was luckier with number six, however. Here the wound, just above the navel, sliced into the abdomen. As the physician excised the tissue, he discovered an intact bullet in a copper-colored metal jacket near Cynthia's hip. If the woman on the table had been standing, she would have immediately fallen, her hip and leg giving out beneath her. Numbers seven and eight hit her extremities and both exited the body.

In addition to collecting the bullet fragments, Dr. McLain did the usual, scraping beneath her nails, taking a sample of her hair, and bagging her nightshirt and underwear. As he assessed the wounds, McLain suspected that although he counted eight they might have all resulted from five or six bullets. Tracing the bullets' paths, he speculated that numbers three and four, the two in the center of the upper chest, appeared to be caused by the same bullet that went through Cynthia's skull before breaking apart and reentering her body.

Of the wounds, McLain judged the first and second as most lethal, the shot through the head and the one that entered her right chest, then traveled through her lung and splintered into her spinal cord.

Half an hour after Dr. McLain began the autopsy on Cynthia, Mike McLelland also lay on a stainless steel table. Over his round figure stood another assistant medical examiner, Dr. Reade Quinton. In his general assessment of the outside of his patient's body, Dr. Quinton noted Mike's heart surgery scar on his chest. Like his wife, for the most part he appeared his age. While his heart disease suggested there might have been medical challenges in his future Mike likely had years to live, if he hadn't been cut down in his living room with a barrage of bullets.

Instead Dr. Quinton considered how to approach the maze of gunshot wounds.

As Quinton worked, it quickly became apparent that of the two physicians, McLain had the easier job. Cynthia's wounds were relatively simple. But the gunman had riddled Mike's body, leaving a jumble of gunshots to track and diagram.

The GSW Quinton designated as number one on his list traveled through Mike's neck, through the left side, out from the right front neck, then reentered into his right chest just below his clavicle, then exited on his right side. Not yet done, the bullet sliced into Mike's right arm. As he assessed the wounds, Dr. Quinton judged that when that bullet hit, Mike must have had his arm pressed against his chest. Remarkably, after cutting through so much of the body, the recovered bullet appeared only slightly misshapen.

In all, Dr. Quinton documented sixteen gunshot wounds in Mike McLelland's body. Most were straightforward, the majority entering from the front or sides, but others hit Mike in the back, presumably as he ran down the hallway. Many of the bullets, or as Quinton labeled them "projectiles," hit Mike's right arm and his chest, some more deadly than others. GSW #5 ranked high on the list of lethal injuries, entering through the right side of the abdomen. On its track through the body, it cut Mike's diaphragm and sliced his aorta. Not yet finished, it pierced the left lung.

As Dr. Quinton drew the entrance and exit wounds and labeled each, he judged the attack a clear case of overkill. So many more bullets dedicated toward killing Mike than Cynthia, it appeared obvious that Mike was the prime target.

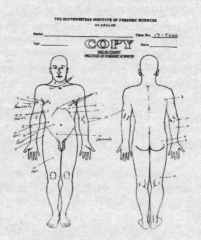

Autopsy diagram of Mike McLelland's wounds

Finishing up, Dr. Quinton put into evidence bags ten bullets and two fragments, many in remarkably good condition, only slightly or partially deformed. Mike's clothes were collected as evidence, samples of his blood and hair, all to be sent to the crime lab. Looking at the bullets and fragments, the two doctors discussed what they'd seen. In their opinions, all the bullets were high-velocity, like those shot from an assault-type weapon, more deadly than other bullets because they traveled at a greater speed and had a shockwave effect. Inside the body, .223 bullets were de-

signed to shatter when they hit bone. The fragments then
spread to do more damage.

As he finished Mike's autopsy, Dr. Quinton wrote out
his conclusions, the same ones Dr. McLain listed on Cynthia's report. The causes of both deaths held no surprises.
Cynthia and Mike McLelland died as the result of multiple
gunshot wounds. Both deaths were clearly homicides.

That afternoon an FBI agent located Tera Bellemare, Eric's
sister, and interviewed her. Later the agent told Wirskye
and Shook that Tera believed her brother was the killer.
"Eric did this and he's laughing at you," she said. "He
thinks he's smarter than anyone."

Chapter 45

Before I was pretty sure it wasn't Eric. Then I saw him on TV, and he'd gained weight. And I thought maybe he was the man I saw murder Mark Hasse.
—Lenda Bush

Despite the team concept, the investigators fluctuated between duties, adapting based on incoming evidence. One investigator turned up video from a neighbor's house that captured a car on the streets early the morning of the murders, headed in the direction of the McLellands' house. The same car left minutes later. Looking at the image, many on the task force speculated that the car resembled a white Crown Victoria, a vehicle often used by police. On the Williams team, Special Agent Laurie Gibbs devoted twelve hours the next day to watching cars coming and going through the area, especially interested in any that resembled the glimpse caught by the neighbor's camera.

One day at the command post, Texas Ranger Major Dockery met with Wirskye and Shook, and the lawyers reviewed what they knew about Eric. One pointed out the timing, that the McLelland killings occurred close to the first anniversary of Eric's theft conviction, and the day before Eric and Kim lost their health insurance. In addition, his appeal had just been set for oral arguments. If that didn't go as he hoped, his conviction would stand. "We wanted everyone to understand that Eric's stress was mounting," said Wirskye.

Later that day, he sent Dockery copies of the theft trial transcript, Eric's health insurance correspondence with the county, and his appeal notices. "Let's concentrate on Eric Williams," Dockery said when the two men talked again.

At 11:20 that morning, two days after the killings, with the help of the FBI profilers assigned to the case, the investigators responded to the latest Crime Stopper tip, the one in which the writer demanded the resignation of a local judge.

Convinced the person who'd sent the tip had to be the killer, they wanted to keep the conversation going. The profilers suggested the response should have a tone of respect, to appeal to the writer's ego. In the e-mail, they wrote: "We have received a number of tips, and yours is the most credible. We are working on your demands. A lot has been put out in the media. In order for us to verify that you are part of a group involved in these incidents, can you give us additional details that are specific to these cases and not known by the press?"

This time, Eric didn't answer.

By then he apparently questioned the wisdom of corresponding with those who hunted him. He did look at the Crime Stoppers Web site off and on, however, at the information listed under "How it works," most likely to reassure himself that it was a secure site, and that the tips remained anonymous.

Enjoying the notoriety of his killings, each day Eric spent hours on the net. He copied videos and photos of the McLellands' house with the crime scene tape, the DPS and FBI cars outside, the mobile crime scene unit. He downloaded a copy of the search warrant authorities secured for the Blarney Stone house before the forensic team went inside. He snipped a photo of Governor Perry from a press conference in which he said the perpetrator would be caught, and the flag at half-staff outside the Kaufman County law enforcement center.

"I can't decide who's next," Eric pondered to Kim at the house. "Glen or Erleigh Wiley."

A day or so later, however, he told her he'd made up his mind: the next one to die would be Glen Ashworth. As he'd planned earlier, he'd shoot the judge with the crossbow, gut him, and then put napalm inside his abdomen. And he wanted to do it soon.

"I have the napalm in the storage unit," he told her.

In Kaufman, Ron Herrington saw Eric Williams's potential involvement in the case as an open secret. The local lawyers speculated about it, as did the staff at the courthouse, yet there'd been only minor mentions of Eric in the media, then only in news articles as a case Mark prosecuted in Kaufman.

When Herrington mentioned Eric to other Kaufman lawyers, some told him not to talk about that possibility. But Herrington worried, afraid others would die, and he remembered what Mark had said, "I think Eric Williams is going to kill me."

Through a friend, Herrington reached out to a local newscaster, who worked for a Dallas network affiliate. "I'm going to give you a name. Let's see what you do with it," Herrington said. "Eric Williams."

The man probed for more information, but Herrington refused. "Talk to everyone around here about Eric Williams," he said. "I'm giving you a bird's nest on the ground."

From that point forward, Eric caught the media's attention.

That afternoon reporters began showing up at his house. The first was Scott Gordon from the local NBC station, a gray-haired veteran. When he knocked on the door, Eric refused to allow him to turn on his TV camera, but

Gordon recorded a cell phone video of Eric denying any anger toward Mark and Mike, or that he had anything to do with the murders. "My deepest condolences go out to the McLelland family," Eric said. "And all the people at the courthouse."

In the interview, Eric revealed that the investigators had taken his phone and swabbed his hands. Based on his history with the victims, Eric said, "If I were an investigator, I'd want to talk to me, too." Through it all, he remained calm, for much of the interview with a slight smirk.

Right after Gordon left, Phil Archer from Houston's NBC affiliate pulled up in a van with his cameraman. Like Gordon, he knocked on Eric's door and waited. No one answered, but he heard barking inside. Back in the TV van, Archer talked to his cameraman, regrouping, when Eric suddenly streamed past on his Segway. They followed him down the street, and when he stopped, jumped out. The camera recording, Eric appeared confident, standing on the Segway insisting that he'd been checked for GSR the night the McLellands died, and he'd been cleared. "Did anyone connected with this investigation suggest to you that you are a person of interest in the investigation?" Archer asked.

Eric shook his head slightly. "No." Again, he expressed his sympathies for the victims' families, and then took it even further, describing Mark and Mike as men who were doing the right thing. "For some reason we're not aware of they paid the ultimate price for that."

The exchange struck Archer as odd. "Eric Williams seemed to be a guy not intimidated by cameras or being questioned about being involved in a murder."

Afterward, perhaps an indication of how much he enjoyed the attention, Eric e-mailed Archer, thanking him for his "objective and journalistic approach to my story."

The investigators, Wirskye and others, watched the interviews as well, remarking about Eric's slight grin. He looked proud, confident. By then, some in the media had begun questioning the Aryan Brotherhood connection. A *Texas Observer* article quoted experts on the ABT as describing the gang as "dumb old white boys who wouldn't kill a DA"; another surmised, "That'd be a big leap for them. I just don't think it's credible that it's them."

Yet ABT tips continued to pour in, perhaps in part spurred by the reward, which had grown to more than $200,000.

At the courthouse, the U.S. Marshals office suggested tighter security measures. And after the Crime Stoppers tip, they added more cameras outside the command post. Still only a few realized how close they worked to the house of the man who many had come to believe had to be considered their prime suspect. Bill Wirskye didn't know until late one night when an officer pointed toward Overlook and mentioned Eric lived one house from the corner. For weeks, Wirskye had used the parking lot as a place to talk on the phone or with one investigator or another when he didn't want everyone in the command post to hear him. Now he knew Eric Williams just needed to walk out his front door and sixty feet over to see him standing there, unprotected and unaware.

One night not long after, Wirskye and the sheriff worked well past dark, and the two men stood outside the building comparing thoughts. Remembering Eric's proximity, Wirskye felt instantly uneasy, his eyes continually drawn in the direction of Eric's house. "Sheriff, let's go inside and finish talking," he said. "That SOB probably has a 308 rifle on us right now."

Inside the house on Overlook, Eric continued to search the Internet for news on the killings and watch TV reports. "Security Reviewed at Kaufman County Courthouse," one article read. In those days following the McLellands' deaths, he clicked repeatedly onto the Dallas NBC station's Web site, one that included his interview with Scott Gordon.

With those first interviews came increased media interest. Now that Eric had publicly admitted he'd been questioned, e-mails arrived from newspaper reporters across the country. Sometimes Eric responded, other times not. He did when the *L.A. Times* reporter got in touch, referring her to David Sergi.

Meanwhile, Leah and Skeet Phillips helped pull together plans for the McLellands' memorial service and funeral. Cynthia had made her wishes known, to be cremated and buried with Mike, so Christina and Nathan picked out a sandstone box for their mother's ashes, one that would deteriorate over time. "So that then they would truly be one," said Leah.

That week a grueling one, Christina suspected FBI agents shuffled through her trash, and Leah and Skeet talked to Texas Rangers and an ATF agent for more than five hours. The atmosphere tense, Leah had difficulty sleeping. Would the killer come after Mike and Cynthia's children or friends? "We had a light on in every room at night. We were nervous."

The memorial service took place on April 4, five days after the murders, at a cavernous Baptist church outside Dallas. That day National Public Radio aired a segment on the killings, and Judge Wood said, "It's not the same county we lived in two months ago. A lot has changed."

Certainly the armed guards at the memorial attested to those changes. The security even tighter than at Mark's service, many of the more than a thousand mourners appeared nervous as they arrived. At the front of the church, Mike's body and Cynthia's ashes shared the same large, flag-draped coffin. Governor Perry talked, carried live on television and the net. The killer would be found, he pledged; "the criminals responsible for the murders . . . will be convicted and they will pay the price." To Cynthia and Mike's family he said, "Millions of people across the state are standing with you during this tragedy, sharing your pain in a very real way."

Beside the coffin hung Mike's army uniform alongside one of Cynthia's quilts, and a portrait of the couple on a stand. Most of the talks involved personal remembrances. Bruce Bryant repeated one of Mike's favorite expressions: "When things get rough, soldier on." Bryant paused, and then said, "I promise we will soldier on."

Many talked of the way Cynthia lit up when Mike walked into a room. In their obituary they'd been described as "a mismatched pair that fit perfectly . . . a true love story."

"They would have done it the same way, because Mike believed in making a difference," said Christina, who in her quiet moments felt an ache, missing her mother's hugs. From the speaker's stand, she then did something that reminded the audience of her dead stepfather. As Mike had after Mark's murder, Christina taunted the killer: "If you have a problem, you can come to my house. I'm a lot younger and meaner."

When the memorial service ended, family members and close friends followed the hearse to First Baptist in Mike's hometown, Wortham, for the funeral. The area again covered by tight security, they positioned the casket at the front of the church, surrounded by stained glass windows. As mourners filed in for the visitation, JR found a seat for his eighty-four-year-old grandmother. As she began to say her good-byes to her son, a friend warned JR, "Get out now!"

In that moment, the doors swung open, and police officers rushed in and ordered everyone to leave. JR put his arm around his grandmother, and hurried her to the limo. The driver peeled out of the lot.

Someone had called in a bomb scare.

No explosives found, guards surrounded the church throughout the night. As added protection, DPS helicopters flew overhead. The next morning at the funeral, Mike's sons and grandsons wore black cowboy hats, as he so often had. At one point, JR removed his and held it over his heart. Nathan wore his Dallas police officer's uniform and saluted the casket.

The funeral in Wortham

At the end, they played a recording of Mike's favorite song, the one he often whistled, "King of the Road." And when they left the church for the short ride to the cemetery, two fire trucks formed an arch with their ladders, one draped with an American flag.

In Dallas the day of the funeral, about five that evening, Bill Wirskye e-mailed Eric's attorneys, following up on his request for an interview. "We would like to visit with your client as soon as possible if he is willing. I think we could be available as early as Monday morning."

When his attorneys forwarded the request to him, Eric responded: "Um, no."

Late at night in Kaufman, a car drove by slowly on a road that bordered the rural ranch house of one of the clerks who worked at the DA's office. As it passed, someone turned off the headlights and pulled over. Inside the house, the woman grabbed a gun. Her heart pounding, she ran outside. She approached the car, watching, when she recognized two local teenagers. "They were just looking for someplace to drink," she said. "I could have killed them."

Chapter 46

A source told me two special prosecutors were appointed for the Hasse/McLelland cases: Toby Shook and his law partner, Bill Wirskye.
    —E-mail signed ERIC sent to a Dallas TV reporter

There seemed little doubt that Eric Williams enjoyed his new role, being sought after by the media, fielding requests from TV and print journalists, e-mailing tips to some when he had new information. Once news broke that he'd been questioned in the notorious cases, he received voice mails and e-mails from the *New York Times*, the *L.A. Times*, the *Dallas Morning News*, and the national TV news networks. Sergi and Sickel issued statements and turned down requests.

At the command post, the conversations were more somber. The week after the McLellands' funeral, an FBI agent found a record on LexisNexis that showed Eric had logged onto the service through his old Kaufman County law library account. With stacks of information to look through, eventually the analyst discovered that the prior January, before Mark's murder, Eric ran a license plate number belonging to Mark Hasse's neighbor. That left many working on the case wondering: Did Eric have Mark under surveillance?

Meanwhile, at the Overlook house, in between playing Mafia Wars, Eric spent most days searching the Internet for information on the killings, on Toby Shook, and on Bill Wirskye. A *Dallas Morning News* blog about the appointments perhaps pleased Eric when he read that in the White House President Barack Obama kept "tabs on the Kaufman County killings."

That day, too, Eric searched for information on Judge Glen Ashworth, the target he'd told Kim he planned to kill next. At one point, he looked at a health article on "10 Ways to Take Charge of Depression." From there, he looked up information on Christopher Dorner's manifesto, then settled in and returned to Mafia Wars.

Nerves continued to plague those working the investigation. One day during a meeting, Bill Wirskye's wife called and said she saw "a suspicious guy" outside their house. "To save my marriage, I've got to head home to Dallas," he told the others, and they understood. When he arrived, the man had disappeared.

Like so many others, by then Shook and Wirskye carried guns. "You think like the guy you're after," said Shook. "What could be better. 'I'll kill the guys who think they're going to get me.' We were armed, but so was Mark and so was Mike McLelland."

At night, Shook placed a shotgun and a pistol next to his bed, another pistol stationed elsewhere in the house. When he left in the mornings, he had a gun in his hand. His wife told him he made her nervous. "It got to be comical," Wirskye said. "We laughed about it. But we were scared."

At an early meeting, Major Dockery had asked if anyone else felt they needed protection, beyond the Kaufman officials who were already under guard. Although frightened, Wirskye and Shook hadn't raised their hands. "We didn't want to appear to be cowards," said Wirskye. But as time passed, their families worried, and they became increasingly anxious.

One day, after the two prosecutors discussed their situation, Wirskye arrived at the command post intent on requesting guards for both him and Shook, but at the morning meeting an FBI agent grumbled about a terrified federal prosecutor who'd walked away from an ABT case. "Can you believe it? Big pussy."

"It wasn't a good day to ask," Wirskye told Shook.

One of the FBI agents, Aaron Beggs, worked on the Williams team off and on, assigned to set up a timeline of Eric's life, find out where he grew up, went to school, where he'd worked. "Everyone we talked to confirmed our belief that he was our guy."

In hopes of finally interviewing their prime suspect, e-mails continued to go back and forth between Eric's attorneys and Bill Wirskye. Then one day, Eric e-mailed Sergi and Sickel and said: "You are authorized to release my email address to the authorities regarding the Hasse/McLelland investigation. . . . If they have some simple questions for me to answer, perhaps it can really be that simple. Thanks for everything. ERIC WILLIAMS."

His attorneys disagreed, wanting to keep Eric distanced from the investigation, musing that if they stepped out of the middle, Eric would lose his layer of protection.

Off and on, Wirskye stopped at the DA's office. With Mike McLelland dead, Wirskye talked to the interim DA, Brandi Fernandez. When he did, "he felt the staff's tension." One paralegal had her whole family sleeping in one room. When she arrived home, she held a gun in her hand while she looked under the beds and in the closets.

"You didn't know who was going to come through the window," she said.

At the same time, at the command post, video kept arriving. Two weeks after the McLellands' murders, on surveillance camera footage from a building half a mile from the Blarney Stone address, someone noticed a white sedan, one that looked like the car in the earlier video. "Look, we've got a photograph," the man said when he handed it to Michael Hillman. "It's a Crown Vic."

Looking at it, Hillman could barely see the outline of the car and wasn't impressed. "Good job," he told the man. "Come back to me when you have something."

"We think this could be it," the man said, pointing out that the time frame matched.

Hillman looked at the photo again, this time more impressed.

Off and on, JR McLelland thought about the day his dad and Cynthia died, trying to figure out how it happened. When he visualized it, knowing what he did about the evidence, what he'd seen at the house, he figured his dad was in his lounge chair and had it pushed back when the gunman burst in. Since Mike rarely locked the door, JR assumed the most likely scenario was that Cynthia sat on the couch. The gunman entered and started shooting, and the way JR saw it, his dad, who'd put on weight since his heart bypass, couldn't jump out of the chair as he needed to in time to grab a gun.

The sadness followed JR until one day he went out to a trailer he kept in the pasture. He stayed there alone for three days, shooting guns like he used to with his dad, letting his grief bubble to the surface.

At work in his Dallas PD uniform, Nathan thought about their parents, too. At times, other officers asked him about the case, where the inquiry stood. He didn't have anything to tell them, because the investigators weren't including the family in their briefings. "It was just bizarre," Nathan said. "Usually I'm the investigator. Now I was on the other side."

American Mensa e-mailed Eric a birthday greeting on April 7. That day he turned forty-six. By e-mail he discussed with his attorneys how to handle Bill Wirskye's continuing requests for an interview and information. While Eric had asked to have them send his e-mail to the prosecutor, David Sergi continued to advise that everything had to go through either him or John Sickel "to preserve the attorney-client privilege." Eric agreed.

"Pursuant to our telephone conversation a few minutes ago, Mr. Williams is declining a face-to-face meeting with representatives of the state of Texas. He has, however, indicated that he will answer written questions submitted by you and Mr. Shook," David Sergi e-mailed Bill Wirskye on the eighth.

The next morning, JR appeared on the *Today* show. After describing the murders as domestic terrorism, he said, "It needs to put all public officials on their toes. It's not just Texas."

Perhaps Eric saw the program that morning. If he did, maybe he had that slight smirk on his face, watching the press coverage mushroom. Later, Eric played Mafia Wars and at 10:38 that night Googled "upper receiver groups AR–15." On a Web site called Bravo Company USA, he looked at upcoming gun shows. Then he searched for information on the Rock River Arms Web site for .223 caliber uppers.

It appeared that Eric Williams was in the market for a new upper for his assault rifle, presumably to replace one he'd disposed of after killing the McLellands. And he planned to buy it through a venue that didn't require background checks.

Nearly two weeks after the McLelland murders, little appeared to be going the investigators' way. They still hadn't interviewed their prime suspect. In response, on April

10, they became more aggressive. Two sheriff's deputies knocked on Eric's door, asking to talk to Kim. Saying she'd been up all night and was sleeping, Eric took their cards.

When Eric informed his attorneys, John Sickel sent Wirskye an e-mail, complaining about the intrusion. Wirskye apologized and claimed he didn't know what the investigators planned. Wirskye "advised that maybe he wasn't clear enough with them yesterday that he was in contact and working with your lawyers," Sickel e-mailed Eric, copying David Sergi.

"Apparently at or about the same time this morning, a ranger and another officer visited my in-laws' house, asking all sorts of interesting questions. Other than being old, sick, and dying, I'm okay with that, since there's nothing for them to tell and nothing to hide—just keeping you up to date," Eric responded.

In e-mails with his attorneys that same day Eric agreed to do as Wirskye requested, to draw up a timeline of where he'd been on the days of the murders. To Sickel, this seemed a reasonable course of action. Someday, if Eric were ever charged, his attorneys would need the same thing, an account of his whereabouts at the times of the murders.

That same day, Eric's attorneys issued a press release, one in which he denied any knowledge of the murders, and David Sergi said, "Eric has nothing to hide."

That night on Overlook, Eric again searched the Internet for gun shows and other venues where he could buy a gun without filing paperwork. He keyed in "law on guns and felons," and "discount guns for sale." He checked gunauction.com, and Armslist classified listings.

The big news that day was that Governor Perry named a replacement for Mike McLelland, Judge Erleigh Wiley. "You can't be fearful. You just have to be prayerful," she told reporters when asked if she worried about her safety. Since the McLelland murders, Wiley's entire family had round-the-clock guards. "You have to know that we've got good people that are going to protect us until justice is done. I think I can do this and not be scared."

Perhaps Kaufman's new district attorney would have felt differently had she known that her name hovered just below Judge Glen Ashworth's on Eric Williams's kill list.

Chapter 47

We got e-mails and phone calls from the *L.A. Times*,
the *N.Y. Times*, CNN, all the local TV stations, CBS,
ABC, *USA Today*. That's when things got out of
hand.

—John Sickel

Just after midnight on Thursday April 11, Eric e-mailed
his attorneys his account of what he'd done on the days of
the murders to turn over to Wirskye. In his account, Eric
referred to phone calls he'd made, e-mails he'd sent, and
said he'd slept in both mornings.

In his query, Wirskye had also asked if Eric had any
theories regarding who may have committed the murders,
perhaps an idea of the profilers intended to appeal to Eric's
ego. At the end of his e-mail to his attorneys, Eric ridiculed
the question: "Are they seriously asking me . . . ?"

That day, Sickel and Sergi discussed concerns about the
growing amount of time committed to handling Eric's af-
fairs. "I couldn't do anything other than deal with Eric's
needs," said Sickel. "If I kept on, I was going to go bank-
rupt. It was clear that Eric couldn't pay us."

While the investigation had moved a step forward—Eric
at least answering questions—the investigators still needed
a big break. It unfolded early that afternoon, when David
Sergi sent Eric an e-mail in which he and Sickel withdrew

as Eric's attorneys on the murder investigation. In it, Sergi said he believed Eric had become a prime target, and he urged Eric to immediately hire another attorney, to prevent law enforcement from swooping in and overwhelming him.

Eric said that he understood, and that he appreciated all they'd done.

Minutes later, as Shook and Wirskye met with the investigators at the command post, Wirskye received an e-mail from Sergi as well, this one informing him that he and Sickel were no longer Eric's lawyers on the murder cases. For the first time in the investigation, Eric's lawyers didn't stand guard over him. "We need to get over there now," Wirskye suggested.

At the command post, the prosecutors and investigators gathered, along with the FBI profilers, Wirskye urging the others to move while they had the opportunity. The others agreed, and the profilers offered advice. As Mike once had, they described Eric as a narcissist and said that his ego made him vulnerable. Flattery could serve the investigators well. "Send someone with a high rank he will see as an equal," they recommended.

The goal was to convince Eric to let them inside his house. Once in, if they saw anything that could connect him to the killings, they might have a shot at a search warrant.

At Overlook early that morning, Eric's mother called, upset because FBI agents descended upon the house in Azle asking questions. "Tell them to leave, Mother," Eric said. "They're trying to pin it on . . ." She lost the end of that sentence, as she paced in the kitchen.

At 3:52 in the afternoon, Eric followed up with his mother via e-mail: "Just checking in to make sure you're okay. Remember—they wouldn't have been there if they had any real evidence on me for their case (which of course they don't since I didn't do anything). But—no good turn goes unpunished—so don't talk to them anymore. ERIC."

Minutes after that e-mail, Chief Deputy Evans and the top Texas Ranger in the region, Major Dockery, knocked on Eric's front door. The dogs barked, but no one answered. They left and walked the block to Kim's parents' house, the other place he'd been most often observed, and rang the bell. At first, no response. Then Eric slowly opened the door. Dockery had a small digital recorder in his portfolio turned on.

"How are you doing, Eric?" Evans asked, his voice sociable. "This is Major Dockery."

"Dewayne Dockery," the major explained, shaking Eric's hand. "Nice to meet you."

"We'd like to ask you a few questions," Evans said. He then explained that they hoped to pin down where Eric had been when the murders took place. Seemingly unconcerned, Eric said he'd answered those questions in an e-mail his lawyers sent to Bill Wirskye. Evans said they hadn't received it. "All we're trying to do, Eric, is figure out a timeframe of where you've been."

Taking it slow, Evans asked questions, including where Eric went the evening after the McLellands died. Along with all the other information, he said he'd included that in the info to Wirskye. Yet, although sounding irritated, Eric answered, saying he and Kim took a drive. "We didn't leave here until eight or eight-thirty."

"Lake Tawakoni?"

"We went north of Quinlan, turned around, came home."

An edge of annoyance in his voice, Eric said, "Here's what I think." Then he contended that nothing he could tell them would convince them to mark him off the list of suspects. "Unless you look at cell phone records . . . My cell phone is always on me."

"You've got to understand," Evans said. "We're working as hard as we can to clear you."

"I know. I know," Eric demurred.

"And you understand why your name pops up." Suggesting their interest only reasonable given the situation, Evans reminded Eric, "You were in law enforcement."

When Eric agreed that he understood, Dockery asked Eric if he had other cell phones, besides the one he'd turned over after the McLelland murders. In response, Eric held out a small flip phone. "You don't have a smart phone?"

"Not when I'm not getting paid," Eric said, and all three men nervously laughed. That was, after all, the crux of Eric's motive, that Mark and Mike stripped Eric of his live-lihood.

After a pause, Evans said, "I want you to believe that we're all trying to do everything we can."

As they stood on the Johnsons' front porch, Evans asked about Eric's arsenal of guns. Eric insisted he no longer had any. He'd sold some, he said, and his father had the others. When the two men asked for particulars, however, Eric said, "I'm not going to get into all that. I know what's going to happen."

"What's going to happen?" Dockery said, with a slight chuckle. "Just so I know."

"From my perspective?" Eric asked. "I know what you're trying to do. I've been through this . . . It's one thing, then it's another thing. Then it's something else."

"Don't you think it's a reasonable thing?" Evans challenged.

Despite their urging, as a lawyer Eric understood the importance of boundaries. "It may be reasonable, but it's also my right as a citizen not to say any more." Employing a term often used by lawyers he said, "When you start asking those questions, it's a slippery slope."

"You don't have any guns?" Dockery asked, after more questions went unanswered.

"I have one gun I'm trying to sell," Eric said, "Nobody wants this stupid forty-four."

"That's all you have left?" Evans said.

The conversation progressed, Evans and Dockery working their way back to Eric's whereabouts on the days of the murders, asking for details. Much of Eric's response involved what he portrayed as time spent caring for Kim's parents. On the Saturday morning of the McLellands' murders, Eric said he received a text at home sometime after nine. "We had dinner here," he said, referring to the Johnson house, where he still stood on the front porch.

As if to throw him slightly off balance, the queries rotated between Eric's actions on the days of the murders and his stock of weapons. "I'm just curious," Dockery said. "How many guns did you used to own?"

This time Eric gave an estimate far lower than the true number, about sixteen. Dockery asked again if he'd sold them all, and Eric said he had. "Some of them were ARs and stuff?" Dockery asked.

"Yeah," Eric said, "Those went quick."

"Were any of the others long guns?"

"One of them was a .223 . . . a rifle, a deer hunting gun."

"You're not going to want us to look at where the guns went?" Evans asked, implying it could help finalize their interest in him. "Let it be done."

"But it's not going to be done," Eric said, contending that once they had the gun information, the investigators would want more. "Look at your credit cards. Look at your bank account. It's going to just keep going and going and going."

Then Evans made a proposal, responding to Eric's repeated contention that nothing he did could convince authorities to cross him off the suspect list. "You show us the gun you own. Let us look in your house and see that there are no weapons there. We can at least draw that one line of the X across your face to get rid of that."

His voice calm and low, Eric responded, "But that's not going to stop anything."

"It'll definitely help," Dockery countered.

"Let us look in the house, so we can tell the others that there are no guns," Evans wheedled.

After repeated pleas, Eric agreed. On his Segway, he led the two officers to his front door. Once inside, Evans and Dockery saw the chaos of Eric's hidden life. Boxes and bags strewn about. Counters piled high. Spotting something interesting, Dockery quickly honed in on an empty box, one for a .357, the type of gun used to kill Mark Hasse. "Yeah, there used to be one in there," Eric said with a slight laugh.

"Did you have shoulder surgery not too long ago?" the major asked, referring to the morning of the Hasse murder when Eric answered the door with his arm in a sling.

"I had what's called frozen shoulder. . . . It's real bad," Eric said. When Dockery asked when he last had a flare-up, Eric answered, "January, when they were here."

In the background, a TV blared and a Dallas reporter described an afternoon rush hour accident, as the men wove through the house. Eric beside them, Dockery and Evans searched boxes, opened closets. When Dockery noticed an empty holster, he asked about Eric's background. "I was military police," Eric said.

Moments later, Dockery pulled what looked like a rifle out of a box, but it turned out to be a paint ball gun. One room to the next, the men searched, making conversation, weaving in questions, asking about Eric's military service and years in law enforcement, subjects he enjoyed. In boxes, Evans and Dockery saw gun parts and ammunition, but no guns.

"Hey Eric, what's in your camouflage bag," Dockery asked, eyeing a sack on a shelf.

"I don't have a clue," Eric said, helping to pull it down. The recorder caught the sound of the bag unzipping and Dockery rifling through it. Conceivably, by then Eric had

had time to think, to realize that he'd made a mistake, a strategic error, allowing the enemy inside his home.

At the command post, Ranger Kasper had just returned from a round of interviews when news spread that they had another break. An analyst in Fort Worth who offered to examine a 325-page LexisNexis report, one that recorded searches done on Eric's county account, discovered that Eric used the service to look for home addresses for Mark and Mike.

One of the investigators called Evans. When he answered, the caller said, "Ask Eric if he searched the Internet for information on Hasse and McLelland, and how he did it."

At the house on Overlook, Evans ended the call but waited before bringing up the subject. Somewhere in the house, a Phil Collins song, "In the Air Tonight," played as Dockery asked about another duffel, one filled with Eric's high school science and math trophies. He asked if Eric had gone to school in Kaufman.

"No, Azle," Eric said.

The rustling continued as the two lawmen scrutinized shelves and bags. Finally Evans casually asked: "Eric, did you ever do any research about this case?"

"Nothing more than I watched the news," he answered.

"Nothing on the Internet?"

"I read stuff on the news Web sites," he offered, saying that it was after the murders, checking for updates on the investigations, on MSN and Google.

That established, Dockery returned the subject to the guns. Earlier Eric said he wouldn't discuss particular weapons, but with prodding he talked about pistols and long guns, all of which he assured them he'd sold. Again, he insisted only the one .44 remained, and that because he hadn't yet found a buyer.

"I wouldn't want to take a hit myself," Evans noted.

"That's why I kept it," Eric said with a chortle, sounding more confident.

The sound of rustling canvas and unsnapping locks filled the air, until Dockery found a box filled with more gun parts, including a rifle scope. "What is this, Eric?"

Sounding tense, Eric said he thought he'd gotten two from the same company, and mounted one on a 5.7 millimeter. "I think it's an AR–57 or 47? That one was just the extra." Then Eric said the scope Dockery held had never been used. But Dockery turned it over in his hands and saw small marks, the kind that result from mounting on a weapon.

In one room, Dockery found four rifle stocks, the back portion of a rifle that rests against the shoulder. Dockery noted that they were the types of stocks used with AR platform rifles.

The longer the investigators remained in the house, the quieter they became, and the more nervous Eric sounded, his voice at times cracking slightly. Inside, his gut must have been churning. Another box opened, and this time Dockery pulled out the one handgun Eric admitted still possessing. "Desert Eagle," he said. "The .44."

The recorder documented the find, but the other men didn't comment. The gun was part of a patchwork the officers were pulling together. Now they had the .357 box, an indication that Eric had owned a gun like the one used to kill Mark Hasse. They had rifle stocks compatible with the type of weapon that shot the .223 caliber bullets that murdered the McLellands. And they had Eric lying about searching for the victims on the Internet. Was it enough?

Despite all they'd uncovered, neither Evans nor Dockery gave Eric any indication that he had reason for concern. Nor did they stop looking. The next discovery consisted of binoculars and a sight that tracked body heat. "Trying to sell that night vision stuff, but it doesn't work," Eric said. "Which does not make me happy."

In the garage Eric bragged slightly about Kim's Trans Am, pointing out that Pontiac stopped producing the car after that year, 2002, while Dockery uncovered a stash of cell phone boxes. "Are there any more phones in here?"

"I have no idea," Eric said. Earlier Eric had offered his phone as evidence of his location on the days of the murders, saying he always had it with him. Now it appeared that he had multiple phones.

In all, Dockery and Evans lingered nearly two hours talking to Eric Williams that day and searching his house. "All right, Eric," Evans said at the front door. "We appreciate it."

"Thank you very much," Dockery chimed in, shaking Eric's hand.

Earlier Eric said his lawyers had e-mailed a timeline of his activities on the days of the murders to Bill Wirskye; now Dockery returned to that subject. "We'll have Mr. Wirskye send you a message."

"If I can think of anything to help somebody," Eric, the former Eagle Scout, said with his crooked smile. "Yeah, I'm gonna do that."

"If we can clear this and go on to something else, we sure would like it," Dockery said.

As they walked away, the investigators knew they had a long night ahead. Instead of heading home for dinner, they returned to the command post, where Wirskye, Shook, and an eager team waited to hear what they'd seen. Would there be enough to get a warrant?

Maybe Eric watched from inside the house, through one of those darkened windows, as Evans and Dockery left. By then he probably realized that allowing them inside the house had been a mistake. At least it appeared that way. For soon after the two investigators departed, as the sun set,

Eric loaded boxes into the back of his Sport Trac and drove a block away to Kim's parents' house.

Later Eric would discover that his actions were observed.

From his car, FBI Special Agent Aaron Beggs watched with great interest as Eric carried something from the Sport Trac into his in-laws' home. Beggs wondered, "What is he trying to hide?"

Chapter 48

Dear Mr. Wirskye. John Sickel forwarded your contact info to me, so that I could send you a response with detailed information. . . . On Saturday, March 30th, I spoke with a friend of mine, Paul Lilly from about 9:15 a.m. to 10:15 a.m. . . .

—Eric Williams

The evening after Dockery and Evans left the house, Eric e-mailed Bill Wirskye his account of what he did on the days of the murders.

On his e-mail account, Eric found a message waiting from his mother, letting him know that after the FBI agents left their house that morning, a *Dallas Morning News* reporter called. "Daddy will not answer the house [phone] anymore, his cell only if it is me? Will see if this works." Then she said someone told her that police had the ability to trace cell phones. Was she warning her son?

Eric advised his mother not to talk to the press. They're "all over it as well."

Meanwhile, at the command post, Dockery and Evans described the gun parts and accessories they saw in the house, some matching the types of weapons used in the murders. They also had Eric's denial that he'd searched for any information on the case other than Internet news articles. That conflicted with the LexisNexis records.

After mulling it over, Wirskye and Shook decided they had enough to justify a search warrant, but would a judge agree?

While the prosecutors worked on the warrant they hoped would allow them to bring a full forensic team into Eric's house, their prime suspect sat at his computer. At 9:39 p.m. he searched the Internet for information on "Texas Ranger Companies," perhaps looking for Major Dockery.

Eric also keyed in "Eric Williams Kaufman County," to pull up the latest on the cases. Just before midnight he again turned his attention to "How to buy a firearm online" and "private gun sales online." He checked reports on the murder in the *Dallas Morning News* and *New York Times*, and Googled reporters covering the killings. He also keyed in "that's karma fuckin' with."

Just after midnight, Eric typed in "Toby Shook."

An hour later at the command post, around one o'clock, with many bits and pieces remaining to pull together, Wirskye and Shook realized they would never get the search warrant signed that night. Instead, they drove home to Dallas, weary from a long day. Before they left, Wirskye glanced around at all the members of law enforcement comparing ideas and strategies. So many times it seemed organizations competed instead of cooperated. This case had drawn them together. "I just want you all to look," Wirskye told them. "There's Texas Rangers, FBI agents, sheriff's deputies, and police officers, and everyone is working together."

On the road, Shook checked e-mails and found one from Eric with a timeline of his activities on the days of the murders attached. Shook skimmed through and quickly decided it was "a bunch of bullshit." While it had details, it contained "nothing of substance" that could verify where Eric had been at the times of the murders.

"I'm glad we're on our way home," Wirskye said, when Shook mentioned the e-mail. Then Wirskye thought about how odd it was that they got the e-mail so soon after they drove off. He considered how close the command post was to Eric's house. "I bet he was watching us."

The only fact easing his disquiet was that by then Eric was under surveillance. "We knew where he was," said Wirskye.

The following morning, the command post again whirred with activity as investigators arrived alongside forensic analysts, who worked on deciphering more of the LexisNexis and cell phone records. Wirskye walked in early, eager to get the search warrant finished and signed. The work went on, until finally they had their document, one that would allow them to seize all computers, disks, USBs, drives, records, notes, correspondence, weapons and weapon components, any trace evidence including DNA and bodily fluids, any clothing that could be tied to the killings, "items related to the criminal investigation, to wit: murder."

Around lunchtime, Wirskye took the document to Judge Chitty to have it signed, along with a search warrant he'd drawn up for Kim's parents' house. The basis for that warrant was that FBI Special Agent Aaron Beggs saw Eric transport boxes to the Johnson house late the previous night, after the walkthrough. The judge read through the warrants, and to Wirskye's relief signed both.

Not long after, Ranger Kasper rang the bell at Kim's parents' house. They knew Eric was there and he answered. "Hi Eric," Kasper said, sociably. "We know that this is your in-laws' and that you're here a lot. We want to know if we can get consent to search the residence."

"I would say no," Eric answered, shaking his head.

"Well," Kasper answered, smiling. "I've got a search warrant."

Despite his usual calm exterior, Eric appeared shaken.

Inside the house with its European decor, Kasper saw Kim's father in bed, weak, with bandages wrapped around his head. As the DPS forensic unit flooded in, Kim's mother said nothing. While they searched, Eric sat outside at a picnic table, circulating to a patio between the house and garage, showing no emotion, at times doing something on his phone.

On Overlook, Kim had just woken up and cared for their three Pomeranians, changing their diapers and feeding them, when Laurie Gibbs and others from the FBI knocked on the door. They showed her the search warrant, and she shrugged and let them inside. While the agents worked, Kim waited on the patio, eager for the search to end so she could return to bed.

Inside, Dianna Strain led the FBI's ten-person ERT (evidence response team). Reviewing the warrant, Strain noted what they were authorized to seize. Then Gibbs gave her a brief overview of the case.

In a previous career, Strain taught kindergarten, but she'd been with the FBI for sixteen years, specializing in terrorism and security investigations. All the agents had multiple functions, and she'd worked crime scenes since 2001. A straightforward woman with shoulder-length dark hair, Strain oversaw agents who sketched the scene, retrieved evidence, and searched for computer evidence. She began by walking the house, assessing the layout.

In the kitchen, she noticed the laptops on the white Formica bar. Then she saw something else, and panicked. Lights flashed on one and "DELETE" lit up on the screen. Hurriedly, she called for the computer expert, who rushed in and turned it off.

Once the crisis passed, Strain continued her walkthrough. For the rest of that day she acted as the primary point person, handling questions and relaying information. The photographers followed Strain in to document the scene before the searchers entered.

The view of the computers in the kitchen, the day of the search
Evidence photo

Throughout, the house appeared disordered. Two-liter plastic Coke bottles piled up in a bathtub and the garage, Kim's empties. Books and papers covered counters. On a secretary in the kitchen they found multiple police radios, all plugged in, set on the state guard channel, and the Forney police and fire departments, where the McLellands lived. Other settings monitored Kaufman PD and the DA's office.

As the two forensic teams worked, a DPS unit at Kim's parents' house and the FBI techs at Eric and Kim's, Wirskye walked back and forth wearing a dark windbreaker, looking like the officers on the scene. Word leaked, reporters showed up but had to stay behind the crime scene tape. Above them blades on TV helicopters beat at the cool spring air.

At the Johnson house, Wirskye watched Eric on the patio, a mousy man, not at all looking like a triple killer. If anxious, Eric didn't let on, and he didn't talk to anyone. At one point, Wirskye's phone rang, and he got more news off the LexisNexis records. As a result, he called Toby Shook. "Hey, guess what?" Wirskye said. "Eric's been searching our names, too."

After Shook sucked his breath in, shocked, Wirskye said, "He's going to jail for something tonight."

"I think you're right, Bill," Shook said. But the problem remained: For what? So far they had nothing that constituted probable cause for an arrest.

The hours passed, more media flooding in, the ever-present television helicopters flying over the houses. When a gun or gun parts were found, Matt Johnson, the ATF agent on the scene, secured and bagged the evidence. Meanwhile, the computer expert ran a preliminary scan on the laptops using OS Triage, a program developed by the FBI. Looking for anything tied to the killings, he checked browser history to find any searches linked to the investigation. Finished, he boxed the computers to be transferred to the lab.

Outside on the patio, Special Agent Aaron Beggs, tall with brown hair, had heard so much about Kim being ill that he expected her to be "at death's door." Instead, she appeared wan, tired, but overall more alert than anticipated. As the search went on inside, she paced, at times chatting. She talked about Honey Nuggets, her Internet business that she'd closed years earlier; her dogs; and her parents.

"Do you and Eric have secrets no one else knows?" Beggs asked.

"No," she snapped. Beggs wondered if she understood the seriousness of the situation.

"Do you think he leads a secret life you don't know about?"

"I don't know," she said, indignant. "Do you?"

Beggs continued to try to get Kim to open up, but she said little about her husband or marriage. After the team finished searching a spare bedroom, they allowed her to go to bed. When someone opened the kitchen refrigerator, they called others over to look at Kim's medications, including liquid morphine. "She took enough to probably put most people into a coma," Beggs said. Pill bottles littered the bathroom. Beggs thought it looked like an episode of *Hoarders*.

In one room, Laurie Gibbs opened a closet and found Eric's trophies, medals, plaques, and ribbons from his high school years. She noticed his framed Mensa certificate. So much potential, and now he'd become the prime suspect in three murders.

Downtown at the DA's office, someone looked out a window and noticed helicopters circling the part of Kaufman where Eric Williams lived. TVs turned on, while some searched local media on their computers. By then Dallas stations carried it live, a search at the home of a former JP, the only identified suspect in the three Kaufman County prosecutor murders.

"It was like finally," said Amanda Morris, Mark's paralegal.

Yet no one celebrated. It was too early.

When the news broke, JR was at his dad's house with other members of the family, cleaning it out after it had been released by the police. They'd all seen Eric's TV interviews, struck by how calm he looked. JR had a cold feeling, not liking the expression, a slight sneer on the man's face. Nathan reacted similarly, astonished by Williams's cool demeanor.

That heartbreaking day at the house, they divided up their parents' possessions. So much reminded them of their loss: Cynthia's shelves filled with quilting material, their library of books. It took three trips to a food bank to clear the larder. In a truck bed, JR and his brother stacked layers of five-gallon pails of flour. In the house, they found scores of boxes of ammo and more than a hundred guns, including three AR–15s. Laid out to be divided, Mike's knives covered the king-size bed.

Still convinced the killer simply walked in, JR said, "If the door had been locked, my dad would have had a chance. He would have had a gun."

So much seemed ironic. For weeks the investigation stalled, but watching the search of the house on the news, it appeared that authorities finally had a suspect, the same man Mike had often pointed at: Eric Williams.

At Kim's parents' house, the crime scene unit found guns, .357s, the caliber weapons used to murder Mark Hasse. Once cleared by the ATF agent, they were logged in as evidence.

Meanwhile, at Kim and Eric's house, the FBI team discovered other things of interest. Along with what Evans and Dockery noted the day before—all the military gear, gun parts, ammunition, and the like—someone noticed a Post-it note on a kitchen cabinet, handwritten, that said, "Kim's Kick-Ass List." On it were names of people Eric bore a grudge against. They were all people who'd taken swipes at Eric, including someone who posted a scathing complaint about his legal services on the net. When Wirskye saw it, he thought Kim and Eric cheered each other on. "It was them against the world, complaining about how they'd been screwed."

Still, that wasn't enough for an arrest.

Then, finally, one of the searchers walked outside and handed Dianna Strain another piece of paper, a tax receipt found in a black computer bag. It had a Web site address written on it—tipsubmit.com—and a series of letters and numbers. Strain called the information in to the command post. There Jolie Stewart worked with others, fielding phone calls as evidence came in. After many in the post looked at the tax receipt, one realized what it meant. When he explained it to Stewart, she looked at him, smiled, and said, "You've got to be kidding me."

Immediately, she called Strain and explained what she held in her hand. The number on the receipt—W695–196—matched the identifiers for the Crime Stoppers tip that came in the day after the McLellands' murders, the tip that correctly described the bullets used to murder Mark. In his e-mail, the sender threatened to continue killing, unless officials followed his orders.

When Bill Wirskye heard what the CSU team found, he called his law partner. "It was like a confession," Shook said.

The two prosecutors discussed what to do next. They didn't want to pursue a charge that might not stand. Although they felt certain that they had their killer, and that others—including themselves and potentially their families—could be in danger, a murder charge seemed premature.

Instead, Wirskye returned to the command post and helped Stewart and others write a different type of arrest warrant for Eric Williams. With the Crime Stoppers number, they had enough to charge him with terroristic threat. "We did what we could to keep him on ice," Wirskye said. "I knew we had him. At that point, he was going away."

Shook drove out to help, and on the warrant the officers wrote: "It was learned that the defendant utilized these unique identifiers to send the threat via electronic communication from his personal computer."

While the search at Kim's parents' house ended, at Kim and Eric's the evening bled into night. The discoveries weren't over. In a cabinet inside the garage an FBI agent found an envelope, one that held a title for a white Crown Victoria, and a copy of an e-mail between a buyer,

"Richard Greene," and the car's owner to set up a time to see it.

When that was called into the command post, FBI agent Michael Hillman thought about the blurry images they'd gathered on surveillance videos of a car that looked like a white Crown Vic coming and going on the morning of the McLelland murders.

No one watching the news reports from the scene knew about the discoveries unfolding, but off and on through the day and into the night, live video continued to beam to TV stations showing the search unfolding at the house. "Well, I'll be damned," Mike Burns said when he saw the reports. "Mike was right all along. It was that JP."

While the others searched, Wirskye and Shook helped finish the arrest warrant. Late at night, they barreled in the darkness down country roads to Judge Chitty's house, getting lost along the way. Finally they found it, and the judge answered the door. Armed guards surrounded the house, while inside Chitty read the warrant, then looked at Wirskye.

"Is this going to end it?" he asked.

"We think so, Judge," Shook replied. At that, the judge signed it.

The house search concluded at 12:30 a.m., and Shook and Wirskye rushed to the sheriff's office to see Eric brought in handcuffed. Just like after the theft arrest, Eric was taken to an interview room. Chief Deputy Rodney Evans, the same man who'd interviewed him two years earlier, tried to get him to talk. "This time he didn't fall for my country dumb act," said Evans.

"Eric didn't say much," Shook agreed. "Just that he was diabetic and needed something to eat." Someone got him a sack lunch, and Shook thought, "He can get used to the shit he's going to eat the rest of his life."

Booked into the Kaufman County jail, Eric's bond was set at $3 million. When Kim heard that her husband had been arrested, she wasn't surprised. She hadn't expected any of it to end well. Worried about what it might mean for her, she took a pill and went to bed.

Chapter 49

They may have gone the wrong way to do it, but they eventually did it. I figured Mike McLelland would have said it was better than a sharp stick in the eye.
—Mike Burns

After Eric's booking, the prosecutors and investigators held a meeting at the command post, discussing what needed to be done. Everyone gathered agreed their prime goals had to be to find the murder weapons and the white Crown Victoria. While they worried that Eric might have disposed of the weapons, dumping a car presented bigger issues, the most likely scenarios that Eric either had hidden it, destroyed it, or sold it. Using state troopers and rangers, Major Dockery offered to take the lead the following morning, to circulate to storage units, especially around Lake Tawakoni, where Eric drove the evening after the McLelland murders.

Early that Saturday morning, Mike's and Cynthia's children were called and told Eric had been booked. JR thought about how sure his father had been that Eric murdered Mark Hasse. Then JR considered the final years with his father, when they'd talked more, and what might have been, the years they should have had to get closer had his father lived. Filled with sadness and anger, JR thought, "Eric Williams stole that from us."

At their homes, Bill Wirskye and Toby Shook woke up grateful for a day off, to finally have leisure to spend with their families at baseball and soccer games. Instead Wirskye's phone rang. It was Eric's guard friend, Roger Williams.

The day before, Roger had watched the search unfold on television. Early that Saturday morning at the unit's regular drill, Roger had talked to Scott Hunt, the guardsman Eric asked about disposing of an upper. After what they'd seen on TV, they decided to contact authorities. "You don't know me. I was given your number. I helped Eric rent a storage unit," Roger said.

"We've got the storage unit," Wirskye told Dockery on the phone. The ranger suggested they set up a meeting with Roger and Hunt, and Wirskye did.

Their plans with their families abandoned, Wirskye and Shook met with Roger Williams and Scott Hunt later that morning at Forney PD headquarters. Dockery and the others joined them, and the rangers handled the interview. In that conversation, Hunt told them about Eric's desire to get rid of an upper, and Roger described renting the Seagoville storage unit. He didn't mention, however, that in early March he'd met with Gibbs and Hillman and never told them about the unit. Wirskye and Shook would only find that out later and wonder, if they had known, if it could have saved the McLellands' lives.

One thing especially surprised those gathered: the way Roger Williams and Scott Hunt even then referred to Eric as "Captain Williams."

When they finished, Wirskye and Shook helped write another search warrant, this one for Eric's storage unit. But they had a problem. Roger Williams didn't remember the name of the facility or its address. Instead, he offered to take them there.

To finish the warrant and get it signed, Shook stayed in Forney, while Wirskye and the rangers followed the two guardsmen to Gibson Self Storage. At the facility they found no one available to unlock the gates, so they called the number on the sign. The manager, Larry Mathis, left his grandchildren's volleyball game. When he got there, he said, "I can't let you in the unit without a warrant."

"There's one on the way," Wirskye said.

In Dallas, Shook had the warrant signed by a judge and then headed to Seagoville. "Don't open it until I get there," he told Wirskye. "I know we're going to find the Crown Vic."

While they waited, Wirskye and the rangers talked to Mathis about how the security system monitored comings and goings at the units. When Mathis printed out records showing when gate codes were used to access Unit 18, Wirskye's "heart skipped a beat." The unit had been entered early on the mornings of both the Hasse and McLelland murders.

The men waited together, talking, until Wirskye decided that perhaps Roger Williams and Scott Hunt needed to leave. Soon the media would descend, and the prosecutor didn't want potential witnesses stopped and asked questions.

After they left, Mathis opened the main gate, and the others clustered outside Unit 18. Lieutenant Stewart and Special Agent Laurie Gibbs arrived, while Gibbs's partner, Michael Hillman, waited at the command post. Before long, Shook drove in, and the fire department cut the steel lock on the unit. Ranger Kasper felt a chill as he pushed the garage-style door up, and at two feet above the ground saw car tires followed by a white bumper, then the Crown Vic. "There were screams, some high fives, and a couple little tears that no one is going to claim," said Lieutenant Stewart.

"It was incredible. There was the car. It was a gold mine," said Gibbs.

Elated, Shook and Wirskye took a photo crouching near the Crown Vic's bumper, a memento from a long and terrifying siege.

The Crown Victoria inside Unit 18
Evidence photo

On her way to a crawfish boil when she heard that a storage unit had been found, Dianna Strain contacted her forensic team, and they headed out in the FBI trailer to Seagoville, arriving about six that evening. On top of the car, they found the key, and one of the team suited in white, wearing gloves and booties, backed out the Crown Vic. By then, word had spread, and news helicopters hovered overhead. At his house, John Sickel watched live as the car emerged from the storage unit. "My God," he whispered.

Once they had the Crown Vic out of the unit, two technicians began processing it on the scene, before deciding it would be easier in the lab. At that point, they locked and towed it.

Meanwhile, all eyes focused on the boxes and bags inside Unit 18. With tarps hung to shield the forensic team from TV cameras, they commandeered a second storage unit, an empty one, to use as a staging area, to catalogue the evidence. The process took hours, and in the end they checked into evidence forty-one firearms, the crossbow, lowers but no uppers for two AR rifles, and nearly every type of gun accessory, from slings to holsters to scopes.

As darkness fell, large lights on posts illuminated the area to allow them to keep working. They found duffel bags and trunks—some with Eric's name stenciled across the top—filled with weapons, machetes, and knives, blue surgical booties, a cleaning agent to wipe away fingerprints, and thousands of rounds of ammo.

In the flurry of activity, Laurie Gibbs stepped in to help the forensic team and spotted a single unfired .223 cartridge in the bottom of a black bag. Struck by the fact that it was the type of ammo used to kill the McLellands, rather than throw it in a box with the others, she bagged it separately and sent it in for processing. Only later would Gibbs understand the importance of what she had done.

The work continued until pickle jars filled with a strange yellow substance were discovered. Worried that they could be explosive, Strain ordered everyone out and called the bomb squad. By then, they'd also found a can of lighter fluid with a dog toy and a lighter attached, a homemade bomb. Some on the scene wondered if Eric planned to eventually use the device to set the Crown Vic on fire and destroy any evidence.

"It was like we found the mad scientist's lair," said Lieutenant Stewart.

When she saw sleeves of badges from different police agencies, bulletproof vests, military duffels filled with gear, T-shirts and jackets that read "POLICE" and "SHERIFF" even "US CUSTOMS," and "TREASURY DEPARTMENT," Stewart looked at all Eric had collected and considered her early impressions of him. He'd wanted to be in the military, but hadn't made it. He'd wanted to be a police officer, but couldn't keep a job. "Eric Williams was the ultimate wannabe," she said, voicing a sentiment Mike McLelland had often expressed.

The FBI's forensic squad worked at the unit until 4:30 the next morning. In the midst of all of it, one seemingly innocuous item caught the attention of Laurie Gibbs—an empty two-liter plastic bottle of regular Coke.

At the house on Overlook, Gibbs had seen the piles of empty Coke bottles, and she'd heard Kim say that Eric didn't drink Coke, that she did. "That bottle suggested that Kim was in the unit," said Gibbs. "And that she knew."

Chapter 50

At first nothing. Then, it was like dominoes falling.
                                                —Laurie Gibbs

At the jail, a guard watched Eric around the clock in Sick 2, a cell in the infirmary. Orders had been put through for a twenty-four-hour suicide watch, a common precaution with inmates who potentially faced severe sentences.

On Sunday morning, the national news dissected the odd situation of a small-town justice of the peace under arrest for murdering two prosecutors and the DA's wife. The following morning, the focus remained on the Kaufman cases, under newspaper headlines and as the leads on national news programs. Some pundits who had endorsed the Aryan Brotherhood angle during the long investigation walked back their previous comments, claiming they'd doubted the link from the beginning. Then mid-afternoon that Monday, two pressure cooker bombs exploded at the Boston Marathon, killing three and injuring 264.

In an instant, the media moved on, along with many of the FBI agents. The Kaufman case coming together, the terrorist attack took its place as the agency's number one priority. A core of agents remained—Michael Hillman, Laurie Gibbs, and Aaron Beggs—while the others boarded planes for the East Coast.

In his office in Dallas that afternoon, Bill Wirskye got

a call from an investigator who relayed lab results on the weapons seized during the searches. Marked as a priority, all the guns found at the storage unit and the two handguns confiscated from Kim's parents' house had been tested. "None of them match the bullet fragments or spent casings," the man said. "Sorry, Bill. We don't have the murder weapons."

While disappointed, Wirskye wasn't surprised. No uppers were found for Eric's assault-type weapons, and the two prosecutors had talked often of Eric's after-dark drive to Lake Tawakoni, a perfect place to dispose of evidence.

Yet they had so much more. By then a unit had tracked down Ed Cole, the man who'd sold the Crown Victoria. When shown a photo lineup, he picked Eric out as the man who bought the retired police car, the man who called himself Richard Greene.

Meanwhile, much of the discussion among the investigators turned to how to approach Kim. Nearly everyone believed that she knew about the killings, some wondering if she could have helped.

The following day, a Tuesday, two sheriff's deputies rang the Overlook house's doorbell. When Kim answered, they asked her to go to the law enforcement center with them, to have her fingerprints taken and her cheek swabbed. Once they arrived, Kim was fingerprinted and her DNA collected. Rather than releasing her, however, they then escorted her to an interview room. Before long, Laurie Gibbs, Michael Hillman, and others walked in and talked casually with Kim. She didn't call an attorney or ask for one. "That's how far out of it I was," she said later.

Bringing her a Coke, chatting calmly, they asked questions, while Bill Wirskye watched on a video hookup. As they spoke, Kim appeared nervous, continually mentioning her sick parents and that they needed her.

"Did you know anything about the McLellands' murders?" one asked.

"No. Nothing," she answered. When they asked about Eric, Kim insisted, "He didn't do it. And I don't know anything about it."

Slowly they revealed what they already knew, including that they had the Crime Stoppers tip that linked Eric to the killings. Not surprised, Kim admitted nothing. "Eric didn't kill those people," she said. "He's a good man. A good husband."

The afternoon wore on, little accomplished. The interviewers never pushed too hard, afraid that if they did she'd lawyer up or leave. Then, about five hours after she'd arrived at the sheriff's office, those gathered felt frustrated and discussed closing it up.

Much of that afternoon the FBI agent who sat with Kim during the search, Aaron Beggs, stood next to Wirskye, watching. Beggs thought the good cop approach wouldn't work with Kim, and he figured he might have a better chance if he played bad cop. In his opinion, Kim deflected questions. If one agent asked a question, she turned and looked at the other and answered. For Beggs, who'd been put off by Kim's attitude at the search, when she'd seemed impatient throughout the process, it seemed time to set aside the niceties. "I could tell she was hiding something," he said.

At about eight that evening when the others left Kim sitting alone in the room, Beggs asked, "Can I take a shot at her?"

"Are you going to ask questions?" Kim asked Beggs when he walked in.

"I'm not going to ask shit. You were there. You know what happened. You need to tell us the truth, to get on the right side of this," he said. Inside the interview room, he pulled a chair close to Kim, sat down and looked her directly in her eyes, then said, "I know you helped your husband kill those people."

"I did not," she said.

"I think you're full of it," he said. "Here's why . . ." With that, Beggs listed the reasons he believed Kim knew, including that she lived in the house with Eric throughout the siege, and that witnesses said someone else drove the getaway car at the Hasse murder. He'd seen the Coke bottle at the storage unit, which by then Beggs called "Eric's little house of horrors." When Kim tried to interrupt, Beggs stopped her. "No! You had your chance. I've heard enough from you," he said. "This is my time to talk. There's no way Eric is sneaking out with you right there in the bed. You're going to notice that. That he's going to dress up like a SWAT guy and go murder those people without your knowing. Why'd you kill Cynthia? Why? What did she do to you?"

In the observation room, Bill Wirskye watched Beggs with Kim and talked to Toby Shook on the phone. When asked how it was going, Wirskye said, "Not so well. Everyone is taking a run at her. She's denying everything. She said Eric is the greatest guy in the world."

Just then inside the interview room, Wirskye heard Beggs shout, "Eric shot that woman in the head, a final fuck-you."

Her stomach churned. Kim hadn't forgotten Eric's words, that Cynthia moaned and he shot her through the head.

In the interview room, Beggs said, "I don't understand how you could sit there and let an old lady who just liked to quilt get killed."

At that, Kim cried, "You wouldn't understand."

"Yes, I would," Beggs answered, lowering his voice. "Are you going to be nice to me now?"

"I just need the truth," Beggs said.

At first only silence, then Wirskye saw Kim lower her head as she said, "I just did what he told me to do. . . . He woke me up and said, 'Today's the day.'"

Unsure if he'd actually heard what he thought he had,

Wirskye asked someone else, "Did she just say what I thought she said?"

"Yes, she did."

"Toby, she just broke," Wirskye told Shook on the phone. "She's giving it up."

Thirty minutes later, Toby Shook arrived at the Kaufman County Sheriff's Office, and Aaron Beggs left Kim in the interview room to confer with the two prosecutors. They instructed him to read her the Miranda warning, and then go over her confession with her again. Beggs did, and Kim repeated that she'd driven with Eric to the murders, that he'd killed Mark Hasse, Mike and Cynthia McLelland.

Under questioning, Kim gave them an outline of the murders. "Yes, we did it," she said, repeating what she'd told him earlier. She also admitted that Eric had already begun preparing for his next murder, and that he'd planned to kill Judge Ashworth that week. "When you talked to me like that, the way you looked at me reminded me of Eric," Kim told Beggs.

When Beggs suggested that Kim did more to help, perhaps opening the door for Eric at the McLelland house, she insisted that wasn't true. "They were trying to put me inside the house," she said later. "I didn't even know what the house looked like inside. I was never there."

In the end, it wouldn't have mattered. Texas had the law of parties, a statute in the criminal code that said that even if a person didn't pull the trigger, if they knowingly participated in an act that led to murder, it held them as culpable as the killer. Whether or not Kim left the car, she could be charged with capital murder and face the death penalty.

Something in particular came through clearly to Beggs; Kim had bought into Eric's anger. She, too, blamed the dead prosecutors for what they'd done. "She talked about how they'd lost their insurance. They'd lost everything," he said. "And she talked about being afraid of her husband. If she hadn't done it, she was afraid he'd hurt her. She was his ride-or-die woman."

As Kim recounted her life with Eric, Beggs believed her. "I thought she was afraid of him, and that he'd controlled her." At the end of the interview, Kim was booked and handcuffed, the charge capital murder. A judge set her bail at $10 million.

When they finished the paperwork, Kim agreed to show Beggs the routes they'd taken to the murders, and they drove the darkened streets to downtown Kaufman, to the parking lot. Kim showed Beggs and FBI special agent Michael Hillman where Eric parked the Sable the day he murdered Mark Hasse, and the routes to and from the McLelland house from the storage unit. Instead of an enemy, Kim warmed up and talked to Beggs like a friend. Yet she called him "the mean guy."

"It's like an adrenaline dump after they confess," Beggs said. "It's almost like being in a shooting. You've expended so much energy, and then it's like, wow, relief."

At the end of the journey, Beggs and Hillman took Kim to her house to tend her dogs for one last time. Her wrists handcuffed, tears in her eyes, she fed them. She panicked when Beggs told her that she couldn't bring her medications. "Just like any addict," he said. He explained that the jail had a medical unit, and they would take care of her, and then he drove to the jail and brought her in. "We'd finally put an end to this thing."

Chapter 51

My mom came to see me at the jail. She asked me if I'd done what they said I did. I told her I did. It was all true. She couldn't believe it.

—Kim Williams

The next morning, Bill Wirskye and Toby Shook went to the Kaufman County jail and had Eric brought out from his cell. They handed him Kim's arrest warrant, which read: "During the interview, Kim Williams confessed to her involvement to the scheme and course of conduct in the shooting deaths of Mark Hasse, Michael McLelland and Cynthia McLelland. Kim Williams described in detail her role along with that of her husband, Eric Williams, whom she reported to have shot to death Mark Hasse on January 31, 2013 and Michael and Cynthia McLelland on March 30, 2013. During the interview, the defendant gave details of both offenses which had not been made public."

The prosecutors hoped Eric might say something incriminating, perhaps even confess, but he stayed silent. Wirskye thought, however, that he could see the jailed man's "wheels turning," most likely contemplating what they did and didn't know.

Later that day at a press conference, the sheriff announced the news of the arrests. By then charges had been filed against Eric for capital murder by terroristic threat for

Mark Hasse's murder, along with capital murder charges for the killings of the McLellands. Both Eric and Kim faced possible death penalties. With the new charges, a judge upped Eric's bail to $23 million.

"It's a relief to know the ones responsible for this are now behind bars," JR told a reporter. ". . . it's only the beginning. There will be a long process before there will be a conviction in this case. But we are ready to see it through."

When Judge Wood and others saw Kim's booking photo, they didn't recognize her. She only faintly resembled the woman they remembered. While many wondered about Eric, they'd never expected her to be involved, especially not after all the years Eric described her as bedridden. Some of their friends wondered if Eric and Kim had ultimately acted out the Mafia Wars game they found so engrossing.

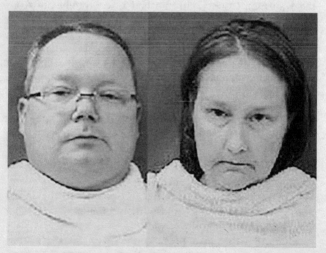

Eric and Kim Williams's mug shots
Kaufman County Sheriff's Office

After the press conference, Kim and Eric signed paupers' oaths, and both were appointed lawyers. In the jail, Kim dried out, the doctor limiting her meds to Tylenol. Although they wanted to know more, much more, Shook and Wirskye held back from attempting to interview her again until she had time to get off the drugs and confer with her lawyer.

Perhaps not surprising, within days of Kim's arrest, letters started arriving from Eric, sent from his jail cell to hers. He reminisced about old times, the dogs, and about sticking together. In some, Eric proposed trips they could take after they were both cleared of the charges, and he reminded her that as his wife spousal privilege laws meant she couldn't be compelled to testify against him. In her cell, Kim wrote back, still attached to him, still feeling the pull of their relationship. "I loved him even then," she said. "Crazy, I know, but I did."

Odds and ends to clear up, mindful that it would come out at Eric's trial and not wanting Judge Ashworth to hear it for the first time in the media, Toby Shook and Bill Wirskye went to the judge's home to explain what Kim had told them, that when he was arrested, Eric was only days away from carrying out a plot to murder the judge.

In Kim's interview with Beggs, much had become clear for the prosecutors, especially the use Eric intended for the bag holding the pickle jars filled with a strange yellow substance and crossbow arrows. "We realized that Kim described exactly what we'd seen in the storage unit," said Shook. "Eric's supplies he'd collected to use to kill the judge."

When Beggs asked Kim why Eric wanted to kill the judge, she'd said, "Because he's arrogant."

Hearing what his former protégé had planned for him had to have been chilling. In the context of his prior relationship with Eric, the way Ashworth had taken his court coordinator under his wing, it must have seemed a particularly bitter pill. "You'll all have to excuse me," the judge said, and left the room, without explaining. It seemed like a long time before he returned.

Afterward, Wirskye and Shook also dropped in on Erleigh Wiley, telling her that she, too, had been on Eric's kill list. The thought occurred to her that Mike and Cynthia had saved her life, since their murders set in motion the events that brought Eric to a jail cell.

A week after Kim's arrest, Wiley was officially sworn in as Kaufman County's new district attorney. She told reporters, "Every day we think about what happened to Mike, Cynthia, and Mark. We miss them."

In her new position, she tried to be more patient than she might have under other circumstances, understanding the trauma the staff had gone through. And although families and friends urged them to leave, nearly all those who worked in the DA's office stayed. "We weren't going to let Eric Williams drive us from our jobs," said one paralegal. "We wouldn't have given him that satisfaction."

At the Kaufman County jail, Tera visited her brother. They'd grown apart and hadn't talked in years. "I wouldn't have expected it to be you," Eric said. Tera cried softly. He ordered her to stop and said, "Everything's going to be okay."

"No, Eric, it's not," she said.

Meanwhile, in his office, Bill Wirskye reviewed lab results. One item in particular jumped out: the stray cartridge Laurie Gibbs had collected from the bottom of the bag in the storage unit, the bullet she bagged separately, bore rifling marks. While it was never fired, Eric had apparently chambered and then removed it from a weapon. The most likely scenario: the final cartridge in a magazine, Eric ejected it when he cleared his rifle.

The reason Wirskye's heart sped up when he read the report: the markings on that .223 cartridge matched those on spent casings found in the McLellands' home. That meant that the storage-unit cartridge had cycled through the murder weapon. "It was the smoking gun," said Wirskye. "It was almost as good as recovering the murder weapon in the storage."

So much coalesced as the case came together, yet the prosecutors and others still wondered if they'd explored every possibility. One thing in particular bothered many. Although Kim hadn't mentioned any accomplices, some wondered if Eric had other help. When they looked at the case, Shook and Wirskye repeatedly wondered most about Eric's fellow guardsmen. They'd shown such loyalty to Eric, continuing to refer to him as "Captain Williams" even after his arrest, that the prosecutors wondered just how far his guard friends would have been willing to go to help Eric carry out his vendetta.

Subpoenas went out, and the prosecutors questioned some of the guard members in front of a grand jury. Many still felt empathy for their former captain, blaming the dead prosecutors for the way they'd come after Eric, destroying his life. "Everyone has a trigger, and you can only push them so far," said one. "And Eric was the last person we thought could do anything like that."

One in particular Wirskye wondered about was Roger Williams. When he'd come forward with the information about the storage unit, they thought he acted as if he should be considered a hero. In contrast, they wondered why he'd taken so long, and why he hadn't told the FBI agents who questioned him weeks earlier.

That left Wirskye and Shook wondering if Roger Williams could be an accomplice. In the end, after questioning the guard members and collecting their DNA, they determined that none had participated in the murders.

In May, Mark, Mike, and Cynthia were honored during National Police Week in Kaufman, and Judge Wood read a proclamation. "Life is precious," he said. "We have folks who give their lives too often. We should not and shall not forget that in this community."

That month, David Sergi dropped Eric's appeal on his theft case. It no longer mattered.

At the Kaufman County jail, Eric's new attorney, Matthew Seymour, had already begun conferring with his client. With a short brown buzz cut and glasses, Seymour had spent his life trying to make the world a better place. Out of college, he traveled to Mali in West Africa as a Peace Corps volunteer. While there, he suffered second-degree burns over eighty percent of his body when a compressed gas cylinder exploded.

After law school he worked as a defense lawyer, then signed on with the Dallas Public Defender's Office in 2007. On the day Mark Hasse died, Seymour was working on a case at the Dallas courthouse. The building seemed to pulsate with tension. "It was all people could focus on," he said. After Mark's murder, Seymour bought his first gun and had his backyard fenced. In March, he'd begun working as a defense attorney for capital cases at the regional public defender's office and was quickly assigned to take on the Eric Williams case.

From the beginning, Seymour saw Eric as an unlikely triple murderer.

In ways, the defense attorney identified with his client. Both had been more nerds than athletes during their school years. Both read a lot, and they'd both been in the marching band. Both played Dungeons & Dragons with friends. Talking with his client, Seymour liked Eric, whom he found to have a dry sense of humor. And early on he realized that the state would throw everything they had against his client. "It was a big case. And it was going to be tough," said Seymour.

Behind the scenes, the investigation quietly continued. In June at the Kaufman County Sheriff's Office, Lieutenant Jolie Stewart collected reports on more evidence coming in from the DPS lab. By then they'd tracked down the Mercury Sable in an auto storage yard. The fleur-de-lis pattern Lenda Bush remembered under hypnosis turned out to be a cat's dirty paw prints over the hood of the car.

While the man who sold the Sable didn't pick Eric out of a photo lineup, the investigators had another break. In the front seat, a DPS trooper discovered a small box that held earplugs. When they were tested, the lab recovered DNA. Eric's DNA. That placed him inside the car. In another lucky break, the owner of the Crown Victoria turned over the envelope the man who described himself as "Richard Greene" used to return his garage door opener. Rather than a stamp, the shipper used a postage meter, the one assigned to Eric's law office.

Meanwhile, computer experts combed through twenty-five terabytes of data off Eric's computers. They found pictures of public officials at press conferences about the killings, and a photo of one of the McLellands' dogs wearing a red campaign blanket over his back that read "MIKE McLELLAND." An inventory Eric made of his firearms two years earlier listed a Ruger and a Smith & Wesson .357, the type of revolver used to murder Mark Hasse. On the same inventory, Eric listed two ARs, the type of weapons used to murder the McLellands.

Possibly most chilling, they discovered the photograph Eric had taken years earlier of the gravestone Judge Ashworth had installed on his cemetery plot.

Unaware of the investigation grinding along behind the scenes, at the Kaufman jail Kim fretted about her parents, worrying much of the day about not being able to care for them. When she conferred with her attorney, she continually turned the conversation to her mother and father. While he listened patiently, her attorney insisted Kim had far more pressing issues. Charged with three murders, she faced a possible death sentence.

As the attorney talked, Kim heard the words, and on one level understood, yet had a difficult time grasping what it all meant.

At times in his letters, Eric threatened Kim. "He told me in one letter that he'd 'tell them everything,'" she said. "I didn't know what to think. I mean, I'd already told them that I knew Eric was going to kill those people and kept quiet. I drove him to one murder. I was with him at the McLellands' house. I wasn't denying that I was involved."

Weeks passed, and Eric's letters kept arriving, Kim writing back as she slowly reconsidered all that had happened. Then one day, "the clouds cleared." Off the drugs, she found clarity, and in place of confusion felt a fiery anger. "I couldn't believe Eric used me like that. And I realized I was responsible for the three people who died. Their blood was on my hands. I didn't stop him."

When her mother visited, Kim asked her to get an attorney. "I want a divorce."

June 27 turned out to be an important day for the case. First, a grand jury formally charged Kim and Eric with all three murders. Secondly, her attorney filed her divorce petition, declaring the marriage "insupportable because of discord or conflict." Kim's mother also filed a lawsuit against Eric to collect $50,000 she'd loaned him.

Two days later, the *Dallas Morning News* ran an article on the case with the headline "State Militia Soldiers May Play a Big Role in Kaufman County Prosecutor Killing Trial." The reporter, Tanya Eiserer, laid out how guard members Roger Williams and Scott Hunt would be called to the stand. And in the piece, she quoted Bruce Bryant, the DA's investigator, as suggesting that Mike felt Kaufman PD's chief, Chris Aulbaugh, seemed unwilling to interrogate the state guard unit. In the piece, Eiserer quoted Aulbaugh as denying that he knew Eric Williams, insisting that they'd never met.

Two weeks later, Aulbaugh resigned from his slot in

Kaufman and took a deputy chief's slot with the Coppell, Texas, police department. While a lesser position, it offered more money.

In the courtroom in July, the visiting judge assigned to the Williams case, Michael Snipes, an ex-army officer who'd been a federal prosecutor and a district court judge, presided over a hearing. Eric entered wearing a business suit brought from home, while guards escorted Kim in wearing her jail uniform. In the audience, JR watched his father and stepmother's killers, thinking about how unlikely it all seemed. When a reporter talked to Mike's mom, Wyvonne said, "I'd like to shoot [Eric Williams] in the knees."

Quickly after being assigned to the case, Snipes asked the prosecutors which of the murders they intended to pursue. In multiple murder cases, it wasn't unusual to split up the murders, giving prosecutors the opportunity—if they didn't achieve the sentence they hoped for with the first trial—to try defendants again on the remaining killings, hoping for a stiffer sentence.

After reviewing their options, Wirskye and Shook decided to try Eric on Cynthia's murder. First: it was the case they had the most evidence on. By then, video had been seized from the Chicken Express near the storage facility. While it should have been trained on the drive-through, the misaligned camera fanned out toward Gibson. On the morning of the McLelland murders, it caught Eric and Kim driving in and out of the facility, on their way to and from the killings.

They also chose Cynthia's killing for another reason: of the three victims, she was truly innocent, the most sympathetic to a jury. Cynthia had no part in the theft trial, had no interaction with Eric Williams, yet in his rage he mowed her down and then pumped a bullet into her head.

To make the charge capital murder—eligible for the death penalty—however, Texas law specified that certain circumstances had to be met; one was that the killing took place in conjunction—during the same event—with a second felony. So they wrote the indictment to specify that Cynthia's murder happened during the commission of a second murder, that of her husband, Mike McLelland.

At the jail, Tera continued to visit Eric, and she took her husband, Zach, with her. Consistently Eric claimed his innocence. When Zach asked what he could do to help, Eric asked him to take a truck like his Sport Trac to a ten-by-twenty storage unit, and see if it "would even fit in one." If it wouldn't, that would have disputed Kim's version of the killings.

Zach did as Eric asked. "But it was stupid. I mean, of course it fit. The unit was the size of a garage. . . . It was like, Eric, if you're really innocent give us something that proves that."

Since she had Eric's power of attorney, Tera cleaned out the Overlook house. They found Eric's stash of high-tech trinkets, and Zach began thinking of his brother-in-law "as a big kid." Eric had ten Mont Blanc pens, one with diamonds. In Kim's closet, they found seventy-five new-looking pairs of shoes, never-worn lingerie, and clothes that still had the store tags.

The weeks, then months ticked past into 2014. As Eric's attorney, Matt Seymour signed for deliveries from the prosecutors, materials turned over during discovery. The computer records alone appeared formidable, and more attorneys were assigned to work with Seymour: Doug Parks and John Wright, out of Seymour's office. Maxwell Peck joined the team as well. A former nuclear missile operator in the air force who'd gone to law school, Peck started out as pro–death penalty but grew to question its fairness.

With much to do, the defense "just started plugging through it," Seymour said.

In her cell at the jail, Kim continued to attempt to explain her situation to her attorney, to make him understand why she did what she did. "I told him about the gun incident, when it went off in the house," she said. "I told him I felt like Eric was threatening me. But he said, 'Well, he was just cleaning his gun.' I said, 'No, you don't understand.' I felt like no one believed me. I couldn't make them understand that I was afraid. I was embarrassed. It all seemed ridiculous. I couldn't believe this had happened."

Off and on, Wirskye and Shook talked to Kim's lawyer, wanting more information. Her attorney explained to Kim that while the prosecutors weren't offering a deal, cooperating offered her best hope of avoiding the death penalty. In July, Wirskye and Shook met with Kim and her attorney for the first time. The things she told them that day matched the physical evidence, including a hole in the wall inside the house where Eric had fired the gun, and holes in the wood fence where Eric practiced using the crossbow he bought to kill Judge Ashworth.

While they had the bones of the case before, Kim offered two important new insights: that Eric had taken her to an underpass where he'd practiced shooting the weapon he used to murder the McLellands, and that he'd thrown a black bag into Lake Tawakoni.

In the car on the way to the deserted underpass, Kim stayed quiet. Once they arrived, she pointed where Eric parked the car, and the cement pillars he shot at. A forensic tech sprayed areas of the pillars that resembled bullet strikes with sodium rhodizonate, testing for copper and lead, elements used to manufacture bullets. The sections glowed pink, the results positive.

Scouring the area, they booked into evidence spent .223 casings. Later, the DPS lab would identify many as matching ones recovered from the McLelland murder scene.

The search of Lake Tawakoni proved vastly more complicated. With Kim, they drove to the lake and onto Two

Mile Bridge, where three months earlier Eric threw something into the water. Standing on the bridge, Kim pointed. "I think it was over there."

At the site, a DPS dive team led by Sergeant Steve Tippett anchored a twenty-five-foot boat marked "Texas Department of Public Safety" on its hull. Each day the searchers, including the FBI's Laurie Gibbs, came and went in a small service boat. In September, the weather sizzled, but by winter, the waters felt cold and the waves became choppy.

Early on, the press showed up, and helicopters hovered overhead. Under the surface, at the bottom of the muddy lake, the divers felt their way, unable to see, methodically searching one section at a time, feeling for the bag, hoping to bump into it. They found shoes, tires, and guns, but none as Kim described. When tested, none of the guns tied back to the murders.

When the search stalled, Gibbs escorted Kim out to the lake again, and she tried to rethink, sending the dive team off to a different area. On the way home, Gibbs asked if Kim wanted to drive past her house on Overlook. She did, and as they slowed down, then stopped, she felt overwhelming sadness. "I wished I'd been more myself, not so drugged up, so I wouldn't have felt helpless," she said. "And I thought it was a pretty house for such a cold relationship."

Again, the searchers worked their way around the lake bottom, only to fail.

Finally in March, the dive team decided to return to the lake and try one last time. Frustrated, blind under the water and relying on touch, they worried that the bag was just beyond the reach of their fingers. If they didn't find the guns, they decided that they had to let go and move on.

For the last time, they transported Kim to Two Mile Bridge. But this time they took her after dark, as it had been the night Eric dropped the bag. Halfway across, she asked them to slow down, and then stop. They did, and she pointed out another area near the crest.

Two weeks passed, the dive team coming up empty. Then on March 5, Tippett returned to the lake bottom for what they all agreed would be a final dive. Although she hated the cold, Laurie Gibbs sat in the boat. She wanted to be there, to see it through. The water a cloudy brown, she couldn't see Tippett and another diver hidden below the waves. But when he swept his hand, he hit something. When he picked it up, he felt a bag with something heavy inside.

As he emerged from the water, Tippett handed Gibbs a muddy black fabric bag. When they inspected what they had, it appeared to be a sack with mesh on one side. Later they realized rather than a bag they'd found a black cloth hood, one that matched the descriptions of witnesses at Mark's murder. From inside, they pulled two revolvers, a Ruger and a Smith & Wesson.

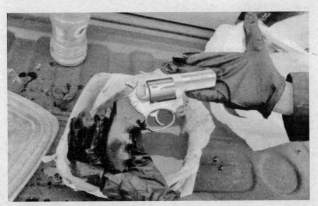

One of the guns pulled from the lake
Evidence photo

In the boat, Gibbs forgot about the frigid cold. Staring down at the guns from inside the bag, she felt certain they now had the Hasse murder weapons. Her only regret was that the upper from the AR weapon used to kill the McLellands wasn't in the bag as well.

When the reports arrived on Wirskye's desk, more pieces of the puzzle snapped into place. Witnesses had described eight shots fired on the morning of Mark's murder. The lab identified the Ruger as the murder weapon. The rifling on bullets fired from it matched the fragment that fell out of Mark's coat at the hospital. That gun was empty; all five bullets had been fired.

Registered to Kim, the Smith & Wesson held three spent casings, totaling the eight. "I didn't know he used my gun," Kim said. "Why would he use my gun?" No one but Eric knew.

Wirskye presumed that Eric had disposed of the missing uppers from the ARs in the lake as well, but doubted they would ever be found. "We were lucky to get what we did. It was a needle in a haystack."

That month more lab reports came in. One in particular caught Wirskye's attention. The lab officially identified the yellow substance in the pickle jars found in the storage unit as homemade napalm.

Chapter 52

You bet the whole pot every time. When we picked the jury, we knew we had to have people able to look Eric in the eye and say, "If he's guilty, kill him." We want to see Eric Williams lie dead on a gurney in Huntsville. We don't apologize for that.

—Toby Shook

Preparing for Eric's trial, Judge Snipes agreed with the defense that it could be hard to seat an impartial jury where such a sensational crime took place, and he moved the proceedings to adjacent Rockwall County. Initially part of Kaufman County, Rockwall splintered off in 1873. The smallest land area of any Texas county, just across Lake Ray Hubbard from Dallas, it was among the fastest growing and most affluent parts of the state.

When the defense asked for more time, Snipes scheduled the trial for the coming December, 2014.

The months passed quickly. Matt Seymour endured long days and sleepless nights, haunted by the task of seating jurors who could be convinced to spare Eric's life. First Seymour would try to persuade the jurors that the state didn't have sufficient evidence, that they should come back with a not guilty verdict. At the same time, however, much of the defense team's focus would be on building sympathy for Eric.

That wouldn't be easy.

Decisions went against the defense; most importantly, the judge ruled they would not be able to include testimony about the validity of the original trial, the theft case. Seymour wanted the jurors to hear Eric's side, that he'd been overprosecuted and unfairly ruined. Now that would be difficult to accomplish.

Yet Eric didn't appear worried. When Tera visited, Eric seemed confident, telling her to "just watch and see what my attorneys have."

In preparation for the trial, the sheriff's department moved Eric from the Kaufman jail to the one in Rockwall. There he had a cell with a TV, a desk, a bunk, a window, and guards who watched him day and night.

Jury selection began in September, when three thousand potential jurors completed a twenty-eight-page questionnaire on everything from their home situations to any experiences with law enforcement, from their jobs to their religions. With Eric facing the death penalty, attorneys on both sides questioned the jurors individually on their views of the ultimate punishment. "If we prove to you that Eric committed this murder, can you vote to put him to death?" they were asked. Some said yes, others, no.

Chapter 53

If looks could kill, Eric gave me looks during opening statements that would have buried me.
—Bill Wirskye

On the morning of December 1, 2014, the sky above
Rockwall shone a pale blue with a hint of lacy clouds. In
the parking lot, attorneys, family and friends, reporters,
and spectators drawn by the notoriety of the impending
proceedings wrapped their jackets to ward off a brisk wind.

As Texas courthouses go, Rockwall's ranked among
the most modern, the front dominated by massive stone
columns. Three years earlier the old courthouse, built
in 1941, had been retired. A well-heeled, white-collar
county, Rockwall had money to splurge on such improvements. Perhaps ironically, the building boasted all the
high-tech amenities Eric once yearned to bring to quaint
little Kaufman, including wi-fi.

On that particular morning a crush of heels clicked on
the impressive terrazzo floor, as the crowd shuffled through
metal detectors. Soaring far above, a Texas lone star marked
the center of the dome. Murmurs rumbled, acknowledg-
ments as investigators greeted one another, entering the
elevators that carried them up to the courtroom.

Preparations for the highly-publicized trial had taken
months. On the first floor a viewing room with large screens

and hundreds of chairs linked to a live feed, in anticipation of an overflow crowd. Across from the courtroom entrance, a small room designated for the media housed a maze of cables, video and audio equipment linked to TV satellite trucks. Although Judge Mike Snipes had a history of not allowing cameras in his courtroom, for the Williams case he'd made an exception.

As the clock ticked toward nine, the key players entered the courtroom. Bill Wirskye and Toby Shook huddled together not far from the judge's bench, their voices low, keyed up by the adrenaline of opening statements. Four other prosecutors from various agencies assigned to help with the case carried files and claimed places along the table at the left front of the courtroom. They were there to back up Shook and Wirskye, to listen to the testimony, and advise them. An unusual situation in a trial, everyone on the prosecution team personally knew one of the victims, Mark Hasse.

Opposite the prosecutors, Matt Seymour anchored the defense table. Beside him an empty chair waited for his client, then the rest of the team: John Wright, Doug Parks, and Maxwell Peck. Each understood their grave responsibility. The state had significant evidence against Eric Williams. If the defense team couldn't help jurors either decide the evidence was insufficient to find him guilty, or decide his actions didn't deserve the ultimate penalty, the cost would be Eric Williams's life.

Watching for his son to enter, Jim Williams sat in the first row behind the defense team, old and frail, heavily wrinkled, his aged skin a patchwork stained by years in the Texas sun. Eric's mother was unable to come; Jessie Ruth Williams had been diagnosed with cancer months earlier. Also missing, Eric's sister, Tera, remained home to take their mother to treatments. Tera's husband, Zach, however, sat beside his father-in-law.

Befitting a precise ex–air force officer, Judge Snipes

walked in just before nine. By then, Mike and Cynthia's family and friends filled much of the left side of the courtroom. Mike's older son, JR, had his black cowboy hat on his lap, reminiscent of his father, in a row filled out by his sister, brother, and aunt. Cynthia's children, Christina and Nathan, with his wife, Julie, sat near Leah and Skeet Phillips. All felt a heavy first-day anxiety.

Throughout the courtroom, armed deputies stood in doorways, others near the front, stationed around the defense table. The judge ordered that the defendant be brought in, and the room fell stone quiet as a door to the far right opened and guards escorted Eric in, dressed in a blue shirt and a dark gray business suit, resembling the lawyer he'd once been.

Jail food apparently hadn't appealed to Eric, for he looked thinner than at his arrest, his light brown hair carefully combed to the side, his blue eyes behind his glasses darting about the room. The trial drew a large crowd, every seat filled, reporters crunched together on benches scribbling into their notebooks, the TV and newspaper cameras competing for a good shot. Many noticed a smirk on Eric's face, appearing self-satisfied at all the attention.

Eric being brought into the courtroom
Courtesy of Ken Leonard

The jurors in place, Wirskye read the indictment charging Eric Williams with the capital murder of Cynthia McLelland, stipulating that the killing took place during the commission of a second felony, the murder of her husband, Mike.

"How do you plead, sir?" Judge Snipes asked. "Guilty or not guilty?"

"Not guilty," Eric answered, his voice exceedingly calm.

"This is my chance to tell you the story of . . . Mike and Cynthia McLelland . . . Who were murdered and died because Mike McLelland prosecuted, convicted, and stood up in a court of law and sought justice against this man." With that Wirskye extended his arm, motioning toward the defense table, echoing what Mark Hasse had done nearly three years earlier during opening statements in another courtroom. "Eric Lyle Williams."

Center stage, Wirskye detailed his account of the crimes, including "a massive investigation" and what the prosecutor branded as a confession, the e-mail sent to Kaufman County Crime Stoppers, one that included details only the killer could know. He insisted the evidence was "air-tight."

As he talked, Wirskye watched Eric. When he became angry, Eric glowered. Determined that the jurors see Eric's expression, Wirskye stood near the defense table. When jurors looked at him, Wirskye knew they'd see Eric, his face a mask of hate.

As Wirskye described that terrible day, the carnage inside the Blarney Stone Way house became real for the jurors. Early that morning, Eric entered carrying an AR–15 and shot a "blizzard of bullets," cutting down Cynthia and delivering a fatal shot directly into her skull. "Then he set his sights on Mike McLelland, his prosecutor, the object of his revenge plot. Eric Williams pulls the trigger repeatedly, hitting Mike McLelland over and over. Finally . . . he falls."

Eric, however, wasn't done, Wirskye said. For then, Eric

Bill Wirskye addressing the jurors
Courtesy of Ken Leonard

stood over his enemy, the man he hated with every ounce of his being, and shot "lead into the body even as the life blood of Mike McLelland pumps out of the many gunshot wounds and pools."

Although a skeletal account, it offered an effective rendering. Days ahead offered the opportunity to fill in details, but the prosecutor wanted the jury to appreciate the coldness of the murders. Yes, Eric had a grudge against Mike. The former justice of the peace lost everything after his theft conviction. But why had Eric murdered Cynthia? What was her sin? "She died because she was married to Mike McLelland, and she died because this man didn't want to leave a witness to a murder."

On the stand, as the prosecution's first witness, Judge Chitty laid the background, recounting the chain of events that led to the murders, explaining Eric had once been a prominent family law attorney and a justice of the peace, one forced out in disgrace after being convicted of a crime.

Judge Chitty on the stand
Courtesy of Ken Leonard

"Is it fair to say he kind of dropped out of sight after he was convicted?" Wirskye asked.

"Yes, sir," the judge answered.

From the motive, Wirskye moved to the discovery of the bodies. In his Dallas PD uniform, C.J. Tomlinson, took the oath. In the nearly two years since her murder, Cynthia's dream had come true. Once she'd predicted that Leah's oldest would one day be her son-in-law. That had happened. In the midst of the turmoil, C.J. and Cynthia's daughter, Christina, had married.

In trials, information builds in blocks, facts brought forward by each witness stacked until a foundation is formed, prosecutors hope one solid enough to hold a case. With C.J., Wirskye introduced the jury to the McLellands in greater detail. That they had good friends, C.J.'s mom, Leah, and his stepdad, Skeet. That they had children. And Wirskye wanted the jury to understand something else, that the morning Eric Williams entered their house and began shooting, Cynthia was truly helpless. When the prosecutor asked C.J. if Cynthia had physical problems, Seymour objected, and the judge asked Wirskye where he was going with the line of questioning. "It goes to her ability to defend herself when she was being murdered," Wirskye said, not mincing words.

With that, the world learned what Cynthia had so steadfastly hidden from even family and friends. As the packed courtroom listened, the reporters wrote in their pads and the cameras recorded Cynthia's most tightly held secret, that she had Parkinson's disease, an illness that trembled her hands when she tried to quilt and made it difficult for her to walk.

The day of the murders, after multiple unanswered phone calls, "we decided to go over there ourselves," C.J. described. The door unlocked, he knew "something was wrong." He stepped inside, and his mother saw the fired shell casings on the entryway rug. Two steps in, and Cynthia's body laid deathly still, a large pool of dried, coagulated blood near her head.

"Upsets you today to talk about it?" Wirskye asked.

Defense attorneys John Wright, Doug Parks, and Matt Seymour (left to right)
Kathryn Casey

"It does," C.J. agreed. When Wirskye asked if they considered calling an ambulance, the Dallas PD officer said no. "There was nothing anyone could do at that point for them."

Instead the sheriff arrived, and before long Blarney Stone Way flooded with activity and all manner of law enforcement.

To further bring jurors to the scene, Wirskye displayed photos of Cynthia's cold, pallid body, and Mike's hulking figure splayed on the hallway floor. And then C.J. identified another photo for the prosecutor, of the McLellands, alive and smiling for a camera.

The McLelland house was a home, Ranger Rudy Flores revealed as he recounted what the DPS mobile crime scene lab team found. Intermingled with an account of the bodies cooling on the floor, he described the house in terms the jurors could picture, a fine four-bedroom on an acre lot. A bedroom filled with large quantities of staples, flour and sugar, platters and silverware Cynthia used when she entertained, the shelves in the study overflowing with books.

The house appeared cluttered, but undisturbed except for the crime scene: the entryway, the den, and the hallway where Mike died. In these areas, spent casings were scattered on the floor, bullets were embedded in walls, furniture was splintered. The forensic team found no signs of forced entry, no indications of a robbery, nothing to suggest any motive other than a resolve to kill. "It seemed to be that the intent of the crime was to commit the murders," Flores said.

Before the jurors saw photos of the bodies, Judge Snipes warned them to prepare, for these were "somewhat grim." As on that horrible night, on the screen Cynthia and Mike lay dead in their home. Two lives ended in a hail of bullets.

In the jury box, some appeared pale as the photo marked state's 90 was displayed on an easel, a close-up of Cynthia, her gaping wounds, a fired .223 casing in blood near her hand.

Documenting the viciousness of the assault, Flores explained that searchers recovered twenty spent .223 casings. Yet the killings presented no mysteries. From the onset, Flores saw it as a straightforward assassination.

On the courtroom's TV screens, Wirskye played the video of the McLelland house, and the horror filled the courtroom. How much hate fueled such a slaughter, a couple at home in their bedclothes while their neighbors slept unaware?

"That's human tissue on the wall," Flores explained as the camera scoped in on what appeared to be a smudge.

Such butchery resulted from the rapid gunfire. Bullets flew so fast Mike had no time to reach the many guns staged throughout the house. Into evidence as state's 211 through 219, Wirskye introduced fragments recovered from the McLellands' bodies during autopsy.

From the scene of the murders, Wirskye led Flores to the underpass on I–175, between Kaufman and Seagoville, where they recovered more spent casings and bullets. The jurors didn't know the significance of the site, that here Eric practiced shooting the weapons used to kill the McLellands.

With only a handful of witnesses, Wirskye had given jurors an overall image of the crime.

On the stand, Dallas medical examiner William McLain, M.D., went point by point through Cynthia's autopsy, describing the eight GSWs. When Wirskye discussed the wound to the top of her head, he asked if it was "kind of a strange wound path if, in fact, she was upright at the time? Is that right?"

Seymour objected, but Judge Snipes allowed it. "It is not a typical wound I see in individuals shot while standing," the physician said. Administered while Cynthia lay on the floor, the assistant M.E. said this particular gunshot caused severe trauma to the brain. "Would this wound be considered a fatal wound?" Wirskye asked.

"Yes, sir," the doctor answered.

When Wirskye asked how McLain knew the bullets were most likely .223 rounds fired from a high-velocity weapon, the physician explained the term "lead snowstorm." When rounds fired from such weapons hit bones, the bullets shatter and scatter throughout the body, destroying tissue and organs, splintering into "hundreds of tiny little pieces."

In the center of the courtroom, deputy chief assistant medical examiner Reade Quinton stood with a clicker in his hand while his diagram of Mike's injuries filled the screen. As he detailed the sometimes tortuous paths the bullets took, Quinton talked of entrance and exit wounds, which bones and organs they struck, what damage they dealt. Some avoided hitting any organs, instead smashing bone and ripping arteries, veins, and tissue. When he described GSW #5, however, he didn't discount the devastation it rendered, cutting through Mike's diaphragm and the body's largest artery, the aorta.

Showing Quinton a photo of Mike's body on his left side, Wirskye asked. "Would what you observed be consistent with this man . . . sustaining these wounds in that position?"

"Yes," he said. As Mike lay dying on the floor, his killer stood over him pulling the trigger, again and again.

On the stand, Roger Williams described his friendship with Eric, one that began when they both joined the guard, and for the first time the debate about Eric's prosecution entered the courtroom. "I had always thought that the burden that Eric carried from being convicted of that crime could have been handled differently," the witness said.

The guard's sergeant major then described how he'd continued to support his former executive officer after his conviction. That support led Roger to agree to rent a storage unit for Eric. "At that point did you still believe in Eric Williams?"

"Yes, sir," he responded.

"You since have found out what was in that storage unit, right?" Wirskye asked.

"Yes," he responded, his voice resigned, as if he'd come to realize that he'd been used.

Sixty-nine-year-old Larry Mathis joked that he considered managing Gibson Self Storage a good job for an old man. Then he detailed the particulars regarding Unit 18, explaining what access codes revealed about the activity at the unit on March 30, 2013. That morning someone entered at 6:06. They left at 6:18, then returned at 7:07 and left again seventeen minutes later. "You don't know what time the McLellands were murdered, do you?" Wirskye asked.

"No, sir," Mathis answered.

The testimony potentially devastating, in the courtroom Eric appeared unconcerned, scribbling on a legal pad. While Mathis hadn't known the time of the killings, the next witnesses filled in the blanks, providing the alarm records that confirmed that the front doors opened for the first time at 6:40 that morning. Inside the house the motion detectors picked up activity. The doors then opened again at 6:42, when the gunman left. Since the system recorded only minutes not seconds, that meant that whoever entered remained inside the house less than two minutes.

After 6:42, the house fell quiet. The monitors sensed no further activity. If someone remained, they no longer moved.

Blocks of information slowly built. Beside Wirskye, Toby Shook lowered his head and whispered to his cocounsel. Their strategy revolved around keeping the presentation spare, putting on only necessary witnesses.

The next Texas State guardsman, Scott Hunt, recounted a peculiar lunch when Eric inquired about body armor–penetrating bullets and how to dispose of an assault weapon's upper.

"Did you ask him if he still had any guns?"

"Yes," Hunt said. "He said that he had gotten rid of them all."

As the conversation continued, Eric had asked Hunt if he could take an upper and "make sure it never saw the light of day."

The defense attorneys asked few questions, but they objected when Wirskye offered photos from the searches of the Williams home and the storage unit into evidence. One photo, state's number 155, the defense attorneys found troubling, that of the homemade bomb. Seymour argued it wasn't germane to the murders, and it could prejudice the jury. Judge Snipes listened, appeared to think about the situation, and then overruled the objection, saying the photograph offered insight into Eric's state of mind.

By the time the FBI's Dianna Strain entered the courtroom, Wirskye had entered into evidence photographs from the search of the Williams house and the storage unit. A businesslike Strain described what each photo depicted. On Overlook, they'd found the Desert Eagle handgun and the three computers sent for analysis, and much more, including the Crown Vic title and the Crime Stoppers tip number.

At the defense table, Eric wrote on the yellow legal pad in front of him, the only evidence of concern a blush of red crawling up his neck from his shirt collar.

The testimony moved on to the next evening, when the ten-hour search commenced at the storage unit. One of the more important matters, Wirskye got out of the way quickly, asking Strain if anyone found anything in the unit tied to anyone other than Eric or Kim Williams.

"No," she said.

Through the photos, she detailed what they found, including the Crown Vic inside the unit. The car removed, they combed through footlockers, bags, and boxes, many holding ammunition and weapons. A chest overflowed with military clothing and badges. SWAT gear hung from the walls. "Now, I can see it looks like a Glock gun box," Wirskye said. "Maybe a sniper's mat? . . . Is that the type of stuff you all encountered in that unit?"

"Yes," Strain answered. When they showed photos of the ballistic vests and a crossbow hanging on the wall, the prosecutor pursed his lips and hesitated, letting the jury take it all in.

The crossbow in the storage unit
Evidence photo

"Would it be fair to describe most of the gear and equipment you encountered as . . . of a tactical nature?" Wirskye asked.

"Yes," Strain answered.

"Like military police officer things? Like that?"

"Yes."

Rather than an individual's storage unit, the contents recalled an armory, the type of weapons and gear used to wage a battle. The owner of that equipment planned carefully, it appeared, based on the spray bottle of Soft Scrub and microfiber cloths for cleanups, and blue booties in a box bearing a mailing label with the name "ERIC WILLIAMS."

The courtroom resembled a weapons class, as Matt Johnson, the ATF agent, gave jurors a primer in how assault-type weapons work. "The upper receiver is going to have the transference or the tool markings on the brass that you could use to trace," he said.

After Johnson confirmed that he'd inspected the weapons found in storage Unit 18, Wirskye asked, "Did you find two AR lowers that were not attached to an upper?"

"Yes," said Johnson.

"If you committed a murder and wanted to get rid of the weapon, what would you do if it was an AR?"

Johnson didn't hesitate. "I would get rid of the upper."

So many tiny pieces pulled together. A few witnesses before Scott Hunt had testified that Eric Williams had asked him to do just that, get rid of an AR upper.

Wirskye asked Johnson about the single round found in the storage unit at the bottom of a bag, the one that had been chambered then expelled from a rifle. Explaining what the "LC" stamped on the bullet's head meant, the ATF special agent said it indicated the brand name, "Lake City."

The next bit of evidence caused a stir in the nearby media room, where reporters listened via an audio feed and watched on monitors. This information Wirskye saw as his "smoking gun": that the unfired cartridge had been chambered and expelled from the murder weapon. "Bullet matches the murder weapon. Bullet is found in Eric Williams's storage unit with his name all over it. Bingo!" one reporter said. The others looked at him and nodded in agreement.

"They've got him," whispered a female TV reporter.

To prove his point in the courtroom, Wirskye displayed state's exhibit 284, a photograph of a marking comparison, which showed that the ridges and valleys of the live round matched those of a spent casing found at the McLelland murder scene.

Perhaps it suddenly became too much, the mounting evidence. Beside his attorneys, Eric remained placid except when he looked at Wirskye, and then hate filled his eyes. For the audience who saw him from behind, the blush on the back of Eric's neck crawled higher and turned a brighter scarlet.

A microscopic comparison of a fired casing from the murder scene (left) and the live round (right)
Evidence photo

On cross examination, Matt Seymour tried to enter some doubt into the jurors' minds by pointing out that Lake City manufactured millions of rounds of ammo every year and that many people owned AR-style weapons. The defense attorney questioned the witness about his science, characterizing his findings as subjective and speculating that since experts hadn't examined every firearm in the world, it was impossible to rule out that another existed with the same markings. He also suggested that the expert may have chosen points on the two projectiles that matched closely, and theorized there were perhaps some that didn't match at all.

"I did not see any or document any areas of varying difference in tool marks," the man responded.

The ballistics evidence had been the most damning thus far for his client, and Seymour went after the witness, suggesting that another examiner might come to another conclusion. The man admitted that was possible, yet held firm that the markings matched.

The defense attorney had attempted to crack an important block of Wirskye's evidence, but the prosecutor came out fighting, asking if a lab that worked for the defense had inspected the evidence. The ballistics expert said they had. If that second lab had come to a different conclusion, the code of ethics required that DPS should have been notified. "Have you been contacted about any disagreement with your work on this case?"

"No, I have not," he answered.

If the prosecutors thought they had a good case, Seymour tried to poke what holes he could in it. When the deputies who'd taken the gunshot residue test from Eric the night of the McLelland murders testified, the defense attorney asked if the lieutenant who conducted the test wore a sidearm, suggesting the test kit could have been contaminated by his own gun.

While the defense attorney made his points, it seemed that the trail his client had left behind was one littered with evidence. The postal inspector who analyzed the barcode on the envelope that the man who called himself "Richard Greene" used to mail the garage door opener left in the Crown Vic said it matched the meter belonging to Eric Williams.

This time, Seymour had no follow-up questions.

It only looked worse for the defense when a witness read the Crime Stoppers tip, beginning with: "Do we have your attention now?" The writer wanted control, and there were veiled threats that more would die. The last sentence of the tipster's final e-mail to the investigators read: "We are not unreasonable, but we will not be stopped."

Then the forensic team found the tax receipt in the search at 1600 Overlook, with the tip's unique reference number written across it. "Up until the time that the FBI located these numbers . . . did anybody in law enforcement have any idea who this person or who these people were?" Wirskye asked the man on the stand.

"No, sir," he answered.

"Obviously when it was found by law enforcement, it was pretty clear who sent this message and where it came from. Was it not?"

"Yes, sir."

"And that was Eric Williams?"

"Yes, sir."

As the hours passed, the forensic experts dominated the trial, evidence lining up and pointing at Eric Williams.

Videos the FBI collected included snatches from the Chicken Express of what appeared to be a black Sport Trac arriving, then a large, light-colored sedan that looked like the Crown Vic leaving Gibson on the morning of the McLelland murders, driving past Martin's Automotive and I–20 Self Storage, on a route that could have taken the car to Blarney Stone Way. Minutes later, what appeared to be the same car left the area, recorded on cameras at Companion Animal Care Clinic and Wrangler Roofing. Then the Chicken Express camera caught Eric and Kim returning to Gibson in the Crown Vic and driving out in the Sport Trac heading for home.

When Matt Seymour pointed out that the FBI special agent who'd analyzed the video couldn't say for sure where the light-colored car in the video went, Wirskye countered by asking how much traffic there had been early that Holy Saturday morning, during the time when the ADP monitors said someone entered the McLelland home. The agent described it as very little traffic. In fact, he "saw one set of headlights enter the neighborhood . . . one set of headlights exit."

Finally, the prosecutors played video from Eric's interview with KXAS, the NBC affiliate out of Fort Worth. With that slight smile on his face, the same one he'd worn off and on in the courtroom, Eric said he'd cooperated with police, that he didn't hold a grudge, and offered his condolences to the McLelland family and those who worked at the courthouse. "I certainly wish law enforcement the best in bringing justice for this incredibly egregious act."

With that, after just three days of testimony, Bill Wirskye announced that the state rested. Many in the courtroom seemed surprised. So many more witnesses were expected, including the woman many greatly anticipated, Kim. And then another surprise; without putting on a single witness, the defense rested behind the state.

Although he'd been a constant in the courtroom, the jurors hadn't heard Toby Shook speak until he opened closing arguments that Thursday morning. While he described the evidence as circumstantial—no one actually testified to seeing Eric Williams fire the fatal bullet into the top of Cynthia McLelland's head—he contended that type of evidence was in many ways the strongest, because it had no bias. "It has no motive," he said. "You put it together, and it's like a net. A net which convicts and traps Eric Williams."

Once inside the house, Eric became "a killing machine," mowing down a defenseless woman who'd done nothing to him, the veteran prosecutor said. Then Eric turned and ran toward Mike as he fled toward the hallway. In his account, Shook built up speed, and his voice had an edge of urgency as he described Mike falling to the floor, helpless, as Eric, fueled by hate, stood over him firing into his body.

Finished with her husband, Eric fired another bullet into Cynthia's head. "Eric Williams wanted to make sure that woman, that sixty-five-year-old woman who just quilts and does no one any harm, is going to be dead before he leaves that house."

A "cocky" Eric Williams then e-mailed what amounted to a confession over Crime Stoppers on Easter Sunday to toy with law enforcement. "He's having fun here, folks," Shook said, shaking his head and looking disgusted.

If Matt Seymour worried when he stood in front of the jury, he didn't let it show. Instead, he started out strong laying out what prosecutors didn't have, forensic evidence that Eric was ever in the McLelland home: "Ladies and gentlemen of the jury, Eric Williams did not commit these murders. And how do you know that? There's not one single piece of biometric evidence that ties Eric to the McLelland home. Not one fingerprint, not one piece of DNA, not one hair, nothing. And the converse is true. There's not one piece of evidence from the McLelland home, blood from the shooting, GSR, that went back to either anything that Eric Williams had or to that vehicle that they say that he used."

The prosecutors had put on their bare-bones case, and Seymour intended to use it against them. Circumstantial evidence, in the defense attorney's assessment, didn't "trump" forensic evidence, and he judged the prosecutors' case as lacking. The prosecutors hadn't put on anyone who could "place Eric Williams in that scene at the McLelland home."

The jurors, he said, had to adhere to the presumption of innocence. They couldn't hold it against Eric that he hadn't testified, nor could they neglect to hold the prosecutors to the high standard of reasonable doubt.

In the center of the courtroom, Seymour attempted to dismantle the prosecutors' case. A long list developed of what Seymour said the prosecutors' case lacked, including cell phone records showing Eric was anywhere near the McLellands' home that morning. "If you build a house of cards," Seymour said, "it has no foundation."

"Follow your oath," he urged. "When you find reasonable doubt, I want you to vote for it. I want you to acquit Eric Williams. I want you to find him not guilty."

From his seat behind the prosecution table, Bill Wirskye unfolded his long frame and stood, then walked over to the jurors. "I submit to you it may be helpful for you folks to ask yourself and ask each other, if not him, then who is the mystery murderer that simultaneously harbors a murderous rage against the McLellands but also bears the intelligence and ill will against Eric Williams to frame him?"

At one point, Seymour had described the prosecutors' case as fictional. Wirskye played off that, saying that he wished that were true. "I wish it were fantasy, but it's not. Two people lost their lives in a hail of lead in under two minutes, twenty shots. This is real life, folks."

While Eric might have looked nonthreatening in the courtroom, Wirskye said "You may be fooled by his veneer of respectability. This mask of normalcy . . . but I'm here to tell you the outward appearances belie what lies inside of this man, which is a seething, murderous rage."

In the final moments of their lives, the McLellands looked into Eric Williams's "soulless" eyes, he said. While Seymour talked of no biometric evidence, Wirskye insisted the murder weapon—although missing—left DNA behind in the markings on the bullets at the crime scene, at the underpass, and on the one live round found in Eric's storage unit, a place that had his name all over it.

When Seymour said the prosecutors had no eyewitnesses, Wirskye objected saying that they did have one, Cynthia McLelland, only Eric Williams silenced her when he put a bullet through her head.

Arguments ended, the jurors filed out of the courtroom,

and the reporters ran out to call in their stories or do live shots to beam back to their stations. No one knew how long it would take. The two prosecutors felt certain the jurors would agree with them, while Matt Seymour wondered if he'd been able to punch any fatal holes into the case. It could have taken days or even weeks, but just a few hours later, the bailiff announced that the jury was in.

When Eric Williams stood and heard the verdict, his head dropped. "Guilty."

From his seat in the courtroom, Sheriff Byrnes watched, and on Eric Williams's face he saw surprise. "I reckoned he thought he'd get off. I thought he could probably say he wasn't guilty and pass a polygraph. Because he felt justified. He figured they'd messed with him. They deserved what they got."

Chapter 54

I was glad they got him, but it felt like Mark was the forgotten man in the trial. No one had even said his name. I wanted Eric to pay for him, just like Mike and Cynthia.

—Mark Ragsdale

The following morning, the mood somber, the lawyers and spectators slipped quietly into the courtroom. Although the McLelland family appeared relieved and happy, even celebrating in the moments after the verdict, they, too, seemed weighed down by the trial. Listening to prosecutors recount Mike's and Cynthia's final moments, the day-to-day grind of such an emotional experience excised a heavy toll.

Yet while prosecutors routinely said juries' decisions couldn't be predicted, the guilty verdict felt predestined. The evidence from the storage unit left little room for mistake. That telltale bullet, the live round ejected from the assault weapon, tied the man on trial inextricably to the murders. Fueled by the hatred that began with a mere $600 in computer monitors, the former justice of the peace executed the district attorney and his wife, by all measures brutal revenge.

The next stage of the trial, however, seemed decidedly less certain: punishment.

Before being chosen, every member of the jury had filled out a questionnaire that included their views of the death penalty. All responded that they believed themselves capable of rendering the ultimate sentence. Yet seated in a courtroom, looking at the face of the man at the defense table, understanding that if they voted as such that person would die? Sometimes jurors changed their minds. To avoid such a situation, the prosecutors had to put on a convincing argument that allowing Eric to live constituted a continuing danger to society.

When the bailiffs walked him in, Eric, too, seemed different, as if he had finally realized the gravity of his situation. Although he'd smirked off and on throughout the trial, looking at times haughty and at other moments like he was holding back rage, on that first morning of the punishment phase, Eric appeared worried. His eyes downcast as he entered the room and his face flushed, he sweated noticeably around his shirt collar.

To begin, Bill Wirskye laid out his strategy for the coming fight, the one over Eric Williams's life. First the prosecutors planned to show that the McLelland murders weren't out of character for the convicted killer. As evidence, the jurors would learn that Eric had committed other crimes, not two slayings but three. Then witnesses would recount his history. Not an anomaly, the murders, Wirskye wanted to show, fit Eric's psyche.

"Last week you heard the story of the murders of Mike and Cynthia McLelland, and how they died because Mike McLelland was one of two prosecutors that prosecuted Eric Williams," Wirskye told the jurors. "There was another prosecutor in that case . . . Mark Hasse."

As "airtight" as the McLelland case, Wirskye said the Hasse murder had even more evidence, including the murder weapon, earplugs with Eric's DNA found in the getaway car, and one more thing, eyewitnesses. "Unlike the McLelland murder, this murder did not go unseen . . . they saw a masked man execute and shoot in broad daylight, a block off the busy city square in Kaufman . . . They saw him gun down Mark Hasse."

Testimony began and painted the picture of what transpired on that cold morning, January 31, 2013, when Mark parked his truck in the lot, got out, and walked toward the courthouse. The first witness displayed blown-up photos of the area, including the courthouse, the town square, the position of the lot, and the modest houses surrounding it. On the photograph, Wirskye pointed at a red mark. "You know that's the location where Mark Hasse died?" he asked. When the witness agreed, Wirskye added, "That's his blood."

Pow! Patricia Luna hit the counter, relating what she heard while working out in the exercise room. Her heart pounding, she turned off her music and looked through the window to see a scene out of a movie, a man in black, his face covered by a hood, walking toward a car while firing a gun into the air. "I was scared!" she said. When she walked outside, she saw that Mark lay dying on the pavement. "I never saw so much blood in my life."

Testifying difficult, Luna apologized for being emotional. She'd liked Mark, whom she saw as a gentle man, one who worked late and always parked his maroon truck in the same place in the lot. Yet her memories of the gunman weren't explicit. "You don't know whether the person you saw firing the gun in the air was a man or a woman?" Seymour asked.

"No, I can't tell," she answered.

Lenda Bush didn't recognize Mark. When she first saw him, he and the man in the hood shoved each other "like kids on a playground." Then she saw the man put a gun up to Mark's neck and fire. When asked if she ever saw Mark with a weapon, she said, "No."

In the courtroom, Wirskye stood in for Mark, and

Martin Cerda, the body shop prep man, demonstrated what he'd seen on Grove Street that morning. The bigger man, he said, grabbed Mark, shoved him, then he heard Mark say, "I'm sorry!" three times. They tussled again, and the man with the gun fired. When Mark fell, the man stood above him and shot again, emptying the gun and pulling another, shooting as he walked away.

Cerda described what he saw as "a vendetta."

The horrendous murder a block from the courthouse square unfolded in the courtroom, but perhaps never as clearly as when Jason Stastny detailed the painful minutes when he gave Mark CPR. The defense attorneys argued that the dash cam video was too inflammatory, but the judge's decision went against them. Wirskye played the video, and the dying man's staggered, labored breaths filled the courtroom. "Come on, Mark. Come on, buddy," Stastny urged. When Mark took a breath, the officer urged, "Keep breathing . . . Come on buddy."

Six, maybe seven times, Mark sucked in air, but then stopped. Stastny pleaded, "They're almost here."

"When you loaded Mark Hasse into the ambulance, did you have any hope at all that this person would survive?" Wirskye asked.

"I hoped," Stastny said.

"He arrived at the hospital not breathing, with a tube. We were breathing for him," the nurse who'd first worked on Mark explained. They found no heartbeat.

Not long after, Mike McLelland walked through the hospital's door. The jury wouldn't hear what he said that day: "Eric Williams killed Mark."

In that emergency room while they cut Mark's clothes off, something fell and rattled to the floor. The nurse reached down and picked it up, a large bullet fragment. During the autopsy, more bullet fragments were collected, including one from Mark's brain.

Experienced prosecutors, Shook and Wirskye brought in the evidence as they had in the previous phase, by bits and pieces, one fact here, another there, so that later in the trial every piece would be available when they completed the picture. One detail was the Mercury Sable purchased just four days before Mark's murder. Another that a contractor working nearby saw Eric's Sport Trac barrel down Overlook minutes before the police knocked on his door. Eric looked sweaty when he answered the door, his arm in a sling.

Trooper Steve Tippett described Lake Tawakoni as having the visibility of "chocolate milk" when his dive team came up with the Ruger and Smith & Wesson. "You're aware. . . . 38 caliber rounds can be fired through a .357 caliber weapon?" Wirskye asked.

"Yes, sir," Tippett replied. "They can."

The bag he recovered the guns in hadn't been a bag at all. In the courtroom a slight gasp escaped the audience as prosecutors produced a Styrofoam head covered by a black hood, mesh in the front—a disturbing looking disguise, one resembling an executioner's mask. "Like a hoodie, grim reaper–type Halloween mask?" Wirskye asked.

"Exactly," Tippett answered.

The Crime Stoppers liaison from the sheriff's department, Brian Beavers, read the anonymous tip: "As proof, Mark Hasse was killed with a .38 caliber +P ammunition, 147 grain Hydra-Shok ammunition, fired from a 3-inch, .357 5-shot revolver."

Did that description exactly match the guns and ammunition that had just been placed into evidence? "That is correct," Beavers said.

Reminding the jurors where the tip number was found, handwritten on a tax receipt in Eric's home, Wirskye then produced the earlier Crime Stoppers' e-mail, sent shortly before the McLellands' deaths, one that claimed a tipster heard a six-foot-tall, 240-pound man talk about killing Hasse for "free gifts, drugs & booze."

The executioner's mask
Kathryn Casey

"Trying to cover his tracks and point the investigation in a bad direction?"

"Yes, sir," Beavers said.

Yet proving Eric also murdered Mark, that he'd killed three times, wasn't enough to qualify Eric for the death penalty. For the jury to give the prosecutors what they asked for, Wirskye and Shook had to show that even in prison, Eric's existence constituted a threat.

That morning during a break, a group of deputies constructed a specially built wooden rack in the middle of the courtroom. Carefully they filled it, gun after gun. Rifle after rifle. Large assault weapons, even an AR–15 on a tripod, bags of knives, and the crossbow intended to kill Judge Ashworth. They displayed so many weapons that it took multiple racks and rows to hold them. Underneath the guns, they piled boxes of ammunition and tactical gear.

The weapons on the display could have supplied a good-size police department.

"This display is horrendous," Seymour argued. "It is cumulative. The jury has seen all the photographs . . . this display is wholly unnecessary, prejudicial in the extreme. I think it's clearly designed for one purpose and one purpose only, to inflame the jury's sentiments and to drive the decision on something other than the facts in this case. I object."

The judge ruled against him, and moments later the jurors reentered. Some must have wondered why anyone would have so many weapons. What they didn't know, but then it wasn't germane since he wasn't on trial, was that Mike McLelland could have filled two such displays with the weapons he kept in his house in Forney. Yet on that fateful morning, by virtue of being taken by surprise, he was outgunned.

The room fell silent when a bailiff carried in the two pickle jars filled with a stringy yellow mixture. "Homemade napalm?" Wirskye asked, and an ATF agent confirmed that it was.

Eric Williams's guns, ammo, and gear in the courtroom
Kathryn Casey

While the display had been impressive, when he took over the witness, Matt Seymour attempted to put it in perspective. This was the punishment phase of the trial. A time when future danger needed to be assessed. If Eric spent his life locked up in a Texas prison, did any of this matter? "How many weapons like this do you expect this jury to believe a prison inmate will have in their cell?" he asked.

"A prison inmate should not have any weapons in their cell," the ATF agent answered.

"I have no further questions," Seymour said.

On redirect, Wirskye attempted to show that there could still be a danger, asking the agent if he knew anything about the Texas Seven, a band of convicts who broke out of a Texas prison and raided the guard shack. "They shouldn't have had access to weapons in the penitentiary either," Wirskye said.

In the courtroom, the battle over Eric Williams's life raged. From that point on, Wirskye put on witnesses to show that even before his feud with Mike and Mark, Eric Williams was a dangerous man. Into the record he put the "killer inside me" e-mail Eric sent to himself, and the "piss napalm" e-mail he'd written to Sandra Harward.

Those days leading up to his arrest, Eric jumped from Web site to Web site on his laptop, playing Mafia Wars, habitually checking out the latest news on the murders. He searched for information on everyone from Judge Wiley to Judge Ashworth, along with Toby Shook and Bill Wirskye. Many of the articles had ominous headlines: "It's Not Open Season on Law, But Kaufman Slayings Show Attacks on the Rise"; "Public Servants the Target of Assassins." The vast number of news stories must have inflated Eric's ego, especially when he read that even the White House watched the Kaufman killings unfold.

On April 9, Eric's searches took an even darker turn, when he perused sites on how to buy firearms on the Internet without a background check. "So this really kind of gives you a glimpse into the mind and the computer of Eric Williams after the McLelland murders. Is that the way you read it?" Wirskye asked.

"Yes, sir," his witness responded.

If anyone in the courtroom still didn't understand Eric Williams, Toby Shook drove it home by displaying photos of the inside of the Sport Trac at the time of Eric's theft arrest, lined with guns, an AR–15 and a 12-gauge shotgun mounted on the headliner.

On the stand, appearing anxious, Janice Gray bravely recounted that evening in a sports bar when Eric told her he had nothing to lose. Prior to that she'd said that she thought Eric was "a nice guy."

When she heard about the Kaufman prosecutors and Cynthia McLelland being murdered, at first Gray couldn't imagine Eric could be responsible. Then she saw one of his interviews, the one where he rode around on his Segway. "I said, 'He did it.' I just, by the look in his face, I said I just knew that he did that."

On cross-examination, Matt Seymour asked if Eric bothered Gray after that evening in the sports bar. He asked if his client ever contacted her in any way. Gray said that he hadn't. When asked if she'd been so frightened she'd sought counseling, Gray said that she hadn't.

"Ms. Gray, when you're talking about your impressions of watching this news report that was just pure speculation on your part?" Seymour asked.

"It was just my opinion. That's all it was," she answered.

In a replay of the testimony at Eric's theft trial, John Burt recounted the time Eric threatened to not only kill him, but his wife and children, over a misunderstanding about a scheduled mediation. Then the prosecutors played their final piece of evidence, the TV interview with Eric on his Segway in which he sent his "heartfelt condolences to the McLelland family and the Hasse family."

After the jurors finished watching the news clip, the prosecutors rested their case. By then they'd painted Eric Williams as a man with a sharp temper, one who threatened violence not once but repeatedly, one who'd patiently planned and executed three people.

When the defense attorneys took over, they had one task. They no longer argued that Eric wasn't guilty. Instead, they simply hoped to save his life.

Chapter 55

I listened to the testimony the defense put on, when
I realized that I'd prosecuted two other murder cases
where the killers played Dungeons & Dragons. It was
eerie.

—Toby Shook

Eight days into the trial, although his attorneys had taken
what swipes they could at the prosecutors' evidence, the
mood in the courtroom felt decidedly against Eric Williams. With the exception of perhaps Eric's father, Jim, and
brother-in-law, Zach, few doubted that the right man had
been convicted. The question remained: Did he deserve
to die?

"Last week you . . . found Eric Williams is guilty of
capital murder," said Maxwell Peck, a heavyset attorney
with dark hair and a matching goatee, as he opened for the
defense. "And we know it would be easy to sidle up to anger
now. To insist that life without the possibility of parole isn't
bad enough. To pronounce Eric deader than dead and dust
off our hands and call it a day. But I want to ask you here, in
Rockwall, Texas, on a mid-December morning, days away
from Christmas, what if Jesus wasn't kidding?"

The defense attorneys understood that Rockwall, like
Kaufman, was Bible-belt Texas, where patriotism, family,
and faith ran deep. The folks in the jury box probably went

to church on Sundays and paused to thank the Almighty before cutting into their chicken fried steak covered in cream gravy. Thus while some might contemplate the Old Testament's "an eye for an eye," Peck suggested they consider Jesus' Sermon on the Mount, in which he urged: "turn the other cheek."

"In the next few days, we'll help you grapple with your emotions and consider what constitutes justice." Then Peck laid out the jurors' options: either imprison Eric for life or send him to his death. Life without parole, Peck argued, offered the more humane alternative and allowed jurors to put their faith into practice.

Impassioned, Peck forged on. The lawyer made no excuses. None of the defense attorneys would attempt to justify what Eric had done. Yet Peck also said that jurors had to answer two questions, the first if Eric posed a continuing threat. Peck said he didn't, because if Eric sought revenge, that had been delivered.

The second question: Were there mitigating circumstances? Peck described it as a simple story: "The walk of Eric Williams from hopeful childhood to ruination."

As Peck portrayed him, Eric spent his life striving for respect and success, working hard to achieve his goals, only to have them unfairly dashed at the hands of men motivated by politics. As a result, Eric felt humiliated. Then Peck asked, what if someone had "taken a breath" and wondered if it was right to ruin anyone over such a small transgression?

To condemn Eric to death simply continued the darkness that resulted in three murders. "Look where we have ended up after chasing revenge. A family has lost their parents and grandparents. A mother has lost her son. Another mother now stands to lose hers as well. . . . What if one of you said let's save . . . this man, this community from one more tragedy instead of killing another person to make it right? What if even one of you said pray, turn, love."

The defense strategy had distinct goals. The first: to get before the jurors what so far had been kept out, the controversy over Eric's theft conviction, the impetus for all the misery that followed, and the belief by many that the man whose life hung in the balance had been persecuted and ruined out of spite.

From the witness stand, Jenny Parks, her shoulder-length blond hair swept to the side, described the Eric she knew, the court coordinator turned attorney who worked his way up to be the go-to person for family law in Kaufman. Over the years, Parks recommended him to clients. At his office, he had a picture of his wife on his desk, and around the courthouse, he was known as a computer geek. The entire theft trial, she said, had resulted because he'd been trying to modernize the courthouse. "It was a ridiculous prosecution. He should never have been brought to court for what they were saying he did . . . It didn't make any sense."

She had watched Mark's aggressive prosecution, yet she expressed surprise at the verdict. To her, it seemed unfathomable that shy, slightly awkward Eric would have stolen the monitors. Months later, she never suspected he could be capable of murder.

Rather than her impressions of Eric, on cross-examination Bill Wirskye suggested another reason Parks hadn't tied Eric to Mark's and the McLellands' deaths. "Really the prosecution wasn't over the top, was it?"

Parks held firm, deeming Eric's prosecution unfair and excessive.

In response, the prosecutor said, "Well, here's my point. If you thought it was over the top, and those two prosecutors who were over the top against Eric Williams both get murdered, then it would seem natural to me, you practice criminal law, that the common denominator is Eric Williams. You understand what I'm saying?"

"I don't correlate murder with being prosecuted, ever," Parks answered.

As he responded, Wirskye smiled. "Exactly my point."

On the stand, the defense team experts portrayed Eric's life as worth saving.

The first, a Bible study leader who'd worked with Eric in the Rockwall jail, had brought him reading material and counseled him. An example of the forgiveness he stressed, the man had a murdered brother, shot through the head because he smiled during a robbery. Instead of harboring hatred, for more than three decades the sixty-five-year-old brought the gospel to prisoners. In the Rockwall jail, Eric attended his Thursday evening Bible studies.

Although understanding Eric had been convicted of a horrible crime, the witness said he believed that allowing Eric to live served a greater purpose. Behind bars, Eric could help others understand "the saving grace and forgiveness of my lord and savior, Jesus Christ."

On cross-examination, Bill Wirskye asked if the man had ever met a psychopath, who could be calculated and reserved. At times, the man admitted, he had been fooled by inmates who professed one thing yet did another. "Have you ever heard the expression: Jesus must live in the jailhouse because that's where everybody seems to find him?"

The man said he had, as some in the courtroom audience softly chuckled.

Matt Seymour asked a second such witness, another jailhouse Bible teacher, if anything stood out about Eric: "Yes, sir," the man said, pointing out that Eric didn't have jailhouse tats, that rather than boisterousness he tended toward shyness. "He looked like my next-door neighbor."

The man said that behind bars Eric had become religious.

Yet Wirskye cast doubt on Eric's sincerity. As evidence, the prosecutor produced a work application given to Eric in the Rockwall jail. Employing the dry sense of humor Kim once loved, Eric filled it out as if he were Jesus Christ. He listed the position applied for as "Lord & Savior." His previous employer: "Kingdom of God."

ROCKWALL COUNTY DETENTION CENTER
INMATE WORKER REQUEST FORM

Inmate's Name: _Christ, Jesus_   Date: _All Eternity_

Position Applying for: _Lord & Savior_

List positions held in previous employment that could be useful while working as an inmate worker for the Rockwall County Detention Center.

1. Previous Employer: _God the Father_

   Position Held: _Son of God_   _Matthew 3:17_

2. Previous Employer: _Kingdom of God_

   Position Held: _Right Hand of Throne of God_ _1 Peter 3:22_

3. Previous Employer: _All of Mankind_

   Position Held: _Sacrifice for penalty of sin_ _John 1:29_

Below please list and describe any skills and training you have received with previous employers that would make you an eligible candidate for the position of inmate worker for the facility. (Carpenter, Landscaper, Cook, etc.)

Carpenter, can turn water to wine, can multiply fish & bread, heal the sick & raise the dead.

Inmate Classification	MIN	MED	MAX
Approved by Jail Administrator			
Approved by Assistant Jail Administrator			
Approved by Maintenance Supervisor			
Approved by Maintenance Supervisor			
Approved by Food Service Supervisor			
Approved by Medical Staff			

• **If you have ever been charged or convicted of any offense involving assault or escape, you will not be eligible for inmate worker status.**

The jailhouse job application

"I guess depending on kind of where you are personally with religion that could be viewed as a blasphemy," Wirskye remarked.

Still, could Eric pose any threat locked up behind bars for the rest of his life? The defense team contended that the humane alternative had to be life in prison without parole, while the prosecutors argued that if Eric Williams lived, could there ever be any guarantees?

To prove their point, the defense put on two jailhouse supervisors who'd overseen Eric's incarceration. They described how carefully the guards watched Eric. They agreed there had been no written reports on security breaches. They described Eric as cooperative.

When prosecutors asked the questions, however, the jailers filled in more details. While nothing existed in writing, they insisted they had concerns. One recalled a trial day Eric dropped a stay off his dress shirt collar in the holding cell. After suggesting it could be used as a pick to unlock handcuffs, Wirskye hinted that Eric had tested jailhouse security.

Another guard observed that the quiet former lawyer had a habit of noting the locations of security cameras. A third talked about a day they discovered that Eric kept a log of all the comings and goings of guards around his cell. Was he hoping to find a weakness in the system, one that might allow his escape?

"What's the jail made of?" Seymour asked one witness.

The man responded: "Concrete, steel, secure."

Back and forth the sides argued, the defense attorneys attempting to convince jurors Eric wasn't a danger, while prosecutors insisted he could escape and kill again.

A parade of prison experts took the stand. "If there's an inmate who has the mindset that he wants to do something, and he decides to do it, he's gonna try," Shook said, and one prison executive agreed. As if to drive that home, Shook mentioned an inmate who pretended to need a wheelchair for a decade before he used a smuggled gun to escape while on a trip to the hospital.

Shook then asked if an intelligent inmate with a mindset to escape or commit murder could be dangerous, and the witness, an expert on Texas prisons, agreed. "Someone who has a history of being able to plan a crime, a murder, to be able to . . . take a lot of time to carry that out? That could be a dangerous inmate?"

"Yes, sir," the expert agreed.

What went unsaid was that Shook described Eric Williams.

After their expert witnesses, Eric's attorneys brought in people out of his past, the intention to humanize their client, to help the jurors identify with the man on trial, perhaps explain him. Despite what Eric had just been convicted of, they'd all agreed to come, drawn by the young man they remembered, someone they deeply cared about.

On the stand, Eric's childhood scoutmaster introduced Eric the Eagle Scout, the boy who hiked trails cut through New Mexico and Texas pine forests with his friends. Then Eric's cousin, Ian Lyles, an army colonel and a faculty instructor at the U.S. Army War College, recounted their shared pasts, from playing in the Williams barn as boys to attending TCU. Eric's arrest for the murders, he said, devastated the family. When asked if he considered Eric an honorable man, Lyles responded, "Yes, I do."

After pointing out inconsistencies between Lyles's memories and the truth about what Eric had done at different times, Wirskye asked, "Not to put too fine a point on it, but you all haven't been very close in some time. Is that right?"

"That is correct," the colonel answered.

Then the prosecutor asked about Lyles's impression of the Eric in the courtroom; was he an honorable man? While the army officer sounded unconvinced that his cousin was a murderer, he said he deferred to the jury. "Well, let me ask you as a hypothetical," Wirskye asked. "Assuming he's guilty and killed three people, he wouldn't be an honorable man?"

"Assuming he's guilty and killed three people," the

colonel said, sounding reluctant. "Eric would not be an honorable man. Yes, sir."

"We were geeks, I guess you'd call us," said Miguel Gentolizo, the first of Eric's school friends to testify. In what would begin a long series of such witnesses, he recounted summers dividing up the yard to imagine they were officers aboard the starship *Enterprise*, or villains who came from far-off galaxies. "It was kind of like the *Big Bang Theory*," Gentolizo said, comparing their group of friends to the uber-popular sitcom featuring four young scientists who indulged in similar pastimes.

As he talked, Gentolizo, who'd been one of the few minority students in Azle High, recounted an afternoon in the high school cafeteria when bullies confronted him. Eric and another friend stepped in. "They're like no, that's not gonna happen, that is not gonna happen. You're gonna have to beat all of us up. And I was—people—that didn't happen to me that often. People, I mean, get beat up . . . He was willing to, to stand up."

A woman with carefully coiffed hair, Dorothy Spears always liked and trusted Eric, who'd been good friends with her sons. Yet she, too, hadn't seen him in more than twenty years.

"From what you could gather from your observations, it appeared that Eric Williams was raised to know right from wrong?" Toby Shook asked.

"He certainly exhibited that when he was at my house," she answered.

"Never appeared to be an abused child in any way, did he?"

"I never saw anything that indicated that," she agreed.

"He seemed to be well fed and cared for by his parents?"

"That would be my impression."

"Thank you, ma'am," Shook said.

Eric's high school friends continued to parade onto the stand, and from appearances many had succeeded well in life. One was a software engineer, another technology director for a computer company, while a third ran a shipboard lab for Texas A&M University. Jesse Spears, a national merit scholar in high school, lived in Austin and had a profession he perhaps prepared for playing D&D with Eric and his other friends decades earlier. He worked for a video game company owned by Nintendo. As they would throughout, the defense put into evidence photos from the early years of Eric's life, smiling photos of a young man no one predicted would have his life hanging in the balance as it did in that courtroom.

On cross-examination, Toby Shook asked Spears about the ball cap Eric had on the day they snapped a certain photo, a hat that bore the emblem "DALLAS COUNTY SWAT." At the time, Eric worked for a small police agency outside Fort Worth. Spears said he remembered that Eric

Eric Williams (left) after high school with Jesse Spears (right)
Evidence photo

liked gun and knife shows. "For rural Texas . . . nothing out of the ordinary."

When Shook asked about Eric's ability to discern between right and wrong, an interesting exchange occurred. The witness recounted a long-ago conversation about driving over the speed limit in which Eric said, "It's only illegal if you get caught."

When Eric's first girlfriend, Tamara, took the stand, the jury saw photos of Eric in a tuxedo for prom and at a wedding, on his high school graduation day, and at her family's resort where Eric worked as a security guard. Like the others, Tamara talked about Eric's intelligence and how he excelled at planning and formulating a strategy. Those abilities, she said, came through when they played Dungeons & Dragons, his tactical abilities making him a sought-after teammate. When it came to the murders, Tamara disagreed with the jurors' verdict. She'd visited Eric in jail, and he'd told her that he wasn't guilty.

"Regardless of what happens in this courtroom this week or next week, you are going to stand by Eric Williams?" Wirskye asked.

"Absolutely," Tamara answered.

Kaufman County's district clerk, Rhonda Hughey, had offered to sing at Eric's wedding, before she'd learned he and Kim planned their nuptials in Las Vegas. An affable woman, Hughey hadn't believed rumors he could be behind the killings. She'd gone to him often over the years when she had questions about the law, and Eric always took the time to patiently answer. As she talked, it became evident that she liked Eric.

"How did you feel about it when you realized that Eric was accused of three murders?" one of Eric's attorneys asked.

"At first I couldn't believe it; and then the more we heard

about it, I mean I started believing that it could have happened and it did happen."

"But it, it just wasn't the character of the person that you had known, was it?"

"Not at first. No."

Wirskye looked kindly at the woman on the stand. "From what you've described, I mean it sounds like you now think . . . he's guilty? . . . He's a triple murderer?"

"Yes, sir."

As the jurors listened, Rick Harrison read Eric's letter from 2006, the one in which he questioned Mike McLelland's character. In the third week of the trial, the defense team continued to attempt to explain what started the freefall of events that led to the murders. Once Harrison finished, he was asked if he thought he was a better choice than Mike for Kaufman's DA. "My level of experience in criminal law as a prosecutor and a defense lawyer was vastly superior to his."

The subject turned to Mike's tenure in the DA's office and any animosity the new DA might have had for Harrison and his supporters, and Wirskye objected. Repeatedly Eric's lawyers asked similar questions, and the judge blocked Harrison from answering. One of the few statements he did get in: "McLelland did not like me during the elections or after."

The mood in the courtroom edgy, the two sides lobbied back and forth. This went to the heart of Eric's motive, that he'd been unfairly prosecuted, financially ruined by a vindictive politician. "As DA did Mike McLelland always seek justice or did he sometimes also seek personal vengeance?" one of Eric's attorneys asked.

"I'm going to object to relevance," Wirskye interrupted, and the judge agreed.

So it went, until the defense attorney passed the witness. Once he did, Wirskye could have asked Harrison questions, but the prosecutor declined. In the courtroom, it felt as if Wirskye wanted to get Harrison off the stand, perhaps fearing that additional testimony could open the door to questions about Eric's theft trial. The proverbial Pandora's Box, once released in the courtroom, it seemed plausible that some of the jurors would feel that while not justified, perhaps on some level they could identify with Eric Williams, to understand what drove him.

In the courtroom, the Kaufman County legal community then marched up to the witness stand one by one, starting with Regina Fogarty, Eric's assistant in the JP office, who testified that he'd been trying to modernize the office. Then one of Eric's friends, Mark Calabria, whose wife, Becky, regularly ate lunch with Eric and Judge Ashworth, answered questions. As he talked, Calabria drew a picture of Eric as a dedicated court coordinator and lawyer.

When asked if he wished he'd done anything differently, Calabria said: "I just felt I was a member of the legal community there, and we all knew Eric. Unfortunate set of circumstances that developed, and the way this matter progressed. . . . I do regret not taking the opportunity or the time to try to make a difference or interject myself into the situation."

"You're not blaming yourself for three murders, are you?" Wirskye asked. When Calabria said he was not, the prosecutor asked, "Eric Williams was fired by your wife?"

"Yes, sir. My understanding is that there was a disagreement over division of fees."

"Eric blamed Mark Hasse for his conviction, isn't that correct?"

"I'm assuming that that's correct, yes, sir."

"As you sit there right now, you know that, don't you, Mr. Calabria?"

"I'm assuming the series of events that led up to Mr. Hasse's death were predicated upon what Mr. Hasse was involved in, yes, sir."

"And as soon as Eric Williams was convicted, Mark Hasse started carrying a pistol everywhere he went because he was concerned about Eric Williams?"

"That's my understanding, yes, sir."

Throughout, the defense team tried to insert the theft case and their contention that their client had been over-prosecuted before the jurors, hoping it might mitigate his guilt. Perhaps the jurors would understand that a man from whom all was taken could turn to violence.

After Cathy Adams talked about the Eric Williams she knew, a proud husband and good lawyer, one who worked hard, Maxwell Peck asked her: "You were Eric's friend when he was prosecuted for the theft case?" When she said she was, he asked, "Why do you think Eric was arrested for those computers?"

Again Bill Wirskye objected. Behind the bench, Judge Snipes looked unhappy. "I previously told you guys that we were not going to relitigate the prior case, and we're not. The objection is sustained."

The sparring continued, and the judge ordered the jurors removed from the courtroom. Once they were gone, Snipes frowned. "Mr. Peck, you are becoming dangerously close to being held in contempt of court. I have ruled on this several times. . . . Do you understand me?"

"I do, your honor," he answered.

"All right. Now, what is it you want to say outside the presence of the jury?"

"This witness was present for the entire theft trial. She's particularly well situated to talk about Mark Hasse's prosecution style, Mike McLelland's demeanor towards the defendant. That goes directly to the prior relationship between the accused and the victim."

In the end, the judge, while not allowing the facts from the theft case, permitted Cathy Adams to talk about the mug shot with "CAPTURED" written across it, perhaps an indication of how personal Eric's prosecution had become. Finally she pleaded for his life: "He's a good person. He's— all of us have a breaking point. You never know what yours is gonna be; and there's, there's parts of him that's worth saving. What, what happened is horrible; but there's still a part of him inside that's good, and it's savable."

"Do you know what a psychopath is?" Bill Wirskye asked. After giving a definition of a psychopath as a person who has no conscience, he continued, "People that aren't psychopaths don't have breaking points where they want to kill people, do they, Ms. Adams?"

"If someone hurt one of my babies, I might could kill them."

"That's self-defense, defense of a third party. You're a lawyer . . . You understand that, don't you?"

"It's still the breaking point," she said.

On the stand, Darlie Hobbs, who'd once owned Twin Points with her family and hired Eric to work there, talked about the boy she knew, one she trusted with her daughter, Tamara, one they loved like a son and took on family trips. It seemed particularly poignant when she spoke of going to Eric's graduation from TCU. "We had always told him work hard and study hard, and you can be anything in this world you want to be. And . . . he's definitely—had done that."

The high achiever, the hard worker, the can't-do-enough-to-help and always-in-a-good-mood Eric Williams, how could he have ended up convicted of such brutal murders? It seemed strange then that when asked what she wanted jurors to know, Mrs. Hobbs answered: "That he's honest, and he's worked hard all his life to live the American dream, and that's what he thought he was doing. And we're very, very proud of him and love him."

The defense attorneys had done what they could to soften Eric's image, in a bid to save his life. As their final piece of evidence they played a video of Eric's mother,

Jessie Ruth, who remained in Azle as she underwent treatments for the cancer that ravaged her body.

On the TV screens throughout the courtroom, Jessie Ruth Williams appeared resigned to the likelihood that all wouldn't have gone well if and when the jurors heard her talk. That had been explained to her early on, that the only time the jury would view her deposition was if it convicted Eric, and if that happened, they would be facing a life and death decision.

As Seymour asked the questions, Jessie Ruth looked at a baby picture of Eric, his first at six weeks old. "Why did you have that picture made?"

"Because he was my baby!" she said, with a smile. When asked if she was proud of him, she said, "Oh, yes."

For more than an hour, they talked of Eric's past, everything from his childhood, to Boy Scouts, to high school band. Off and on, Seymour put photos into evidence, visual representations of the memories: baby pictures, junior high, and high school. There were chuckles when Jessie Ruth

Eric in the band room and as a Boy Scout. In the group photo, Eric, wearing a neckerchief, is to the left just above the Worth Ranch sign. Jim Williams is the middle man in the back row.
Evidence photos

said Eric played the trumpet in junior high, but was only mediocre. When Seymour asked if he practiced around the house, she said with a smile, "When we'd let him."

The video continued, and at times Eric's mother dabbed at her eyes. At a good memory, she smiled, even laughed. When Seymour asked about Eric's high school triumphs with the math team, Jessie Ruth said she'd been proud. "That's what mommas do," she said. During a poignant pause, her eyes tracked off to the left as if to prevent tears, and then she said, "A lot different than now." She then shook her head and took a deep breath, as if fortifying herself to go ahead.

Eric's mother talked of his college years, his diagnosis with diabetes, which she pegged as the reason he hadn't been able to continue on into the army. When asked if the turn of events disappointed her son, Jessie said she felt certain it had, although Eric never complained. She recounted her ill feelings about Kim, saying that she'd never seemed right for Eric.

When Eric went to law school, Jessie Ruth said she didn't understand why, when he already had one college degree. She hadn't become involved when he ran for justice of the peace, because she voted for Democrats and her son ran as a Republican. On the video, Jessie Ruth Williams appeared a strong, judgmental person, one who'd early on been deeply involved in her son's life, but who over the years stepped back from it. Still, she wore her love for her son proudly, recounting the better times, before he'd lost his judgeship and his reputation, before he'd been indicted for three murders.

Her testimony continued until Seymour asked Eric's mother what she wanted the jurors to know. "I've never been on a jury except one time, when they were taking a child . . . away from his father. So I don't know what I'd do," she said, looking tearful. "I only know that he's still my child. He'll always be my child. I'd certainly hope to say he

A still of Jessie Ruth Williams taken from the
video
Evidence photo

hasn't done anything wrong, but I cannot believe that at this
point. I don't think he's done everything though."

"Why should they choose life?" Seymour asked.

"Because I think he has a lot in him that he could help
children. He has shown that before." Asked if he could help
people in the penitentiary, Jessie Ruth wiped away tears as
she said that he could, "more so than in death."

Throughout all the prior witnesses, Eric sat nearly mo-
tionless, exceedingly quiet, often staring down at the table
before him. Now, for the first time, listening to his mother,
many of those in the audience saw tears fall from Eric's
eyes and roll down his cheeks. Embarrassed, he quickly
wiped them away. If he'd been able to distance himself
through much of the testimony, he had no wall to keep out
his dying mother crying over his fate.

"And if Eric is convicted of capital murder for the killings he's accused of, what if anything would you want to
say to the families of those victims?"

". . . It would be horrible if Eric did something as horrible as they believe that he did," she said. "I'm certainly

sorry, and I would give anything if I could take that back, but I can't. And neither can he, if he did it. But are you really going to be serving any purpose by taking his life?" Her tears had stopped, and she stared directly into the camera, almost defiant. "I can't answer that question. They'll have to answer that themselves."

One of the prosecution team then asked a few questions, including did Eric have advantages growing up, was he a smart child, did he know the difference between right and wrong? To each, Eric's mother answered, "Yes, sir."

When asked if she believed her son was a murderer, she said, "That I just can't say for sure. It's very hard as a mother to say one way or the other."

"You could see how people would view someone who could kill three people as an extremely dangerous person? You could agree with that?"

On the screen, Mrs. Williams had her hand covering her mouth. "Yes."

Chapter 56

We worked a lot with Kim. We had to get it through to her that codefendants hurt themselves if they try to make themselves look good. Juries like to hear the whole story. So she just needed to go up there and tell the truth.

—Toby Shook

Throughout the trial rumors floated, speculation about which witness would be called next, what jurors would hear about Eric Williams's plot to kill the men he blamed for his demise, or what glimpse would be afforded into his bitter mind. Of them all, those attending whispered one name most often, a witness everyone in the courtroom eagerly anticipated, one who lived with Eric while he planned the murders, assisted him when he carried out his war.

On the morning of December 16, the twelfth day of the trial, wearing a thick-striped black-and-white jail uniform, her long, light brown hair spread like thin straw to her shoulders, Kim looked nothing like the woman in her wedding photos. In prison, she'd gained weight, and her illnesses had taken a heavy toll. Her missing front teeth gave her a slight lisp when she talked. Spheres of shadow darkened her eyes, and she appeared exhausted, but determined.

Kim Williams testifying
Courtesy of Ken Leonard

"Are you charged in all three of these murders with capital murder, is that correct?" Wirskye asked.

"Yes," she answered.

"Are you guilty?"

"Yes, I am," she said.

"Do we have any deal?"

"No, we do not," she said.

When the prosecutor asked what he'd requested of Eric Williams's wife, Kim said only to tell the truth, and when asked if she pulled the trigger, personally murdering any of the victims, she shook her head and said, "No, I did not." Who committed the murders? "Eric Williams."

"Were you a willing participant?"

"Yes, I was," she admitted.

The next point would be critical, an indicator of her husband's likelihood to, if given the chance, commit future violence. "After the McLellands were killed, were there more people on his hit list?" Wirskye asked.

"Yes," Kim answered. "Erleigh Wiley . . . and Judge Ashworth."

"They were the next to be killed by Eric Williams?"

"Yes," Kim answered. When asked if in years prior she'd been a good person, Kim said that she was, yet she admitted that at the time of the murders she was heavily addicted to prescription medicines: "OxyContin, morphine, Valium, Provigil . . . a lot of stuff."

Their marriage started with great promise, but stumbled. Three years into her marriage, Kim went on disability, her days gradually spent in the bedroom of the Overlook house, in the dark, her world numbed by the drugs. At one point, Eric wanted a divorce. "I thought we would work it out," Kim said, explaining why it didn't happen, "and eventually he did, too."

Then in 2011, Eric won his slot as the justice of peace in Precinct 1, and the phone rang one afternoon, leading Kim to scurry out of the house with a computer monitor to hide at her parents' house. "You stood behind him at this time with respect to those charges?"

"Yes," she answered. "Because I believed in him, and I loved him."

The portrait of her husband Kim drew depicted an angry man, furious that he'd been convicted on the theft charge and at the loss of his law license. "He thought that they set him up," she said, adding that again she believed him.

"Who was he mad at?" Wirskye asked.

"Mark Hasse . . . Mike McLelland . . . He mentioned that he would like to kill them."

"Did you think he was serious?" Wirskye asked.

". . . I ignored a lot of it in the very beginning, until he just kept talking about it."

Thanksgiving 2012, Kim said her husband's plans crystallized, as he entertained a variety of revenge scenarios that would have begun with Judge Ashworth. At times, Eric described shooting Judge Ashworth with the crossbow, another scenario played out with Eric abducting Ashworth and hiding his body in their chest freezer or burying him in the backyard flower bed.

"Did he go so far as to dig out that flowerbed to see if a body would fit?"

"Yes, he did," she said, nodding.

"At some point, did he start talking about specific plans for Mark Hasse and Mike McLelland?"

"Yes," she said, with a nod.

As her husband hatched then discarded plots, Kim went along on scouting trips. Finally he landed on the ambush in the parking lot, and he told Kim that she would drive the car. "You knew someone was going to lose their life?" Wirskye asked.

"Yes, I did. I was so drugged up, and I so believed in Eric and everything he told me. His anger was my anger."

At that point, Kim told jurors about the plot her husband christened "Tombstone," an execution in broad daylight on a public street. "Was the plan that this brazen murder would kind of freeze people and bystanders in shock?" Wirskye asked.

As the jury listened, many stared at the woman on the stand in wonderment, so matter-of-factly discussing a plan that took a life and terrorized a community. "Yes," she answered.

Questions and answers, and the scene in the Williams house unfolded, Kim describing how Eric showed her the guns he would use in the murder. During a dry run, in the seat beside her, he sized up the location. At the house, Eric's anticipation built as the plans developed. One day he modeled what he would wear. "How would you describe the mask?" Wirskye asked.

"Like a ghoul, like a ghost."

The prosecutor held up the strange black hood that had

already been put into evidence, state's exhibit 417. "That's the mask he wore," she confirmed. When he produced the two guns retrieved from the lake, Kim covered her mouth, as if troubled when he asked if she recognized those as well. "Yes," she said. She shook her head, appearing disgusted, as she described one gun as hers and the other as a gun she'd seen in the Overlook house.

"There was excitement in the air," she said about that awful day.

"You all wanted to murder Mark Hasse?"

"Yes," she said.

At that point, Kim described Mark's murder, from sitting in the parking lot waiting, to Eric jumping out of the car. "Did you watch?" Wirskye asked.

"No . . . I couldn't. . . . Because it hurt. I, I couldn't watch him kill someone." At that moment, Kim closed her eyes, her head dropped, and she appeared caught in a horrible memory.

But "you were happy moments earlier?"

"Yes, I was," she said, frowning. She loved her husband, yet she feared him. She blamed the prosecutors, but had

Bill Wirskye showing Kim Williams the Hasse murder weapons
Evidence photo

to numb herself to tolerate the killing. She fed off Eric's anger, his excitement, but felt overwhelming dread. Again she admitted, "I was."

After putting the Sable in the storage unit, back at the house Eric put on the sling and watched news reports, elated, while Kim took a Valium and returned to bed. The sling, she said, served one purpose, "to fool the police."

"Did police come?"

"Yes." She heard their voices, and Eric gave her orders. "He didn't want me talking . . . to be quiet, don't say a word."

In the weeks that followed, Eric prepared to kill the McLellands, taking her to the underpass where he fired his rifle, buying the Crown Vic. "Eric looked happy. He was ready," Kim said. "He had already killed one person, and he was ready to kill Mike McLelland."

Wirskye asked, "Why did Cynthia McLelland have to die?"

Her eyes downcast, Kim shook her head. "I don't know why she had to die." For the first time, Kim appeared near tears, her eyes red. She shut them, as if trying to erase the memories. When Kim asked, Eric described Cynthia as "collateral damage."

In the courtroom, the McLellands' children quietly sobbed.

The plans in place, Eric appeared ebullient. They drove into the McLellands' driveway. Kim waited while her husband disappeared into the house. Moments later, she heard gunfire.

Demonstrating how long the firearm was, Kim held up her hands slightly less than a yard apart. At that, Wirskye brought to her the lower part of an AR–15, asking her if the rifle had a shoulder sling on it like the one in his hand.

"Yes, it did," she said.

Their moods as they left the scene? Not sugarcoating her feelings, again acknowledging the conflict inside her, she answered: "Happy and satisfaction."

Eric Williams listening to his wife testifying
Courtesy of Ken Leonard

When Kim repeated what her husband said about Cynthia McLelland's death, that he'd shot her through the head because she moaned, in the gallery the McLellands' children leaned together, Cynthia's daughter-in-law with her hand on her husband's back, as he softly cried.

That afternoon, Kim said she and Eric celebrated at her parents' house with steaks. Afterward, he threw the hood with the guns inside into Lake Tawakoni. An hour later, deputies contacted him, and they made arrangements to meet at the Denny's in Kaufman. "Once you got the phone call, did you stop anywhere . . . did he wash his hands (after he handled the guns to throw them away)?" Wirskye asked.

"No," she said, shaking her head. Later that test had proved positive for gunshot residue.

The questioning continued, and Kim talked of her husband's fascination with another self-appointed vigilante, Christopher Dorner. Perhaps that killer's manifesto inspired

Nathan and Julie in the courtroom
Courtesy of Ken Leonard

Eric to e-mail tips and taunt the police, then laugh about the chaos it would cause. In the days following the Mc-Lelland murders, Eric even granted interviews to reporters. Afterward Kim described Eric as proud. "He enjoyed showing off his Segway. He acted like nothing had happened."

Despite three murders, Kim said Eric hadn't finished killing. On the stand she described the plans Eric had for Judge Ashworth, the next on the hit list, to be shot with a crossbow, his abdomen gutted, then filled with napalm. "I guess to drive in an extra kind of F U," she said.

"You weren't angry about the fact he was going to kill Judge Ashworth. You were angry about the holes in the fence" Eric made practicing with the crossbow? Wirskye asked.

"Yes," she admitted.

As her testimony continued, Kim revealed the other side of her marriage to the jurors. She talked of the night Eric held a flashlight on her ailing father's eyes, while trying to take away his cell phone. And the times she wondered if her husband intended to kill her.

The napalm in the backpack with the crossbow bolts
Evidence photo

Those incidents, Wirskye pointed out, predated the loss of his bench and his law license.

Despite everything, Kim had been afraid or unwilling to turn on her husband. Even days after his arrest, when she reported to the sheriff's department to give finger-prints and DNA, she initially defended him. Still sedated by large amounts of painkillers and drugs, she refused to cooperate until the questioning wore her down. Then the truth came in curt facts with little embellishment. Why was she testifying now? Wirskye asked.

"Because those families have had a terrible, terrible loss, and they deserve this," she said. "I want to give it to them."

"Did I ever ask you to say anything other than the truth?" the prosecutor asked.

"No," she said.

When asked if she still loved Eric Williams, Kim answered, "No."

In response to Matt Seymour's questions, Kim relayed her thoughts on her years with Eric. "He provided all the things that you needed?"

"Yes," she answered. The breadwinner, Eric bought her clothes and paid the household expenses, paid for her cigarettes and cars. When Kim's father fell ill, Eric helped clean his wounds.

While prosecutors denied they'd made any deal for her testimony, Kim admitted that she hoped her cooperation would buy her a pass from the death chamber.

Seymour cited discrepancies, some small, some large, between Kim's original interrogation and her testimony. "Do you recall failing to mention at all that Eric was wearing a vest of any kind?" Seymour asked.

"I may have. Yes," she said.

"Do you recall telling the officers that when you arrived back at your home you went to bed and couldn't remember anything after that?"

"Yes, I recall that."

After a series of questions in which Kim admitted she'd left things out during her interrogation, Seymour asked, "Mrs. Williams, your story today that you told in court of your recollection is much sharper than it was back then, is that correct?"

"Yes, it is."

"Do you recall after, Mrs. Williams, you attempted to maintain a relationship with Eric by writing him letters while in jail. Is that correct?"

"Yes," she said. "We stayed in contact." When asked how many letters she'd written, she speculated perhaps twenty-five.

"You wrote him because you wanted to maintain your relationship?"

"In the beginning, yes," she said.

"Because you loved him?"

"Yes, I did."

Despite all they'd been through, all they had planned and done together, the violence and the killing, when Seymour asked if the same feelings had been there as when they'd first met and married, Kim agreed they were.

Moments later, both attorneys released her from the witness stand. A bailiff came forward, handcuffing Kim to the thick leather belt secured around her waist, and led her from the courtroom. When she walked out, Kim relaxed. It was over. When Wirskye saw her, "She seemed almost euphoric, thinking that she'd finally done the right thing."

Chapter 57

We wanted the jurors to see the face of someone else Eric Williams planned to kill, so they'd understand that he wasn't done.

—Toby Shook

After the jury returned from a short recess, the sentencing trial continued. Bill Wirskye brought Dianna Strain, the FBI forensic officer who'd supervised the scene at the storage unit, back to the stand. Through her, he introduced more evidence, things that backed up the testimony the jurors had just heard, including Eric's "SHERIFF" patch and "tactical helmet," similar to ones worn by SWAT officers responding to potentially violent scenes, the ones Kim said Eric wore when he killed the McLellands.

Although Kim had told jurors that the next person Eric planned to kill was Judge Ashworth, he didn't take the stand. Having him testify might have opened up too many opportunities for the defense to ask about Eric's early years, when the judge thought so much of his court coordinator that he'd urged Eric to attend law school and even put Eric in his will.

Instead the other person who remained on Eric's list testified: Erleigh Wiley, Kaufman County's present district attorney. For the jurors, Shook had the former judge recount the day she called Eric into her office to discuss

Erleigh Wiley on the stand
Courtesy of Ken Leonard

overbilling on CPS cases. "You thought he was padding his bill?" Shook asked.

"He was padding his bill," she said.

When asked about the mood in the office after the McLellands' murders, Wiley said it was "unbelievable." Not only were people in the courthouse frightened, but she said, "We're still scared." At that, she closed her eyes, as if overcome by emotion.

"You'll recall we asked so many questions about the death penalty and how you felt about it, and we put all our cards on the table. . . . We feel we have the type and quality of evidence that we believe will prove this defendant guilty beyond a reasonable doubt, and that these special issues should be answered in such a way that will result in his execution," Toby Shook said, starting closing arguments. "That it was our goal in this case, one we wouldn't back away from, that Eric Williams lie dead on a gurney in Huntsville, Texas someday."

Toby Shook with Judge Snipes behind him

One of the first things Shook asked the jury to consider was whether Eric Williams was a continuing threat to society. Implying an answer to that question, he pointed out how quickly Eric came to the decision that he would kill Mark Hasse. "Mark Hasse was gonna die. And that's what's so scary and makes Eric Williams so very, very dangerous, folks, because this wasn't done in hot blood, in a split-second decision. He had months to change his mind . . . Every day he woke up and could have stopped himself. He could have gone back to the way he was raised. The church, his family, his friends, but he didn't do that."

What made it particularly heinous, Shook said, was that Eric hadn't ambushed and run that morning in the parking lot. Instead, he confronted Mark. "He wanted Mark Hasse to know exactly what this was about and who was gonna kill him."

Mark begged for mercy, but Eric offered none. "That tells you exactly how dangerous Eric Williams is, you see, because he could see the fear in Mark Hasse's eyes, and it had no effect on his soul."

Rather than being upset by the killing, Eric felt exhilarated. Instead of being satisfied at what revenge he'd exacted, Eric planned his next murders, the McLellands.

Cynthia tried to shield her face from the bullets. "What does he do? Walks calmly over to her, takes that rifle, points it at the top of her head, and shoots her . . . And that tells you all you need to know about how dangerous Eric Williams is and what a threat he's going to be." Even at that, Eric wasn't finished. He still had Erleigh Wiley and Glen Ashworth on his hit list.

"Nothing has stopped Eric Williams. The only people that can stop Eric Williams are the twelve of you, and that's what we'll ask you to do today."

"**Y**ou're to follow the law, follow the evidence; and you're to do what your own conscience tells you to do. I will say from the, the defense standpoint that we believe that all life is sacred," one of Eric's attorneys, John Wright, began. "There are only two punishments for capital murder in Texas. One the death penalty. The other life in prison."

While Shook had described the horrific two minutes in the McLelland house and on the street as Mark begged for his life, Wright classified the accounts as conjecture. The jurors heard no evidence about what pain the victims suffered or what they felt or thought in their final moments. And when Shook talked of future danger, Wright said the more proper word was "threat." The question was: Would Eric, if incarcerated in a state prison for the rest of his life, be a threat to society?

Addressing the jurors, Wright insisted his client would not. "This is not the first time that prison officials have dealt with somebody who was sent to prison for premeditated capital murder. They've got a lot of experience."

If any of the twelve jurors didn't agree to the death penalty, they didn't have a unanimous verdict, and the sentence then automatically defaulted back to life in prison. Any tiny bit of evidence could be mitigating and allow Eric to live. If any of the witnesses convinced them that Eric shouldn't be executed, that was enough. The jurors needed nothing more.

Once Wright sat down, Matt Seymour stood. He picked up where his cocounsel left off, arguing that to vote for the death penalty the jurors had to come to the conclusion that Eric remained dangerous even in a prison setting. "The overwhelming and resounding answer is no!"

To support his argument, Seymour referred to the testimony of the expert witnesses who explained that Eric would be housed in a maximum security prison. "They can control inmates. They do control inmates. They will control Eric Williams without any problem." Seymour's voice had a pleading edge when he said, "He will not be a danger to anyone."

Finally, Max Peck, who'd opened the punishment phase talking of the Bible and what God expected, took over to close for the defense. "Mercy doesn't come from comradery or compatibility. We bestow it upon even our enemies, whom we rarely understand, and share very little with. Mercy doesn't claim to comprehend the sin. It doesn't require believable excuses. Instead, it overcomes the wickedness we cannot understand. Sometimes it requires great personal sacrifice, as in Jesus on that old rugged cross."

The final attorney to speak at the trial, Bill Wirskye said, "Now you've heard about the murder of Mark Hasse. You've heard about this man's first murder; and just as surely as Mark Hasse has risen from the grave and come into this courtroom and told you who his murderer was, the evidence we've introduced to you lets you know without a shadow of a doubt, it points the accusing finger of guilt at the right person. Eric Williams is a murderer. A double murderer, he's a triple murderer. He's a serial killer. He has the blood of three people on his hands. He has launched an unprecedented assault on our criminal justice system. He has crossed a line that others do not dare to approach. He has murdered in cold blood two prosecutors along with one of their wives. He plots to kill two judges. He must be held accountable for these actions, folks."

As Wirskye talked, he walked toward Eric and urged the jurors not to be fooled by his "benign" appearance, but to understand that Eric was a psychopath. "He has a special sort of darkness within him, and that special sort of darkness lets you know beyond any shadow of a doubt that he is a danger. He was a danger in his past, danger in the present, and he will be a continuing danger in the future."

Where Peck invoked biblical allegories, Wirskye said jurors had only two questions to answer. "Yes, he is a future danger; and no, there is nothing sufficiently mitigating that would spare his life and spare him from the ultimate penalty . . . It's that simple, folks."

In his last statement to the jurors, Wirskye said, "I stand up, like Mike McLelland and like Mark Hasse and ask for justice, and ask for those certain final answers. He must be stopped. It's that simple. How many people have to die before someone stops him?"

With that, the judge gave the jurors their final instructions and they were led from the room. For hours, those who'd watched the trial wandered about the Rockwall courthouse, some in the lunchroom, some on benches outside, talking softly and waiting. As the hours ticked off the clock, they waited until the judge returned to say that the jurors were retiring for the night.

The scene repeated the next morning, those involved again hovering. Then when word spread that the jury had a decision, the attorneys, the victims' families, Eric's father and brother-in-law, many of the investigators who'd worked on the cases, and dozens of reporters flowed back into the courtroom. Before long, Judge Snipes sat behind the bench, and Eric walked in surrounded by guards.

The jury's decision: death.

For just a moment, Eric swayed, as if it hit him like a physical blow.

Affirming the jury's decision and officially sentencing Eric to a lethal injection, Judge Snipes voiced his own thoughts on the case. "Mr. Williams, you made yourself out to be some sort of Charles Bronson death wish vigilante in this case. I never bought that. And to any deluded souls out there who may have bought it, at the end of the day, you murdered a little old lady; and you would have murdered two other innocent people if you had the opportunity. That puts you right there with Charles Manson, Jeffrey Dahmer, and Richard Speck."

The judge's eyes left the man behind the defense table, and scanned the crowd in the courtroom: "To the people of Kaufman County, I know you've been scared for the last couple of years. No reason to be scared anymore."

Epilogue

> Someday, I tell my wife, when we're older in the nursing home with blankets on our laps in the wheelchairs, we'll look back at this, remember, and know life goes on. You have to go on.
>
> —Judge Bruce Wood

On December 30, 2014, Eric Williams sat in a cell in the Texas Department of Corrections Polunsky Unit, on death row. Matt Seymour was off of his case, but Eric's other attorneys prepared his appeal. His execution date hadn't been set yet, and probably wouldn't be for years to come, while his appeals worked through the courts. One of the issues they would cite was that scans showed Eric had signs of possible brain damage either from birth, due to injuries, or as a result of poorly controlled diabetes. The appeal contended among other things that had the jurors been presented with that evidence, they might have opted against the death penalty.

Inside the Kaufman County courthouse on that date, Kim pleaded guilty to murdering Mark Hasse, approximately one hundred feet away from the parking lot where he died. The yellow metal arches over the entrances had been cut off to prevent trucks from hitting them. Judge Wood had the one closest to where Mark died turned into a cross and painted white. Some complained that religious symbols shouldn't be

A 2016 photo of the cross marking where Mark Hasse died
Kathryn Casey

on county property, but others appreciated the monument to a painful time. Once in a while people still dropped off tributes, silk flowers and the like, that they placed nearby. Although it had been nearly two years, Kaufman hadn't forgotten.

Others had memorialized the victims. In Kaufman's courthouse, a quilted banner hung in the victim's assistance room, one in Cynthia's favorite pattern, log cabin, with hearts around the outside. In the center, the members of the quilters' guild stitched the scales of justice, in her honor and Mike's. Others erected a marble bench in her memory on the grounds of Terrell State Hospital, where she'd worked. And Mike's and Mark's names had been inscribed on the National Prosecutor Memorial in Columbia, South Carolina. They became the twelfth and thirteenth names on the monument. The oldest case dated back to William Foster, a Virginia prosecutor who died in a gun battle in 1912.

The decision had been made for Kim to plead on the Hasse case rather than the McLelland murders. Eric had been convicted on the McLelland killings, and this meant that someone took responsibility for Mark. The deal included a forty-year sentence, making Kim eligible for parole in 2033 at the age of sixty-six.

From the stand that day, Cynthia's son, Nathan, told her that he felt relief not having to endure another trial, and that "these murders have torn apart my family and Mark

Hasse's family." Rather than look down as Eric had during his victim impact, presumably to avoid looking his victims' families in the eyes, Kim met Nathan's gaze and nodded.

"At least she has a little conscience," JR said. But he also told her that he held her responsible. "You had too many opportunities to stop it, and you didn't take that."

Later recalling Eric's trial, all he and his family had endured, JR said, "When they came back with the death penalty against Eric, it felt like a letdown. I guess I thought it would make things feel like they'd changed. But they didn't. It didn't bring my dad back. It didn't take the hurt away. The only good thing was that Eric Williams would never hurt anyone else."

Thinking about all that had happened, he paused, then shook his head in disgust. "You know, this whole thing was basically small-town politics gone bad."

When I talked with Matt Seymour, living by the rules governing attorneys, he said little about his representation of Eric, but one thing came through clearly. "I think the day they gave Eric the death penalty was among the worst in my life," he said, his eyes clouded with tears. "I saw part of myself in Eric. And when the jury came back and said that he was to be put to death . . ."

At Toby Shook's office on a Saturday morning, I met with Shook and Bill Wirskye. Both dressed for family day, planning to spend the time watching baseball, they looked happy and proud of the sentence, neither one voicing any qualms about the death penalty.

They did express one regret, that no one solved the cases before Cynthia's and Mike's murders. "We came tantalizingly close a few times," Wirskye said. "But we just weren't quite there."

I'd heard after the trial that Kim and Eric had turned down all media inquiries, so I wasn't hopeful. But as I always do,

I put in requests for interviews. Their agreement, then, left me surprised but pleased.

"I've read one of your books," Kim wrote to me. ". . . Yes, I'll talk to you."

Eric responded as well, sounding eager. Over the coming year and a half, I'd drive periodically to their prisons, showing up with my tape recorders, pens, notepads, and camera.

By the time I arrived for that first visit, I'd already heard a lot about Kim. Some had told me that they saw her as not a reluctant coconspirator, but perhaps the mastermind, someone who'd urged Eric to "get even and pull the trigger." Some of Eric's lawyer friends still didn't see him as capable of the murders, but they had a more sinister view of Kim.

In contrast, most of the investigators viewed Kim as another victim, someone who'd fallen under Eric's trance. As

Kim Williams in prison, Gatesville, Texas, 2016
Kathryn Casey

dependent as she'd been on Eric, Ranger Kasper wondered if perhaps Kim had Stockholm Syndrome, where hostages bond with their captors. "I did think she was genuinely frightened," Bill Wirskye said. "But I thought she was cheerleading him, too."

I wasn't sure what to think.

The woman I met in prison, however, appeared truly regretful. She talked often of her drug addictions during the final years she lived in the house on Overlook with Eric, describing it as a fog that anesthetized her to all that unfolded around her. And she fumed. "I couldn't believe he did this, and that he insisted on including me. Why would he do that?"

In prison, Kim took only anti-inflammatories for her rheumatoid arthritis, and then not every day. But she looked well, fairly content. She smiled often, and she always seemed happy to see me. She asked about the outside world, and she looked wistful realizing she'd probably never again be part of it. More often than not, we spent part of our time together with her musing over Eric's intentions. She talked of his intellect, his gifts, and she wondered why he'd do the things he did, sending in Crime Stoppers tips and the like. "Did he want to get caught?" she asked me one afternoon.

"No, I think his ego got the better of him," I said, and she nodded.

In detail, she described the plans and the murders, and the uneasy feeling—despite the drugs—she had living with Eric. Yet in the same interviews, she repeated often that she'd loved him. "What he wanted, I wanted," she said. "And I was mad at those people. Those two men ruined our lives."

While I sensed sadness about her, it wasn't until late in our second visit that she sobbed as she talked about Cynthia's murder. "I think about it every day. I have the blood of three people on my hands. I try not to let people here see me cry, but at night, sometimes, I think about her. How frightened she must have been. And I think about what I did to their families. And my own family. And I'm sorry."

For a long time, she didn't ask me if I visited Eric as well, and I didn't mention it. Then it came out, and one day, in a letter, she wrote: "What do you think about Eric?"

For months, I'd struggled with that same question.

Interestingly, many of those who tried to solve the mystery of Mark Hasse's murder doubted Eric would have ever been caught if he'd stopped after that first killing. "I don't think we would have found enough evidence," said the sheriff with a shrug.

"Eric had all the criminal gods with him. He did it without being recognized. He executed and got away. He had the suckers at the guard who weren't turning him in. He had Kim doped up. That must have been an ecstatic sixty days," Erleigh Wiley told me. "And then he decided, it went so well, to kill Mike."

But could Eric have stopped? I didn't think so. I didn't think his ego would have let him. How much better would it have been to get away with killing two or three people than one?

The Polunsky Unit, Texas's death row, was an austere place, off-white walls, concrete and metal, gates and razor wire, guard towers and phone booth–size compartments to confine inmates while talking on telephones to visitors. The Eric Williams on the other side of the Plexiglas window appeared much as others described him. Eric wasn't a big man or a muscular one. Rather than a triple killer, he looked like a computer programmer. When I arrived, he always smiled. He had a calm manner and a dry sense of humor. When I asked a question he deemed silly or strange, he had a crooked smile and dimples.

If I repeated a question, he sometimes appeared to lose patience with me, as if he talked to a child or someone whose intellect didn't equal his.

Eric Williams in prison, 2016
Kathryn Casey

One Kaufman friend of Eric's told me that, looking back, she wasn't sure she ever knew him, although they'd been close for years. "Because he was our friend, we overlooked a lot of things. No one wanted to think he was that diabolical."

"He doesn't look like a killer, does he?" a prison employee said one day, as I walked from Eric's unit. "Maybe that made him more dangerous?"

On my trips into Kaufman, I'd met a lot of Eric's friends, who continued to believe that he'd been pushed too hard by Mike McLelland and Mark Hasse, and that he'd snapped. The guard members I interviewed talked of what happened to Eric as a trigger. "Everyone has one," a guardsman told me. "There's always something capable of setting a person off."

In truth, there were days I shared that opinion. Ruining a life, taking away someone's livelihood for $600 worth of monitors, especially when one sat on his county desk, did seem excessive. On one trip, I told Eric that, and he nodded. Yet, it didn't matter in the wake of what he'd done. Nothing, after all, could account for assassinating three people. Nothing mitigated the malevolence of the murders.

While Kim talked in detail with me about their lives and the killings, Eric never admitted the murders. Instead, he talked in riddles. Suggesting the things in the storage unit weren't his, one day he prodded: "Did it bother you that no one found the key to the storage unit in my things? If you find the person who has the key, you'll find the killer."

What he failed to take into account was that all the possessions in the unit tied to him. It reminded me of what Zach, Eric's brother-in-law, told me, that Eric had asked him to pull a Sport Trac–size vehicle into a ten-by-twenty storage unit. "It was silly," Zach said. "Of course, it fit."

On a trip when I told Eric that I saw nothing to suggest he hadn't committed the murders, he nodded at me. He didn't frown, and he didn't look surprised. As on so many of my other visits, he seemed emotionally detached, as if he'd expected it. Then we just continued talking, as if I hadn't just said that I believed he'd murdered three people.

"Eric sent me a letter," Kim told me on one of my visits. "He said he forgives me."

"He forgives you?" I said. By then, Eric and I had written often, and he'd told me that he'd converted to Catholicism, and that he studied the Bible. At one point he sent me a page torn from a pamphlet, a profile of Saint Lucy, a patron saint to writers. I wrote and thanked him, posted it on my office wall. During lockdowns, when the prison guards scour through the cells and try to rid them of contraband, he didn't respond to my letters, explaining that he spent the time meditating on his newfound faith.

Two aspects of Christianity, of course, are confession and repentance. So while I felt glad for Eric, that he'd found something to believe in, I did have nagging doubts. While I assumed he meant he forgave Kim for testifying against him, it seemed he had larger issues to address. "Shouldn't he have asked you for forgiveness, for tying you up in all this?" I asked Kim. "Even more, what about the victims and their families?"

"Exactly," she said. "Then he asked, 'How am I?' Really Eric? He's not a stupid man. Certainly he realizes the toll this has taken on me and my family." She thought about that and then she frowned and said, "Honestly, I don't think he gives a thought to the three other people or their families. What he's done. Everyone he's hurt."

In one of Eric's many letters to me, he quoted Mother Teresa. "In the final analysis, it is between you and God," he wrote. "It was never between you and them anyway."

When I read that, I wondered if it was a way of telling me that he felt justified in all he'd done. In that same letter, he said that he could go "to the execution chamber tomorrow with a clear conscience."

On one visit when he again insisted on his innocence, I asked if he knew who'd committed the murders. "I do." But then when I asked who, so I could investigate any evidence he had, he refused to divulge a name but said, "The attorneys have all that information."

"So there's no one I can look at?" I said.

Eric shook his head. What he said next reminded me of a line out of a novel or a movie. "Take me completely out. Say it is unsolved. Unless that person's DNA gets in the system. That's the wild card."

In the end, I decided that Eric Williams didn't live in the soil-and-water physical world the rest of us inhabit, but in his imagination.

As I looked at all I'd learned, I believed part of Eric remained that kid who excelled in Dungeons & Dragons. Somehow the lines blurred between fantasy and reality. He bought the Segway after seeing one in a movie. He called

Mark Hasse's murder "Tombstone," after his favorite Western. He dressed in costumes when he committed the murders, in the Hasse case not unlike a character out of a comic book wearing what looked like an executioner's mask.

Perhaps that helped make him so dangerous. Since Mark Hasse, Mike and Cynthia McLelland, and their families weren't real to him, he could never identify with them. He felt nothing but satisfaction when he killed them.

"Death row isn't like what I would have expected," he told me one day. "Not like in the movies. Most of the time, I'm simply alone."

"Do you feel like you belong here at all?" I asked, after he said that while some of the pieces in the case did appear to point to him on the surface, he still thought the jurors should have had reasonable doubt.

"I believe God sent me here. Why, I don't know," he said.

We talked about what lay ahead if his appeals failed, his execution. At that he looked worried. He flushed and said he used to believe in the death penalty but didn't any longer. "With a few exceptions I haven't seen anyone here who needs to be executed."

We talked more about the death penalty, and he shook his head. Then he said, "You know, in the end, it's really all about revenge."

A Challenge for Readers

For the trial, much of what was on Eric's computer was entered into evidence, and I had access to it to write this book. One thing in particular caught my eye: a series of six strange e-mails that were sent to Eric around the time of the McLelland murders. I asked Bill Wirskye about them, and he told me that the investigators wondered about them, too. "We thought it might be some fantasy thing he played online," Wirskye said. "We had different theories, but no one could figure it out, and we didn't focus on it. . . . We didn't need them, so we went on. At the end of the day, we couldn't make anything out of them."

The e-mails all had chapter numbers, and I ended up wondering if they were some kind of a cipher, especially when I realized that the lines in the messages came out of Mark Twain's original text for *The Adventures of Huckleberry Finn*. Yet the phrases didn't come from the chapters cited in the e-mails, which seemed odd.

On one round of visits, I brought printed copies of the e-mails to the jails. Kim said she'd never seen them before, and she had no guess as to what they meant. She added, however, that they were vintage Eric, that he loved playing such games.

When I held them up to the glass for Eric to look at, he appeared taken aback, uncomfortable, and said he didn't

remember them. His reaction left me wondering even more
if they had some hidden meaning.

So, I now leave it up to any reader who enjoys solving
puzzles. Was Eric playing a game of some sort? Do these
six e-mails have anything to do with the murders?

Below are the e-mailed messages in order. To be as clear
as possible, I added the headings: date and time, re, and message. For some reason, the fourth e-mail has an extra chapter
number at the end. That isn't a mistake, at least not mine.

The e-mails are printed as I found them, including
errors in spelling and grammar.

> E-mail 1: Date and time: 3/26/2013 10:19:54 A.M.;
> Re: Chapter XXII; Message: Louis one, in St. So I
> never said nothing.

> E-mail 2: Date and time 4/3/2013 8:06 A.M.; Re:
> Chapter XX; Message: Id a shot him, That was where
> it pinched. I was scared.

> E-mail 3: Date and time: 4/3/2013 6:55 P.M.; Re:
> Chapter III; Message: There warnt anything to say,
> They backed water. Hungry, too, I reckon.

> E-mail 4: Date and time: 4/6/2013 6:52 P.M.; Re:
> CHAPTER XXXI; Message: You could tame it, THEY
> aint a? goin to suffer. CHAPTER XXXVIII

> E-mail 5: Date and time 4/7/2013 5:45 A.M.; Re:
> CHAPTER XXX; Message: Oh, I see, now, Thatll
> answer. You didn't want to come.

> E-mail 6: Date and time: 4/10/2013 5:30:25 P.M.; Re:
> CHAPTER XXXVIII; Message: In Hookerville, seven
> mile below, We never thought of that. The family was
> at home.

Is it interesting that the last one concludes with "the family was at home?" The McLellands were in their home the day they were killed. Perhaps a coincidence? You tell me.

Good luck!

Acknowledgments

As always with a project like this, there are many people to thank.

- All those who told me their stories, who explained to me what they saw and heard and knew about the case.

- All the wonderful people I met in Kaufman County who advised me about their slice of Texas and introduced me to those involved.

- Edward Porter, my good friend, who read the manuscript and discussed issues about the law and facts about firearms.

- Carey Smith who pulled together some of the news articles for me.

- To my William Morrow editor, Emily Krump; Guido Caroti, who designed the cover; and Eleanor Mikucki, who copyedited the manuscript.

- To my readers, who have been incredibly supportive over the years. This is my fourteenth book. I wouldn't be here without you. Thank you for standing by me and for recommending my books to others.

As always, a big thank-you to my family and friends. I appreciate all your love and patience.